# OXFORD STUDIES IN DIACHRONIC AND HISTORICAL LINGUISTICS

GENERAL EDITORS

Adam Ledgeway and Ian Roberts, University of Cambridge

ADVISORY EDITORS

Cynthia Allen, *Australian National University*; Ricardo Bermúdez-Otero, *University of Manchester*; Theresa Biberauer, *University of Cambridge*; Charlotte Galves, *University of Campinas*; Geoff Horrocks, *University of Cambridge*; Paul Kiparsky, *Stanford University*; Anthony Kroch, *University of Pennsylvania*; David Lightfoot, *Georgetown University*; Giuseppe Longobardi, *University of York*; David Willis, *University of Cambridge*

RECENTLY PUBLISHED IN THE SERIES

For a complete list of books published and in preparation for the series, see pp. 278–79

# Syntactic Reconstruction and Proto-Germanic

GEORGE WALKDEN

OXFORD
UNIVERSITY PRESS

# OXFORD

UNIVERSITY PRESS

Great Clarendon Street, Oxford, OX2 6DP,
United Kingdom

Oxford University Press is a department of the University of Oxford.
It furthers the University's objective of excellence in research, scholarship,
and education by publishing worldwide. Oxford is a registered trade mark of
Oxford University Press in the UK and in certain other countries

Published in the United States of America by Oxford University Press
198 Madison Avenue, New York, NY 10016, United States of America

British Library Cataloguing in Publication Data
Data available

Library of Congress Control Number: 2014930363

ISBN 978-0-19-871229-9

Printed and bound by
CPI Group (UK) Ltd, Croydon, CR0 4YY

# Contents

# Acknowledgements

More people than I can name have helped me in more ways than I can name during the time that this book was put together, so my first acknowledgement is to those people who I've unjustifiably failed to acknowledge below. Sorry.

This research originated as a doctoral dissertation with the same name at the University of Cambridge, which was supported financially by Arts & Humanities Research Council Doctoral Award AH/H026924/1.

For comments and discussion at workshops and conferences, I am grateful to Laura Bailey, Kristin Bech, Kersti Börjars, Sarah Courtney, Tonya Kim Dewey, Roland Hinterhölzl, Richard Ingham, Brian Joseph, Ans van Kemenade, Ruba Khamam, Tony Kroch, Svetlana Petrova, Susan Pintzuk, Gertjan Postma, Laurie Reid, Christine Meklenborg Salvesen, Eva Schlachter, Ann Taylor, Ewa Trutkowski, Phillip Wallage, Joel Wallenberg, Richard Waltereit, and Wim van der Wurff. I am particularly grateful to Svetlana Petrova and to Susan Pintzuk and Ann Taylor for looking after me during research visits to Berlin and York respectively, during which I learned a lot. Thanks also to the anonymous reviewers of the journal articles stemming from my research for this book.

Various of the people who taught me languages and linguistics as an undergraduate deserve thanks: Debbie Anderson, Anne Breitbarth, Michelle Crowe, Richard Dance, Stephen Fennell, Mari Jones, Kirsty McDougall, Sheila Watts. Other linguists in Cambridge helped out in various different ways, in particular Theresa Biberauer, James Clackson, Kasia Jaszczolt, Adam Ledgeway, Chris Lucas, Ian Roberts, Michelle Sheehan, and Bert Vaux.

Thanks to Cambridge coursemates and friends: Alastair Appleton, Tim Bazalgette, Alison Biggs, Cat Davies, Fiona Hanlon, Ena Hodzik, Minyao Huang, Petros Karatsareas, Elliott Lash, Dimitris Michelioudakis, Moreno Mitrović, Iain Mobbs, Neil Myler, Elena Pala, Artūras Ratkus, Latifa Sadoc, Liane-Louise Smith, David Thomas, Anna Tristram, Jen Wainwright, Liv Walsh. Thanks to two friends from further back, Alastair Mailer and David Woods, who reminded me that there was life outside linguistics, if not outside academia, and thanks to all my other non-linguistics friends. Craig Gibson, my personal trainer, helped keep me in shape mentally as well as physically, going far beyond the call of duty.

Many thanks to linguists in Manchester, particularly Yuni Kim and Danielle Turton, for helping me settle in there—and thanks for giving me a job. I'll try not to let you down. Thanks also to Laurel MacKenzie for help with ggplot2.

My parents Bob and Diana Walkden have been wonderfully supportive, and my brother Michael is the best source of distraction I know.

Theresa Biberauer deserves a special mention for her seemingly infinite energy and unfailing enthusiasm, and for continually pointing me in useful directions. Ian Roberts has been an amiable, accessible guru, who has been extremely supportive during my years as a graduate student and beyond, quite apart from being a fantastic source of information on virtually every conceivable linguistic topic. My adviser, Sheila Watts, taught me more about linguistics than anyone else during my seven-and-a-half years at Cambridge, from my first baby steps to where I am now, and I am tremendously grateful to her for that.

Finally, David Willis was a model dissertation supervisor. He always knew when I needed prodding and when I needed to be cut some slack; his comments on my work were always constructive, thoughtful, and thorough; he provided invaluable advice not just on the process of writing, but on every aspect of how to be an academic linguist. It's mainly thanks to him that I now have a shot at spending the rest of my life doing what I love: thinking, and learning, about language. I can't thank him enough for that.

This book is dedicated to the memory of my grandmother, Joy Houlton.

# List of abbreviations

| | |
|---|---|
| ACC | accusative |
| CL | clitic |
| DAT | dative |
| DEF | definite |
| FEM | feminine |
| GEN | genitive |
| INF | infinitive |
| INSTR | instrumental |
| INTJ | interjection |
| MASC | masculine |
| NEG | negative |
| NOM | nominative |
| OPT | optative |
| PL | plural |
| PRET | preterite |
| PRT | particle |
| REFL | reflexive |
| SBJV | subjunctive |
| SG | singular |

| | |
|---|---|
| BCC | Borer–Chomsky Conjecture |
| EF | Edge Feature |
| HPSG | Head-Driven Phrase Structure Grammar |
| L1(, L2 . . . ) | first language (etc.) |
| LFG | Lexical-Functional Grammar |
| OE | Old English |
| OHG | Old High German |
| ON | Old Norse |
| OS | Old Saxon |
| PIC | Phase Impenetrability Condition |
| PIE | Proto-Indo-European |

| | |
|---|---|
| PLD | primary linguistic data |
| SVO(, SOV...) | Subject-Verb-Object (etc.) |
| UG | Universal Grammar |
| V2(, V3...) | verb-second (etc.) |
| $V_{fin}$ | finite verb |

# List of figures

# List of tables

# 1

## Introduction

### 1.1 Preamble

We know that English, German, Dutch, and the Scandinavian languages are related by descent from a common ancestor, and that they are related, more distantly, to languages such as Spanish, Persian, Armenian, and Greek. We know this because of the development of two tools in particular—the family tree model (*Stammbaumtheorie*; Schleicher 1853, 1861/2, 1863) and the notion of the regularity of sound change (Osthoff and Brugmann 1878)—in the nineteenth century. With these two tools it became possible to make massive strides forward in corroborating the vague hypotheses about relatedness that had been put forward for centuries. Many of the achievements of scholars of this period are still widely accepted today; see Campbell and Poser (2008) and Morpurgo Davies (1998: 170–1, 251–4) for an overview. The 'best fit' Indo-European family trees generated by Ringe, Warnow, and Taylor (2003), Dunn et al. (2008), and Longobardi and Guardiano (2009), using computational methods as well as extensive up-to-date scholarship, are extremely similar to the classical tree presented in Schleicher (1853), which is still used as a yardstick against which to measure newer attempts at constructing family trees. Of course, as with everything in science, it is impossible to be sure that such hypotheses are on the right track, however many insights we accumulate and however many correct predictions are made. However, an alternative explanation with greater empirical coverage and explanatory power has yet to be presented.

Assuming that the Germanic languages are indeed related in this way, a natural next question to ask is: what was their common ancestor like? The process of trying to answer this question is known as reconstruction, and nineteenth- and twentieth-century linguists have had great success in reconstructing the sounds and words of such 'protolanguages'. For example, we can hypothesize that the Proto-Germanic word for 'wolf', in the nominative case, was *wulfaz, on the basis of the attested forms given in (1).[1]

---

[1] The versatile little asterisk serves a number of functions in this book. When prepended to a word or expression in an ancient language or protolanguage, it signifies that that form is a reconstruction, i.e.

(1)  Old English         *wulf*
     Old Saxon           *wulf, wolf*
     Old High German     *wolf*
     Old Norse           *úlfr*
     Gothic              *wulfs*

We can do this because the sounds that make up the word correspond systematically across the languages, in a way that will be made more precise in Chapter 2. The tools of traditional reconstruction thus enable us to reconstruct large swathes of the lexicon, phonology, and morphology of protolanguages.

However, as has been noted by many authors (e.g. Brugmann 1904: viii; Watkins 1964: 1035; Clackson 2007: 157), comparative-reconstructive linguistics as practised in the nineteenth and early twentieth centuries has not always accorded syntax a central place. Beekes (1995), an introductory volume to comparative Indo-European philology, omits syntax entirely, as does Szemerényi (1996), another standard reference work. Even the father of historical-comparative syntax, Berthold Delbrück, questions whether it is appropriate to reconstruct in syntax as is done for the lexicon, phonology, and morphology (1900: v–vi). A number of works attempting to reconstruct aspects of the syntax of protolanguages have appeared: for Proto-Germanic, Lehmann (1972), Hopper (1975), and Kiparsky (1995, 1996) are a few key examples. On the other hand, these approaches have met with extreme scepticism: see, for example, Jeffers (1976), Winter (1984), and Lightfoot (1979, 1980, 1999, 2002a, 2002b, 2006). The debate was at its fiercest in the pages of *Journal of Linguistics*, 38, in which Lightfoot (2002a) criticized the reconstructive techniques of Harris and Campbell (1995), meeting with a response by Campbell and Harris (2002) which in turn was replied to by Lightfoot (2002b). A full review of the literature on syntactic reconstruction can be found in Walkden (2009, 2013a).

This book is a discussion of the problem of whether it is possible or profitable to reconstruct the syntax of unattested stages of linguistic family trees. A related, though not coextensive, question is whether the methodology used in lexical-phonological reconstruction can be straightforwardly applied to syntax. My answer to this second question will be 'partially'; my answer to the first question, in all its guises, will be an unalloyed 'yes'. I start by discussing the epistemological and methodological issues involved in the reconstruction of syntax, including the important objections raised by Lightfoot and others (Chapter 2). The bulk of the book is devoted to case studies from the Germanic language (sub-)family in support of the approach to syntactic

---

unattested but hypothesized to exist, as is the norm in historical linguistics (see e.g. Campbell 1998: xix). When prepended to an expression in a language for which we have access to native speakers, it signifies that that form is ungrammatical, as is the norm in syntax. Finally, when appended to a syntactic phrase label it signifies that that phrase may occur zero or more times in the derivation; this is the Kleene star, roughly as used in mathematical logic.

reconstruction developed, dealing with main clause constituent order (Chapter 3), the system of *wh*-words (Chapter 4), and the occurrence and distribution of null arguments (Chapter 5); these should also serve as stand-alone contributions to the historical syntax of the Germanic languages. Chapter 6 concludes. The rest of this chapter outlines the aims of the book in more detail, as well as the basic assumptions I make throughout.

## 1.2 The mythmaker's handbook: a constructivist approach to historical syntax

> Being reflective creatures, thanks to the emergence of the human capacity, humans try to make some sense of experience. These efforts are called myth, or religion, or magic, or philosophy, or in modern English usage, science. (Berwick and Chomsky 2011)

Reconstruction can be defined as the process of constructing forms that are nowhere attested but which are 'posited, on the basis of some evidence, as having existed in some earlier or ancestral form of a language' (Trask 1996a: 302–3). The most pessimistic view on reconstruction to be found in the literature is that of Lightfoot (1979, 1980, 1999, 2002a, 2002b, 2006). For Lightfoot (2002a), reconstructions are 'myths'; for Lightfoot, myths may have functions, as in the case of 'formulist' statements about the historical relatedness of languages, but the term can also be used in a pejorative sense, and this is what Lightfoot intends in using it to characterize 'realist' efforts to reconstruct a prior linguistic reality (2002a: 115). Campbell and Harris (2002), in response, suggest that it is damaging to the field to label hypotheses about prior realities 'myths'.

It is instructive to compare these perspectives with the one taken by Lass (1997). In contrast to many historical linguists, whose expertise is vastly more linguistic than it is historical, Lass has engaged with the literature on the philosophy of history. Such an engagement is important, since, as noted by White (1978: 126–7), 'every historical discourse contains within it a full-blown, if only implicit, philosophy of history'; this is true no less of historical linguistic discourse than of other branches of history, and means that 'metaworries' (Kiparsky 1975: 204) must be accorded a central place in historical linguistic theorizing rather than dismissed in favour of 'get[ting] on with the serious business of doing linguistics', an attitude criticized by Lass (1980: ix–x).

Lass draws a trenchant distinction between 'history', i.e. the events that happened, and 'historiography', the interpretation and explanation of those events. As is widely accepted within the academic discipline of history (cf. e.g. Jenkins 1991: ch. 1 for an accessible introduction), our only access to 'history', to those events, is through witnesses, which themselves must be identified and interpreted. But this identification and interpretation is an act of historiography.

Our approach to history, as Lass (1997: 17) emphasizes, must therefore be at least partially constructivist in the sense of Ortony (1979): there can be no access to history without constitutive historiography. This is not to say that there exist no such things as 'truth' or 'facts'; indeed, Lass is at pains to deflect charges of 'flabby postmodern relativism' (1997: 5). Sokal (2008: ch. 3, ch. 6) provides a good summary of the practical dangers of the relativist position. Crucially, even those who characterize history as a search for truth make the distinction between history and historiography, and do so willingly without supposing that the problem makes their work somehow 'unreal' or 'illegitimate' (cf. e.g. Elton 1967: 70, 112–13; Zagorin 1999; Jarrick 2004). There is, or was, a truth about history, and this assumption is 'a conceptual necessity' for the study of history (Zagorin 1999: 16; cf. also Hobsbawm 1997: 6); the key issue is our access to this truth.

For Lass, then, all hypotheses about the past are myths (1997: 5); the term here is used in its technical sense, which is not inherently pejorative, as emphasized for social history by Tindall (1989: 2), for political science by Flood (2002: 44), and for the comparative study of mythology by Puhvel (1987: 2). A myth, under this view, can be defined as a story 'which embodies and provides an explanation, aetiology, or justification for something such as the early history of a society, a religious belief or ritual, or a natural phenomenon' (*OED*).[2] The constructivist viewpoint suggests that Campbell and Harris (2002: 602) are being overly defensive in characterizing the suggestion that reconstructive hypotheses are myths as 'inaccurate and deleterious to the field'. However, Lightfoot (2002a) makes a more serious error, not in labelling such hypotheses as myths but in implicitly contrasting them with an unexemplified type of non-mythological historiography. The gravity of this error lies in the fact that, as Lass has argued, *any* hypothesis about linguistic history is mythical in a non-trivial sense. For instance, Lightfoot's account of the loss of case in English and its syntactic consequences (2006: 102–23) rests on a framework of interpretations and assumptions, including interpretations of the Old English textual record, the assumption that this reflects in any direct way the grammar of some (or indeed any) Old English speakers, and so on. Mythology in historical syntax, then, may be more pervasive than assumed in Lightfoot (2002a). Honeybone (2011) makes a similar point: since past I-languages cannot be observed, 'all historical linguistics deals with reconstructed forms' (2011: 30).

As Lass additionally observes (1997: 19 n. 22), the problem of access is not one that is unique to the historical sciences: direct observation of synchronic states of the language faculty, for instance, is also impossible. Campbell and Harris (2002: 602) observe, rightly, that 'for Lightfoot to suggest that reconstructions are myths, rather

[2] Cf. Bierce's (1911) tongue-in-cheek definition of mythology in *The Devil's Dictionary*: 'The body of a primitive people's beliefs concerning its origin, early history, heroes, deities and so forth, as distinguished from the true accounts which it invents later.'

than hypotheses, raises the question of whether the supposed "hypotheses" of synchronic linguists are also "myths"'. Following Lass (1997: 18) and Honeybone (2011: 30 n. 6), I would argue that the answer to this question is probably yes, but that it should not matter in the slightest to the practising linguist, whose task remains the same in this case.[3]

But are some myths more mythological than others? Perhaps. Lass (1997: 19–20) observes that comparing our sources of historical knowledge to witnesses leads to comparing the historian's task to a courtroom setting:

> [Accepted truth] arises through argument, evaluation, consideration of often conflicting testimony, discussion of the relative credibility of witnesses, precedent, even rhetoric. Witnesses may tell the truth; they may be mistaken or confused, or be liars; advocates may be sophists or demagogues. The historian, like a magistrate or jury, has to produce the best verdict he can. This is why historiography contains an irreducible conventionalist element, whether or not its ultimate pretensions are realist.

According to this view, the myths we construct in historical linguistics are, in virtue of their function, subject to criteria of empirical responsibility and rationality; in other words, when assessed against these criteria, some of the myths we construct will turn out to be more convincing than others. Similarly, Dressler (1971: 6) refers to the process of reconstruction as a *Wahrscheinlichkeitsschätzung* ('estimation of probability'). Lightfoot (2002b: 625) closes his paper with an exhortation to the effect that the myths constructed thus far are not palatable to him:

> If somebody thinks that they can reconstruct grammars more successfully and in more widespread fashion, let them tell us their methods and show us their results. Then we'll eat the pudding.

What follows is an exploration, assuming the constructivist approach to history advocated by Lass (1997) and by much mainstream histori(ographi)cal practice at the same time as a realist attitude towards the past itself, of the extent to which plausible hypotheses (and thus tasty puddings) about the syntax of protolanguages can be constructed on a methodologically accountable basis. The first two chapters of this book lay down some guidelines for the prospective mythmaker; the remaining chapters put these guidelines into practice.

With all that said, the term *myth* may nevertheless be unpalatable to some readers, perhaps due to its pejorative prior associations, or due to the necessity of a distinction between 'religious' and 'non-religious' myths (Lass 1997: 5). The reader is, in that case,

---

[3] Evans and Levinson (2009) claim that many of the hypotheses of synchronic linguists, namely those postulating language universals, are in fact myths, in the sense that such universals do not exist. Their claims are, however, hard to evaluate, since they reject analyses above a certain (unspecified) level of abstraction (Baker 2009; Longobardi and Roberts 2010), and their article contains a large number of factual and logical errors (Harbour 2010).

invited to substitute *theory* or *hypothesis* for (non-religious) *myth* for the remainder of this book; these are also the terms I shall be using hereafter.

## 1.3 Syntactic framework

The syntactic framework I assume here is, broadly, the one developed in the context of the Minimalist Program (e.g. Chomsky 1995, 2000, 2001) and refined in subsequent work. I do not view this work as Minimalist, as it does not seek to contribute to the goals of the Minimalist research program itself by investigating the Strong Minimalist Thesis, the idea that language is an optimal solution to legibility conditions (Chomsky 2000: 96). Instead I draw upon the results of the Minimalist approach to syntax in order to inform my own historical investigation, which has its own goals, as outlined in section 1.1; namely, to assess the possibilities for the reconstruction of syntax and 'to recover as much as possible of the actual language spoken in the past' (Campbell and Harris 2002: 600) with respect to the syntax of earlier stages of Germanic. As Chomsky (2001: 41) puts it:

Internalist biolinguistic inquiry does not, of course, question the legitimacy of other approaches to language, any more than internalist inquiry into bee communication invalidates the study of how the relevant internal organization of bees enters into their social structure. The investigations do not conflict; they are mutually supportive.

I take it that Minimalist investigation and investigation into the diachronic development of languages (in the pretheoretical sense) can be mutually supportive in this way.

The specifics of the approach I take to syntactic variation are discussed in section 2.2, as these bear heavily upon the general question of whether it is possible to reconstruct syntax at all. Here I will simply outline some of the basics of the syntactic framework I am adopting, particularly its two core operations, Merge and Agree, as well as locality conditions and the order of Merge of functional lexical items. Readers with no interest in the technicalia should feel free to skip the rest of this subsection. For a more detailed overview of a Minimalist theory of syntax assuming no prior knowledge of the framework, see Adger (2003).

Simply stated, Merge 'takes two syntactic objects α and β and forms the new object γ = {α, β}' (Chomsky 2001: 3). Much ink has been spilled over the precise formulation of Merge. For our purposes it is sufficient to note that it is a structure-building operation which operates on sets and makes no reference to linear order. I assume that linear order is derived through a mapping algorithm of the sort proposed by Kayne (1994), resulting in heads uniformly preceding their complements and specifiers uniformly preceding their heads. Constituent order variation must then be derived via movement. Although in Chomsky's earlier Minimalist work (e.g. 1995, 2000) Move was required as a separate operation, it is argued in Chomsky (2001,

2005) that movement comes for free as part of the formulation of Merge. Given α, β can be Merged to it either from outside α or from inside α. The former, 'external Merge', is the classic case of Merge of an item new to the derivation; the latter, 'internal Merge', corresponds to classic cases of movement (Chomsky 2005: 12). If movement is 'free' in this sense, no separate operation need be postulated, though the question of featural 'triggers' for internal (and external) Merge still remains.

Agree, the second core operation, 'establishes a relation...between an LI [lexical item—GW] α and a feature F in some restricted search space (its *domain*)' (Chomsky 2000: 101). Features may be interpretable or uninterpretable; uninterpretable features must be checked, as they play no role at the conceptual-intentional and sensorimotor interfaces. Following Chomsky (2001) and much recent work, I will assume that the process of checking is a process of valuation, and that interpretable = valued and uninterpretable = unvalued (though cf. Pesetsky and Torrego 2001, 2004 for an approach which takes these notions to be distinct). In Chomsky's framework, the *probe* is the uninterpretable feature F associated with a head α higher in the structure, and it seeks a *goal* in its c-command domain, which must bear a value for the feature F. In addition, a goal must be *active*: in Chomsky's terms, it must also bear an uninterpretable feature (distinct from F). Structural Case features, for instance, may serve this role. Uninterpretable features will be indicated, following common practice, by a prepended *u*, e.g. [*u*Tense]; interpretable features by a prepended *i*, e.g. [*i*Tense], or simply by a value, e.g. [Tense:Past].

If an *inactive* goal, i.e. a goal bearing a value for the feature F but no uninterpretable feature, is closer to the probe than an active goal, then the effects of matching are blocked. This latter property of Chomsky's model is termed a *defective intervention constraint* (2000: 123), which is the first type of locality condition that will play a role in the analyses in this book. Defective intervention has its roots in earlier theories of intervention-based locality constraints, most notably Rizzi's (1990, 2001a) Relativized Minimality and the Minimal Link Condition of Chomsky (1995). It is a relative rather than absolute locality restriction in the sense of Rizzi (1990: 2), in that it is relativized to the feature F for which Agree must take place.

The second type of locality condition is an absolute one: that of phases. I assume the Phase Impenetrability Condition of Chomsky (2000).[4]

(2) **Phase Impenetrability Condition (PIC)**
   In phase α with head H, the domain of H is not accessible to operations outside α, only H and its edge are accessible to such operations.
   (Chomsky 2000: 108, his (21))

---

[4] The version of the PIC given in Chomsky (2001: 13) is more permissive, and not assumed here.

Phase heads are the spiritual successors of barriers (Chomsky 1986a), being conceptually justified by mapping their complements to the interfaces and thus ensuring that 'mappings to the two interfaces can forget about what they have already done' (Chomsky 2005: 16). Their role partially overlaps with that of intervention constraints. The traditional assumption is that $C^0$ and $v^0$ are phase heads (Chomsky 2005: 17), and possibly also $D^0$ (Svenonius 2003).

Agree and phase heads play an important role in the typology of movement-triggering that I will assume. Following Biberauer (2008) and Biberauer, Holmberg, and Roberts (2010), I assume that there is only one movement-triggering feature, ^, but that this can and must be parasitic on another type of feature wherever it occurs. When associated with a probing feature (e.g. φ-features), ^ triggers A-movement; when associated with the Edge Feature that is the crucial property of a phase head, ^ triggers A'-movement.[5] I also assume, following Roberts (2010b), that head-movement is not derived via internal Merge. Instead, head-movement is the result of an Agree relation in which the features of the goal are a proper subset of those of the probe; some mechanism of chain reduction then enforces the non-overtness of the goal.

The hierarchy of projections that I will assume is the standard one: CP, TP, $v$P, VP in the clausal hierarchy, and PP, DP, $n$P, NP in the nominal hierarchy. In line with the assumptions of the 'cartographic' research tradition (Rizzi 1997; Cinque 1999; Cinque and Rizzi 2010) I assume that each of these is shorthand for a more fine-grained array of projections, which largely occur in a fixed order,[6] with only one specifier available per head (cf. also Kayne 1994). For my purposes, it will only be necessary to 'expand' the CP and zoom in on the left periphery of the clause, in a tradition following Rizzi (1997). Rizzi divides CP up as in (3).

(3)   ForceP > TopP* > FocP > TopP* > FinP   (Rizzi 1997: 297)

ForceP hosts elements related to clause type: declarative, interrogative, etc. TopP, which may be iterated indefinitely, hosts topics, while FocP hosts foci. Finally, FinP specifies the finiteness of the clause.

Building on Rizzi's work, Frascarelli and Hinterhölzl (2007) present a slightly more nuanced picture of the left periphery, illustrated in (4).

(4)   ForceP > ShiftP > ContrP > FocP > FamP* > FinP
                    (adapted from Frascarelli and Hinterhölzl 2007: 112–13; their (37))

---

[5] ^ may also be associated with the c-selectional features of a lexical root, in which case it triggers linearization movement ('L-movement'). This latter type, often referred to as 'roll-up' in the literature, is largely used to derive orders in consistently head-final languages, and hence plays no further part in this book.

[6] Cinque (1999: 127) notes that variation does arise, but in the TP domain at least seems to be limited to negation and agreement morphemes.

The main advance made is the distinction between three different types of topic: shifting or Aboutness topics, hosted in ShiftP, indicating what the clause is about; contrastive topics, hosted in ContrP, which create oppositional pairs with respect to other topical elements; and familiar topics, hosted in FamP, which are typically given constituents, often realized in a pronominal form (Frascarelli and Hinterhölzl 2007: 88). I will adopt this hierarchy here, since it makes slightly stronger predictions than Rizzi's pioneering hierarchy in (3). I also assume, with e.g. Aboh (2010) and Cruschina (2009), that information-structural features are present in the syntax, added in the numeration; the element bearing these features must then enter into an Agree relation with a left-peripheral head.

These are the core details of the syntactic framework I am adopting. Other, more minor details will be introduced as and when they are needed in the relevant chapter.

## 1.4 The Germanic languages

The case studies drawn upon throughout this book are drawn from the Germanic language family, and in this subsection I discuss the family, as well as the key individual languages used as sources of data. Germanic is a sub-branch of the Indo-European family, which emerged as a distinct grouping at around 500 BC (Ringe 2006: 213). Its internal structure is generally assumed to be as in Fig. 1.1.

Fig. 1.1 shows the earliest stages of the Germanic family tree (before AD 1000); robustly attested stages are in italics. Acceptance of the tree in Fig. 1.1 is not universal among Germanicists; Krahe and Meid (1969: 37–8), for example, prefer to assume a subgrouping of Gothic and the North Germanic languages together as opposed to West Germanic due to a number of apparently innovative features that these languages share. However, the majority of scholars nowadays (e.g. Harbert 2007:

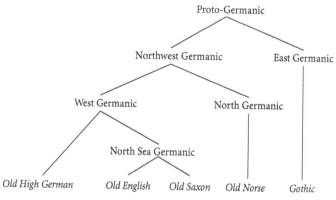

FIGURE 1.1 The Germanic family tree

7–8; Nielsen 2000a: 23; Ringe 2006: 213) take the hypothesis of an early Northwest Germanic unity as a given. In any case, since the early Germanic varieties were geographically contiguous (Harbert 2007: 8), it is likely that East Germanic and West Germanic both individually shared innovations with North Germanic, and that the binary branching tree in Fig. 1.1 is essentially an artefact of the method.

The correct internal subgrouping of West Germanic is more controversial (Ringe 2006: 214; Nielsen 2000b). Old English and Old Saxon (together with the later-attested Old Frisian and Dutch)[7] are often assumed to form a North Sea Germanic or Ingvaeonic subgroup to the exclusion of Old High German. This hypothesis is not uncontroversial; however, the debate centres around the affiliation of Old Saxon, which shares certain features with Old High German that the two do not share with Old English (see Nielsen 2000b for discussion). For our purposes it is important simply to note that Old Saxon can be considered phylogenetically and geographically intermediate between Old English and Old High German.

The Germanic family is an appropriate one to use as a test bed for syntactic reconstruction for a number of reasons. First, the older languages are comparatively well attested, and well studied, if not always well understood; cf. Robinson (1992) for an introduction to these languages, and Harbert (2007) for an overview with references. Secondly, as Harris (2008: 90) observes, focusing on a clearly delimited language (sub-)family at a relatively shallow time depth renders the task of reconstruction more manageable and less speculative. As discussed in Walkden (2009: 7–21), most past attempts at syntactic reconstruction (e.g. Lehmann 1974; Friedrich 1975; Watkins 1964, 1976) have attempted to address Proto-Indo-European, and are therefore dealing with a much more amorphous language family at a much greater time depth; Clackson (2007: 157–86) provides a useful discussion of work in this area. Such long-distance, big-picture syntactic reconstruction is by no means excluded in principle by the methodology outlined in this book. The most profitable way to proceed, however, would be to work from the 'bottom up', starting with smaller pieces of the puzzle such as the details of the common West Germanic or Northwest Germanic and proceeding to a greater time depth only when acceptance of some of these details is reached.

The italicized languages in Fig. 1.1 are those that will form the basis of my discussion in Chapters 3, 4, and 5. The rest of this subsection is devoted to considering those languages in more detail, since each poses unique questions of attestation and interpretation. Many of the issues are shared, however; for general issues relating to the use of written records, including verse texts and translations, I follow the

---

[7] These languages are largely excluded from the present study both due to their late attestation (de Haan 2001, for instance, argues on linguistic grounds that Old Frisian should really be called Middle Frisian) and for reasons of space and time.

strategies suggested by Lass (1997: 44–103).[8] There is little that is new here, since it has long been known that historical linguistics can be thought of as 'the art of making the best use of bad data' (Labov 1994: 11). Where it becomes useful to test for statistical significance, Fisher's exact test (Fisher 1922) is used unless otherwise stated.

### 1.4.1 *Gothic*

Gothic is the earliest robustly attested Germanic language, and the only member of the East Germanic branch with such attestation. Spoken by the Visigoths and Ostrogoths, two highly mobile tribal groupings (see Robinson 1992: 43–7 for a brief history), it has survived primarily in fragments of a translation of the New Testament from Greek, attributed to Bishop Wulfila (*c*.310–383). The manuscript, known as the *Codex Argenteus*, dates from the sixth century and was most likely produced in Italy; see Ebbinghaus (1997) for discussion.

The primary difficulty when dealing with the syntax of Gothic is the degree to which the translation is dependent on the syntax of the New Testament Greek original. A recent study of the adjectival syntax of Gothic describes the Gothic Bible as 'a near-wholesale importation of Greek presented in Gothic guise' (Ratkus 2011: 24). The two poles of opinion are represented by Curme (1911), who argues that the affinities between Gothic and New Testament Greek are due to shared inheritance rather than slavish translation technique, and Bennett (1980: 127), who claims that in view of translation influence the Gothic texts are 'all but useless for the study of Germanic syntax' (cf. also Hopper 1975: 60; Lehmann 1994: 21).[9] Ratkus (2011: 32–3) describes these as the 'idealist' and 'agnostic' positions respectively.

From a purely logical perspective, it is not clear that there is anything 'agnostic' about the claim that Gothic syntax was heavily influenced by Greek, and nor is it clear that this should be the null hypothesis when investigating the syntax of Gothic. Similarities between languages may be the result of language universals, shared inheritance, convergent development, parallel development, or language contact (Blevins 2004: 47–52; Aikhenvald 2006: 1–2). Common practice in the literature is to assume that a feature is not due to contact unless the evidence is clear and overwhelming (e.g. Lass 1997: 201, 209; though cf. Farrar and Jones 2002 and Filppula 2010: 449 for criticism of this 'if-in-doubt-do-without' mentality); among

---

[8] Dewey (2006: 17–21) argues that using verse for syntactic investigations is even advantageous in some respects, as this text type is likely to be conservative and in addition intonational information may help us to determine syntactic features. See also Pintzuk and Kroch (1989), who use this logic to differentiate between extraposition and Heavy NP Shift in *Beowulf.*

[9] Bennett's claim is made with reference to both the Gothic Bible and the *Skeireins*, an incomplete short commentary on the Gospel of John. Though the *Skeireins* is generally thought not to have been composed by Wulfila, it is likely that it is nevertheless a translation from a Greek original: see Schäferdiek (1981). In addition, the newly discovered *Gothica Bononiensia* manuscript (Finazzi and Tornaghi 2013) came to my attention too late for it to be incorporated into my study.

Gothicists, the logic seems to be reversed.[10] Furthermore, many scholars have presented evidence for 'genuine' Gothic syntactic phenomena in the Gothic Bible, often supported by sophisticated quantitative argumentation, e.g. with regard to the relative order of the verb and its complement (Koppitz 1900, 1901; Fourquet 1938; Jasanoff 2004), use of the dual (Seppänen 1985; Keidan 2006), verb position in imperatives, *wh*-questions, and negation (Eyþórsson 1995; Fuß 2003), relative clauses (Harbert 1992), the absolute construction (Dewey and Syed 2009), pronouns (Ferraresi 2005), and the order of elements in the noun phrase (Ratkus 2011). Many of these studies are based on the principle of lexical deficiency: instances where the Gothic text translates a single Greek word with multiple Gothic words. In these cases, it is argued, no model was available, and so the word order is likely to have followed the unmarked native pattern. Furthermore, instances where the Gothic text deviates from its Greek model also indicate native Gothic phenomena (provided that other influences, such as that of Latin or Coptic, can be ruled out). In contrast, I am unaware of any study presenting clear data and explicit argumentation to the effect that the similarities between Gothic and New Testament Greek *are* due to narrow translation: Metlen's (1932: 46–7) conclusion to this effect has been criticized by Berard (1993) as based on an insufficient range of phenomena. Instead, the judgement that the Gothic Bible represents 'Greek syntax garbed in the dress of Gothic grammar' (Metlen 1932: 47) seems to be based, more often than not, on simple intuition; an intuition that is perhaps circular, as will become clear from the next paragraph. It is equally unclear, then, that 'idealist' is an appropriate term to apply to those who, like Curme (1911), wish to claim that similarities are due to common origin. The issue is an unresolved one.

In any case, for those working on the syntax of Gothic it is necessary to attempt to rule out structural calquing from New Testament Greek, even though this necessity has more to do with the sociology of the field than with logic or empirical evidence. The important question then becomes: since we do not know what manuscript Wulfila himself had access to, and there is no single original Greek text, which version of the New Testament Greek Bible do we use as a comparator? Ratkus (2011: 28–32) provides a useful guide to this issue. Many scholars, e.g. Berard (1993), Fertig (2000), and Ferraresi (2005), primarily use the version provided in Streitberg's (1919) edition, which has survived through later editions and is often reproduced elsewhere. The problem with this is that Streitberg was not a Bible scholar, and his version of the Greek New Testament is a hybrid which does not derive from any single manuscript; furthermore, observed differences between other versions and Streitberg's edition make it clear that Streitberg's version is closer to the Gothic than

---

[10] One could object that the 'if-in-doubt-do-without' methodology is intended to be applied to cases of language change across populations rather than individual cases of loan-translation. The burden of proof would then be on those who wished to claim that the two types of contact influence were significantly different.

any other (Ratkus 2011: 31). Using Streitberg's version to investigate correspondence with the Greek is dangerously circular, then, as it cannot be ruled out that Streitberg was guided in his 'reconstruction' of the Greek original by the form of the Gothic.

Another version often used is the Critical Text (most recent edition Nestle et al. 2001), which has a wide circulation and is widely regarded as the standard edition for academic purposes. It is used for studies of Gothic syntax by Thomason (2006) and Dewey and Syed (2009) *inter alia*. Ratkus (2011: 33–9) has conducted a three-way comparison in terms of omissions, word order, lexical choice, and grammatical form between the Gothic, the Critical Text, and another version, the Majority Text (Robinson and Pierpont 2005), which is based more heavily on Byzantine than on Alexandrine manuscripts: his aim is to establish which manuscript tradition the Gothic translation can be attributed to. His findings are unequivocal: 'Gothic follows the Majority Text much more closely than it does the Critical Text, and the former should thus be used as a point of reference in the comparative study of Gothic and Greek' (2011: 39). I will therefore use the Majority Text as comparator in subsequent chapters where Gothic becomes relevant to the discussion.

### 1.4.2 *Old Norse*

Old Norse (ON) is a North Germanic language. North Germanic bifurcates early into East Nordic (precursor to Danish and Swedish) and West Nordic (precursor to Faroese, Icelandic, and Norwegian); ON in this book refers to West Nordic texts. The texts investigated are Old Icelandic, mainly because of the availability of a pre-final version of the Icelandic Parsed Historical Corpus (IcePaHC; Wallenberg et al. 2011). Unless otherwise stated, Old Icelandic is here taken to stand for early North Germanic in general, though material on Old Swedish and Old Norwegian will also be drawn upon, particularly Håkansson (2008) and Kinn (2013) on null arguments. In addition to the corpus, the grammars drawn upon for this book are Gordon (1927), Wessén (1966), Heusler (1967), Barnes (2004), and Faarlund (2004).

The study of ON poses problems that are different from those familiar to the student of Gothic or the early West Germanic languages. A large number of autochthonous prose texts are available, so that the philological issues of dealing with translations and verse texts do not need to concern us. On the other hand, the earliest texts at our disposal date from around 1150, which is markedly later than for the other Germanic languages under consideration; the 'Old' Norse period is thus contemporaneous with Middle English and Middle High German. The language has thus had a considerable amount of time to undergo changes, and we find that ON is indeed substantially different from the other early Germanic languages, e.g. in having generalized verb-second in subordinate clauses. A further issue is the extent to which the comparatively uniform grammar underlying the transmitted texts was representative of many, any, or all North Germanic speakers at the time of production (cf. Faarlund 2004: 2).

The texts used in this book are the earliest texts found in IcePaHC; the *First Grammatical Treatise* and samples of the *Íslensk hómilíubók* (twelfth century), the *Jarteinabók*, *Þorláks saga helga*, the *Íslendinga saga*, the theta manuscript of *Egils saga*, the *Jómsvíkinga saga*, the *Grey Goose Laws*, and the *Morkinskinna* (thirteenth century).

### 1.4.3 *Old English*

'Old English' (OE) refers to the West Germanic language spoken in parts of Great Britain from the earliest migrations until circa 1150. In contrast to the other West Germanic languages, a substantial body of prose material is available from the period between 800 and 1150, much of it original and not translated from Latin (e.g. Wulfstan's *Homilies*, the Anglo-Saxon Chronicle). A large amount of this material is contained within the York-Toronto-Helsinki Parsed Corpus of Old English Prose (Taylor et al. 2003), which I have used as my primary data source. Even in cases of translation it is in general safe to assume that we are dealing with native OE syntax, except in biblical translations (see Allen 1980a: 262 and Taylor 2008 for discussion). The parsed version of *Beowulf* from the York Parsed Corpus of Old English Poetry (Pintzuk and Plug 2001) has been used to supplement this large prose corpus.

Four main dialects of OE can be distinguished: Northumbrian, Mercian, Kentish, and West Saxon. Northumbrian and Mercian are often grouped together as 'Anglian'. Since the vast majority of texts in the YCOE are West Saxon, other material, such as the data of Berndt (1956), has occasionally been used to supplement this; this becomes particularly relevant for work on null arguments. Reference works used in addition are Mitchell (1985) and Mitchell and Robinson (2007). Citations of OE examples are given from corpus tokens where possible; elsewhere, the short titles given in Mitchell, Ball, and Cameron (1975, 1979) are used. A vast amount of work, both generative (e.g. Allen 1977, 1980a, 1980b; Koopman 1985, 1992, 1995, 1996, 1997, 1998; van Kemenade 1987; Pintzuk 1993, 1999, 2005; Fischer et al. 2000; Biberauer and Roberts 2005, 2008) and non-generative (e.g. Visser 1963–73; Kohonen 1978; Bean 1983; Mitchell 1985; Bech 2001; Davis and Bernhardt 2002; Cichosz 2010) has been done on the syntax of OE, particularly with regard to constituent order, and as a result discussion will often focus on whether the proposals made in these works are transferable to the less well-studied Germanic languages.

### 1.4.4 *Old High German*

Old High German (OHG) is a cover term for a group of West Germanic dialects whose unifying feature is that they have all undergone the phonological change known as the Second Sound Shift to some extent (see e.g. Sonderegger 2003: 31; König 2005: 63); early texts from the north of the German-speaking area are thus not included (see section 1.4.5 on Old Saxon). OHG is usually taken to range from the earliest texts, in the eighth century, to around 1050. The surviving texts are mainly manuscripts from monasteries, and can be divided into 'dialects' according to their place of origin: Franconian, Alemannic, or Bavarian.

We are not as fortunate with the OHG texts as we are with OE: all substantial texts are either verse texts or translations, although some of the latter, such as the *Isidor* translation, have been argued to be relatively free (Schlachter 2010: 13–15). Perhaps because of this deficit, there exists as yet no parsed corpus of OHG, and hence few recent quantitative studies. For the present work I have not attempted to remedy this, instead relying solely on grammars such as Braune and Eggers (1975) and recent theoretically informed secondary work such as Schlachter (2010) and in particular Axel (2007).

### 1.4.5 *Old Saxon*

The third and final West Germanic language to have a textual tradition dating back to the first millennium AD is Old Saxon (OS), sometimes known as Old Low German. Two main texts exist from this period: the *Heliand*, a Gospel harmony written in alliterative verse of 5,983 lines, and fragments of a version of the Genesis story, also in verse. Both can be dated to the first half of the ninth century.

Given the antiquity of these texts, it is surprising that, in comparison to the vast amount of work dealing with the syntax of OE, that of OS has rarely been given any serious attention, a lack noted elsewhere in the literature (e.g. by Linde 2009: 366). The extensive survey of verb position in the early Germanic languages by Eyþórsson (1995) only mentions OS in passing. Moreover, for the most part, traditional philological works on syntax (e.g. Behaghel 1897) and grammars in the philological tradition (e.g. Cordes and Holthausen 1973; Gallée and Tiefenbach 1993) have had nothing to say about the aspects of clause structure considered here. Among the few works dealing with the syntax of OS are Ries (1880), Rauch (1992), Erickson (1997), Dewey (2006), Breitbarth (2009), and Linde (2009); it is clear that the language is in need of further theoretically informed empirical work. My own data, which I hope represents a step in this direction, consists of all 6,229 finite clauses in the *Heliand*, using the Behaghel and Taeger (1996) edition.

Clauses were manually tagged for clause type (main, conjunct, subordinate, relative, *wh*-question, yes-no question, imperative) and for verb position (initial, second, third, or later), polarity (the negation morpheme *ni/ne* proclitic to the finite verb), and various characteristics of the subject. It should be noted that subordinate clauses can be introduced by a wide range of elements. Some of these elements, such as *thar* 'there' and *thô* 'then', as well as serving as sentence adverbials of place and time in main clauses, can also introduce subordinate clauses; these two then receive the readings 'where' and 'when' respectively. In practice it is often difficult to distinguish between the two readings; verb position is a potential distinguishing factor, but, since the investigation of correlations between verb position and clause type is one of the objects of this study, using word order preconceptions to decide clause type would be unforgivably circular. Instead I have followed the readings indicated by the punctuation in Behaghel and Taeger (1996), though it may well be that some of these readings—and other editorial decisions—are wrong.

### 1.4.6 *Other sources of evidence*

The five languages mentioned above are the main ones I shall draw upon. However, as noted in section 1.4.2, mention is occasionally made of Old Swedish and Old Norwegian where relevant, as well as Old Dutch. In addition, it is necessary to say a few words here about the Germanic runic inscriptions. Modern scholarship usually takes these inscriptions, written in the Elder Futhark alphabet and attested between AD 200 and 800, to be representative of the Northwest Germanic node of Fig. 1.1, for the most part (Antonsen 1975, 2002; Nielsen 2000a). Few such inscriptions have survived, and many of these do not constitute full sentences; Faarlund (1989: 172, 1990: 21) estimates that of the 129 runic inscriptions known at the time of writing, 69 were full sentences, and Antonsen (1975: 24) states that there are 34 inscriptions in Northwest Germanic in which the position of the verb can be determined. In light of this extremely limited attestation, which is not unequivocal as regards the areas of investigation of this book (cf. Faarlund 1990: 29; Eyþórsson 1995: 180–9), I will not treat the language(s) represented by the runic inscriptions as a comparator in the same way as e.g. OE. Instead the evidence of the runic inscriptions will only be used as the broadest of heuristics against which to assess the reconstructions postulated. A similar stance is taken by Hopper (1975: 80).

# 2

# A methodology for syntactic reconstruction

## 2.1 Introduction

This chapter lays out a framework for the reconstruction of syntax. To do this it is necessary to establish a clear view on the locus and nature of syntactic variation across space and time. Section 2.2 of this chapter is therefore dedicated to the question of syntactic variation: here I defend an implementation of Principles & Parameters theory known as the Borer–Chomsky Conjecture (BCC) against the criticisms of Newmeyer (2004), showing that it makes more, and clearer, predictions than Newmeyer's rule-based alternative while remaining descriptively and explanatorily adequate. Section 2.3 addresses the question of syntactic change, arguing that it is desirable to reduce 'language' to individual grammars as assumed within the generative tradition, and that the task of diachronic linguistics then becomes to investigate the historical relationships between these grammars, mediated by transmission and acquisition. I also show, broadly following Roberts and Roussou (2003) and van Gelderen (2004, 2011), that directionality in syntactic change is not incompatible with this view of diachronic syntax as long as statements of directionality are reducible to properties of the acquirer's interaction with the primary linguistic data (PLD). These serve as precursors to section 2.4, in which an attempt is made to draw parallels between lexical-phonological and syntactic reconstruction, and, where these fail, to work around them as far as possible. It is shown that the BCC adopted in section 2.2 provides a straightforward way of extending the traditional notion of cognacy to syntax, although it is not always as straightforward to *establish* cognacy as it is in lexical-phonological reconstruction due to the 'correspondence problem' raised by Lightfoot and others. I then suggest that if cognacy can be established, then the postulation of items for the protolanguage is just as easy or difficult as it is in lexical-phonological reconstruction.

## 2.2 Modelling synchronic syntactic variation

### 2.2.1 *The structure of syntactic variation*

The general approach to the synchronic study of language taken here is a mentalist one, in which the object of enquiry is I-language, the linguistic knowledge of individual speakers (Chomsky 1986b; see Isac and Reiss 2008 for a recent introduction). Whatever the architecture of the innate universal endowment for language, it must be possible for the faculty of language to exist in different states, as even the most superficial glance at linguistic diversity reveals. The rest of this subsection concentrates on the form that this variation takes, since the nature of syntactic variation is crucial to establishing whether or not traditional notions such as cognacy can be transferred into the syntactic domain. This subsection focuses on the general case of variation across individuals; variation within individuals, in some sense, is another logical possibility, and this question will be addressed in section 2.2.2, since it is highly relevant to the question of the spread of linguistic changes across both space and time. The 'primitives', syntactic features, will be discussed in section 2.2.3.

I shall take the position that the distribution of states of the faculty of language across the human population is a question that is not solely answerable in mentalist terms: in other words, that while the innate universal endowment for language delimits the hypothesis space, the state that an individual's I-language will attain is contingent on a wide range of other factors, the incorporation of which into a model of grammar would be redundant and misleading. This 'evolutionary' or 'substance-free' position has been most clearly and frequently stated with respect to phonology (e.g. Blevins 2004; Hale and Reiss 2008; Samuels 2011), though Chomsky (1995: 17–20) emphasizes the role of 'historical accident' and other idiosyncrasies, and Newmeyer (2005) offers a forceful defence of the position. The historical study of syntax may shed light onto these factors, and in this sense is complementary to internalist biolinguistic enquiry, as argued in section 1.3.

I thus concur with Kayne (2005) when he states that 'there is no problem' in the fact that a very limited number of choice points generates an astronomical number of possible grammars. There is no reason to expect the space of attested grammars to map to the space of possible grammars, or for the former to be randomly distributed among the latter, given what we know about diachrony. Furthermore, this large space does not necessarily present a learnability problem: poverty of the stimulus considerations only requires that it be logically *possible* to acquire language on the basis of limited input in our theory, not that it be maximally easy.[1]

---

[1] In any case, most parametric theories of acquisition only require acquirers to set a limited number of parameters, not to search the space of possible grammars (Kayne 2005: 14; though cf. Yang 2002).

The perspective I shall assume on the relation between variation and the innate endowment is as stated in (1).

(1)  **The Borer–Chomsky Conjecture** (Baker 2008: 353)
     All parameters of variation are attributable to the features of particular items (e.g. the functional heads) in the lexicon.

The approach, also known as the Lexical Parameterization Hypothesis (Manzini and Wexler 1987), is associated with current Minimalist syntactic theories, but has its origins in an earlier stage of the Principles & Parameters programme (Borer 1984). Frameworks outside the Minimalist Program have also made use of the notion: Buttery (2006: 99) employs it in building a computational model of first language acquisition in Categorial Grammar, and the notion of Constructicon in Construction Grammar bears some similarities (cf. Barðdal and Eyþórsson 2012). The explanatory advantages of the approach are outlined by Borer (1984: 29):

The inventory of inflectional rules and of grammatical formatives in any given language is idiosyncratic and learned on the basis of input data. If all interlanguage variation is attributable to that system, the burden of learning is placed exactly on that component of grammar for which there is strong evidence of learning: the vocabulary and its idiosyncratic properties.

I am not the first to suggest that syntactic reconstruction should be approached on the basis of (1): the possibility is suggested by Pires and Thomason (2008: 47) and Bowern (2008: 195). However, its implications for reconstruction have not been explored in detail, and this will be the main focus of section 2.4.

To fully understand the implications of the BCC it is necessary to contrast it with its conceptual predecessors. The Principles & Parameters approach, of which the BCC is usually considered part,[2] originated in Rizzi (1978) and Chomsky (1981). Parameters under this view were points of variation associated with particular principles (Chomsky 1986b: 150–1). Classic examples, often seen as 'macroparameters', are the *pro*-drop parameter of Chomsky (1981) and Rizzi (1982) and the Subjacency Parameter of Rizzi (1982: 49–76). On this view, the initial state of the language faculty was seen as a 'switchboard' attached to UG, with various options that could be set; Chomsky (1986b: 146) attributes this metaphor to James Higginbotham.

This model has come under fire from all sides in recent years (see Pica 2001; Newmeyer 2004, 2005, 2006; Boeckx 2010). Newmeyer's critique has been particularly influential, and will briefly be discussed here, along with the response of Roberts

---

[2] Boeckx (2010) takes a different view, distancing himself from the defence of parameters in Holmberg and Roberts (2010). However, the controversy seems to be mainly about whether it is appropriate to call the new, arguably epiphenomenal, points of variation 'parameters'. As such the question is terminological rather than contentful.

and Holmberg (2005) and Holmberg and Roberts (2010). Newmeyer takes issue with
what he terms the 'standard story', given by (2) (his (8)).

(2)  (a)  Parameters are descriptively simple, whereas rules are (generally) not.
     (b)  Parameters have binary settings (an idea which is inapplicable to rules).
     (c)  Parameters are small in number; the number of rules is open-ended.
     (d)  Parameters are hierarchically/implicationally organized, thereby account-
          ing for both order of first language acquisition and typological generaliza-
          tions (there is nothing comparable for rules).
     (e)  Parameters are abstract entities with a rich deductive structure, making
          possible the prediction of (unexpected) clusterings of morphosyntactic
          properties.
     (f)  Parameters and the set of their possible settings are innate (and therefore
          universal). Rules are not (normally) assumed to be drawn from an innate
          set.
     (g)  Parameter settings are easily learned, while rules are learned with greater
          difficulty.
     (h)  Parametric change is markedly different from rule-based change (such as
          grammaticalization and morphological change).

The thrust of Newmeyer's argument is that the empirical expectations of the traditional Principles & Parameters model, in which it was hoped that a small number of
parameters would be discovered along with 'clusterings' of properties, have not been
met. This point is usually conceded by researchers in the framework (Baker 1996,
2008; Pica 2001). As a result, he concludes, points (a)–(h) are impossible to maintain.
Instead Newmeyer advocates an alternative position in which 'language-particular
differences are captured by differences in language-particular rules' (2004: 183).

Points (a), (b), and (e) are largely issues of notation. With regard to (a), Newmeyer
(2004: 189) assumes that 'parameters are motivated only to the extent that they lead
overall to more formal simplicity', and that a descriptively adequate theory of
parameters and a descriptively adequate theory of rules are notational variants of
one another; hence, for him, rules should be preferred. Roberts and Holmberg (2005)
do not dispute the latter assumption, but reject the former, since their motivation in
positing parameters is explanatory adequacy rather than formal simplicity, and the
two do not always coincide. Similarly, Roberts and Holmberg suggest that (b),
binarity, is simply 'a matter of formulation' and thus does not bear on the issue of
parameters vs. rules, since the key assumption, discreteness, is shared by both. Point
(e) can be treated likewise: both rules and (macro- and micro-)parameters can
predict clusterings if properly formulated; obviously the extent to which the cluster-
ing holds is an empirical question.

With regard to (c), Newmeyer's case is stronger: he points out that, if we take the
'switchboard' approach, then a parametric model becomes increasingly evolutionarily

implausible under the assumption that those parts of the language faculty related to syntax are most likely to have evolved via a simple mutation (cf. Berwick and Chomsky 2011: 29). The question is then one of 'evolutionary adequacy' (Longobardi 2003). Roberts and Holmberg (2005) concede this point, suggesting that 'parameters are not really primitives of UG, but rather represent points of underspecification which must be filled in in order for the system to become operative'. Under this view, compatible with the BCC, parameters are no longer genetically specified (in any direct sense), and the switchboard metaphor is no more than a metaphor.

Point (d) relates to the hierarchies of parameters developed by Baker (2001) and subsequent work. In this view there are implicational relationships between parameters, such that, for instance, a language only has a value specified for the Subject Placement parameter if it has a positive value for the Verb Attraction parameter, which in turn only has a value specified if the Subject Side parameter is set to 'beginning' rather than 'end'. Newmeyer (2004: 199–201) raises a large number of empirical problems for Baker's (2001) parameter hierarchy, and implies on this basis that the attempt to develop such hierarchies is futile: 'they do not work' (2004: 201). Roberts and Holmberg (2005) take issue with this, and suggest that the predictive power of such hierarchies is worth the difficulty of attempting to establish them. In more recent work (e.g. Holmberg and Roberts 2010), specific implementations of parameter hierarchies have been proposed, along with the suggestion that macroparameters are aggregates of microparameters acting together (cf. also the 'principles and schemata' approach of Longobardi 2005).[3] Assuming the underspecification view of 'parameters' sketched in the previous paragraph, such hierarchies, *if* they can be established in such a way as to be plausible empirically and from the point of view of acquisition, are in principle compatible with the BCC insofar as they are taken to be epiphenomena, not genetically specified per se but representing a way in which we can understand the learning process. This is close to the way in which these hierarchies are understood by Holmberg and Roberts (2010: 51), who suggest that they 'arise from third-factor properties' in the sense of Chomsky (2005: 6). The question of hierarchical organization, then, remains an open one.

Points (f), (g), and (h) are related in that innateness feeds into learnability, which in turn feeds into change, and in all cases Newmeyer assumes that 'parameters are complemented by rules in the marked periphery' (2004: 213). If such a periphery exists and is acquirable, he argues, then 'learners have to acquire rules anyway', and this undermines the need for a distinct parametric core. In their response, Roberts

---

[3] This is comparable to the view sketched by Baker (2008: 354 n. 2) according to which 'languages can differ in the properties that large classes of lexical items have'. A model of variation based on this notion, along with 'generalization of the input' (see section 2.3.2), is highly compatible with the conception of regularity in syntactic change outlined in Walkden (2009: 38–40) and in section 2.4. In this model it may be that the notion of hierarchy can be dispensed with.

and Holmberg (2005) argue that this assumption is unnecessary, and that there is no need for a 'marked periphery' (following the mainstream view; though cf. Smith and Law 2009). They concede that Lightfoot's (1991) diagnostics for parametric change as opposed to rule-based change are not reliable, as argued by Harris and Campbell (1995: 37–45). Instead they suggest a model in which there are only two types of change: parametric change and lexical change.[4] In the model I assume here, based on the BCC, there is only one type of change, namely lexical change. In any case, I concur with Roberts and Holmberg (2005) that the issue is not a telling one with regard to parametric theory in general.

Roberts and Holmberg's (2005) main objection to Newmeyer's proposal is that the alternative he suggests, language-particular rules, is unrestrictive. Newmeyer (2004: 185) in fact acknowledges this potential criticism but does little to stave it off, beyond arguing that performance factors may be implicated in shaping individual grammars. The influence of such factors is in my view inevitable, and here I find Newmeyer's argument compelling; see section 2.3. But issues with the rule-based alternative remain. As Holmberg and Roberts (2010: 25) point out, the class of potential rules is infinite, giving rise to a potential acquisition problem. Furthermore, it is not clear what the primitives of a rule-based system are, or what constrains them. Newmeyer states his rules in natural language, as in (3).

(3)   English: Complements are to the right of the head. (2004: 184)

But nothing in Newmeyer's system prohibits the introduction of rules such as (4).

(4)   Move the second word in the sentence to the beginning of the sentence.

However, it has long been known that acquirers do not posit rules such as (4): this restriction is known as *structure-dependence* (Chomsky 1957). It is not straightforwardly possible to formulate a lexical specification equivalent in derivational outcome to (4), assuming the BCC. It will not do to point at performance factors to explain the unviability of (4); the rule is certainly logically possible, and toy 'languages' can be constructed that make use of such a rule without becoming unprocessable. At the very least a plausible argument from performance against rules such as (4) would need to be constructed. The rule-based alternative seems, then, to be too permissive.

In sum, a view of syntactic variation based on the BCC (1) is demonstrably superior, in terms of descriptive and evolutionary adequacy, to the traditional approach adopted

---

[4] A reviewer also suggests that there may be an important distinction to be drawn between lexical change, qua change in the properties of open-class lexical items, and change in the inventory of functional heads (closed-class items). This is also suggested by the mention of functional heads in the definition of the BCC in (1). While in principle this distinction may prove important, the trouble is that it is difficult to draw a firm line between the two: for instance, are prepositions lexical or functional (see Mardale 2011)?

within the Principles & Parameters framework, while at the same time being immune to the bite of Newmeyer's (2004) criticisms of the latter. Furthermore, while not being overly restrictive, it makes more, and clearer, predictions about possible languages than the rule-based alternative advocated by Newmeyer.

### 2.2.2 *The question of free variation*

In linguistic theory, a postulate such as (5) is commonplace.

(5)  **Blocking Effect**
     Within a grammar, interpretatively identical lexical items cannot exist.

Motivation for (5) comes from two different sources. First, as well documented for morphology (Aronoff 1976) and imported into syntax by Clark (1992) and Kroch (1994), such an effect seems to be a reasonable empirical generalization, at least to a first approximation. Children who overgeneralize regular morphology during the acquisition process, for instance, do not admit variation between regular and irregular forms when they eventually learn the latter (Kroch 1994: 6). Furthermore, on the lexical level, formations such as *clearness* appear to be blocked by pre-existing competing forms such as *clarity* (Kroch 1994: 8). Kroch views the effect as 'a global economy constraint on the storage of formatives' that is active during acquisition (1994: 17), and argues that 'there are good conceptual reasons to accept the universality of the blocking effect'. Assuming the BCC, (5) applies to syntax as it does to the rest of the lexicon.

Second, a version of the Blocking Effect can also be derived from the principles of early Minimalism, namely Last Resort ('don't do too much') and Full Interpretation ('don't do too little'); see Chomsky (1995), Biberauer and Richards (2006). Fox (2000) and Reinhart (1995) argue on this basis that 'optional' operations are only permitted when they allow an interpretation that would not otherwise be available: in other words, 'an optional rule can apply only when necessary to yield a new outcome' (Chomsky 2001: 34).[5] Optionality understood this way, then, is not optionality at all.

In addition to (5), two further assumptions often implicitly adopted are (6) and (7), which will be elucidated in what follows.

(6)  **Monoglossia**
     A single speaker has a single grammar for a single language.

(7)  **Derivational Determinism**
     For a given selection of lexical items, there is only one possible derivational outcome.

---

[5] The original rationale, as proposed by Fox and Reinhart, is not available in current Minimalism, since Last Resort and comparison of derivations are no longer admitted. Chomsky's formulation therefore follows from nothing directly, though can be argued to be a 'third factor' effect.

The conjunction of (5), (6), and (7), however, excludes the possibility of 'free variation' at the individual level, in the traditional sense of interpretatively vacuous alternations. To avoid this consequence, there are three obvious options: deny (5), deny (6), or deny (7). All of these options have been proposed in the literature, and I will discuss each in turn.

The most commonly taken option is to deny (6), the assumption of monoglossia. The theory of 'competing grammars' resulting from this is due to Kroch (1989, 1994), who maintains that the Blocking Effect holds within individual grammars but that grammars can compete with one another within the mind of a single individual, with cognitive/acquisitional pressures then leading to one grammar being favoured over the other in diachrony (see also Yang 2002). Competing grammars theory has been applied to various languages, particularly historically attested ones, e.g. Pintzuk (1999) on OE. Several considerations speak in favour of a variant of this approach. Most important is the fact that (6) must be rejected in any case, since it is entirely possible for individuals to be natively bilingual, and indeed bidialectal (see e.g. Roberts 2007: 324). The innovation is the extension of this concept of 'syntactic diglossia' to more fine-grained intra-speaker differences.

It is worth noting that, although studies in the competing grammars framework have typically assumed a theory of syntax containing headedness parameters rather than the asymmetric view due to Kayne (1994) and adopted here, nothing about the framework per se requires such a theory: a Kaynean view of linearization is perfectly compatible with competing grammars, as shown by Wallenberg (2009: 117), who develops an account involving both. Another necessary clarification is that 'competing grammars' are not thought to involve massive redundancy for the many identical features involved; instead, the two grammars share a large amount of material (under the approach adopted here, to be understood as lexical items), diverging only where differences are found.

Since (6) is so obviously false, some form of the competing grammars hypothesis must be correct. However, certain problems remain.[6] As Roberts (2007: 325) notes, the concept of 'syntactic diglossia' is often generalized to cases in which no functional motivation for the use of one or other grammar is adduced. For instance, in the work of Pintzuk (1999, 2005), grammars with head-initial IP and head-final IP are argued to be at work in a single OE text, Alfred's translation of Gregory's *Cura Pastoralis*, but no discussion is provided of the contexts in which each grammar is appropriate; indeed, there seem to be no such contexts, and there is then no principled distinction to be drawn between the competing grammars approach and positing ad hoc 'diacritic' features [+F], [−F]. This becomes a problem when we examine the notion of 'grammar'. Kroch (1989, 1994) does not provide an explicit

---

[6] The argument that competing grammars give rise to learnability problems is controversial (cf. Kroch 1994: 184, 2001: 722; Niyogi 2006: 336; Roberts 2007: 328), and I do not consider it further here.

definition of this notion, which must therefore remain intuitive. But the notion is problematic in the context of the BCC. Since differences between grammars are attributable to differences in lexical items, the only sensible way to view competing grammars under the BCC is as two separate mental bins that separate, for instance, the lexical items that constitute a 'high' grammar from those of a 'low' one (in the terminology of Ferguson 1959). This is not clearly distinguishable from the result of postulating lexical features [+high] and [+low] (or [+English] and [+French]). As I will argue in the next section, this is not an unreasonable way of representing conceptual knowledge, and obviates the need for reference to the ill-defined concept of 'grammars'. But in cases where the two grammars are not functionally/contextually distinguishable, simply [+Grammar1] and [+Grammar2], we would expect the Blocking Effect in (5) to rule out the postulation of two separate grammars just as it would rule out two interpretatively identical lexical items.[7]

My conclusion as regards competing grammars, then, is similar to that of Roberts (2007: 331): in principle they represent a useful tool for understanding variation and the process of change, but they need to be employed with caution, as positing two grammars in free variation is no more plausible than postulating two lexical items in free variation. In addition, I have suggested that what have been called 'competing grammars' are better viewed as 'competing lexical items' like any others, with distinct feature specifications.

Henry (1995, 2002; Wilson and Henry 1998) takes a different route, rejecting the Blocking Effect in (5). She concludes (from debatable premises) that competing grammars are unable to allow for differing frequencies of use across sentence types and for stable variation across long periods of time, and criticizes Kroch for failing to 'grasp the nettle' (2002: 272) and accept variability within a single grammar: 'a better characterization seems to be that individual structures/parameter settings are variable, rather than that there are actually separate grammars' (2002: 274). Adger (2006a) likewise rejects (5), or at least weakens it. In Adger's scheme (2006a: 510), featurally identical lexical items may not exist, but featurally non-identical lexical items may be non-distinct in their contribution to interpretation as long as they differ only in uninterpretable features. Interpretatively identical lexical items with differing feature specifications can thus coexist: Adger refers to this as 'underspecification'. Since I find the empirical and conceptual arguments for (5) compelling, not least because it enforces greater restrictiveness in theory-construction, I cannot here adopt Henry's or Adger's account of variability.

---

[7] This problem is particularly severe for the model of acquisition of Yang (2002), in which the proliferation of vast numbers of probabilistically activated grammars during acquisition would be predicted to remove all semblance of discreteness in child linguistic judgements and production of possible variants, rendering the Blocking Effect vacuous.

A third possibility is explored by Biberauer and Richards (2006) and exploited for diachronic purposes in Biberauer and Roberts (2005, 2008, 2009). The core of their proposal is that, while movement-triggering EPP features associated with agreement relations must be satisfied, the computational system simply 'doesn't mind' whether they are satisfied by movement of the Goal alone or by pied-piping of additional structure. In modern spoken Afrikaans, for instance, an alternation between embedded V-final and V2 obtains, as in (8) and (9), and is claimed to be semantically vacuous.

(8)  Ek   weet   dat   sy   dikwels   Chopin   gespeel   het
     I    know   that  she  often      Chopin   played    has

(9)  Ek   weet   dat   sy   het   dikwels   Chopin   gespeel
     I    know   that  she  has   often     Chopin   played
     'I know that she has often played Chopin.'

This is derived if the finite verb is in $T^0$ and the EPP feature of $T^0$ may be satisfied either via movement of the DP subject from SpecvP to SpecTP, yielding V2, or via pied-piping of the entire vP. Though (5) and (6) are maintained in Biberauer and Richards's (2006) account, then, the assumption of derivational determinism (7) is abandoned, since one and the same numeration may lead to different outcomes at the interface.

Though the account elegantly exploits a loophole in Minimalist syntactic theory with regard to satisfaction of movement-triggering features, some of the assumptions it makes are not uncontroversial. In particular, it is not clear that it is more Minimalist for the grammar to be indifferent with regard to the size of the moved category; one might alternatively expect that in such cases the category moved would always be the smallest possible structure, in order to minimize 'heavy lifting', as proposed by Chomsky (1995: 262) (or indeed the largest, in order to maximize the amount of lifting being done in one go). Biberauer and Richards (2006) do not argue for the 'computationally innocuous' nature of their system as opposed to these alternatives. Similarly, the data does not support their account of variability over others, since it is possible to account for it in other ways, for instance in terms of competing grammars (cf. Wallenberg 2009: 100–45). Most problematically, the abandonment of (7) leaves it entirely unclear what determines which of the two options will be taken in a given derivation. Biberauer and Richards imply that nothing determines this choice. But this cannot be the case, since such a nondeterministic algorithm is unimplementable: faced with complete indeterminacy, the derivation must 'roll the dice' or crash, neither of which are desirable outcomes. It is also not clear that the approach of Biberauer and Richards (2006) can be generalized to all cases of syntactic variation beyond Germanic verb position.[8]

---

[8] A dramatically different approach to the question of free variation is to encode probabilities in the grammar itself, as in Stochastic Optimality Theory: see Clark (2004) for an application of this to historical syntax.

I have argued, then, that none of the approaches to the 'question of free variation' has succeeded in solving it without considerable cost: the abandonment of (6), though it is trivially false, does not resolve the situation, and (5) and (7) cannot reasonably be abandoned. There is, however, a fourth possibility, namely the rejection of the implicit assumption made throughout this section: that free variation exists. Obviously, if free variation did not exist then predicting its non-existence would not be a problem. In fact, the history of syntactic research reveals a gradual whittling down of the numbers of cases of what appear to be free variation. As Diesing (1992, 1997) shows, for instance, the possibilities for scrambling in the German *Mittelfeld*, which on the surface exhibit a great deal of freedom, are actually restricted by subtle considerations of specificity and scope:

(10)  Er   hat   oft    ein   Buch   gelesen
      he   has   often  a     book   read
      'He often read a (non-specific) book.'

(11)  Er   hat   ein    Buch  oft    gelesen
      he   has   a      book  often  read
      'There is a book that he often read.'

Similarly, in recent years the alternation between V2 and non-V2 in Mainland Scandinavian subordinate clauses has been shown to be related to illocutionary force (Julien 2007; Wiklund 2010). If the considerations in this section (including (5)–(7)) are on the right track, then true free variation is psychologically implausible.

Biberauer and Richards (2006) claim that 'true, semantically vacuous optionality is . . . prevalent in human language'; however, apparent cases may reduce to instances of variation with subtle conditioning, which may not be 'semantic' in the strict (truth-conditional) sense, but rather functional or contextual. I take it that the conceptual-intentional component of the mind contains such notions in a way to be elaborated upon in section 2.2.3. At any rate a methodological point must be made: our inability to perceive the conditions on variation does not mean that those conditions do not exist.[9] Roberts (2007: 331) makes a similar point:

we cannot exclude the possibility that the competing grammars postulated by Kroch, Pintzuk, and others for the early stages of various languages for which we have little or no sociolinguistic information, did have a social value whose nature has been completely obscured by the passage of time and the nature of the extant texts.

---

[9] It is telling that those languages for which the competing grammars framework has been most heavily used in its 'diacritic' form are those with no living native speakers, e.g. earlier stages of English, French, and Yiddish.

Extrapolating from an artefact of our methodological limitations to making an ontological claim about the status of variation in a historically attested language is clearly a category error.

A reviewer objects that studies of sound change in progress show that sometimes 'there is simply probabilistic variation', and even that 'all social conditioning of linguistic variants is stochastic in nature'. However, no such thing has been demonstrated: all that can be shown (from a falsificationist perspective) is that the factors *so far explored* do not deterministically capture all variation. It is not possible to demonstrate that there is no factor such that, when properly understood, a deterministic account will be possible. That is, whenever we assume probabilistic variation, we are either ontologizing ignorance on the part of the researcher—see, for instance, Hale's (2007: 180–90) discussion of Bresnan and Deo's (2001) 'Fallacy of Reified Ignorance'—or assuming an unfalsifiable hypothesis. In effect, then, the only methodologically sensible interpretation of probabilistic variation is an epistemic one. In what follows I will therefore assume, where I am unable to establish the exact nature of a conditioning factor, that such a factor existed in the form of a lexical feature of some kind. Admission of ignorance is only healthy.

### 2.2.3 *Syntactic features*

In this subsection I discuss the features entering into syntactic computation. First, observe that the alternation between (12) and (13) is not normally taken as parallel to the alternation between (14) and (15).

(12)    Thus you have washed the dishes.
(13)    Thus have you washed the dishes.
(14)    You have washed the dishes.
(15)    Have you washed the dishes?

In (15), it is usually assumed that there is a feature present in the derivation that is absent in (14), for example [Q] associated with $C^0$ (e.g. Radford 1997: 108), and that its presence is related to movement of the auxiliary. By contrast, (13) has a markedly more archaic flavour than (12), yet it is not usual to account for the difference in terms of a feature [archaic] associated with $C^0$ in this case. Instead, it is usually assumed that the speaker has access to multiple varieties, and that a 'user's manual' regulates the choice between them (e.g. Culy 1996: 114). The question is: why are these two alternations not treated in a parallel fashion? In what follows I argue that there is no principled reason for this disparity, and that 'social knowledge' should be treated as part of the lexicon, with the possibility to 'enter into' syntactic computation.

In approaches to phonology that are similar to the one that I assume here for syntax, it is usually assumed that among the universal aspects of phonological knowledge, alongside some combinatorial process for constructing phonological representations, are phonological features (Blevins 2004: 41; Samuels 2011: 576). However, these features are substance-free in that their phonetic interpretation does not play a role in phonological computation, as Samuels emphasizes. A crucial consideration pointing in this direction comes from signed languages: although it is uncontroversial that these languages have phonology (see e.g. Brentari 1998), it is even clearer that the phonological primitives cannot make reference to, for example, bilabial articulation, or voicing; see Mielke (2008) and Samuels (2009: 46–72) for extended arguments against the innateness of specific distinctive features in phonology and in favour of an 'emergent' alternative. What is universal, then, can only be a schema for features rather than contentful features themselves. If hooked up to different production and perception systems, phonological computation may operate identically on a different set of primitives.

I would like to suggest that the same is true of syntactic features. Specifically, universally available is a format for features, which (consistent with section 1.3) I assume is an attribute–value pairing. In addition, there is an Edge Feature marking a lexical item as a phase head, and the possibility for a diacritic ˆ triggering movement.[10] The semantic–pragmatic specifics of features are taken not to play a role in the syntactic computation per se. This picture seems consistent with a Minimalist view of the syntactic component; in the ideal case, even these few specifications are (virtually) conceptually necessary. The intuition is that, if hooked up to a different conceptual-intentional system, syntactic computation may operate identically on a disjoint set of primitives.

It follows that there is no set of features 'provided by UG' in the sense of being specified in the *syntactic* component. Whether there is a set of semantically or pragmatically universal features, of course, remains an open question, as does the issue of the cartographic hierarchy: insofar as it is correct (see e.g. Nilsen 2003), it must be derived exclusively from semantic/conceptual considerations rather than encoded as a selectional sequence of heads as implied in Cinque (1999). Again, from a Minimalist perspective I take this to be a welcome result. Questions of learnability also play a role in what features enter into the syntax, of course: as Plaster and Polinsky (2010) emphasize, acquirers cannot be expected to build linguistic systems around complex, culture-specific conceptual-semantic information to which they have no access.

The approach taken here is similar to that of Zeijlstra (2008). In terms of Zeijlstra's *Flexible Formal Feature Hypothesis*, features are analysed as formal features able to project a functional projection if doubling is present in the input during acquisition (2008: 145). Abstracting away from his implementation and the question of whether doubling is a correct diagnostic, the crucial point is that positive evidence is required

---

[10] I do not take a stance here on the issue of c-selection features.

in the primary linguistic data in order for a feature to be analysed as 'formal' and enter into syntactic computation.[11] Like the present approach, this hypothesis avoids 'stipulating a set of formal features that is uniform across languages' (2008: 145).

Once these considerations are taken into account, there is no reason to distinguish between traditional 'semantic' features such as tense and negation and more 'social' features such as register. This too is a welcome result, for various reasons. First, it allows us to bring alternations such as that between (12) and (13) within the ambit of syntactic theory and out of the less well-understood realm of the 'user's manual'; in fact, it renders the notion of such a manual redundant. Second, it meshes with a body of work on 'social meaning' (e.g. Campbell-Kibler 2010) that focuses on social knowledge as it enters into cognition; this type of knowledge is compatible with, and in fact presupposes, a mentalist approach to language. Note that there is no blurring of the competence–performance distinction here. Society and social situations do not enter into the theory; knowledge of language and use of language are kept strictly separate, with knowledge of the situational appropriateness of specific linguistic forms a part of the former. The theory of variation expounded upon here remains a theory of competence.[12]

Culy (1996), after considering three theories of null objects in English recipes and concluding that an empty-category approach is the most promising, does an about-turn and abandons the approach on the basis that 'the regularities of registers... should not be expressed in the grammar per se' (1996: 112). Culy does not provide justification for this perspective beyond asserting that 'we must distinguish between a language and its uses'; while I agree with this statement, it is still possible and necessary to incorporate *knowledge of use* into a theory of linguistic knowledge, as I have argued.[13]

To summarize section 2.2, the main features of the model of syntactic variation I have proposed are presented in (16).

(16)  (a)  The human language faculty delimits the space of possible grammars.
       (b)  'Parameters' are attributable to differences in the feature specifications of lexical items (the BCC).

---

[11] The precise definition of PLD varies in the literature, as noted by Hale (1998: 1 n. 1). I here take it to be the input to the linguistic learning system in the acquirer's mind rather than a raw acoustic stream.

[12] For other critiques of the strict separation of social and grammatical knowledge, see Hudson (1996), Bender (1999), and Paolillo (2000). The approach taken here is similar to that of Bailey (1996) in modelling the varieties at the speaker's disposal within a single grammar; Bailey himself, however, rejects the notion that social knowledge should be part of the grammar per se (e.g. 1996: 61).

[13] Cf. Bender (1999) for further critique. Culy's further claim that a null pronoun analysis involves 'complicating the ontology of categories' (1996: 113) by admitting empty categories would not be taken seriously by many researchers nowadays, since the motivation for phonologically null elements has been repeatedly demonstrated independently of this specific case.

(c) For some features of individual grammars or apparent generalizations, a historical explanation may be more enlightening than a synchronic one ('substance-free' or 'evolutionary' syntax).

(d) There is no such thing as 'free variation'.

(e) The set of features that enter into syntactic computation is not universal, but those features have a universal format.

(f) 'Social' and 'pragmatic' features as well as 'semantic' features may enter into syntactic computation, which is blind to featural content.

With these points in mind, let us turn to variation over time, and change.

## 2.3 Modelling diachronic syntactic variation

### 2.3.1 *I-language, acquisition, and change*

The approach to syntactic change taken here is based on the approach to syntactic variation outlined in section 2.2. In that sense it is an 'I-language approach', in the tradition of Lightfoot (1979, 1999, 2006), Hale (1998, 2007), and Roberts (2007), among others.[14] It is important to realize, however, that there can exist no pure I-language approach to diachronic syntax, in that a crucial element of all diachronic linguistics is the postulation of historical relations between grammars. Crisma and Longobardi (2009: 5) provide a semi-formal version of this implicit notion:

(17)    An I-language L2 derives from an I-language L1 iff
   (a) L2 is acquired on the basis of a primary corpus generated by L1, or
   (b) L2 derives from L3 and L3 is derived from L1.

(18)    **H-relation:** Two linguistic objects X and Y (I-languages or subparts of them) are in an H-relation if and only if one derives from the other or there is a Z from which both derive.

Change, then, refers to the case in which L1 and L2 are non-identical. It is straightforward to see that this definition is not free of E-language notions. The idea of 'primary corpus' itself, for instance, cannot be defined in I-language terms: since we know that speakers cannot pass structures directly to hearers, the primary corpus must be a set of sentences, plausibly a proper subset of the weak generative capacity of L1. But weak generative capacity is an E-language notion, as Chomsky (1986b:

---

[14] The idea that 'language is not an object which has a reality of its own independent of its speakers' is associated with Chomskyan linguistics, but was also an important founding principle of the Neogrammarian school, setting them apart from earlier thinkers such as Schleicher (Morpurgo Davies 1998: 230–3).

   Under the Minimalist assumption that the syntactic component itself is invariant, with change limited to the lexicon (the BCC), syntactic change as such does not exist; this point is made by Hale (1998, 2007). Though this may seem a terminological triviality, the BCC does have consequences for a theory of change, as section 2.4 shows.

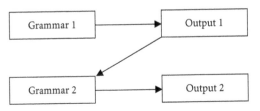

FIGURE 2.1 The Z-model of Andersen (1973: 767)

149–50 n. 89) makes clear. Moreover, it is not a random subset, since the sentences that the primary corpus consists of are determined by all sorts of contingent facts about the environment, the desires and motivations of the speaker, which way the wind is blowing (determining whether or not the sentences are audible to the hearer), etc. In addition, since speakers are fallible in production, speech errors—sentences that are not generated by L1—may occur as part of the primary corpus, such that the primary corpus can no longer even be defined as a proper subset of L1's weak generative capacity.

Furthermore, the definition in (17) is insufficient in a crucial respect: the 'primary corpus' on the basis of which L2 is acquired is, in the standard case, *not* generated by the grammar of a single individual: rather, it consists of sentences uttered by many different individuals, e.g. parents, carers, and peers, who may very well have grammars that differ in subtle ways. In other words, the classic 'Z-model' of language transmission due to Andersen (1973), given in Fig. 2.1, is an idealization that is untenable.[15] By consequence, the notion of H-relation in (18) becomes either very permissive or very restrictive: is L2 in an H-relation with all of the grammars underlying the primary corpus? Does this hold when one of these grammars is of a different 'dialect', or a different 'language', or in the case that the primary corpus contains sentences produced by a second-language speaker? And how do we define 'change'?

All this is not to say that a more adequate definition of historical relation could not be formalized; merely that such a definition would inevitably require reference to non-I-language notions. As Andersen (1973) makes clear, the transmission of language must pass through the gulf between speaker and hearer, through a cloud of murky E-language.[16]

---

[15] For technical discussion of this idealization, and an attempt to establish a class of models of acquisition that do not assume it, see Niyogi and Berwick (2009).

[16] For this reason I reject Lightfoot's (2006: 66–86) characterization of work such as Gibson and Wexler (1994) and Clark (1992) as 'E-language approaches' to acquisition, as opposed to his own 'I-language approach'; in fact, all three of these works subscribe to the E-language/I-language distinction, differing only in that they model the interaction between innate capabilities and experience in varying ways. Lightfoot, however, is usually careful to highlight the relevance of E-language notions to historical syntax (see e.g. 2006: 15).

It is clear that a diachronic linguistics without historical relations would be toothless and bizarre.[17] As Hale (1998: 1) observes:

If we adopt I-language as the proper object of study for diachronic linguistics, as it is for synchronic, such traditional questions as 'How was V2 lost in English?' cease to be sensible. In spite of this seemingly dire consequence, I will argue here that, contrary to much theoretical work in the area of historical linguistics, we must make I-language the object of our study.

Although Hale correctly identifies this consequence as dire, he does not draw the obvious conclusion: if the questions we want to ask turn out to be unformulable in purely I-language terms, then a purely I-language approach to historical linguistics must be rejected.[18] In Hale's approach to the pretheoretical notion of 'change', however, such questions are not in fact unformulable, and can be answered with reference to an actuation event (Weinreich, Labov, and Herzog 1968: 102; Hale's sense of the word 'change') plus an explanation of its diffusion. Although Hale classes diffusion as 'simply not an I-language phenomenon' and thus 'irrelevant for those interested in studying the properties of I-language' (1998: 6), he closes his article by discussing 'the loss of [a] ... property of Latin on the way to Romance' (1998: 16–17): this 'loss' (a change in the pretheoretical sense) must involve both actuation and diffusion, of course, and is stated here not in terms of individual grammars but in terms of vague E-language notions ('Latin' and 'Romance'). There is nothing wrong with this; indeed, there is no other approach to historical linguistics. The point is simply that the questions that historical linguists are interested in asking cannot be answered exclusively by reference to I-language. This does not, of course, entail that we should give up on looking at I-language; in fact, I argue in what follows that thinking of 'change' in I-language terms enables us to gain a much better understanding of it, following Hale, Lightfoot, and others.

The actuation–diffusion distinction, as Hale views it, is also not clear-cut from a nuanced I-language perspective. Diffusion, for Hale, 'represents the trivial case of acquisition: accurate transmission' (1998: 5). However, once we allow that the input to the acquirer may consist of data generated by multiple grammars, the question then becomes: accurate transmission of what? Hale rejects the view expressed in Niyogi and Berwick (1995) and Lightfoot (1997) that 'mixed PLD' may be involved in change, suggesting that this is 'strongly counterindicated by known observations regarding the acquisition process' (1998: 4), observing that children exposed to an environment in which 70 per cent of their input is in French and 30 per cent in English do not typically acquire a 'mixed' grammar. However, it is then asserted that

---

[17] Faarlund (1990: 32) makes a similar point: 'If a language only exists in the minds or brains of each individual speaker, then it will die with the speaker. Thus it does not make sense to talk of linguistic change except in the trivial case of changes in one person's language through his or her lifetime.'

[18] On this basis, Bailey (1996: 244) denies the fruitfulness of the I-language ('static', 'minilectal') approach altogether.

'acquisition of multiple "dialects" of one "language" is just as trivial as is the acquisition of multiple "languages"', and that therefore 'acquisition of more than one grammar (given sufficient exposure to both) is the *only* outcome we should be considering' (1998: 4–5). While it is true that there is no distinction between 'language' and 'dialect' in I-language terms, it does not follow that the acquirer will always be capable of discerning which grammar underlies the input. While 'English' and 'French' grammars are sufficiently different to render this possible, it is not necessarily so easy when the two input grammars are varieties of 'English' that differ in subtle ways: here it is conceivable that the acquirer would be unable to distinguish. There is no logical basis, then, for the implicit denial that acquirers ever conflate input from different sources, and hence no argument against 'mixed PLD' explanations for change. More-over, even assuming that a definition of historical relation can be formulated that distinguishes actuation and diffusion on a principled basis, some cases of apparent diffusion as 'accurate transmission' may nevertheless in fact be instances of 'multiple reactuation', where the same actuation process is triggered in multiple speakers (see Willis 1998: 47–8). Hale simply states that this 'does not seem *a priori* particularly likely'. (See also the discussion of transmission and diffusion in section 2.3.4.)

In the preceding discussion it has been assumed that, taking an I-language-informed view of historical linguistics, an instance of 'change' can be defined as two distinct grammars in a historical relation with one another. This is presumably what authors such as van Kemenade (2007: 156) mean when they refer to 'grammar (I-language) change'; if this and only this is to be classed as 'change', it follows that the locus of language change is language acquisition, as van Kemenade argues. Another logical possibility, of course, is change in the I-language over the course of a speaker's lifetime. This possibility is usually glossed over by generative syntacticians interested in historical linguistics: Crisma and Longobardi assert that 'within an I-language, there seems to be no such a thing as change' (2009: 4), though they admit that changes do in fact occur later in life (2009: 5).[19] Hale (1998) does not mention change during the lifetime. Faarlund (1990: 9) claims to defend 'on the basis of logical inference' that the locus of linguistic change is language acquisition by new generations. This logical inference seems to amount to stipulation: although 'the internalized grammar of an adult speaker may change', Faarlund states that 'such changes do not constitute a diachronic linguistic change until a future generation of speakers have adopted the mixed system as their own' (1990: 10).

There is by now substantial evidence that speakers' grammars may change in non-trivial ways throughout their lifetimes. For instance, Sankoff and Blondeau (2007) demonstrate a change from apical to posterior /r/ in Montreal French, and Wagner and Sankoff (2011) discuss a syntactic change, namely replacement of the

---

[19] In addition to the obvious case of the radical changes that take place within a single I-language during acquisition.

inflected future with the periphrastic *aller* 'to go' + infinitive, in which age-grading in a retrograde direction is found. Assertions such as that of Meisel (2011: 123) that such lifespan changes 'do not involve reanalyses of grammars' (see also the 'A-rules' of Andersen 1973) simply beg the question. The claim that the locus of language change is language acquisition, then, is subject to the same criticisms that Campbell (2001: 133) levels at the notion of unidirectionality in grammaticalization: either it is built into the definition of I-language approaches to syntactic change (as with Faarlund 1990), and is thus true but empirically vacuous, or is an empirical hypothesis stating that I-language change during the lifespan does not occur, and is false.[20]

However, this should not be taken to undermine the thesis that first language acquisition is of great importance for language change. Evidence for a 'critical period' in acquisition, a hypothesis first proposed by Lenneberg (1967), has accumulated over the years.[21] The central idea is that the interaction between the innate human capacity for language and the PLD is different in young children from that of adults. Much acquisition research is devoted to exploring the extent of this difference, the ages at which it holds, whether there is a precise cut-off or rather a tail-off in acquisition 'ability', and whether the differences are qualitative or quantitative, and these are all interesting empirical questions; see Hawkins (2001) and White (2003) for two generative introductions, and Meisel (2011) for a recent discussion bearing on diachrony. Though it has its origins in the mentalist approach to language, some version of the critical period hypothesis is accepted by all serious linguists nowadays (see e.g. Dahl 2004: 294; Trask 1999: 63–4; Trudgill 1989, 1996, 2011: ch. 2). While Hale (2007: 44) states that he does not believe in 'what is sometimes called the Critical Age Hypothesis', it is clear that this relates to a very strong version of the hypothesis, since three pages earlier he suggests that 'adults may be highly constrained in the types of changes they can make to their grammars' (2007: 41). Though the details are controversial, then, the central idea is not. One striking piece of evidence comes from the creation of a new signed language, Idioma de Señas Nicaragüense, in Nicaragua, reported by Kegl, Senghas, and Coppola (1999). According to these authors, this language was created virtually *ex nihilo* by first language acquirers under 10 years old, who converted a range of idiosyncratic homesign systems into a fully-fledged natural language (1999: 180). Discussion of the implications of this

---

[20] As a reviewer points out, however, all demonstrated cases of language change across the lifespan have so far involved relatively subtle changes in frequencies rather than the emergence of radically new structures. Further research into whether there is in fact a qualitative difference between acquisition-driven change and change across the lifespan is an urgent desideratum.

[21] *Pace* Roberts (2007: 322), the existence of a critical period is not necessary to account for the independent fact that the amount of data available to the acquirer is finite (Niyogi and Berwick 1995: 2; Niyogi 2006: 19); this fact already follows from human mortality, in conjunction with limitations on production and perception. The existence of a critical period serves to reduce the amount of relevant data even further, though.

incident, and of the critical period hypothesis in general, for diachrony can be found in Lightfoot (2006: 156–66) and Roberts (2007: 427–38).

A major advantage of incorporating the study of I-languages into historical syntax, then, is that we can apply our conceptions of the processes of acquisition—whether gained through experimental work or computational simulations such as those of Niyogi and Berwick (1995), Yang (2002)—to help us characterize the changes that we see. This includes differences in approach between adult learners and young children when faced with the same set of data (see also section 2.3.4). Paul (1880) is usually credited with being the first to highlight the importance of first language acquisition for diachrony. Crucially, it is not clear how these insights could be incorporated in a non-reductionist theory of diachrony in which languages, in the pretheoretical sense, are taken as abstract objects moving along a vector in a multidimensional phase-space, such as that of Lass (1997: 370–83).[22] I will not commit to a specific model of acquisition here (for some candidates, see Lightfoot 1991; Clark and Roberts 1993; Niyogi and Berwick 1995; Fodor 1998; Yang 2002; Buttery 2006; Niyogi 2006; Lightfoot and Westergaard 2007; Westergaard 2009), though I will outline some desiderata in section 2.3.2.

A further gain of the reductionist position is that it allows us to sidestep a persistent problem that has hounded traditional reconstruction. It has often been observed that traditional reconstructive methods result in a product which is timeless and non-dialectal (e.g. Twaddell 1948; Campbell 2013: 142–3). Pulgram (1959: 422) points out that 'Anything in linguistics that is timeless, nondialectal, and nonphonetic, by definition does not represent a real language.'[23] This problem evaporates as soon as the pretheoretical conception of 'language' plays no role in our theory, as Hale (2007) observes. Hale proposes to define a protolanguage as the 'set of all (chronologically) anterior grammars which do not differ in recoverable features' (2007: 228). Under this definition, there is no implication that a community of speakers were all possessed of a single grammar; rather, what variation existed among this community (the sociohistorical details of which are unknown or unimportant) is postulated to lie in precisely those features that we are unable to recover using traditional methods. The result of the methods then becomes an existential claim about a portion of a mental grammar, not spatiotemporally located except in the trivial sense of anteriority to its daughters. Of course, as a scientific hypothesis, the claim could be false or only partially correct. In any case, there is no longer anything weird about the entity postulated.

---

[22] Though I share Lass's scepticism about speakers as 'agents' of change (1997: 366–9), I disagree that 'we don't gain anything by invoking them' (1997: 377 n. 42), at least in the realm of syntax. Section 2.3.2 suggests some potential gains.

[23] On Pulgram's distinction between 'Real PIE' and 'Reconstructed PIE', as well as the assertion that reconstructions are non-phonetic, see Walkden (2009: 27–9).

In sum, though there is no 'pure' I-language approach to diachronic linguistics, I have argued that taking I-language into consideration in work on syntactic change is worthwhile in that it enables us to incorporate insights from acquisition into our approach to change and to avoid a conceptual problem often encountered in traditional reconstruction—in addition, of course, to allowing access to the tools and methods of analysis of synchronic generative linguistics. In section 2.3.2 I consider syntactic change itself, and its causes, in more detail.

### 2.3.2 *Mechanisms and causes*

In the previous section, an instance of 'change' was defined as two distinct grammars, L1 and L2, in a historical relation with one another. This includes both 'actuation' and 'diffusion', in the traditional sense (Weinreich, Labov, and Herzog 1968). One obvious question that can be asked is: why do changes happen when they do? In other words, what causes L2 to be different from L1?

A natural assumption about acquisition is (19) (see also Hale 1998: 9).

(19)   The acquisition of syntax is a deterministic process.

The intended meaning of (19) is that, for any temporally ordered set of sentences (PLD), any and all learners exposed to it will converge on the same grammar: there is no '"imperfect" learning or "spontaneous" innovation' (Longobardi 2001: 278). This may turn out to be false, but such an assumption is desirable for the same reasons that it is desirable to exclude randomness from models of grammar; see, for instance, the discussion in Hale (2007: 180–90) of Bresnan and Deo's (2001) stochastic approach to English dialectal 'be'. Though some models of acquisition assume determinism (e.g. Fodor 1998; Lightfoot 1991), not all do: the models of Gibson and Wexler (1994) and Yang (2002), for instance, contain probabilistic components. See Walkden (2012) for further discussion.[24]

Given (19), then, why does any syntactic change occur at all? Clearly the cause of a particular change, in the traditional sense of 'sufficient condition', cannot be an innate predisposition, as innate factors (the first and third factors, in the terminology of Chomsky 2005) are assumed to be universal and constant: all else being equal, we should not expect one acquirer to be driven by UG to 'fix' the language they are acquiring if the previous generation was able to acquire it unproblematically. See Hale (1998: 8 n. 9). As Niyogi and Berwick (1995: 1) note, the occurrence of language change is particularly problematic under the widespread assumption that children converge on the grammar of the previous generation without error: this is the 'logical problem of language change' (Clark and Roberts 1993: 299–300).

---

[24] Furthermore, if one believes that the language faculty itself matures with age independently of the input received (as do e.g. Borer and Wexler 1992), then we must also stipulate that (19) will only be true if the learners are exposed to the same sentences in the PLD at the same stage of development.

There is no real problem, however, since the assumption of error-free convergence turns out to be untenable.[25] Niyogi and Berwick explain this as follows (1995: 2):

> ... even if the PLD comes from a single target grammar, the actual data presented to the learner is truncated, or finite. After a finite sample sequence, children may, with non-zero probability, hypothesize a grammar different from that of their parents.

There are infinitely many sets of PLD that may be 'generated' by a particular L1. The 'cause' of a given change, then, assuming (19), must be a difference in the PLD as received by the learner of L2. This is what is standardly assumed in the generative literature: see Lightfoot (1999: 218, 2006: 15), Hale (1998: 9–10), Kroch (2001: 699–700), Roberts (2007: 126).[26]

Under a view of diachrony that takes I-languages into account, then, the cause of change lies in the triggering experience, Chomsky's (2005) second factor. What causes this triggering experience to be different is something that is not well explored in the generative literature, since it is tangential to the concerns of mainstream theorizing; Lightfoot (1999: 207) states that we have 'no theory of why trigger experiences should change'. It is possible to conceive of various influences, some performance-related: contact, production biases, speech errors, as well as the simple matter of what the speaker said and why. Though ideas can be advanced, and have been, a Theory of Everything would be necessary in order to capture the vast numbers of contingent factors that could potentially play a role. If the precise distribution of the PLD is not 'random', then, it is certainly 'chaotic' in the technical sense (see Hale 1998; Lightfoot 1999: ch. 10). Furthermore, invoking differences in PLD to explain attested historical changes is inevitably post hoc, since the specifics of the PLD of acquirers of previous millennia are forever beyond our grasp. The core argument of Lass (1980, 1997)—that there exist no satisfactory causal explanations of linguistic change—therefore applies in equal measure to the proposals made by Lightfoot, Hale, and others.

Fortunately, causal explanation is not a prerequisite for successful reconstruction: causal explanations have been pursued with no greater success in historical phonology than they have in historical syntax, and the few such explanations attempted by the Neogrammarians have not been accepted; see McMahon (1994: 18) and Morpurgo Davies (1998: 263–4) for discussion. Reconstruction itself, on the other hand, has yielded genuine results. This is so because for reconstructive purposes it is far more important *how* languages change than *why* or *when*; this question of the

---

[25] In addition to the logical argument given by Niyogi and Berwick (1995), Dąbrowska (2012) provides numerous empirical reasons to doubt the assumption. I will assume, with Roberts and Roussou (2003: 13), that the goal of acquisition is simply to acquire a grammatical system on the basis of experience.

[26] This cuts both ways, in fact: it is impossible to ensure that the L2 acquirer's PLD will guarantee convergence on the grammar of L1, and hence, as argued in Walkden (2012), there is no theoretical basis for 'inertia' in the sense of Longobardi (2001).

'mechanisms' of change, as distinct from its causes, therefore needs to be addressed with regard to syntax.

The central mechanism in the literature on syntactic change of the last forty years has been that of reanalysis. A term that gained weight in the 1970s (Andersen 1973; Timberlake 1977; Langacker 1977, 1979), reanalysis has been understood in subtly differing ways. Harris and Campbell (1995: 61), building on Langacker (1977), define it as 'a mechanism which changes the underlying structure of a syntactic pattern and which does not involve any immediate or intrinsic modification of its surface manifestation'. The process by which the effects of a reanalysis become apparent, affecting more contexts, patterns, or words, is then known as actualization (Timberlake 1977) or extension (Harris and Campbell 1995). A further important notion in this approach to reanalysis is the exploratory expression, an expression produced as a by-product of the ordinary operation of the grammar which may then 'catch on' and become the input to reanalysis as an obligatory part of the grammar (Harris and Campbell 1995: 72–3).

Another definition of reanalysis, closer to that implicit in Lightfoot (1979, 2002a), is as a process whereby the hearer assigns a parse to the input that does not match the structure assigned by the speaker.[27] I will assume the latter here, since it is not clear how to define 'surface manifestation' or 'underlying structure' in the framework I have adopted; in particular, it is not clear what 'a change in the surface manifestation of a syntactic pattern that does not involve immediate or intrinsic modification of underlying structure', Harris and Campbell's (1995) definition of extension, would involve. The alternative proposed here, though very similar, is more parsimonious, as there is no need for a separate process of 'extension': cases of extension can simply be viewed as either direct results of the reanalysis itself, or as smaller subsidiary reanalyses. This solves part of the problem noted by McDaniels (2003), who argues that it is not always possible to distinguish between reanalyses, extensions, and exploratory expressions on principled grounds (see also García 1990).[28]

Reanalysis here is a 'mechanism' in that it is a descriptive term for both process, misparsing, and results, instances of misparsing: it has no independent existence psychologically or genetically, nor is it causal, except in the very limited sense that the reanalysis 'causes' the hearer to update his syntactic lexicon, which is better viewed as an inextricable part of the whole process. Reanalysis does not cause syntactic change: it *is* syntactic change.

---

[27] In Lightfoot's approach, the learner/hearer is in fact only sensitive to certain 'cues', and filters out the vast majority of the input. The definition of reanalysis given here is applicable whether the learner/hearer takes in a little or a lot of the input, however.

[28] 'Exploratory expressions', though not crucial to the approach adopted here, could be seen as utterances that are strictly speaking ungrammatical and created by conscious manipulation. The methodological problem of identification still remains.

De Smet (2009: 1729) argues that ambiguity cannot be seen as the cause of reanalysis, since the ambiguity itself only arises when the newer analysis is in principle available. Under the approach to reanalysis taken here, this issue does not arise. For a given hearer, there is no ambiguity and no period in which multiple analyses are 'available'; rather, following the principle of determinism in (19), only one analysis is available and selected. If this analysis differs from that of the previous generation it is due to differences in the PLD the two generations were exposed to. Ambiguity is neither causal nor necessary.

A further argument against reanalysis adduced by de Smet (2009: 1731) is that, unlike analogy, it does not have independent status as a mechanism of synchronic grammatical organization:

The double status of analogy—as a mechanism of change and as a strategy of language use and synchronic organisation—is what gives analogy its substance as an explanation of language change... Reanalysis, by contrast, appears to show no direct correspondence to a principle of synchronic grammatical organisation, it enjoys no privileged status in synchronic model-building, and it is, consequently, confined to the realm of historical change. The only synchronic process with which diachronic reanalysis could be equated is misparsing, but it is doubtful that misparsing could be an independent strategy of language use—rather, misparsing can be expected to arise through application of the same strategies as are employed in correct parsing.

Here an ontological issue is conflated with a terminological one. 'Analogy' as de Smet uses it is multiply ambiguous between a 'mechanism' of change, an instance of change by that mechanism, and a principle active synchronically. Reanalysis, by contrast, does not have the last of these three senses. Rather, as de Smet correctly identifies, reanalysis can be equated to misparsing, which is a by-product of parsing (of course, the string is only 'misparsed' in the sense that its parse does not match the structure underlying its production; there is no absolute sense in which a parse can be 'wrong'). What appears to be needed, then, is a term 'false analogy', 'analogical change', or 'misanalogy', to differentiate between cases in which the application of analogy by the hearer results in structures which converge with those of the previous generation and cases in which it does not. Morpurgo Davies (1998: 233) points out that *falsche Analogie* was in fact the traditional term for analogically driven change in nineteenth-century linguistics. False analogy, then, arises through application of the same strategies as are employed in correct analogizing.

Analogical change, in fact, can be considered to be derivative of reanalysis. This is because, as we have seen, internal 'constant' principles can never be causal. The role of analogy then becomes to mediate in the parsing/acquisition process, selecting favoured structures over disfavoured ones; it will only be able to affect change if the PLD is already skewed, since otherwise we would have expected the previous generation to analogize in the same way (given determinism). For instance, a child might hypothesize, by analogy, that the past participle of *bring* is *bringed*, in the specific case in which no tokens of *brought* are present in the PLD. Analogy may have a role to play in more purely syntactic cases, too, in the guise of 'generalization of the input' (Roberts 2007: 275); cf. also Hawkins's (1983: 134) 'Cross-Categorial Harmony', Mobbs's (2008: 41) 'Generalize Features', Boeckx's (2011: 217) 'Superset Bias'. In these cases—as a reviewer observes—analogy is active as a cognitive/acquisitional pressure with a tendency to lead to 'harmonic' parameter settings (see also Culbertson, Smolensky, and Legendre 2012). In all cases, however, we are dealing with a grammatical decision based on a parse. Analogy may thus have an important role to play in 'how'-explanations, though not 'why'-explanations, just as reanalysis does.

I do not assume that reanalysis is 'abductive' (Andersen 1973). This is because the notion of abduction as employed in historical linguistics is not straightforwardly interpretable; Deutscher (2002) demonstrates that Andersen's conception of abduction was based on a conflation of two different ideas, and concludes (2002: 484) that 'the term "abductive innovation" is neither adequate nor necessary for a typology of linguistic innovations'; see also Itkonen (2002: 413–14) for a different conception of abduction. It is also argued in Walkden (2011) that 'abduction', if meaningful, entails a rejection of the assumption of determinism in (19), and that as a result it is abduction that should be abandoned.

### 2.3.3 *Directionality*

In the 1970s it was common for theorists of syntactic change to speak of changes as being ongoing over hundreds of years and following similar pathways over such periods (e.g. Lehmann 1973, 1974; Vennemann 1974), a phenomenon that Sapir (1921: 150) had already characterized as 'drift'.[29] As observed by Lightfoot (1979: 391), under the natural assumption that such changes must be reduced to sequences of I-language acquisition events, this view of long-term change creates more problems than it solves:

> Languages are learned and grammars constructed by the individuals of each generation. They do not have racial memories such that they know in some sense that their language has gradually been developing from, say, an SOV and towards a SVO type, and that it must continue along that path.

Adopting the I-language perspective on historical syntax, then, there can be no *independent* principles of syntactic change governing the directions that change may take. Lightfoot in fact takes this further: 'We have no well-founded basis for claiming that languages or grammars change in one direction but not in another' (2002a: 126); in other words, cross-generational tendencies of change should not

---

[29] Furthermore, 'cycles' of change had already been noted by Bopp (1816), as van Gelderen (2009a: 93) observes.

exist. Though Lightfoot admits on the same page that grammaticalization is 'a real phenomenon', the implication is that the opposite changes might just as well occur.

Both cross-generational changes and recurrent tendencies of change have, however, been identified. For instance, Kroch (1989), drawing on data from Ellegård (1953), has shown that the rise of *do*-support in English took place over a period extending at least from 1400 to 1700, at a rate that can be modelled using the logistic function. With regard to recurrent tendencies, a large number of 'cycles' and 'pathways' of change have now been catalogued; see Heine and Kuteva (2002) and van Gelderen (2011) for a selection. The challenge, then, is to account for these phenomena in a way that is consistent with the reduction of language change to series of historically related I-languages.

A number of authors have since argued that the conclusion that there can be no (consistent or recurrent) directionality in a framework that takes I-language, and acquisition, as crucial to the understanding of change, does not follow. In particular, Roberts and Roussou (1999, 2003) and van Gelderen (2004, 2009a, 2009b, 2011) have reconceptualized grammaticalization in a way that they claim is consistent with the basic assumptions of an I-language approach to linguistic change. The principles these authors claim to underlie grammaticalization are presented in (20)–(22).

(20)    **Featural Simplicity Metric** (Roberts and Roussou 2003: 201, their (23))
A structural representation R for a substring of input text S is simpler than an alternative representation R' iff R contains fewer formal feature syncretisms than R'.

(21)    **Head Preference Principle** (van Gelderen 2009b: 136, her (4))
Be a head, rather than a phrase.

(22)    **Late Merge Principle** (van Gelderen 2009b: 136, her (5))
Merge as late as possible.

These principles are used to account for a number of clear-cut cases from the grammaticalization literature. Van Gelderen (2009a: 105–8, 2009b: 186–9) suggests that both (21) and (22) follow from a principle of feature economy similar to (20), which prefers uninterpretable features over interpretable features over semantic features. Two key categories are worth mentioning.

First is the case in which a specifier of a phrase becomes the head of that phrase. Rowlett (1998: 89–97) conceptualizes Jespersen's Cycle as the reanalysis of SpecNegP elements as $Neg^0$, offering Haitian Creole *pa* as a potential recent example of this. Similarly, Roberts and Roussou (2003: 158–60, 199) present the Greek negator *dhen*, which was reanalysed from a DP to simply $Neg^0$. Willis (2007a) discusses the Welsh affirmative main clause complementizers *mi* and *fe*, arguing that they originated as preverbal subject pronouns in SpecCP and were reanalysed as $C^0$ elements. Van Gelderen (2009b) argues that the same is true of OE *whether* (see

Chapter 4) and other *wh*-elements. Roberts and Roussou (2003: 199–201) illustrate how such cases follow from (20); in addition, all of these examples fall straightforwardly under (21).

Second is the case in which a moved head originating lower in the structure becomes a head first Merged in its moved position. Roberts and Roussou (2003: 36–47) illustrate this using the English modals, which could originally be analysed as lexical verbs but became reanalysed as heads of higher functional projections (see also Lightfoot 1979, Warner 1993, and much subsequent work). Willis (2000) examines the case of conditional auxiliary forms in Slavonic, originally moved to $C^0$, becoming reanalysed as uninflected markers of conditional mood first Merged there. Van Gelderen (2009b: 153–4) mentions that, in some Dravidian languages and Indo-European languages in contact with them as well as in Jamaican Creole, verbs of saying have been reanalysed as clause-final complementizers, e.g. Sinhala *kiyəla*; another example is Ewe *bé* (Heine and Kuteva 2002: 263). Roberts and Roussou (2003: 198–202) illustrate how such cases follow from (20); in addition, all of these examples fall straightforwardly under (22).

A word of caution is in order here, however. In the approach to syntactic change adopted in this section so far, it is clear that such principles of acquisition cannot be causal in change, *contra* van Gelderen (2009b: 189):

Thus, for Lightfoot, change can only come from the outside, i.e. triggered by variable data... I have argued the opposite: that change can come from the inside.

As argued by Hale (1998) and in section 2.3.2, 'constants'—including the first and third factors of Chomsky (2005)—can never be causal in change, as this would lead to a regress problem.[30] What, then, is the role of principles such as (20)–(22)? I would suggest that they help to answer the 'how' question of syntactic change: they do not tell us when or why a change will take place, but they aid in predicting the form it will take by acting as part of the parsing and acquisition process. In this formulation there is no conflict between the view, attributed to Lightfoot, that change can only come from the PLD, and the view that 'third factor' principles guide acquisition and thus shape change.[31]

There is no 'diachronic grammar' involved, and no unidirectionality (see Newmeyer 1998, Campbell 2001, and especially Janda 2001 for criticism of this notion): changes do not have to go in the direction these principles point towards (Norde 2001, 2009; Willis 2007b). The distribution of cases of 'directional' change is entirely a function of the distribution of different sets of PLD and how the learner/hearer responds to them, i.e. the cases in which (20)–(22) and similar principles will

---

[30] See also Labov's (2001: 503) 'Principle of Contingency'.
[31] See also Niyogi and Berwick (2009: 10127); their SL model combined with a cue-based learning algorithm building on Lightfoot (1999) yields directionality straightforwardly.

be active. But of course nothing prevents the PLD from taking an entirely different form and resulting in an entirely different grammar: if a grammar is a possible one, then it follows that it must be possible for a change to result in that grammar.

It should also be noted that although (20)–(22) imply comparison of different derivations (or representations), it should not be assumed that the learner/hearer has access to two (or more) analyses and actively compares them. Instead it can be posited that at any time the learner only has access to one derivation for a given string, namely the most economical derivation as defined by (20)–(22) or similar principles that is compatible with the PLD received. Thus in the implementation of (20) there is no comparison of derivations with more or fewer syncretisms, for instance, and in the implementation of (21) there is no comparison of derivations with head elements vs. derivations with phrasal elements. This is a good thing if one believes, with Frampton and Gutmann (2002), that comparison of derivations is otiose. Similarly, (22) can be seen as a reflex of the fact that, given certain sets of PLD, it may very well be simply impossible for the learner/hearer to determine the site of first Merge of an item. There is no need to assume a 'Merge over Move' preference that is active as a synchronic principle; again, this is a good thing, as Castillo, Drury, and Grohmann (2009) and Motut (2010) observe that there are conceptual and empirical problems with such a principle.

It is possible, then, for directionality to coexist with the basic assumptions of an I-language approach to syntactic change, including discontinuity of transmission, reanalysis, and determinism. In the terminology of Willis (2011), 'universal directionality', insofar as it is applicable, can be reduced to 'local directionality', the interaction of the acquisition algorithm with the PLD leading to reanalyses whose form is predictable; see also the discussion in Willis (2011: 421–4).

### 2.3.4 *Transmission, diffusion, and language contact*

To close the section on diachrony, I will briefly discuss sociolinguistic and contact-related aspects of syntactic change, as these are necessary to give a full picture not only of how changes begin but also of how they run to completion across a speech community. Though the analysis of social and contact situations at a time depth of 2,000 years can only be coarse-grained, it still has the potential to supplement our understanding of the progression of specific linguistic changes.

Much work in the second half of the twentieth century and beyond, in the Labovian tradition, has enriched our knowledge of how linguistic innovations spread. Weinreich, Labov, and Herzog (1968) provides a manifesto for the approach, and Meyerhoff (2006) is an accessible modern introduction. Labov (1994, 2001, 2011) attempts to bring the findings of half a century's work together. Here just a few aspects of interest will be touched upon.

Many of the specific hypotheses proposed in the sociolinguistic literature, such as those to do with the social stratification and evaluation of particular linguistic variants in terms of class and gender, can obviously not be assessed with regard to the early Germanic languages, for which the surviving material is too sparse and homogeneous in origin. However, sociolinguistics has also led to findings that are of interest to any attempt to explain language change. One of these is the finding that linguistic changes typically follow an S-curve, in terms of the relative frequencies of two competing variants (see Osgood and Sebeok 1954; Bailey 1973; Kroch 1989). Another is the finding, corroborated many times since the Milroys' research reported in Milroy (1987), that change spreads more slowly through dense and multiplex social networks, and that peripheral members of networks can be instrumental in introducing changes. See Pratt and Denison (2000) for an application of this logic to syntactic change; on a macro-level, this sort of work offers hope for linking rates of language change to differences in population structure.

Another important development is the distinction between transmission and diffusion (Labov 2007). Some scholars draw no firm distinction between these two terms, considering both together as near-synonyms for the process of spread of linguistic variants through speech communities. Hale (1998), as we have seen, regards diffusion as accurate transmission, and is primarily concerned with the process of actuation or innovation, which he terms 'change'. Croft (2001), similarly, though from a very different theoretical standpoint, distinguishes 'innovation' from 'propagation'. Labov (2007) was the first to draw the distinction. Transmission, in Labov's sense, refers to an 'unbroken sequence of native-language acquisition by children' (2007: 346); diffusion, by contrast, involves the (often unfaithful) replication of linguistic features between adults.

Labov illustrates the difference between transmission and diffusion with reference to the New York short-*a* system (2007: 353–72), among other case studies. He demonstrates that the alternation between tense and lax variants of this variable is conditioned by a complex array of factors, ranging from phonological and grammatical to lexical and stylistic: function words, for instance, have lax short-*a*, while the vowel is tense in corresponding content words, and there are a number of lexical exceptions to the general phonological rules. The New York system has diffused to other communities, but typically imperfectly: for instance, in New Jersey and Albany the function-word constraint has been lost. Diffusion, according to Labov, typically leads to a 'loss of structural detail' (2007: 357), typical of adult-language acquisition.

Labov (2007) explicitly links diffusion with language contact. Contact must feature in any discussion of the early Germanic languages, since contact both within and outside the Germanic family was all-pervasive: for instance, between Brythonic Celtic and OE, and between ON and northern OE. As a basic framework, I will follow Winford (2003, 2005), who himself builds on van Coetsem (1988). Using 'transfer' as an umbrella term referring to any kind of cross-linguistic influence from a source language to a recipient language regardless of agentivity (2005: 376), Winford further distinguishes between 'borrowing'—transfer of linguistic material under recipient language agentivity—and 'imposition', transfer under source language agentivity. The distinction is based on the notion of language dominance, understood in psycholinguistic terms as the language in which the speaker is most proficient. Speakers dominant in the recipient language are likely to bring about borrowing, while speakers dominant in the source language (i.e. less proficient in the language which ultimately receives the transferred material) are likely to bring about imposition.

The distinction is important because—as Winford argues at length—borrowing and imposition are likely to have different kinds of effect on the recipient language. The prototypical example of borrowing involves open-class vocabulary items. Structural borrowing, though not impossible, is less usual; phonological and syntactic features are usually transferred through imposition (van Coetsem 1988: 25; Winford 2005: 377). In BCC terms, this can be understood in terms of more functional items being less liable to borrowing.

Of course, not all contact-induced change is transfer from one language to another, as Winford acknowledges (2005: 376 n. 3). Lucas (2009) argues that another type of contact-induced change is possible in this situation, which he labels 'restructuring': 'changes which a speaker makes to an L2 that cannot be seen as the transfer of patterns or material from their L1' (2009: 145). Lucas illustrates this possibility using several case studies of L2 acquisition in which systematic deviations from the target grammar have been observed that cannot be interpreted as resulting from the acquirer's L1 (2009: 135–8), particularly in the domain of word order. Håkansson, Pienemann, and Sayehli (2002) show, for example, that speakers of Swedish (a V2 language) learning German (another V2 language) as an L2 regularly produce non-V2 structures in their German output: a simple imposition story is clearly inadequate here.[32] Restructuring will be important later in the book, especially in Chapter 5.

Like Labov (2007), Trudgill (2011) argues that certain types of linguistic change are more likely to happen in certain sociohistorical situations, ultimately due to the balance of psycholinguistic dominance in a given area. Borrowing (to use Winford's terms) is likely to lead to additive complexification, while restructuring is likely to lead to simplification. Conclusions of this kind must be drawn with caution, since different types of change can and do coexist in the same contact situation (Winford 2005: 378). Nevertheless, contact-based explanations of this kind have the potential to satisfy Labov's (2001: 503) 'Principle of Contingency', according to which specific instances of change require specific (rather than universal) explanations.

---

[32] For an early application of this logic, see Weerman (1993: 918–22), basing himself on Clahsen and Muysken (1986).

With a framework for understanding the basic mechanisms of syntactic change in place, we can now turn to the core question of this chapter: can syntax be reconstructed, and if so to what extent?

## 2.4 Lexical-phonological and syntactic reconstruction: parallels and pitfalls

### 2.4.1 *Background to the debate*

As noted in Chapter 1, syntactic reconstruction is often thought of as having lagged behind lexical-phonological reconstruction. In this section I explore whether there is a principled reason for this, such as the inapplicability of all or part of the methodology of lexical-phonological reconstruction, and, if so, whether syntactic reconstruction is thus rendered impossible.[33] The question is lent added urgency by the emergence in recent years of phylogenetic work attempting to use syntactic properties as the basis for establishing historical relatedness, e.g. Dunn et al. (2008) and Longobardi and Guardiano (2009), on the grounds that structural features of a language are likely to be more diachronically stable (cf. Nichols 2003, Keenan 2003) and hence allow for construction of phylogenies at a potentially greater time depth. Both for phylogenetic and reconstructive purposes it is necessary to know how to proceed when the languages under consideration do not exhibit identity in syntactic properties. The two enterprises should be able to inform one another, as they are two sides of the same coin.

I take for granted here that lexical-phonological reconstruction is possible and profitable, including the reconstruction of phonological systems; though this too can be questioned (cf. Lightfoot 1979: 166), the advances in understanding brought by this form of reconstruction seem obvious.[34]

Numerous prior attempts at syntactic reconstruction have been made, e.g. Delbrück (1893–1900), Watkins (1964, 1976), Givón (1971, 1999), Lehmann (1972, 1974), Friedrich (1975), Miller (1975), Campbell and Mithun (1981), Harris (1985, 2008), Campbell (1990), Harris and Campbell (1995), Campbell and Harris (2002), Costello (1983), Kortlandt (1983), Hock (1985), Kiparsky (1995, 1996), Roberts (1998, 2007), the papers in Gildea (1999) and Ferraresi and Goldbach (2008), Willis (2011), Barðdal and Eyþórsson (2012), Barðdal (2013). Much of this work is reviewed in Walkden (2009: 7–21; 2013a). Rather than discussing these prior attempts in detail here, I approach

---

[33] Some of the material in this section overlaps with material presented in Walkden (2009, 2013a).

[34] In earlier work (Walkden 2009) I sought to investigate whether 'the Comparative Method' was applicable to syntax. However, the term is understood in many different ways (cf. Meillet 1954; Fox 1995; Baxter 2002; Harrison 2003), such that the definite article and capitalization do not seem appropriate: there is no single, clearly defined method for comparative reconstruction. In what follows I will refer to 'the methods of lexical-phonological reconstruction', a wording which I feel is less misleading.

the question from a more abstract perspective, comparing lexical-phonological and syntactic variation in order to see where parallels can and cannot be drawn. The questions will be framed around the problems that have been raised by sceptics such as Jeffers (1976), Jucquois (1976), Winter (1984), and Lightfoot (1979, 1980, 1999, 2002a, 2002b, 2006). I will term these the *directionality problem*, the *radical reanalysis problem*, the *correspondence problem*, the *pool of variants problem*, and the *transfer problem*.

In phonological reconstruction, statements about the predictable direction of sound changes help us to reconstruct proto-sounds: for instance, b > p / V___V is a highly unlikely change, whereas p > b / V___V is natural and often found (Harris and Campbell 1995: 361). On the basis of his view that a theory of change should reduce to a theory of grammar and acquisition, Lightfoot (2002a) denies the existence of (uni)directionality.

(23)  **Directionality Problem**
      we have no well-founded basis for claiming that languages or grammars change in one
      direction but not in another (Lightfoot 2002a: 126)

In response to (23), Campbell and Harris (2002: 612) argue that, although unidirectionality is rightly controversial, tendencies of directionality can be established, and that appeal to directionality is not only a valid criterion in the application of the comparative method but is fundamental to it. As seen in section 2.3.3, even those who have criticisms of grammaticalization theory or of the strong conception of unidirectionality are prepared to admit that instances of change from less grammatical to more grammatical are vastly more common than changes in the opposite direction (Campbell 2001: 133). Directionality of syntactic change is a fact, and 'grammaticalization is a real phenomenon' (Lightfoot 2006: 177). Furthermore, it is not true that 'a distinction between possible and impossible changes is in principle a necessary prerequisite for reconstruction' (1979: 154), since lexical-phonological reconstructions are a matter of qualitative probability rather than of mechanical certainty (Dressler 1971: 6; Ohala 1981). In syntax, as in lexical-phonological reconstruction, then, a minority of counterexamples to the prevailing tendency should not concern us much when carrying out reconstruction.

Directionality cannot be established for all types of sound change, of course; the change /a/ > /o/ and the change /o/ > /a/, for instance, seem to be equally possible (cf. Barðdal 2013), and lenition and fortition are mirror-image processes that appear equally natural (Kiparsky 1988). The same holds for syntax: for instance, claims of directional tendencies in constituent order change, e.g. Newmeyer's (2000) proposal that OV > VO is more natural than VO > OV, are controversial and rarely backed up with the sort of cross-linguistic study found in work on phonological directionality (e.g. Blevins 2004) or grammaticalization (e.g. Heine and Kuteva 2002). It follows that it will not always be possible for reconstruction to be guided by directionality considerations, either in phonology or in syntax. However, as in phonological reconstruction, further criteria are available to guide us; these will be the subject of section 2.4.3. The 'directionality problem' in (23), then, is no more problematic in syntax than it is in lexical-phonological reconstruction.[35]

As regards the radical reanalysis problem, Lightfoot has repeatedly emphasized that the lack of continuity between grammars, and the reanalytic nature of syntactic change, is an obstacle to reconstruction:

(24)   **Radical Reanalysis Problem**

> grammars are not transmitted historically, but must be created afresh by each new language learner...If this is correct, one can deduce very little about the form of a proto-grammar merely through an examination of the formal properties of the daughter grammars (Lightfoot 1980: 37)

Two points should be made here. First, although it is true that grammars are created afresh by each generation, it is also true that language acquisition is incredibly successful most of the time; indeed, this was, and remains, one of the key motivations of generative theory, in the form of the poverty-of-the-stimulus argument (Chomsky 1980). Given a finite array of data there are infinitely many theories consistent with it but inconsistent with one another (cf. Hauser, Chomsky, and Fitch 2002: 1577; Roberts 2007: 140), but it should follow from the first and third factors of Chomsky (2005) that grammars actually acquired on the basis of similar PLD do not vary substantially from one another, otherwise the acquisition task becomes intractable. Roberts and Roussou (2003: 13) explicitly assume that convergence with the adult grammar is successful in the normal case. This vitiates Lightfoot's criticism in (24), as under these assumptions there is no reason to assume that the grammars of successive generations will be drastically different (though such difference is entirely possible); in fact, quite the contrary.

A second relevant point is that, 'if Lightfoot's objection were valid, it would presumably apply equally to that portion of the grammar that handles phonology. This would equally mean that phonological reconstruction were impossible' (Harris and Campbell 1995: 372). Therefore, if one accepts the validity of lexical-phonological reconstruction, the objection in (24) has no purchase. The fact that change occurs by way of discrete reanalyses is also unproblematic, as there is evidence that the same is true of phonology: Ohala (1981) has shown that reanalyses of the speech signal on the part of the listener commonly lead to phonologically abrupt sound changes, e.g. of the type $VN > \tilde{V}N > \tilde{V}$ (see also Blevins 2004). Yet these changes are just as reconstructable as any other; the methods of lexical-phonological reconstruction do not require sound change to be gradual.

---

[35] For more on the non-problematicity of (23) from a generative perspective, see Roberts (2007: 362) and Willis (2011: 421–4).

A third, and more significant, objection is the correspondence problem.

(25)   **Correspondence Problem**

   It is hard to know what a corresponding form could be in syntax, hard to know how one could define a sentence of French which corresponds to some sentence of English, and therefore hard to see how the comparative method could have anything to work with. (Lightfoot 2002a: 119)

As Watkins (1976: 312) puts it, 'the first law of comparative grammar is that you've got to know what to compare'. Lightfoot is neither the first nor the only person to raise the issue of what can be compared in syntax (see also Jeffers 1976; Winter 1984: 622–3). The methods of lexical-phonological reconstruction involve hypothesizing correspondence sets in which *both* the lexical item and the sounds that constitute its phonological form are cognate, in the traditional sense of diachronic identity between those items and a single item in the proto language through transmission across generations.[36] I will state this crucial assumption as in (26):

(26)   **Double Cognacy Condition**

   In order to form a correspondence set, the contexts in which postulated cognate sounds occur must themselves be cognate.

In English *pipe* and German *Pfeife*, for example, we know that the initial /p/ and /pf/ are cognate because many other instances of /p/ and /pf/ corresponding in initial position are found (e.g. *pepper* ~ *Pfeffer*). The lexical items themselves are also cognate, as each of their component sounds is part of a systematic correspondence in this way, and so a proto-lexeme could be reconstructed. But *pipe* and *Pfeffer*, for instance, would not qualify as part of a correspondence set in the traditional sense, since although initial /p/ and /pf/ can be argued to be cognate the other sounds that make up the item do not correspond.

   Semantic similarity is a useful heuristic in establishing correspondences, but no more than that. Consider French *bureau* 'office' and Spanish *buriel* 'a coarse cloth'. If any two lexical meanings are irreconcilable, these are they; yet we can establish straightforwardly on phonological grounds that these words are entirely cognate. Moreover, in this case the meaning change that took place in French can be traced back through textual records, but this is not always possible, especially when (as is frequent in reconstruction) we are working with the earliest attested stage of a language. Since we have no restrictive, universal theory of semantic change (see McMahon 1994: 184), the notion of functional irreconcilability is essentially vacuous.

---

[36] Although the term is usually applied only to words (cf. the definition in Trask 1996a: 78), I use the term to apply to sounds in the clear sense mentioned by Harris and Campbell: 'sounds which are related to each other...by virtue of descent from a common ancestral pronunciation' (1995: 345); see also Harrison (2003: 221). Cognacy can be considered the equivalent of the historical relation between grammars argued to be necessary in 2.3.1; both are fictions, but useful ones.

In contrast, we have a very stringent criterion for formal irreconcilability: if the sounds in two words do not correspond as one would expect them to given the sound changes established for that language on the basis of other correspondence sets, then the two words are simply not cognate.

The notion of context is fundamental to phonological reconstruction. Correspondence sets can be constructed because we can observe that the sounds constituting the phonological form of a lexical item are themselves cognate. We can do this because we know that sounds develop regularly according to the phonological environment they find themselves in:[37] this is the Neogrammarian regularity hypothesis (Osthoff and Brugmann 1878: xiii). Only this way can we see how sounds (as individual items) have developed systematically *across* lexical items.

In phonological reconstruction, then, two types of unit can be said to correspond: sounds (phonemes) and words (lexical items). Correspondences are established on the basis of both, since the sounds that constitute the phonological forms of two words under comparison must be identifiable as having developed regularly, systematically, from a proto-form in order for the two words to be identified as cognate.

What would these two types of unit be in syntax? As for the lower level unit, corresponding to the sound/phoneme, I will defer the answer until section 2.4.2. The higher level unit, however, corresponding to the context in which the lower level unit occurs, is a problem. The only meaningful context that any syntactic element could occur in is the clause or sentence. However, it is clear that sentences, in the vast majority of cases, cannot be cognate in the traditional sense, since 'languages do not have finite inventories of sentences' (Harris and Campbell 1995: 347). Harris and Campbell (1995: 344) nevertheless refer to cognate sentences 'in an intuitively clear sense', although Campbell and Harris (2002: 606) add an important clarification:

Cognate sentences cannot, of course, be descended from a shared sentence;...they are examples of shared patterns descended from a pattern in the proto-language.

As Lightfoot (2002a: 123) and von Mengden (2008: 103) note, this use of the term is out of step with its general use in the phonological comparative method, since for two items to be cognate in the traditional comparative method requires there to be a diachronic identity between those items and a single item in the proto language, in the sense of transmission across generations.[38]

---

[37] A circularity thus emerges: in the comparative method, the cognacy of words is demonstrated by the cognacy of the sounds within them, which itself is demonstrated by the cognacy of the words in which they occur. This circularity is acceptable, however, to the extent that alternative explanations (chance similarity, or massive borrowing) are less plausible in accounting for the data. The account is justified by its internal coherence, which goes some way towards defending against the charge of circularity.

[38] As section 2.4.2 should make clear, although the arguments of Lightfoot (2002a) and von Mengden (2008) with regard to the cognacy of *sentences* are sound, it does not follow that the notion of cognacy has no role to play in syntactic reconstruction. Insofar as they have psychological validity, patterns (Harris 2008), constructions (Barðdal and Eyþórsson 2012), and functional lexical items all have the potential for cognacy, since they are all units that are hypothesized to be acquired and transmitted across generations.

Patterns, in and of themselves, do not provide a way out of this problem, however. In a pattern-based theory of syntax such as Construction Grammar, sentences are still formed through composition (combination) of patterns/constructions (see e.g. Michaelis 2012: 59–60). Although abstract schematic constructions in such a framework may make a number of slots available to be filled, considerable freedom is possible in filling these slots, and must be, in order to account for the discrete infinity of sentences that are grammatical in any language. The phonological matrices of lexical items also involve combination, in this case combination of phonemes, but here the combination is crucially not free: the phonological matrices are made up of a fixed set of phonemes in a fixed order, not analogous to the looseness of selectional restrictions in syntax. Patterns and constructions in syntactic reconstruction, then, cannot be quite parallel to lexical items in lexical-phonological reconstruction: the patterns/constructions themselves may be cognate, but the sentences they generate are not.

If the context in which lower level syntactic items occur must be the sentence, and if sentences are not transmitted across generations in the standard case, then a clear lack of parallel between syntactic and phonological reconstruction is observed, since the Double Cognacy Condition in (26) cannot be met. In other words, *pace* e.g. Watkins (1976: 306), Fox (1995: 105), Harris and Campbell (1995), and Barðdal and Eyþórsson (2012), the correspondence problem is real, and the comparative method as employed in phonology cannot be unproblematically applied to syntax.

The remaining two problems, the pool of variants problem and the transfer problem, are reducible to the correspondence problem. The pool of variants problem, a term coined by Vincent and Roberts (1999), can be presented as follows, following Roberts (2007: 362):

(27) **Pool of Variants Problem**
     Future tense forms in Romance:
     French:       *chanterai*
     Italian:      *canterò*
     Spanish:      *cantaré*
     Romanian:     *voi cînta*
     Sardinian:    *appo a cantare*
     Calabrese:    Ø (no form)
     Salentino:    Ø (no form)
     How are we to decide what the original form might have been on this basis? (Roberts 2007: 362)

The forms in (27) 'correspond' only in terms of function/meaning. The problem has an analogue in lexical-phonological reconstruction: English *dog* and German *Hund* are words fulfilling the same function and with the same broad meaning, but diachronic identity can be excluded on the basis that phonological regularity shows that they are not cognates. Because of the correspondence problem, however, there is no such clear criterion for syntax. The 'pool of variants' problem thus reduces to the correspondence problem: if a reliable way of reinforcing hypotheses about correspondence can be stated, we would have an independent criterion for stating that the Romance forms listed above do not correspond.

The term 'transfer problem' is from Willis (2011):

(28) **Transfer Problem**

> If a grammatical rule is present in two languages, this could be because there is a continuous line of transmission from an ancestor grammar where that rule was present or alternatively the rule could have been transferred via contact from one to the other. (Willis 2011: 414)

The difficulty is in identifying the two cases. Lexical transfer can be ruled out in the study of phonological change by the fact that transferred items typically fail to fit the system of regular sound correspondences established for the recipient language.[39] But under the analogy we have been pursuing, one equivalent of phonological transfer in syntactic reconstruction might be the transfer of functional lexical items, and so our syntactic comparative method is not necessarily able to identify this. Independent methods do exist for identifying such syntactic transfer: Harris and Campbell (1995: 372–4), Bowern (2008: 208–10), and Erschler (2009: 417–19) discuss some. For example, 'exotic' constructions that are counterexamples to strong typological principles or exceptional within the language or language family itself may be cases of transfer if a source can be identified (Bowern 2008: 209; Erschler 2009: 418). These criteria can be used to aid us in identifying syntactic transfer up to a point; however, they (and we) are not infallible. Due to the correspondence problem, then, transfer is an unavoidable confounding factor in syntactic reconstruction, and may obscure the history of the languages involved, leading us to incorrectly reconstruct retention of a feature rather than innovation: 'structural similarity may mislead a historian' (Lightfoot 2002a: 117).

### 2.4.2 *Establishing correspondences*

It is worth starting by recapitulating the main finding of the previous subsection. What would a correspondence set look like in syntactic reconstruction? In

---

[39] However, it should be noted that direct phonological transfer can also occur: Dravidian influence may well have caused Indic to develop retroflex consonants (Emeneau 1956: 7; Thomason and Kaufman 1988: 141–4; though see Hock 1996 for a different view), and it may have been as a result of influence from other Caucasian languages that Eastern Armenian developed ejectives (Vogt 1988: 458; Chirikba 2008: 45). Lexical-phonological methods are not able to identify such transfer in all circumstances. If the problem is greater for syntax, then, it may be only quantitatively and not qualitatively so.

phonological reconstruction, a correspondence set consists of words presumed to be cognate on the basis that the sounds within them can all be analysed as cognate. Pursuing the isomorphism, a correspondence set in syntactic reconstruction would consist of sentences presumed to be cognate on the basis that the lexical items or constructions 'within' them could all be analysed as cognate. But, as we have seen, sentences *cannot* be cognate, if we interpret cognacy to mean 'diachronic identity' in the sense of von Mengden (2008: 103). And if sentences are not transmitted, it is not meaningful to say that sentences preserve the evidence of lexical/constructional change in the same way that words preserve the evidence of phonological change. We therefore arrive at a real dilemma, one that vindicates Lightfoot's criticism, and the isomorphism between phonological and syntactic reconstruction partially breaks down here. This leads to the pool of variants problem (27) and the transfer problem (28), for the reasons discussed above. If the correspondence problem is real, then, additional work is required in order to demonstrate that (a) correspondences (cognacy) can in principle exist in syntax, and that (b) methods for establishing correspondences can be found. This section attempts to demonstrate both of these, using as a test case the ON middle ending *-sk*.

A crucial component of the comparative method in phonology is the notion of context, as shown in 2.4.1: sounds develop regularly according to the phonological environment they find themselves in. This is the Neogrammarian regularity hypothesis (Osthoff and Brugmann 1878). How can this be captured in syntactic reconstruction?

Let us first consider the nature of phonological inventories. Current rule-based phonological theories represent variation across items in phonological inventories as variation in feature matrices; the feature specification for English /t/, for example, might be as in (29).

(29)

$$/t/ = \begin{pmatrix} + \text{ coronal} \\ -\text{voice} \\ -\text{cont} \\ + \text{ ant} \\ + \text{ dist} \end{pmatrix}$$

A parallel can here be drawn between phonological variation and the view of syntactic variation outlined in section 2.2, given the Borer–Chomsky Conjecture in (1) (repeated below):

(1)   **The Borer–Chomsky Conjecture (BCC)** (Baker 2008: 353)
      All parameters of variation are attributable to the features of particular items (e.g. the functional heads) in the lexicon.

A possible specification for the tense head T in English is given in (30) (after Adger and Smith 2005).

(30)
$$T = \begin{pmatrix} \text{tense:past} \\ \\ u\text{Case:nom} \\ \\ u\text{Num:} \\ \\ u\text{Pers:} \end{pmatrix}$$

This approach enables units of syntactic variation, lexical items, to be seen as analogous to the units of phonological variation. Most usefully for the purposes of comparative reconstruction, both types of (lower level) unit occur in context, as part of a higher level structure containing more such units: a word or morph in the case of phonological items, and a sentence in the case of lexical items. The isomorphism between phonological and syntactic reconstruction is thus almost complete: whereas in phonology we might reconstruct the lower level unit, sounds, through their context of appearance in lexical items attested in the daughter languages, in syntax we might reconstruct the lower level unit, lexical items, through their context of appearance in sentences attested in the daughter languages. Later in this section this is illustrated on the basis of the ON ending -sk.

The issue of the parallels between syntax and phonology is certainly more complex than this, and different views have been advanced. The basic idea that sentences are (in some sense) permutations of words which are themselves permutations of sounds goes back at least to Hockett (1960), and Hjelmslev (1943) argues that syntax and phonology are entirely isomorphic. Bromberger and Halle (1989: 69) argue that 'syntax and phonology are essentially different'; van der Hulst (2005) and Anderson (2006) take issue with this position, arguing that differences between 'levels' should be minimized, and if possible eliminated, on methodological grounds. Hale (1998: 15) is sceptical:

A syntactic representation results from the concatenation of lexical items (its component parts) via the processes Merge and Move, while a phonological representation does not involve the concatenation of individually-stored segments (its component parts).

However, some sort of concatenation *is* required in phonology, e.g. the Concatenate operation proposed by Samuels (2009: 254), in order to account for the phonological effects of the concatenation of word-internal morphemes.[40] Hierarchical organization with binary branching is commonly assumed at both levels. Chomsky also characterizes phonology as 'at least partially compositional' (2004: 151). I will assume here that the parallels between syntax and phonology, if not perfect, are extensive enough for the analogy to hold.

Crucially, we know that lexical items can be cognate. If all syntactic variation is encoded on lexical items as stated in (1), then the lower level unit in syntactic reconstruction can be cognate too, meaning that correspondences (cognacy) can, in principle, exist in syntax—though we still need a method of identifying them.

It should be noted that the logic of this approach to syntactic reconstruction as laid out so far follows from the architecture of the system within Minimalism, since it employs an 'item-based' view of syntactic variation in which syntactic primitives are stored in an inventory (the lexicon). As such it illustrates that derivational models of syntax can approach the question of proto-syntax in much the same way as representational models. However, the logic of the approach is valid not only for Minimalist theories of syntax but in any approach that assumes such an 'item-based' view of syntactic variation. Construction Grammar, with its Constructicon, is one such approach (cf. Michaelis 2012 and Barðdal and Eyþórsson 2012), as is the implicit pattern-based theory of syntactic variation assumed by Harris and Campbell (1995) and Harris (2008). It is less obvious how to extend this logic to a model which assumes variation to be encoded in the form of phrase-structure rules (as in early transformational approaches and LFG), as constraints (as in HPSG), or as the values of a fixed universal set of parameters (as in early Principles & Parameters theories of syntax).

The parallels only run so far, however. Central to phonological reconstruction is the fact that both sounds and the units that contain them are transmitted from generation to generation. This allows hypothesized sets of cognate sounds and hypothesized sets of words containing them to provide mutually reinforcing evidence: in effect, a 'fossil record' of phonological change. As discussed in section 2.4.1, however, sentences are not transmitted in this way—the Double Cognacy Condition in (26) does not hold of syntax—and so this fossil record is absent, and the isomorphism is incomplete.

---

[40] Unlike the symmetric Merge we see in syntax, this Concatenate operation may turn out to operate asymmetrically, as argued by Samuels and Boeckx (2009).

Does this mean the end of the road for syntactic reconstruction? In the remainder of this section I will argue that it does not. Correspondences can be established in other ways: first, through the use of phonological clues, and secondly, through the distribution of lexical items across structures.

Where overt phonological material is present, cognacy of lexical items can usually be established. Once this is done, working out the syntactic properties of those lexical items can then follow. This forms the starting point for Willis (2011: 425–42), in which a number of forms are identified which can be shown to be cognate with the modern Welsh free-relative marker *bynnag*. Similarly, in Old East and West Nordic texts a 'middle voice' verbal ending can be found (Barnes 2004: 146; Faarlund 2004: 123–7; Ottósson 1992; Ottosson 2008, 2009). In Old West Nordic it primarily functions as a reflexive, reciprocal, or anticausative marker, depending on the verb to which it is attached (Ottósson 1992: 66–8); although a passive function can frequently be found in Old Swedish and Old Danish, Ottosson (2009: 32) notes that the passive function is extremely rare in Old West Nordic texts. In Old East Nordic the ending surfaces as -*s*; in Old West Nordic it mainly surfaces as -*sk*, although -*mk* is found in the first person and -*zk* in the second person plural (Eyþórsson 1995: 234).

(31)  Úlfrinn  gapði  ákafliga  ok  fekksk  um  mjök  ok  vildi  bíta  þá
      wolf.DEF  gaped  greatly  and  got.REFL  about  much  and  would  bite  them
      'The wolf gaped terribly and thrashed around and wanted to bite them'
      (*Prose Edda*, 34)

This ending has no obvious morphological parallels in the early Germanic languages outside Scandinavia. However, a third person reflexive pronoun with a phonologically similar shape is attested in some of the other early Germanic languages, e.g. Gothic *sik*, OHG *sih* (Wright 1910: 123).

(32)  Jah  gawandida  sik  Iēsus  in  mahtái  ahmins  in  Galeilaian
      and  turned  REFL  Jesus  in  power.DAT  spirit.GEN  to  Galilee.ACC
      'Jesus returned in the power of the Spirit to Galilee'
      (Gothic Bible, Luke 4: 14)

(33)  muor  varsuuilhit  sih
      sea  swallows  REFL
      'the sea swallows itself'
      (*Muspilli* 53)

On the basis of both phonological and semantic criteria it can be argued that the ON -*sk* ending is cognate with this pronoun. The alternation between -*sk* and -*mk*, in particular, is indicative of this.

There is also a partial parallel in the regularity of syntactic change. Although unconditioned changes in the featural composition of phonemes may occur, many changes are represented in terms of conditioning environments, as in (34):

(34)   r > Ø / V ___ [C, +coronal] #

This is a change that happened in some varieties of English around 1300, according to Lass (1997: 284–5), yielding forms such as *hoss* 'horse', *cuss* 'curse', and *passel* 'parcel'. Do environmentally conditioned syntactic changes, analogous to phonemic splits and mergers, occur?

There is evidence that they do. Longobardi (2001) provides an example from the history of French, where the Latin noun *casa(m)* 'hut, house' developed in two different ways: into Old French *chiese*, a noun that was later lost except in a few fixed expressions, and into Old French *chies*, which became the modern French preposition *chez* (2001: 276). Using a variety of evidence from the Romance languages he demonstrates that a construct state construction is present in some of these languages, in which common nouns move leftward to $D^0$ under certain conditions, and that French *chez* shared enough of the properties of this construction to be plausibly derived from it. The phonological alternation is then explained on the grounds of differing stress patterns (2001: 293). Importantly for our purposes, the single lexical item *casa(m)* develops in two different ways in different contexts: where it moves to $D^0$, it becomes the preposition *chez* (presumably through string reanalysis of a D head as a P head at some point during the history of French), and elsewhere it remains syntactically the same. This type of change, where the 'new' and 'old' items coexist in the same grammar, is referred to as 'divergence' in the literature on grammaticalization (e.g. Hopper 1991: 22; Hopper and Traugott 2003: 118–22), and is analogous to a phonemic split. In addition to the *chez* example, the fixed item *methinks* in early modern English coexisted with its full lexical sibling, the verb *think* (Palander-Collin 1997: 374). Similarly, the conditional marker *by* in fourteenth-century Old Russian, an uninflected form first Merged in $C^0$ which had been reanalysed from the second/third person form of the perfect auxiliary *byti* 'to be', coexisted with other forms of this verb, and the two could even co-occur in the same clause (Willis 2000).

We can thus see that an effect akin to the Neogrammarian regularity hypothesis is at work. Syntactic change of a given lexical item may occur within a correctly defined context, and will normally be exceptionless. This in fact follows from the nature of syntactic change. If a speaker reanalyses an item in a certain context, e.g. a noun as a preposition, there is no reason for that speaker also to postulate the original ('correct') analysis of that item in that context. More generally, given the parallels presented above in which functional lexical items are analogous to sounds, it is difficult to imagine that *irregular* syntactic change could even exist. Irregular phonological changes are those which affect only specific individual words in which the sounds occur, with no phonologically definable context. Pursuing the analogy, an irregular syntactic change would affect only specific individual sentences in which the functional lexical items occur, with no syntactically definable context. Such 'sentential diffusion' is, however, ruled out by the simple fact that sentences are normally not transmitted from generation to generation, as discussed by Lightfoot (2002a) and in section 2.4.1.

Pires and Thomason (2008) challenge the idea that there can be regularity in syntactic change, arguing that the analogical spread of animacy through Slavic noun declension paradigms is not regular in the sense of regular sound change, although they admit that 'the analogic changes that led to the current states of [Russian and Čakavian Serbo-Croatian] were regular in that they affected all nouns in the relevant class, case, and number categories' (2008: 53). This appears to be a misunderstanding of the nature of regularity, since, as the above quotation shows, their example in fact provides evidence for it.

In a footnote, Pires and Thomason (2008: 53 n. 17) also cite personal communication from Longobardi, stating that he has never argued for regularity of syntactic change, 'considering, for instance, that change of syntactic features may spread regularly [*sic*] and incompletely through similar lexical items'. Again, this is not a problem if we wish to maintain that syntactic change is regular. The sounds /p/, /t/, and /k/ are similar phonological items, and yet in phonological change /p/ > /pf/ word-initially may perfectly well occur regularly without /t/ > /θ/ and /k/ > /kx/ also occurring in the same context, as happened as part of the German Second Sound Shift (König 2005: 63). There is no need for 'similar' lexical items to pattern together in regular syntactic change, just as there is no need for 'similar' phonemes to pattern together in regular phonological change.

Evidence, then, can be adduced from distributional patterns of the lexical items in question, i.e. the syntactic environments in which they can be found in the daughter languages. As with phonology, surface formal similarity is not enough, although it is a useful criterion. Environmental alternations brought about by the regularity of syntactic change are key, where they exist; as in phonological reconstruction, these help to differentiate between similarity caused by genetic relationship and similarity due to other causes. For instance, in the case of the Old West Nordic *-sk* ending a lexical split can be observed, since Old Icelandic itself also retains the reflexive pronoun alongside the middle ending:

(35)  Grettir  lá   kyrr   ok   hrœrði  sik    hvergi
      Grettir  lay  quiet  and  moved   REFL   nowhere
      'Grettir lay quietly and did not move an inch' (*Grettis Saga*, 35)

The distribution of the two cognates is different: the middle ending is only found postverbally, while the pronoun has greater syntactic freedom of position. This suggests a change in which the pronoun became reanalysed as an ending in this position.[41]

Round (2010) suggests a related criterion for syntactic reconstruction. If a sound change that occurred in the history of a language can be established to have affected words in a certain position in a phonological domain (such as its right edge), then words that have descended as doublets, in which one has undergone the change and the other has not, must have been able to occupy different syntactic positions, on the reasonable assumption that there exists some alignment between prosodic and syntactic domains (2010: 67). If the two doublet forms have slightly different meanings or functions, then again lexical split is a possibility. Round gives some illustrations of this criterion from the Tangkic language family.

Finally, formal and functional similarity are additional criteria for determining correspondences, although nowhere near as reliable as the Double Cognacy Condition-based method of lexical-phonological reconstruction. (To illustrate this, consider 'false cognates' such as English *day* and Spanish *día* 'day', English *dog* and Mbabaram *dog*, or the list of formally similar words between Ancient Greek and Hawaiian given in Trask 1996b: 220.) 'Formal' similarity in a syntactic context is taken to include properties such as word order and agreement patterns as well as purely phonological similarity.

To sum up: correspondences and cognacy can exist in syntactic reconstruction, given the BCC in (1), but identifying them is difficult and cannot depend on the methods of lexical-phonological reconstruction applied by analogy. Instead, lexical-phonological methods can be used directly to identify cognates, but only when the lexical items in question have phonological form; as Hale (1998: 16) points out, many of the most interesting items do not. The regularity of syntactic change as outlined in this section provides another criterion, supplemented by formal and functional similarity. The prospects for identifying correspondences are therefore not as rosy as might be hoped, but using these criteria we can at least do better than reconstructing under identity, which according to Lightfoot (2002a: 120) is as far as one can go.[42]

### 2.4.3 *Establishing proto-forms*

Harris and Campbell (1995: 344) recognize two steps in traditional methods of lexical-phonological reconstruction, each of which feeds into the other: the establishment of correspondences and the reconstruction of proto-forms. The preceding sections have argued that the establishment of correspondences in syntax is possible, though

---

[41] The exact synchronic morphosyntactic status of the ending is debated; see e.g. Eyþórsson (1995: 238–41), Ottósson (2008), Walkden (2013a). I here analyse it as a suffix.

[42] One might question why, under Lightfoot's assumptions, it is even feasible to reconstruct identity. Is there any more basis for determining correspondence when two grammars exhibit 'identical' patterns than when differences are found? Structural similarity may be misleading, as Lightfoot (2002a: 117) observes.

not in exactly the same way as in phonology. In this section I argue that no such disparity exists with regard to the step of establishing proto-forms: all the criteria used for this purpose in lexical-phonological reconstruction are in principle equally applicable in syntactic reconstruction. The discussion will be based around Lass (1997: 228–32), which provides a recent statement of these guidelines for lexical-phonological reconstruction (cf. also Lass 1993).

(36)   'Quasi-conventionalist' guidelines for reconstruction
        (a) Process naturalness
        (b) System naturalness
        (c) Simplicity
        (d) Legality
        (e) Family consistency
        (f) Oddity condition
        (g) Portmanteau reconstruction

Guideline (a), process naturalness, suggests that a postulated proto-form ('projection', in Lass's terms) ought, where possible, to reflect the natural starting point of a pathway of change. The issue of pathways in syntactic change has been covered in 2.3.3. In the case of the ON middle voice ending -*sk* and its cognate pronoun *sik*, for example, we should assume that the pronoun is the starting point, since the development from pronoun to verbal suffix is well attested and reasonably well understood (see Fuß 2004).

Guideline (b), system naturalness, suggests that the full system of postulated proto-forms should be one that is compatible with known implicational universals as established through typological study. For instance, no VO language appears to contain clause-final complementizers (Dryer 1992: 102; Hawkins 1990: 225; see Biberauer, Holmberg, and Roberts 2010 for a theoretical account). Proceeding naturally to the inductive generalization that this combination is an impossible one in human languages, we should be wary of positing such a system at any point during a language's history (see also von Mengden 2008). Of course, the usefulness of typological generalizations is dependent on their accuracy; see Wichmann (2008) for discussion of the dangers of assuming that properties correlate when in fact they do not. The typological criterion does not replace traditional reconstructive techniques; rather, it is a heuristic to be used alongside them, and with care.

Lass (1997: 229) states guideline (c) in biological terms: 'Apomorphies should be single rather than multiple: avoid homoplasy.' In other words, we should minimize the number of innovations posited, and parallel innovation should not be the default assumption: this can be seen as a criterion of methodological economy (cf. Willis 2011: 424). Hale (2007: 240–2) argues that it is dangerous to apply this criterion, since the change under investigation may itself be evidence for subgrouping: if three related languages show one variant and another related language shows another, and if the variant shared by the three languages is likely to be innovative, it would be sufficient grounds for subgrouping the three languages together as against the fourth. Hale's point is well taken as a cautionary note when applying the criterion of economy; in cases where subgroupings have already been safely established, however, such as the West Germanic languages as opposed to Gothic, we can make confident inferences on the basis of such a criterion. In the case of the ON middle ending, positing that the suffix rather than the pronoun was original to Proto-Germanic, or that both were present in Proto-Germanic, would require us to suppose that the suffix was lost independently in both East and West Germanic. As stressed by Lass (1997: 229), this guideline needs to be applied with particular care, especially when it conflicts with another guideline such as (a).

(d), legality, is another typological criterion: 'no reconstructed segment may be inconsistent with our present knowledge of the capabilities of the human vocal tract' (Lass 1997: 229); analogously for syntax, no reconstructed lexical item may be inconsistent with our present knowledge of the capabilities of those elements of the human language faculty that deal with syntax. For instance, if we believe for whatever reason that the No Complex Values hypothesis of Adger (2010), given in (37), is well motivated, then we should not reconstruct a lexical item with the specification in (38).

(37)   **No Complex Values**
       Features cannot embed other features in a lexical item.

(38)
$$T = \begin{pmatrix} \text{tense:}[u\text{Past:perfect}] \\[1em] u\text{Case:Nom} \\[1em] u\text{Num:} \\[1em] u\text{Pers:} \end{pmatrix}$$

Our knowledge of the limitations on syntactic computation is arguably less, or less concrete, than our knowledge of the limitations of the vocal tract, but there is no qualitative difference in the application of the guideline. Legality is closely related to system naturalness: while system naturalness states that reconstructions should not violate implicational universals, legality states that reconstructions should not violate absolute universals.

Guideline (e), family consistency, speaks for itself: 'No segment type ought to be reconstructed for a protolanguage that does not occur in at least one descendant language' (Lass 1997: 229). Applied to lexical items rather than segments, and concretely to the case of the ON middle voice, this suggests that we should not reconstruct, for instance, a noun *sik for Proto-Germanic as the origin of the cognate pronoun and endings, even though it is known that reflexive pronouns commonly originate as nominals (cf. van Gelderen 2000). This guideline must be used with caution, however, especially where it conflicts with one of the others.

Guideline (f), the 'oddity condition', essentially states that the rarer an item is, the more evidence we should require to reconstruct it. This amounts to a uniformitarian principle based on the extrapolation of (qualitative) likelihoods to the past, also referred to as the Panda Principle: 'in the absence of powerful evidence, the improbable probably wasn't' (Lass 1997: 230).[43] Although basic OVS orders are argued to exist, for instance Hixkaryana (Derbyshire 1979), the amount of evidence required to motivate a reconstruction of Proto-Germanic as OVS in neutral declarative clauses would be comparatively high.

Finally, portmanteau reconstruction, (g), is a procedure designed to deal with cases where positing an existing item as primitive, as preferred by guideline (e), yields extreme process unnaturalness. This is the case in lexical-phonological reconstruction for the Indo-European interrogative pronoun, whose initial consonant survives variously as labial, dental, velar, and labialized velar (Lass 1997: 231). The optimal response, according to Lass, is then to ensure 'maximal coding', ensuring that as much of the variation found in the daughters as possible is packed into the proto-item.

I end this section with a further quotation from Lass (1997: 232):

projection... [is] guided by a network of partial prohibitions and procedural desiderata, which co-operate with whatever other argumentative strategies one uses. The network of procedural, conventionalist and empirical constraints underwrites our claims to epistemic respectability.

## 2.5 Summary

This chapter has argued that, given an appropriate theory of syntactic variation (2.2) and syntactic change (2.3), it is possible to approach the question of syntactic reconstruction (2.4). Under the approach to variation adopted here, the BCC in (1), stipulation would be required in order to argue that cognates could *not* exist in syntax; however, identifying these cognates remains difficult, and parallels with lexical-phonological reconstruction cannot universally be maintained. In some instances, cognacy can be hypothesized on phonological grounds; in other instances, the distribution of syntactic items can be used to identify correspondences, based on

---

[43] This Panda Principle must be clearly distinguished from the unrelated use of pandas as an expository device in Lass (1980: 84–5 n. 18), intended as an argument against functionalism. For more on giant pandas, see Dudley (1997).

the idea that syntactic change, like phonological change, is 'regular' by a certain definition. Finally, if correspondences can be established, reconstruction of proto-forms may take place along the same lines as in lexical-phonological reconstruction.

A simple example of reconstruction, concerning the origin of the ON middle voice suffix, was used to illustrate the method. The intuition that the ending originated through reanalysis of the reflexive pronoun is not a new one: it has been accepted for over a hundred years (e.g. by Nygaard 1906, Gordon 1927, Faarlund 2004, Ottosson 2008). By its very straightforwardness, though, it weighs heavily against Lightfoot's (2002a: 120) contention that reconstruction of syntax is possible only in cases of identity, since in this example two different lexical items with differing forms, functions, and syntactic distribution descend from a single source.

The rest of this book presents a number of case studies dealing with aspects of early Germanic clause structure, drawing on the approach outlined in this chapter.

# 3

# Verb position in early Germanic main clauses

## 3.1 Introduction

This chapter represents an attempt to put the methodology for syntactic reconstruction outlined in Chapter 2 into practice, by reconstructing aspects of the structure of Proto-Northwest Germanic main clauses. The focus throughout is on the position of the finite verb in declarative main clauses: other types of clause, such as subordinate clauses, imperatives, and interrogatives, are left out of consideration here, though interrogatives are discussed extensively in Chapter 4.

Second and subsequent conjoined declarative main clauses ('conjunct clauses') are also left out of consideration. It has often been observed for OE (e.g. Andrew 1940: 1; Mitchell 1985: 694) that these frequently appear to pattern with subordinate clauses with regard to constituent order, as in (1). Similar cases can be found for OHG, as in (2), though these are rare (Axel 2007: 77–9), and for OS, as in (3).

(1)  Her        for    se    ilca    here   innan  Myrce  to   Snotingham  
     this-year  went   the   same    army   inside  M.     to   N.  
     &      þær     wintersetle          **namon**  
     and    there   winter-quarters   took  
     'This year the army travelled inside Mercia to Nottingham and took up winter quarters there'  
     (cochronE,ChronE_[Plummer]:868.1.1098)

(2)  Inti  fon    mir selbomo  niquam      óh   her  uuár  **ist**  ther  mih  santa  
     and   from   me  self     NEG-came    but  he   true  is     who   me   sent  
     'I have not come here of my own accord, but he who sent me is true'  
     (*Tatian* 351,29; Axel 2007: 78)

(3)  Si    ni    uueldun  im    hôrien  te  thiu,      ac   sie  simla  mêr
     they  NEG   wanted   them  hear.INF  to  that.INSTR  but  they  still   more
     endi  mêr    oƀar   that   manno      folc  hlûdo  **hreopun**
     and   more   over   the    men.GEN    folk  loudly  called
     'They did not want to listen to them, but instead called out more and more
     loudly over the crowd of people'
     (*Heliand* 3568–70)

Campbell (1970: 93 n. 4) goes so far as to suggest that 'even co-ordinating conjunctions are syntactically subordinating' in OE. More recent work (Stockwell and
Minkova 1990: 512–13; Kiparsky 1995: 148–9; Pintzuk 1999; Bech 2001: 86–93;
Ohkado 2005: 196–282) has indicated that this is an overstatement of the case.
Kiparsky (1995: 148), for instance, observes that long-distance *wh*-dependencies
into subordinate clauses can be found, but that the same is not true of conjunct
clauses; furthermore, conjunct clauses permit V1 order even when there is no parallel
in the initial conjunct, whereas this order is extremely rare in subordinate clauses.
Stockwell and Minkova (1990) observe that subjunctive verb forms, frequent in
subordinate clauses, are rare in conjunct clauses. Bech (2001) adduces quantitative
evidence demonstrating that there is no strong tendency for conjunct clauses to be
verb-final, contrary to what is often implied in the literature, but that there are
statistically significant differences in the distribution of verb-positions between main
and conjunct clauses in OE. I will therefore follow Bech (2001: 93) and other authors
in keeping the two types of clause apart.

    Gothic will also be left out of consideration for the greater part of this chapter, due
to (i) the special interpretative difficulties arguably involved with the Gothic data (see
section 1.4.1), (ii) the preponderance of clauses introduced by the conjunction *jah*,
and (iii) the fact that it appears to behave differently from the other early attested
Germanic languages with regard to main clause word order (see Eyþórsson 1995).
Reconstructions will therefore be posited here initially only for a Proto-West Germanic or Proto-Northwest Germanic stage, though section 3.5 will make some
further tentative suggestions on integrating Gothic.

    Finally, word order in subordinate clauses will not be investigated here. It can be
observed that there is an asymmetry in verb position between main and subordinate
clauses in all the early West Germanic languages, but that the verb is not consistently
final in subordinate clauses as it is in modern German: see e.g. van Kemenade (1987)
and Fuß and Trips (2002) on OE, and Axel (2007) on OHG. The same is true for ON
poetry (Kuhn 1933; Þorgeirsson 2012), though in ON prose there seems to be no such
asymmetry (see e.g. Faarlund 2004: 191). I leave this interesting issue aside.

    Section 3.2 focuses particularly on the V2/V3 alternation that has often been observed
in OE main clauses. Some scholars (e.g. Westergaard 2005; Hinterhölzl and Petrova
2009) have speculated that the V3 pattern resulted from an innovation. Sections 3.2.1

and 3.2.2 lay out the situation in OE, OHG, OS, and ON. Section 3.2.3 presents
an analysis involving multiple, information-structurally determined positions for subjects and other constituents in the clausal left periphery (C-domain) as well as verb-
movement to the left periphery. It is argued in section 3.2.4 that the possibility of V3 is
more likely to be the result of shared retention than of innovation among these
languages; thus, an active left periphery is reconstructed for Proto-Northwest Germanic.

In section 3.3 I consider V1 main clauses, which are found in all the early Germanic
languages. Following much previous research I argue that they are associated with a
special (non-assertive) interpretative value, and that the possibility of V1 can be
reconstructed for Proto-Northwest Germanic at least.

In section 3.4 I discuss 'verb-late' main clauses, which have so far resisted insightful
analysis. After demonstrating the presence of such clauses in all the early West
Germanic languages, I propose an account based on the discourse status of these
clauses as presupposed. Section 3.5 is an attempt to integrate Gothic into the picture,
in particular tackling the question of whether verb-movement to the left periphery
should be posited for Gothic or for Proto-Germanic; section 3.6 then summarizes the
reconstructions proposed in this chapter.

## 3.2  V2 and V3

### 3.2.1  *V2: the data*

A first glance at the syntax of OE main clauses 'suggests a strong parallelism' between
OE and modern Germanic V2 languages such as Dutch and German (van Kemenade
1987: 42). Examples (4)–(6) illustrate this.[1]

(4)  We   **habbað**   hwæðere     þa    bysene     on    halgum   bocum
    we    have      nevertheless  the   examples   in    holy     books
    'We have, nevertheless, the examples in holy books'
    (cocathom1,+ACHom_I,_31:450.315.6332)

(5)  On   twam   þingum   **hæfde**   God   þæs   mannes   saule   gegodod
    in    two    things    had     God   the   man's    soul    endowed
    'With two things had God endowed man's soul'
    (cocathom1,+ACHom_I,_1:184.161.166)

(6)  Þa   **ongan**   he   ærest   sprecan   to   þam   munece
    then  began    he   first   speak.INF  to   the   monk
    'Then he first began to speak to the monk'
    (comary,LS_23_[MaryofEgypt]:65.42)

---

[1] References to OE examples are given from the YCOE (Taylor et al. 2003).

In all of these examples the verb follows the first constituent. Where an adverbial 'operator' such as *þa* or *þonne* is initial, as in (6), this pattern is dominant (see e.g. Koopman 1998: 141; Fischer et al. 2000: 106). Moreover, it is the majority pattern in main clauses in general. Cichosz (2010: 72–6) shows that in samples of non-conjunct declarative main clauses from OE poetry, original prose, and translated prose, V2 is the most common position for the verb. Searching the YCOE reveals that 2,739 of 4,173 such clauses in Ælfric's *Lives of Saints* (65.6%) are V2, and 1,138 of 2,717 such clauses in Bede's *Historia* (41.9%).

It has long been observed that OHG exhibits a robust variant of the V2 property (e.g. Reis 1901; Lippert 1974; Robinson 1997; Axel 2007). Lippert (1974) counts 280 of 380 main declarative clause examples in *Isidor* as verb-second (73.6%). Examples of subject-initial and non-subject-initial verb-second are in (7) and (8).

(7)  der    antichristo   **stet**    pi    demo    altfiant
     the    antichrist    stands    with    the    old-fiend
     'The Antichrist stands with the devil'
     (*Muspilli* 44)

(8)  pidiu   **scal**   er    in    deru    uuicsteti    uunt       piuallan
     thus    shall    he    in    the    battlefield    wounded    fall
     'Thus he shall fall, wounded, on the battlefield'
     (*Muspilli* 46)

Cichosz (2010: 72–6) shows that in samples of non-conjunct declarative main clauses from OHG poetry, original prose, and translated prose, V2 is the most common position for the verb, and that V2 is even more firmly established in OHG than it is in OE.

As observed by Rauch (1992: 24), Erickson (1997), and Dewey (2006: 60), V2 seems to be the dominant pattern in OS as it is in OE and OHG. My quantitative data enables this to be stated more precisely: a total of 1,597 of the 2,348 main clauses in the *Heliand* (68.0%) have the verb in second position, as in (9) and (10).

(9)  Godes    engilos    **antfengun**    is     ferh
     God's    angels    received    his    spirit
     'God's angels received his spirit'
     (*Heliand* 3350–1)

(10)  Mattheus    **uuas**    he    hêtan
      Matthew    was    he    called
      'He was called Matthew'
      (*Heliand* 1192)

Finally, in ON the finite verb in declarative main clauses is typically in second position (Nygaard 1906; Eyþórsson 1995: 189; Faarlund 2004: 191; Þorgeirsson 2012:

234–6), as in (11) and (12). Examples in which the verb is later than second are vanishingly rare; see Table 3.1.

(11)  Stýrimaður **þarf**  byrinn      brýnna     en     sá
      helmsman   needs  breeze.DEF  sharper    than   that.NOM
      er    nautunum   skal   brynna
      that  cows.DAT   shall  water.INF
      'A helmsman needs a sharper breeze than someone who waters the cows'
      (1150.FIRSTGRAMMAR.SCI-LIN,.75)

(12)  Nú    **skal**tu    drekka   blóð    dýrsins
      now   shall-2SG   drink    blood   beast.DEF.GEN
      'Now you shall drink the beast's blood'
      (*Hrólfs saga kraka* 34: 101)

In all of these languages, however, a substantial number of non-V2 clauses can be observed, of a kind that would be unexpected in a corpus of a strict V2 language such as modern German or Dutch. These exceptions are classifiable 'into a relatively small number of easily distinguishable and clearly describable types' (Axel 2007: 63), for which distinctive interpretative properties can be posited. Much of the rest of this chapter is devoted to describing and explaining these types across the early Northwest Germanic languages.

### 3.2.2  V3

A pattern in which two constituents precede the finite verb, as in (13), (14), and (15), has long been recognized for OE.

(13)  æfter   his   gebede   he   **ahof**   þæt   cild    up
      after   his   prayer   he   lifted   the   child   up
      'After his prayer he lifted the child up'
      (cocathom2,+ACHom_II,_2:14.70.320)

(14)  Fela    spella    him   **sægdon**   þa    Beormas
      many    stories   him   told      the   Permians
      'The Permians told him many stories'
      (coorosiu,Or_1:1.14.27.243)

(15)  Nu    se    rica   mann   ne    **mæg**   her    habban...
      now   the   rich   man    NEG   can      here   have...
      'Now the rich man cannot here have...'
      (coaelive,+ALS[Ash_Wed]:110.2758)

Where the subject is pronominal, as in (13), it almost invariably precedes the verb in main clauses not introduced by *þa* or *þonne* (Haeberli 1999a: 335). Van Kemenade

(1987: 138–40) was aware of such examples, in which the second-position constituent is a subject. Pintzuk (1999) additionally observed that examples such as (14) involving object pronouns existed.[2] The existence and relative prevalence of examples such as (15), in which a full DP subject precedes the finite verb, was first brought to light by Allen (1990: 150–1), Swan (1994), Bech (1998, 2001), Koopman (1998), and Haeberli (2002). Bech (2001: 96–8) demonstrates for XP-Subj-$V_{fin}$ non-conjunct main clauses that 22 of 101 subjects (21.8%) in her early OE sample, and 21 of 86 (24.4%) in her late OE sample, are full nominals. Haeberli (2002) found that subject-verb non-inversion (i.e. V3) occurred 188 times (28.7%) of the time in a small corpus of 654 clauses with full nominal subjects in second position and a fronted constituent in initial position, taken from ten text samples. Speyer (2008, 2010: 187–210) additionally demonstrates that examples of V3 of this kind in OE cannot all be written off as instances of verb-late structure where the verb is 'accidentally' in third position.[3]

Tomaselli (1995) presents a number of cases of V3 main clauses in OHG:

(16)   erino   portun   ih   **firchnussu**
       iron    portals  I    destroy
       'I destroy iron portals'
       (*Isidor* 157)

(17)   Dhes     martyrunga   endi   dodh    uuir   **findemes**
       his      martyrdom    and    death   we     demonstrate
       mit     urchundin    dhes           heilegin   chiscribes
       with    evidence     the.GEN   holy        writings
       'We demonstrate his martyrdom and his death with evidence from the holy scriptures'
       (*Isidor* 516)

Tomaselli argues that subject pronouns are the only elements found in the second position of a V3 clause (1995: 348). Furthermore, she claims that V3 clauses are only found in the *Isidor* translation and in the Monsee Fragments. As Axel (2007: 239) points out, these are dated earlier than most OHG prose texts.

Tomaselli's first claim appears to be falsified, at least on the surface, by clauses such as (18), from Harbert (1999: 258), and (19), from Axel (2007: 239). Pronouns are often inserted in this position counter to the source text in translations (Axel 2007: 248).

---

[2] Adverbs may also occur in this position (Koopman 1996, 1997: 84–5).

[3] The V3 'pattern' referred to here, as opposed to V3 as a surface word order, refers to a particular configuration (discussed in section 3.2.3) in which the verb has moved leftward and is preceded (typically) by some XP constituent followed by a discourse-old subject. It is not intended to encompass the cases of V3 word order discussed by te Velde (2010) with *Vor-Vorfeld* elements in modern German, or embedded V3 in Scandinavian as discussed by e.g. Angantýsson (2007).

(18) Ih  inan     **chistiftu** in minemu dome
     I   him.ACC  install    in  my     house
     'I install him in my house'
     (*Isidor* 629)

(19) forlazan  imo      **uuirdit**
     forgiven  him.DAT  becomes
     'he will be forgiven'
     (Monsee Fragments 6,9)

A difference between OHG and OE is that, whereas XP-Subj-$V_{fin}$ order is almost always found when the subject is pronominal in main clauses not introduced by *þa* or *þonne* in OE, in OHG it appears to be optional: 'it is not the case that personal pronouns must appear before the verb, but they may' (Robinson 1997: 17). Furthermore, Axel (2007: 248–50) argues that non-pronominal elements are not attested in second position, other than a few examples with short adverbs such as (20), again unlike the situation in OE.

(20) siu  tho  **giuuanta** sih
     she  then turned    REFL
     'she then turned herself'
     (*Tatian* 665,19)

Like Speyer (2008, 2010) for OE, she also demonstrates that not all such examples can be written off as instances of verb-late order (*contra* Lenerz 1984), since further pronouns may follow the verb, which they may never do in ordinary verb-late clauses:[4]

(21) Vnde do   iu            habeta si  leid     in-fangen in iro herzen
     and  then you-DAT.PL    had    she sorrow   received  in her heart
     'and then her heart was filled with sorrow for you'
     (Notker's *Psalter* VII 23,26)

In OS, however, unlike in OE and OHG, V3 does not appear to be a productive pattern. In total, 93 of the 2,348 non-conjunct declarative main clauses (4.0%) are V3 in having two constituents preceding the finite verb. This proportion is low, and there are reasons to suspect that V3 does not have an underlying representation/derivation distinct from verb-late in OS. Whereas a large proportion of clauses in which the verb surfaces in third position in OE and OHG are of the form XP-SubjPron-$V_{fin}$

---

[4] The rationale for treating V3 and verb-late as separate 'patterns' with potentially differing derivations is explained in the next section (3.2.3). Examples (17) and (18) do not provide decisive evidence either way, since the possibility of unmoved verbs and a process of rightward movement must be independently assumed for the older Germanic languages, as noted by Tomaselli (1995: 365 n. 3).

(Haeberli 1999a: 335), this order is rare in OS. Only 4 of the 93 examples (4.3%) have this order: (22) and (23) below, as well as instances in lines 2,834 and 4,757.[5]

(22)  Thanna  thu  **scalt** lôn    nemen fora   godes ôgun
      then    you  shall reward take  before God's eyes
      'Then you shall be rewarded before God'
      (*Heliand* 1563–4)

(23)  Bethiu    man  **sculun** haldan thene       holdlîco
      therefore one  should hold  that.MASC.ACC favourably
      'Therefore all should keep him in their favour'
      (*Heliand* 1869–70)

Three of the four examples of XP-SubjPron-V$_{fin}$, including (22) and (23), begin with adverbs that may also be used as subordinators, rendering them potentially ambiguous between main and subordinate clauses although traditionally read as the former. Since no adverbs or postverbal pronouns are present in any of these examples, furthermore, there is the possibility that these are in fact instances of the verb-late pattern rather than V3 as found in OE and OHG.[6]

Hinterhölzl and Petrova (2009: 320) suggest that (24) (their (12)a) is an example of V3 with verb movement as in OE:

(24)  Thar  imu  tegegnes  **quam** ên idis     fan    âdrom    thiodun
      there him  against   came a   woman  from   different tribe
      'There, a woman from another tribe approached him'
      (*Heliand* 2984–5)

However, this example is as inconclusive as (22) and (23) with regard to underlying structure. Since a rightward movement process must be postulated for OS as for OE, it is possible to argue that the verb in (24) is unmoved and that the postverbal constituent *ên idis fan âdrom thiodun* 'a woman from another tribe' has in fact been moved rightward over it.[7] Furthermore, as for (22) and (23), in context it is entirely

---

[5]  Van Bergen (2003) shows that indefinite *man* in OE behaves as a personal pronoun rather than as a full nominal. I assume this holds for OS, though it remains to be demonstrated.

[6]  I have found only one example of a V3 clause with a pronoun in postverbal position:

(i)  Than  thoh   **gitrûoda** siu  uuel  an  iro   hugiskeftiun
     then  though trusted she  well  in  her   understandings
     'Still she had faith in her mind'
     (*Heliand* 2028–9)

Here, however, *thoh* seems to behave like modern German *jedoch* and *aber* in marking a preceding constituent as contrastive, and this example can thus be seen as an instance of V2: see e.g. Frey (2004: 20) and Axel (2007: 217–22).

[7]  Since this constituent represents new information, as acknowledged by Hinterhölzl and Petrova (2009: 320), this state of affairs is all the more likely, as rightward movement (at least in OE) appears to be driven partially by information-structural considerations (Pintzuk 2005: 124 n. 12; Taylor and Pintzuk 2009).

possible to analyse (24) as an embedded clause with the meaning 'where a woman from another tribe approached him': see the expanded version in (25).

(25)  Thô  giuuêt  he  imu  ober  thea  marka  Iudeono,  sôhte  imu Sidono
      then  went   he  him  over  the   region  Jews.GEN  sought  him S.
      burg, habde gesîdos      mid imu, gôde iungaron. **Thar** imu
      town  had   companions  with him  good  disciples  **there** him
      tegegnes  quam  ên  idis      fan    âdrom      thiodun
      against   came  a   woman     from   different   tribe
      'Then he travelled across the lands of the Jews and sought out the town of Sidon—he had companions with him, good disciples—where a woman from another tribe approached him'
      (*Heliand* 2982–5)

The appositive clause *habde gesîdos* ... between the main clause and (24) should not be taken as an argument that (24) must be a main clause: compare (26), without capitalization or punctuation between the clauses, in which an appositive element also intervenes between the main clause and the locative adjunct.

(26)  Thô  uuard  is  uuisbodo        an Galilealand, Gabriel cuman,
      then  became his  wise-messenger  in G.-land      G.      come
      engil  thes      alouualdon,   thar   he   êne  idis      uuisse
      angel  the.GEN   Almighty.GEN  where  he   a    woman     knew
      'Then his wise messenger, Gabriel, came to Galilee—the Almighty's angel—where he knew a woman'
      (*Heliand* 249–51)

The extreme rarity of the XP-SubjPron-$V_{fin}$ order in my corpus must also be taken as an argument against its productivity. For OE, the order XP-SubjPron-$V_{fin}$ is 'used consistently' (Haeberli 1999a: 335) when an element other than *þa* or *þonne* is fronted. In contrast, in the *Heliand* there are 462 examples of V2 declarative main clauses in which the subject pronoun follows the finite verb, e.g. (27), and 223 examples of V2 declarative main clauses in which the subject pronoun precedes the finite verb, e.g. (28). All of these can be seen as 'missed opportunities' (Faarlund 1990: 17–18) for V3.

(27)  mildi  **uuas**  he  im        an   is    môde
      mild   was   he  them.DAT  in   his   mood
      'He was gentle in spirit to them'
      (*Heliand* 1259)

TABLE 3.1. Frequency and percentage of V1, V2, V3, and V-later main clauses in ON pre-1300

| | V1 | | V2 | | V3 | | V-later | | Total |
|---|---|---|---|---|---|---|---|---|---|
| | N | % | N | % | N | % | N | % | N |
| 1150.FIRSTGRAMMAR.SCI-LIN | 21 | 18.1 | 85 | 73.3 | 8 | 6.9 | 2 | 1.7 | 161 |
| 1150.HOMILIUBOK.REL-SER | 172 | 13.5 | 1069 | 84.0 | 31 | 2.4 | 1 | 0.1 | 1273 |
| 1210.JARTEIN.REL-SAG | 70 | 30.3 | 161 | 69.7 | 0 | 0.0 | 0 | 0.0 | 231 |
| 1210.THORLAKUR.REL-SAG | 73 | 27.8 | 186 | 70.7 | 4 | 1.5 | 0 | 0.0 | 263 |
| 1250.STURLUNGA.NAR-SAG | 318 | 24.7 | 962 | 74.8 | 6 | 0.5 | 0 | 0.0 | 1286 |
| 1250.THETUBROT.NAR-SAG | 49 | 34.8 | 92 | 65.2 | 0 | 0.0 | 0 | 0.0 | 141 |
| 1260.JOMSVIKINGAR.NAR-SAG | 49 | 10.7 | 406 | 88.6 | 2 | 0.4 | 1 | 0.2 | 458 |
| 1270.GRAGAS.LAW-LAW | 15 | 9.0 | 150 | 89.8 | 2 | 1.2 | 0 | 0.0 | 167 |
| 1275.MORKIN.NAR-HIS | 235 | 23.0 | 783 | 76.6 | 3 | 0.3 | 1 | 0.1 | 1022 |

(28)  Thu   scalt   for     allun      uuesan   uuîbun      giuuîhit
      you   shall   before  all.DAT    be.INF   women.DAT   hallowed
      'You will be hallowed above all women'
      (*Heliand* 261–2)

I therefore conclude that V3 as found in OE and early OHG is not a productive feature of OS, or at least of the variety represented by the *Heliand*.

Finally, in ON V3 orders are not found (Faarlund 1994: 64). The distribution of word order types in the texts of the IcePaHC (Wallenberg et al. 2011) is given in Table 3.1, and illustrated in Figure 3.1.[8]

In all but the earliest two texts, instances of V3 or V-later are very rare, and all can be analysed as involving left-dislocations or constituents in apposition, or (in the *Íslensk hómilíubók*) involve the Latin word *sicut* in initial position, which appears to function as a conjunction. XP-Subj-V$_{fin}$ orders are not found.

### 3.2.3 *Analyses of V2 and V3*

Two core classes of analysis of asymmetric V2 in the Germanic languages have been proposed.[9] According to the first, based on an intuition going back to den Besten (1977) and Evers (1981, 1982), the finite verb moves to C$^0$ in all main clauses, as in the tree in (29), illustrated by an example from modern German.

---

[8]  For the full names of these texts, see section 1.4.2.

[9]  I do not discuss 'symmetric V2', as found in Icelandic and Yiddish, here. See Rögnvaldsson and Þráinsson (1990) on Icelandic, and Santorini (1994) for a comparative perspective.

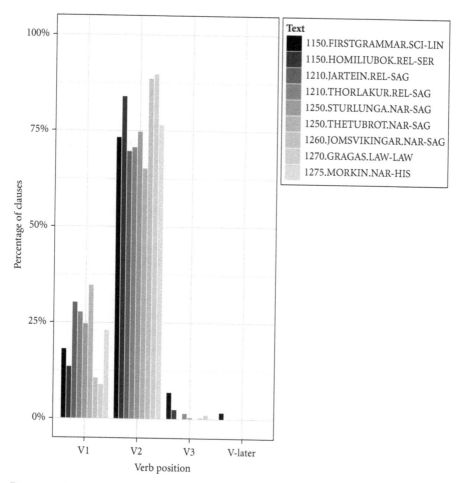

FIGURE 3.1 Percentage of V1, V2, V3, and V-later main clauses in ON pre-1300

(29)

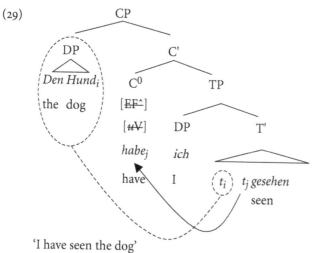

Two separate movements are involved. First, the finite verb moves to $C^0$. Second, a single constituent is moved to SpecCP.[10] Following the theoretical assumptions laid out in section 1.3, the head-movement operation can be recast here as triggered by a $[uV]$ feature on $C^0$ (see Roberts 2010b): this $C^0$ agrees with the finite verb, and, since the featural content of the finite verb is by assumption a subset of that of $C^0$, the verb is spelt out in $C^0$. The movement of the verb, here and elsewhere in this book, is represented by a solid line. The second movement, of some constituent to SpecCP (in (29), the direct object), can be viewed as triggered by an instance of ˆ associated with the Edge Feature of the phase head $C^0$. This demands that a constituent be moved to SpecCP, but is agnostic about the nature of that constituent; this is equivalent to Fanselow's (2003) 'stylistic fronting', and Frey's (2004) 'formal movement'.[11] This and other phrasal movements will be represented in this book by a dashed line.

This approach has the major advantage of explaining the asymmetry between main and subordinate clauses in modern German and Dutch: on the assumption that the complementizer is first Merged in $C^0$, this position is no longer available for the verb to move to, and so it remains in its base position. Under the head-movement-as-Agree account, we can assume that the complementizer $C^0$ does not bear a $[uV]$ feature. As a result, no Agree relation is established between $C^0$ and the finite verb, precluding head-movement in the sense of Roberts (2010b).

The second major class of approach is associated with Travis (1984, 1991), Zwart (1991, 1993), and is referred to by Diesing (1988, 1990) as the 'two-structure hypothesis'. Under this approach, in present terminology, a derivation such as (29) is proposed only for main clauses in which a constituent other than the subject precedes the finite verb. In other cases, the verb moves only as far as $T^0$, and the subject is in SpecTP, as in (30).[12]

---

[10] I here abstract away from the movement of the subject from Spec$v$P and from the internal constituency/ordering of the $v$P.

[11] Almost any constituent may fulfil this requirement. Finite TPs are one major exception: see Abels (2003), Wurmbrand (2004).

[12] As noted by Schwartz and Vikner (1996: 46), for this approach it is crucial that TP be head-initial and that the finite verb fail to move to $T^0$ in subordinate clauses. Haegeman (2001) provides data from West Flemish that casts doubt on this assumption. I will leave the issue aside here.

(30)

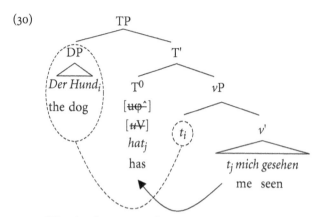

'The dog has seen me'

This approach is characterized by the presence of [EF^] and [*u*V] on main clause C⁰ only when a constituent precedes the subject, with an interpretative effect (topicalization, focus, or interrogation). Motivation for this approach is provided by morphological alternations in verb forms in eastern dialects of Dutch and in Swabian depending on whether the subject precedes the verb (Zwart 1991, 1993),[13] as well as by the desire to eliminate movements that are string-vacuous.

Schwartz and Vikner (1989, 1996), however, argue that this approach is inadequate to account for the facts of the modern Germanic languages. A first problem (1996: 12–13) is that adjunction to TP must be stipulated to be possible in subordinate clauses but impossible in main clauses, in order to derive the contrast between modern German (31) and (32).

(31) Ich weiß, dass letzte Woche Peter tatsächlich ein Buch gelesen hat
     I know that last week Peter actually a book read has
     'I know that Peter actually read a book last week'

(32) *Letzte Woche Peter hat tatsächlich ein Buch gelesen
     last week Peter has actually a book read
     'Peter actually read a book last week'

---

[13] A similar alternation in verb endings is found in OE with first and second person plural pronominal subjects (see van Gelderen 2000: 157–67), as well as in Middle Low German (Lasch 1914: 227).

Secondly, the approach is unable to account for the contrast between (33) and (34)–(35) with respect to the absence of the expletive (see also Tomaselli 1986). On the hypothesis that *es* is a SpecCP expletive, that the verb is uniformly in C⁰, and that SpecCP must be filled, the facts in (33)–(35) fall out naturally: the expletive may not be Merged in SpecTP, so is prohibited in (33), but is necessary in (34) to fill the otherwise empty SpecCP (cf. (35)).

(33)  Gestern    ist   (*es)     ein  Junge  gekommen
      yesterday  is    (*there)  a    boy    come
      'A boy came yesterday'

(34)  Es    ist   ein  Junge  gekommen
      there is    a    boy    come
      'A boy came'

(35)  *Ist  ein  Junge  gekommen
      is    a    boy    come
      'A boy came'

These, and other facts, indicate that the two-structure hypothesis is on the wrong track for the modern Germanic asymmetric V2 languages; see Diesing (1990: 60–1), Lenerz (1993), Branigan (1996), and van Cranenbroeck and Haegeman (2007) for further data militating in the same direction.[14] However, the V3 data discussed in section 3.2.2 has been taken by many authors (e.g. Pintzuk 1993, 1999; Eyþórsson 1995; Haeberli 1999a, 1999b, 2002; Fuß 2003) to indicate that a version of this hypothesis is in fact correct for OE. Typically, this class of analysis assumes that verb-movement to C⁰ takes place only in contexts introduced by *þa*, *þonne*, or a *wh*-item; in all other cases, the verb moves to T⁰. The canonical OE sentence under this analysis can be represented in present terms as in (36).

---

[14]  Further types of analysis of V2 exist in the literature. These include: (a) the 'V2-inside-IP' analysis of Diesing (1990) and Rögnvaldsson and Þráinsson (1990), also shown to be inadequate by Schwartz and Vikner (1996: 30–46); (b) 'Münchhausen-style' analyses such as Fanselow (2003), in which the movement of the finite verb is XP-movement rather than head-movement; and (c) Müller's (2004) remnant-movement analysis, in which a *v*P emptied of all constituents except its head and edge moves to SpecCP. Analyses of types (b) and (c) are motivated by the desire to exclude head-movement as a syntactic operation; in the present work, the theory of head-movement of Roberts (2010b) is adopted, making this unnecessary. Biberauer and Roberts (2004) also show that Müller's (2004) approach makes a number of incorrect predictions for the V2 Germanic languages, especially with regard to adverb fronting.

(36)

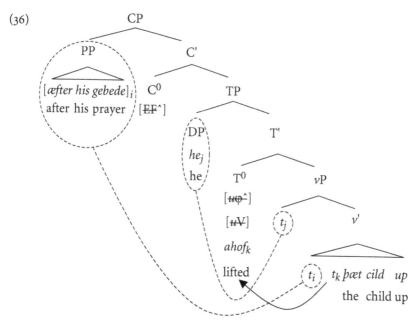

'After his prayer he lifted the child up'
(cocathom2,+ACHom_II,_2:14.70.320)

Within the two-structure family of analyses, different variants exist. Pintzuk (1993, 1999), for example, assumes that TP may be head-initial or head-final, thus accounting for the existence of verb-late main clauses (see section 3.4). Eyþórsson (1995: 302–3) and Fuß (2003: 225 n. 15), meanwhile, acknowledge the existence of verb-late main clauses but do not provide an analysis for them. Haeberli (1999b, 2002) differs from the other accounts in that the verb is in AgrS⁰, with the subject occurring variably in SpecAgrS or SpecTP; Haeberli's account is also adopted in important recent work by Speyer (2008, 2010).[15] Nevertheless, similar concerns arise for all these accounts. These concern (a) the occurrence of objects in preverbal position, (b) the occurrence of multiple pronouns in preverbal position, (c) the absence of V1 orders in subordinate clauses, and (d) the clause-type asymmetry.

The occurrence of objects in a position ostensibly reserved for subjects, as in (14) from OE and (18), (19), and (21) from OHG, is a problem for any account positing that 'high' subjects occur in SpecTP or SpecAgrSP, since these are typically viewed as A-positions restricted to subjects. Pintzuk (1993: 24 n. 25), Eyþórsson (1995: 314), and Haeberli (2002) avoid this problem by assuming that subject and (optionally) object pronouns are clitics not occupying a specifier position, a hypothesis to which I will return. Fuß (2003: 226 n. 22) speculates that these object pronouns might behave like

---

[15] I do not assume Agr projections here, basically for conceptual reasons (see Chomsky 1995: ch. 4).

modern Icelandic quirky subjects, but the latter typically occur systematically in the context of the case frames of particular lexical verbs, and there is no evidence that this is the case for OE preverbal objects.

There are proposals in the literature (e.g. Diesing 1990; Barbosa 1995, 2001) to the effect that SpecTP may be an A'-position in certain languages; however, as well as being non-standard, such a proposal would overgenerate with regard to OE and OHG. All else being equal, we would expect the same range of constituents to occur in SpecTP as occur in SpecCP, including prepositional phrases and full DP objects. However, as shown in section 3.2.2, the constituents which may occur in this position in OE and OHG are pronominal subjects, pronominal objects, and light adverbs; in addition, there is evidence for full DP subjects in this position in OE, and more rarely full DP objects (Koopman 1997: 82). PPs, as far as I know, are essentially unattested. It will be shown that a simple generalization links the attested items: they are all discourse-given (Bech 1998, 2001; Westergaard 2005; van Kemenade and Los 2006; Walkden 2009; Hinterhölzl and Petrova 2009). If this information-structural approach is correct, then analyses assuming the two-structure hypothesis are unen-lightening with regard to OE and OHG V3 unless additions are made.

A further, related problem is presented by occasional cases in which multiple pronouns intervene between a fronted XP and the finite verb (see W. Koopman 1992).

(37)  Nu    ic eow hebbe to hæftum   ham   gefærde alle of earde
      now   I you   have to bond.DAT home  led      all of native-land.DAT
      'Now I have led you all from your native land to a place of imprisonment'
      (*Sat* 91–2)

SpecTP and SpecAgrSP are usually assumed to be single positions, making examples such as (37) problematic for any theory that requires preverbal pronouns to be in one of these positions.

A third problem, raised by Haeberli (2005: 273), is that two-structure analyses typically predict that V1 structures should be possible in subordinate clauses. This is so because if subject movement to the higher specifier (SpecTP in most theories; SpecAgrSP in Haeberli 1999b and 2002) is optional, the subject may stay low while the verb moves, leaving the higher specifier unfilled and the verb adjacent to the complementizer. However, this word order is extremely rare.

The final core problem with the two-structure analysis of the early Germanic languages, also noted by Haeberli (2005: 273–4), is the asymmetry in verb position between clause types. Under the traditional view going back to den Besten (1977), the complementizer in $C^0$ in subordinate clauses and the verb in $C^0$ in main clauses are in complementary distribution, with the former blocking the movement of the latter. If the verb only moves as far as $T^0$ or another IP-domain-internal head in subject-initial V2 main clauses, the prediction is made that subordinate clauses should also always exhibit subject-initial V2, a prediction that is false at least for German and Dutch. Zwart's (1991) workaround for this, adopted by Eyþórsson (1995: 202–3), is to assume that verb-movement to $AgrS^0$ is driven by $AgrS^0$'s need to check its N-features, and that when the complementizer is present $AgrS^0$ achieves this by moving to $C^0$, making verb-movement unnecessary. But as well as creating a lookahead problem in a derivational approach—when $AgrS^0$ is Merged, how does it know whether a complementizer will be Merged above it or not?—this approach lacks independent motivation. As noted above, Pintzuk (1993, 1999) makes a virtue out of necessity by indicating that orders that she considers both IP-final and IP-initial are found in OE in both main and subordinate clauses. However, as observed by Koopman (1995: 142), and as Pintzuk (1999: 223) acknowledges, this provides no clear explanation for why IP-final should be more frequent in subordinate clauses than in main clauses, especially if with Fuß and Trips (2002: 211) we make 'the plausible assumption that a speaker cannot switch from one grammar to another in mid-sentence'. Though Pintzuk and Haeberli (2008) claim that verb-late order in OE is more common in main clauses than previously thought, it still appears to be substantially more common in subordinate clauses (see their table 14, 2008: 398, and section 3.4). A clear asymmetry between clause types can also be observed in OHG (Axel 2007: 6–8) and in OS (see Table 3.2 and Figure 3.2; the difference is statistically significant, $p < 0.0001$).[16]

Haeberli (2005) solves the latter two problems by positing that the verb moves higher in main clauses than in subordinate clauses (effectively reinstating a key aspect of the original V-to-$C^0$ analysis of van Kemenade 1987): to $AgrS^0$ in main clauses, but only to $T^0$ in subordinate clauses. This rules out V1 in subordinate clauses, and

TABLE 3.2. Frequency and percentage of V1/V2 vs. V-later main vs. subordinate clauses in the *Heliand*

| | V1/V2 | | V-later | | Total |
|---|---|---|---|---|---|
| | N | % | N | % | N |
| Main | 2078 | 88.5 | 270 | 11.5 | 2348 |
| Subordinate | 567 | 25.8 | 1629 | 74.2 | 2196 |
| Total | 2645 | – | 1899 | – | 4544 |

[16] The problems raised in this section do not arise for ON, since here verb-movement to (at least) $T^0$ *is* found in subordinate clauses. Eyþórsson (1995: 214–88) discusses facts relating to negation in the Poetic Edda that indicate that negated verbs occupied a position below topics and above canonical subjects, arguing that this position is $C^0$. It could therefore be the case that the two-structure account is correct for ON, but false for the West Germanic languages. However, the problems raised by Schwartz and Vikner (1996) remain for ON; in addition, the negation facts are also compatible with a split-CP account of the type I develop in this section.

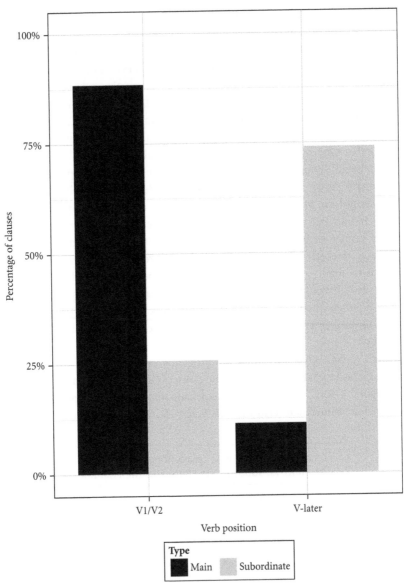

FIGURE 3.2 Percentage of V1/V2 vs. V-later main vs. subordinate clauses in the *Heliand*

permits a clause-type asymmetry; however, the issues of preverbal pronominal objects and multiple preverbal pronouns are still problematic for this analysis. I therefore conclude that the two-structure hypothesis is unable to account convincingly for the full range of constituent order variation in the early Germanic languages without stipulation.

For approaches to early Germanic constituent order that posit uniform V-to-$C^0$ movement, it is necessary to make additional assumptions in order to account for the occurrence of V3. Most usually, as in van Kemenade (1987), Tomaselli (1995), and Roberts (1996) as well as the non-V-to-$C^0$ approaches of Pintzuk (1993, 1999), Eyþórsson (1995), and Haeberli (2002), this assumption is that personal pronouns are clitics (rather than weak pronouns in the sense of Cardinaletti and Starke 1999) and thus 'do not count' as preverbal constituents.[17] However, van Kemenade (1987: 126) and Pintzuk (1999: 189 n. 17) are obliged to admit that there is no written evidence for clitic forms in OE. The hypothesis of clitichood has been challenged for OE by Koopman (1997) and Bech (2001), and for OHG by Axel (2007: 254–77). Clitichood is usually associated with phonological reduction, yet there is almost no evidence for this: in OE the subject pronoun *þu* 'you.SG' is reduced when postverbal, and *hit* 'it' is sometimes spelled without an <h> in late OE, but otherwise no reduction is visible (Koopman 1997: 89–90). Koopman therefore concludes that '[t]he virtual absence of evidence for reduced forms makes it difficult to use the term "clitic"'. Axel (2007: 254–77) investigates the situation in OHG and comes to a similar conclusion. She cites evidence from Nübling (1992) that vowel reductions are found, and that postverbal pronouns are often written together with the preceding verb, though word boundaries are not consistently marked in general. However, there is not enough evidence to posit 'a fully fledged paradigm of…clitic forms' (2007: 260).

It could, of course, be argued that the absence of phonological evidence is not telling, since written records might under-represent cliticization processes. In addition, it could be argued that syntactic clitichood and phonological clitichood need to be kept apart: this is suggested e.g. for Old French by Adams (1987a) and Vance (1997), and for Proto-Germanic by Hopper (1975: 31). However, the evidence for syntactic clitichood is equally dubious. Koopman (1997) takes the eight morphosyntactic criteria formulated by Kayne (1975) for distinguishing clitics from full pronouns, e.g. inability to be conjoined, and applies them to OE. He concludes that 'personal pronouns show syntactic behaviour that differs from that of full NPs, but not all of them do and those that do, not in every position in which they occur' (1997: 90). Axel (2007: 262–4) shows for OHG that personal pronouns could be modified and conjoined, and concludes (2007: 277) that preverbal pronouns in V3 constructions are XP-elements. For both OHG and OE, then, it seems more plausible to analyse personal pronouns as either weak or strong pronouns in the sense of Cardinaletti and Starke (1999).

Furthermore, for both OE and OHG, assuming that personal pronouns are clitics does not solve the V3 'problem', because other elements, such as adverbs, are found in the preverbal position in V3 main clauses. Koopman (1996, 1997: 84–5) argues that such adverbs cannot be analysed as clitics in OE due to their distributional properties. In addition, the prevalence of full DP subjects in preverbal position in V3 main

---

[17] The analysis given in Haeberli (2005) is agnostic as to the clitic status of OE pronouns.

clauses in OE means that assuming clitichood gains us little, merely replacing one V2 tendency with a slightly stronger V2 tendency. As Bech (2001: 98) puts it:

The fact that one fifth of the subjects in the [XP-Subj-V$_{fin}$] pattern cannot be clitics, but nevertheless occur in exactly the same position as the clitic elements, can hardly be overlooked, especially if a clitic position is defined as a position where only clitics can occur.

The clitic hypothesis, then, even if correct, does not solve the problem it set out to solve. An alternative account for V3 orders needs to be sought. Bech (1998, 2001) has provided the generalization upon which such an account can be based: the elements that occur in second, preverbal position are discourse-given. In Bech's corpus of early OE, 86 of 101 subjects of XP-Subj-V$_{fin}$ clauses (85.2%) had low information value, a notion roughly equating to givenness in Bech's terms, vs. 180 of 301 subjects of XP-V$_{fin}$-Subj clauses (59.8%), and the latter figure falls to 53 of 174 (30.5%) when clauses with initial *þa* or *þonne* are discounted (2001: 160–1). This difference is statistically significant (p < 0.0001).

The fact that the figures are not absolute is of course a problem for any study making the assumptions about syntactic optionality outlined in section 2.2.2 (i.e. that it does not exist). However, the non-absoluteness of the figures could result from a number of things: (i) inconsistency of annotation and other human error; (ii) givenness not quite being the right notion to characterize the generalization; (iii) chance, especially given that historical data is typically noisy, and Bech's sample contains a number of texts which themselves were worked on by a number of scribes. All in all I consider the generalization to be a fair starting point for an analysis that will probably have to be revised in the fullness of time.

Support for this type of generalization is derived from a similar case in a modern language: Westergaard (2005) and Westergaard and Vangsnes (2005) present a close parallel from a recent synchronic study of Tromsø Norwegian. In this variety, certain types of *wh*-questions exhibit a V2/V3 alternation, with subjects preceding the finite verb if contextually given and following if new. In OE (and possibly in OHG), then, as in Tromsø Norwegian, the prevalence of subject pronouns in second position in V3 clauses receives a natural explanation: unstressed subject pronouns are 'the canonical instance of a given nominal' (Westergaard and Vangsnes 2005: 137).

Walkden (2009: 60) and Hinterhölzl and Petrova (2009: 324) proceed to formalize the information-structural patterns in terms of the cartography of the split CP in the tradition of Rizzi (1997). Following Hinterhölzl and Petrova (2009), here I will base my analysis on the more nuanced split-CP hierarchy discussed in section 1.3 and repeated here in (38).

(38)   ForceP > ShiftP > ContrP > FocP > FamP* > FinP
       (Frascarelli and Hinterhölzl 2007: 112–13; their (37))

Mohr (2009) in fact proposes a split CP analysis for V2 in modern German, the details of which I will adapt and adopt for main clauses in the early Germanic V2 languages

(OS, ON, and late OHG). Under this analysis, the verb's landing site is Fin⁰. This head also bears an Edge Feature associated with a movement-triggering ˆ, causing one (and only one) item to move to SpecFinP.[18] This [EFˆ] may move any constituent to SpecFinP, including a constituent that will ultimately move higher in order to check and value an uninterpretable feature on a higher probe, since otherwise the merger of such constituents would cause the derivation to crash; when no such constituent exists, the structurally highest constituent is moved to SpecFinP (cf. Mohr 2009: 154; also Frey 2000, Fanselow 2003), in order to avoid derivational indeterminism.

The derivation of a neutral subject-initial declarative in the early V2 Germanic languages therefore proceeds as in (39) (=(9), from OS).

(39)

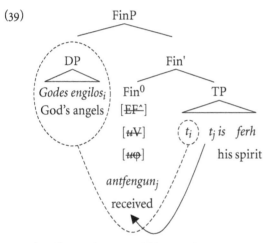

'God's angels received his spirit'
(*Heliand* 3350–1)

When a constituent that is not the subject is in first position, the derivation is as in (40) (=(10), from OS). Structure without relevant material (e.g. ShiftP and FamP in this example) is omitted for clarity.

---

[18] In Mohr's analysis, this is a subject-of-predication feature rather than [EFˆ]. However, Mohr must stipulate that expletives (2009: 150), adverbs (2009: 152 n. 14), and focused XPs (2009: 155 n. 17) are able to check this feature, since these elements must be able to move through SpecFinP. In consequence it is no longer clear that the initially attractive semantic notion of subject-of-predication retains any semantic content.

I assume a single specifier per head (cf. Kayne 1994; Cinque 1999). Chomsky (1995, 2000) has argued that Merge permits multiple specifiers. I retain the single-specifier assumption because (i) it is a cornerstone of the cartographic approach to phrase structure and (ii) it allows the construction of more restrictive theories.

My argument here forces me to suggest that Fin⁰ bears [EFˆ] despite not being a phase head, *pace* Biberauer, Holmberg, and Roberts (2010). It could be that Fin⁰ is a 'weak phase' in the sense of Chomsky (2001), or that phase head properties are distributed across the heads of the split CP. Alternatively it could simply be that all heads bear [EF], as suggested by Chomsky (2005), and that the presence or absence of ˆ is parameterized.

(40)

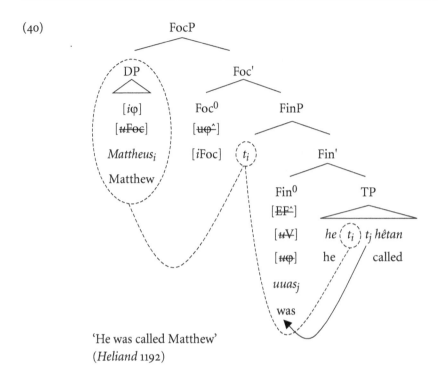

'He was called Matthew'
(*Heliand* 1192)

The initial constituent (here, *Mattheus*) first undergoes fronting to SpecFinP by virtue of the Edge Feature on Fin$^0$. Foc$^0$'s [$u\varphi$ ˆ] feature then probes and in the process attracts *Mattheus* to SpecFocP. The movement of a constituent to the initial position in informationally non-neutral clauses is thus a two-stage process, as in Mohr's (2009) account.

Movement of more than one XP to the left periphery is ruled out as follows. By assumption, in OS and ON, the information-structural left-peripheral heads bear [$u\varphi$ ˆ]-probes. The verb, however, which is in Fin$^0$, bears φ-features that have (already) been valued by the subject. It therefore acts as an intervener in terms of agreement-based Relativized Minimality: the only constituent accessible to probing by an information-structural left-peripheral head is the (single) constituent in SpecFinP— or the finite verb itself, which, as a head, is unable to move and satisfy ˆ, causing the derivation to crash. The account is thus a 'bottleneck' approach to V2 in the sense of Rizzi (2006), Roberts (2004: 316–17), and Mohr (2009: 155): even though the left periphery is in principle fully available in main clauses in V2 languages, SpecFinP provides a bottleneck through which one and only one element may pass to reach it.[19]

---

[19] Frascarelli and Hinterhölzl (2007) propose for modern German, and Hinterhölzl and Petrova (2009: 321–2) for OHG, that the finite verb and XP-movement-trigger are both in Force$^0$. They present apparent cases of postverbal Aboutness topics in modern German as evidence for this. I will not adopt this proposal here, as it is not compatible with my analysis of null arguments (Chapter 5).

This analysis predicts that V2 with a non-DP constituent in initial position is possible, through EF-triggered movement to SpecFinP; however, since left-peripheral heads other than Fin⁰ probe for φ-features, they should not be able to attract adverbs or PPs to their specifiers, and hence V2 with a non-DP constituent may not be information-structurally motivated. This prediction seems to be false. I leave this issue for future research, noting that Roberts and Roussou (2002) independently suggest that certain non-DP constituents may bear φ-features in order to account for non-nominal subjects in English.

For OE and OHG, where multiple elements may occupy the left periphery, a different account is clearly needed: the intervention-based locality constraint does not seem to hold. This can be captured if in OE and OHG the left-peripheral heads probe not for φ-features, but for interpretable information-structural features, i.e. they bear features such as [*u*Shift^] or [*u*Foc^]. A sample derivation of a V3 clause is given in (41).

(41)

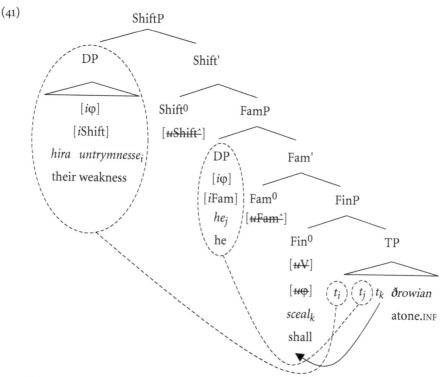

'He shall atone for their weakness'
(cocura,CP:10.61.14.387)

Again, levels of structure not relevant have been omitted. Whether or not Fin⁰ bears an Edge Feature in OE and OHG as it does in OS and ON is immaterial, since its role in shipping a phrase to the left periphery is redundant in these languages due to the lack of intervention effects.

In these languages, then, DP material is assigned interpretable information-structural features upon entering the numeration, rather than uninterpretable features; similarly, the left-peripheral heads bear the uninterpretable version of their signature feature rather than the interpretable version. This difference could be the key property that defines so-called 'discourse-configurational' languages and sets them apart from languages such as modern English in which the possibilities for information-structure-related movement are severely limited.

The proposal is able to overcome many of the shortcomings of earlier accounts of OE and OHG. Second-position elements in V3 clauses, including pronouns, occur in SpecFamP, as they are discourse-given, and surface after all left-peripheral material apart from the finite verb; the position may be iterated, accounting for examples such as (37) containing multiple preverbal pronouns.[20] Clause-type asymmetries in verb position are accounted for if we assume, with Roberts (1996: 160, 2004: 300), that complementizers in these languages are Merged in $Fin^0$ and move to $Force^0$ if it is present. This is so because English-style complementizers such as *that* encode two pieces of information: clause type and finiteness (Rizzi 1997). If the complementizer is Merged in $Fin^0$, then the verb cannot move there. The classic den Besten (1977) account of these asymmetries is thus maintained for all the early Northwest Germanic languages.[21] Variable verb position in subordinate clauses, as amply demonstrated e.g. by Pintzuk (1999) for OE, can be accounted for by assuming varying targets of movement below $Fin^0$ in these clauses (cf. Fuß and Trips 2002), a matter which falls beyond the scope of this chapter.

Though the account given here develops split-CP proposals by Roberts (1996) and Frascarelli and Hinterhölzl (2009), it is also similar in its predictions to the two-structure account of Haeberli (2005). Like Haeberli's account, the present proposal adopts the idea that there are two distinct subject positions as well as two distinct targets of verb-movement (at least in OE and OHG), and predicts clause-type asymmetries. The key difference here is that the targets of movement are higher in the structure than under Haeberli's account, and the information-structural sensitivity of subject position as demonstrated by Bech (2001) and others is accounted for. In other respects, however, the two accounts are very similar, as noted by a reviewer. In particular, there is no conflict between the proposal here and the considerable evidence adduced by Speyer (2008, 2010) from the diachrony of English for a Haeberli-style account, since this evidence is equally compatible with the present proposal; Speyer himself resists a split-CP account for OE, but does not rule it out

---

[20] Strictly speaking, by Relativized Minimality the different FamP heads should count as interveners with respect to one another, predicting (falsely) that only one element can occur in this position after all. This may indicate that further decomposition of FamP is needed.

[21] Though this account is not without its problems: how is the acquirer to discern the first-Merge position of the complementizer? In the framework of Roberts and Roussou (2003), one might expect it to 'grammaticalize' upwards by eliminating the movement and treating $Force^0$ as its first-Merged position, but this has clearly not happened in OE.

for pre-OE (2008: 210–27). It is the earlier history of Northwest Germanic to which we now turn.

### 3.2.4 *V2 and V3 in Proto-Northwest Germanic*

In the account given in the previous section, the crucial difference between OE and OHG on the one hand and OS and ON on the other is that OE and OHG probing left-peripheral heads bear uninterpretable information-structural features such as [$u$Shift^], [$u$Fam^], or [$u$Foc^] rather than [$u\varphi$^] as in OS and ON. For the rest of this section I assume that the relevant properties were the same in early OHG as they were in OE, though, as observed in section 3.2.2, this is an oversimplification.

Even for those scholars who have advocated syntactic reconstruction, constituent order has often been recognized as posing special problems: see e.g. Campbell and Harris (2002: 605 n. 1). In the context of the correspondence problem as laid out in Chapter 2, this is unsurprising. Those cases in which syntactic reconstruction is most intuitive, such as the ON -*sk* ending discussed in Chapter 2 and the examples discussed by Harris (1985), Willis (2011), and Barðdal and Eyþórsson (2012), are those in which cognacy can be independently established on lexical-phonological grounds, with the problem of reconstruction then reducing to the (simpler) task of determining the most likely syntactic properties of the proto-form by 'undoing' plausible reanalyses. In contrast, the properties determining constituent order at the clausal level are usually thought of as pertaining to phonologically null functional heads (cf. Hale 1998: 15–16), making the establishment of cognates substantially more speculative, and this is the case here.

I will assume that the relevant left-peripheral heads—Shift$^0$, Foc$^0$, and Fam$^0$ in particular—are all cognate with their counterparts in the other early Northwest Germanic languages. This is on grounds of formal similarity alone. This assumption having been made, we can ask which system—the OE/OHG one or the OS/ON/late OHG one—was closer to that of early Northwest Germanic.

Westergaard (2005) suggests that V3 in OE was an innovation, although she admits (2005: n. 14) that 'OE was presumably never a true V2 language in the same way as e.g. present-day Norwegian'. Hinterhölzl and Petrova (2009), too, speculate that V3 was an innovation. The diachronic scenario they posit is as illustrated in (42) (their (28)) for OE and OS, and (43) (their (27)) for OHG:

(42) a. Stage I:   [Aboutness] [$_{ForceP}$ (familiar topic) [$_{TP}$ ... V$_{fin}$ ... ]]
     b. Stage II:  [$_{ForceP}$ [Aboutness] (familiar topic) [$_{TP}$ ... V$_{fin}$ ... ]]
     c. Stage III: [$_{ForceP}$ [Aboutness]$_i$ [$_{TP}$ Subject V$_{fin}$ t$_i$] ... ]

(43) a. Stage I:   [Aboutness] [$_{ForceP}$ V$_{fin}$ [TP ... ]]
     b. Stage II:  [$_{ForceP}$ [Aboutness] V$_{fin}$ [TP ... ]]
     c. Stage III: [$_{ForceP}$ [Aboutness]$_i$ V$_{fin}$ [t$_i$ [TP ... ]]]

In other words, they posit that OE and OS underwent a process of reanalysis that caused clause-external Aboutness topics to be integrated into a clause with a clause-internal, TP-external familiar topic ((42)a–b). In OHG, on the other hand, this clause-external Aboutness topic is integrated instead into a clause in which initial position is occupied by the finite verb ((43)a–b). These topics are then reanalysed as originating inside the clause ((42)b–c, (43)b–c). V3 as a syntactic possibility in OE and OS thus results from the innovation in (42)a–b.

Hinterhölzl and Petrova's (2009) general approach is appealing in many respects, since they offer a detailed consideration of the interaction between information structure and constituent order which makes nuanced predictions; furthermore, they attempt to account for a wide range of data. However, the specifics of their diachronic proposal are unsatisfactory for a number of reasons, both empirical and theoretical. For a start, Hinterhölzl and Petrova are incorrect in stating (2009: 324) that in OS 'clauses expressing subordinating discourse relations [topic-comment structures—GW] pattern with OE rather than with OHG' in exhibiting V3; as I have shown in section 3.2.2, XP-$V_{fin}$-SubjPron rather than XP-SubjPron-$V_{fin}$ is almost ubiquitous in the *Heliand*, and there is no clear evidence that clauses in which the verb has moved from its first-Merged position into the left periphery as in OE, but in which a constituent still intervenes between it and an XP in initial position, are possible at all in OS.

Hinterhölzl and Petrova's reanalysis schema in (42) for OHG also cannot account for the fact that V3 orders do exist in this language, as clearly demonstrated by Tomaselli (1995) and Axel (2007); see section 3.2.3. Though they mention in passing earlier in their paper (2009: 316) that these are possible as 'a very rare declining pattern', Hinterhölzl and Petrova would either have to argue that the unequivocal examples of this kind (such as (21)) are ungrammatical, which seems unlikely, or that V3 in OHG is in fact the product of a similar innovation to that which took place in OE.

There are also a few conceptual problems with this analysis. The schemata in (42) and (43) make numerous assumptions about the syntax of earlier stages of the languages in question. For instance, in order for (42)a to be possible, Proto-West Germanic (or just Proto-Ingvaeonic) would have had to allow clause-internal pre-verbal familiar topics, suggesting that a V2 pattern, of a kind, was already possible. But for (43)a to be possible, Proto-West Germanic (or at least prehistoric OHG) would have had to allow verb-initial clauses with verb-movement to Force$^0$. Hinterhölzl and Petrova's analysis thus either requires both V1 and V2 to have been possibilities in Proto-West Germanic—a state of affairs which they do not support with diachronic argumentation—or requires extra changes, which they do not discuss, to have taken place between Proto-West Germanic and the individual prehistoric OHG/OS/OE languages. Furthermore, evidence for stages (a) and (b) in their schemata is lacking, as they acknowledge (2009: n. 7). Finally, Hinterhölzl and

Petrova (2009) motivate neither of the changes that they propose as initiating the reanalysis chains: why would the reanalysis involve a clause with a familiar topic for OE/OS acquirers only, and a verb-initial clause for OHG acquirers only?

The alternative I will pursue here is simpler, in that it only involves a single type of change: the reanalysis of information-structural probing as $[u\varphi\hat{\ }]$-probing, and thus the reanalysis of 'accidental V2' structures as necessarily V2. In terms of the analysis in the previous section, I am proposing that the information-structural probing language type, found in OE and OHG, was the original one, and that the change that occurred in OS and ON (independently, as a result of language contact) was towards $[u\varphi\hat{\ }]$-probing. The only plausible alternative is to assume that the change happened in reverse in OE and OHG, which is not as diachronically parsimonious: the well-established family tree structure of West Germanic, in which OE and OS (together with the later-attested Old Frisian and Dutch) are often assumed to form a North Sea Germanic or Ingvaeonic subgroup to the exclusion of OHG (see section 1.4), prevents one from positing that these two languages shared an innovation, and so one would need to posit two separate (but parallel) identical innovations. The syntacticization of an originally information-structurally conditioned pattern is also, arguably, more plausible a priori than the reverse.

Contact is also not a likely explanation, since OE and OHG occupied areas of the Northwest Germanic dialect continuum that were not geographically contiguous, with the OS-speaking area between them. By contrast, the generalization of $[u\varphi\hat{\ }]$-probing could plausibly have spread as a single wave of diffusion across the Proto-Northwest Germanic dialect continuum. That V2, a constituent-order phenomenon, can be affected by language contact is suggested by evidence from northern Middle English, which was more strongly V2 than southern varieties, plausibly due to contact with Scandinavian (Kroch and Taylor 1997).

I can only speculate as to why V2 became generalized in OS, ON, and later OHG but not OE. The solution must inevitably be particularistic, given that certain Germanic varieties which by hypothesis share a starting point underwent the change and others did not. The Subset Principle (Berwick 1985; Biberauer and Roberts 2009) may have a role to play: a grammar which sanctions V3 as an interpretatively licensed variant generates a larger variety of structures than one which permits only V2.[22] A certain brand of computational conservatism may therefore have been relevant. However, it is difficult to imagine that V3 clauses, which are robustly attested in OE, could have been simply ignored by the acquirer, or have fallen below a critical threshold.

---

[22] Though there are problems with the Subset Principle as applied to syntactic acquisition, and it only holds if we assume a model of acquisition in which indirect negative evidence is impossible: see Fodor and Sakas (2005), Clark and Lappin (2011: 95–7).

Several further, language-specific changes must be posited in order to capture the intricacies of the data. For instance, V2 must have become generalized in OE *wh*-questions, since both in OHG (Axel 2007: 244–5) and Gothic (Eyþórsson 1995: 25) pronouns were able to intervene between *wh*-elements and the finite verb (see Chapter 4). Furthermore, if it is the case that only pronouns and not full XP topics could intervene between the initial XP and the finite verb in OHG, then an explanation for this qualitative difference as compared with OE is required. I leave these questions for future research.

To summarize: under the scenario sketched here, Proto-Northwest Germanic had generalized V2/V3, i.e. verb-movement to $Fin^0$ and no further, in ordinary declarative clauses, with the surface occurrence of V2 or V3 depending on the information-structural status of clausal constituents. The development of generalized V2 was the result of a later reanalysis.

## 3.3 V1

### 3.3.1 *V1: the data*

Verb-first main clauses are found in all the early Germanic languages. For OE, 465 of 4,173 main clauses in Ælfric's *Lives of Saints* (11.1%) are V1, and 760 of 2,717 main clauses in Bede's *Historia* (28.0%). Cichosz (2010: 72–6) finds that 104 of 418 main clauses (24.9%) in her OE poetry sample, 15 of 122 main clauses (12.3%) in her OE original prose sample, and 7 of 140 main clauses (5.0%) in her OE translated prose sample are V1. An example is given in (44).

(44) **Wæs**   he   se    biscop   æfest   mon   &   god
     was   he   the   bishop   pious   man   &   good
     'He the bishop was a pious and good man'
     (cobede,Bede_3:22.250.23.2556)

For OHG, Cichosz (2010: 72–6) finds for her samples that 50 of 224 main clauses (22.3%) in poetry, 2 of 144 (1.4%) in original prose, and 54 of 188 (28.7%) in translated prose are V1. Axel (2007: ch. 3) provides extensive discussion of the phenomenon, including references. An example is (45).

(45) **Floug**   er   súnnun   pad
     flew   he   sun.GEN   path
     'He flew the path of the sun'
     (Otfrid's *Evangelienbuch*, I, 5,5; Axel 2007: 114)

For OS it has often been observed that the V1 pattern is common (e.g. by Ries 1880, Linde 2009). In the *Heliand*, 481 of 2,348 main clauses (20.5%) are V1, as in (46).

(46)  **Fellun**  managa  maguiunge  man
      fell     many    young      men
      'Many young men fell'
      (*Heliand* 743–4)

Finally, for ON Faarlund (2004: 192) observes that V1 is a common variant in main clauses. In the early texts from the IcePaHC, between 9.0 per cent and 34.8 per cent of main clauses are V1, with the sagas generally exhibiting higher percentages (see Table 3.1). An example is (47).

(47)  **Er**  það  komið  til  eyrna     mér
      is    it   come   to   ears.GEN   me.DAT
      'It has come to my ears'
      (1260.JOMSVIKINGAR.NAR-SAG,.1377)

Eyþórsson (1995: 182–4) observes that (48), a Northwest Germanic runic inscription from the Vimose Chape, may be analysed as a V1 declarative main clause, although he notes that the interpretation is debated.

(48)  **maridai**  ala   makija
      praised    Alla  sword
      'Alla praised the sword.'

### 3.3.2 *Analyses of V1*

One factor relevant to the presence of V1 in declarative main clauses is negation. It is observed by van Kemenade (1987) and Eyþórsson (1995) that negation is often initial in OE, and that it is often followed by the finite verb. Wallage (2005: 111) notes that 'negation is most commonly placed clause initially in OE main clauses (n=1698/2547, or 67%)', and that the initial element is most usually *ne* immediately followed by the finite verb, as in (49).

(49)  Ne   **het**     he   us   na    leornian  heofonas  to   wyrcenne
      NEG  ordered   he   us   not   learn     heavens   to   make
      'He did not order us to learn to make the heavens'
      (coaelive,+ALS_[Memory_of_Saints]:127.3394)

Wallage also shows, however, that examples of V2 with a fronted constituent, a negated finite verb, and a postverbal subject pronoun existed throughout the OE period (2005: 137, his table 3.6): for the years 850–950, for example, 61 examples were found out of 450 negated clauses (13.6%), with some of the fronted XPs being arguments. It appears, then, that though initial placement of the negated finite verb is not compulsory in OE, the negated verb must move to a position that is above SpecFamP and below SpecShiftP. Similar facts appear to hold for OHG (Axel 2007:

151–3) and for OS, in which V1 with negation is common but far from obligatory; see also Eyþórsson (1995: 258–64) for similar data involving the negative -*at* suffix in ON.

Non-negated V1 declaratives are often described in the theoretical literature (e.g. by van Kemenade 1987: 44–5; Kiparsky 1995: 163; Cichosz 2010: 78) as characteristic of dramatic, lively narrative and continuity (often termed 'Narrative Inversion').[23] This approach to V1 relates it to similar examples from colloquial modern German and Dutch (see Önnerfors 1997). It is, however, important to make this vague notion of lively narrative explicit. Reis (2000a, 2000b) argues that verb-first declaratives in the modern languages are associated with a systematically different illocutionary force, merely expressing/recounting a true proposition rather than asserting its truth.[24] More work needs to be done to establish whether this holds of V1 in the older Germanic languages, and whether differences obtain between them; however, the possibility is plausible and opens up an analysis in which the verb moves further than in ordinary declaratives, to Force$^0$, the locus of illocutionary force specification (Rizzi 1997).[25]

Since the possibility obtains in all the early Germanic languages, it can be straightforwardly reconstructed for Proto-Northwest Germanic alongside the neutral V2/V3 options discussed in section 3.2.

## 3.4 Verb-late and verb-final main clauses

### 3.4.1 *Verb-late main clauses: the data*

All of the early West Germanic languages, as well as some ON poetry but not prose (Þorgeirsson 2012: 239–42), exhibit clauses in which the verb occurs later than third position. These are often termed 'verb-late' or 'verb-final' clauses.[26] I conflate these two categories here as 'verb-late', treating both as instances in which the verb does

---

[23] In addition, Cichosz (2010: 77) observes that V1 has been said to be characteristic of poetry, though she notes that her own data does not entirely support this view. Axel (2007: ch. 3), meanwhile, comes to the conclusion that there are a number of different V1 constructions with heterogeneous motivations in OHG: in addition to V1 conditioned by negation and Narrative Inversion and by preverbal null subjects, she mentions V1 with verbs of saying, existential/presentational constructions and unaccusative verbs. Future research should establish whether these categories of V1 clause are shared by the other Germanic languages and whether they can be reconstructed for an earlier stage.

[24] For a different approach, associating V1 with highly novel information, see Roberts and Roussou (2002).

[25] This makes it unnecessary to posit a phonologically null element such as a narrative continuity operator (as suggested by Sigurðsson 1993 and Faarlund 2004 for ON) in initial position. However, *þa* and *þonne* in OE are characterized by the function of narrative continuity when inducing V2. It could therefore be the case that these elements are lexicalizations of such a null operator, though the question of their optionality (alternation with V1) would then arise.

[26] With possible differences in categorization. For instance, Smith (1971) classes clauses in which the verb is in third position or later (including those discussed in section 3.2) separately from clauses in which the verb is in clause-final position. Koopman (1995) and Pintzuk and Haeberli (2008) deal with 'verb-final' main clauses, but include examples such as (49) in which the verb is not in absolute final position. Cichosz (2010) leaves clauses in which the verb is both second and final out of consideration. Here I broadly follow the diagnostics proposed by Koopman (1995) and Pintzuk and Haeberli (2008), but using the term 'verb-late'.

not occur in its expected clause-early position. For OE, Cichosz (2010: 73–4) finds that 69 of 418 main clauses (16.5%) in her OE poetry sample, 19 of 122 main clauses (15.6%) in her OE original prose sample, and 15 of 140 main clauses (10.7%) in her OE translated prose sample are verb-late. Similarly, Koopman (1995) found that between 0.5 and 6.0% of OE main clauses had late finite verbs, depending on the text, and Pintzuk (1993: 22 n. 22) found that 16 of 252 main clauses (6.3%) had late finite verbs in a corpus of OE prose texts from between 900 and 1100. Examples are (50) and (51).

(50)  Her    Cenwalh   adrifen    **wæs**   from   Pendan     cyninge
      here   C.        out-driven  was     from   Penda.DAT  king.DAT
      'This year Cenwalh was driven away by King Penda'
      (cochronA-1,ChronA_[Plummer]:645.1.324)

(51)  Baloham   ðonne   fulgeorne     feran       **wolde**
      B.        then    full-gladly   proceed.INF  wanted
      'Ballam then very much wanted to proceed'
      (cocura,CP:36.255.22.1674)

In a more recent study, Pintzuk and Haeberli (2008) use elements such as particles and negative objects as diagnostics for the 'true' prevalence of verb-lateness, since the existence of processes such as extraposition and scrambling means that surface V2 clauses may in fact be derived in a way that does not involve leftward movement of the verb. Their working assumption is that if a diagnostic element such as a particle precedes the finite verb, the clause must be analysed as verb-late, since these diagnostic elements are not susceptible to movement. They find that 56.6 per cent of main clauses including particles (111 of 196), 31.5 per cent of main clauses including negative objects (17 of 54), and 16.3 per cent of main clauses including stranded prepositions (20 of 143) are verb-late.

The figure for particles, which is much higher than that for other diagnostic elements, may be problematic: as van Kemenade (1987: 30) showed, it may have been possible to move the particle leftward along with the verb in clauses like (52) and (53). A reviewer suggests that some of these particles may have switched from separable to inseparable.

(52)  Stephanus   up    **astah**   þurh      his   blod    gewuldorbeagod
      Stephen     up    rose       through   his   blood   crowned-with-glory
      'Stephen ascended, crowned with glory through his blood'
      (cocathom1,+ACHom_I,_3:205.198.633)

(53)  Ut    **eode**   se    sædere   hys   sæd    to    sawenne
      out   went      the   sower    his   seed   to    sow
      'The sower went out in order to sow his seed'
      (cowsgosp,Mk_[WSCp]:4.3.2387)

Pintzuk and Haeberli are aware of this possibility (2008: 396–7), which they term 'parasitic' movement (2008: 389), and state that in their data evidence for this type of movement is restricted to the particle *ut*.[27] In any case, the existence of such examples means they must weaken their conclusion substantially: 'the frequency of preverbal diagnostic elements represents an upper limit' to the frequency of verb-late structures (2008: 390).

For OHG, Cichosz (2010: 73–4) finds frequencies of surface verb-late of 10.7 per cent (24/224) for poetry, 1.2 per cent (2/144) for original prose, and 10.1 per cent (19/88) for translated prose. These figures are lower than those found for OE. Indeed, Axel (2007: 62, 77) has argued that such cases are more restricted and less frequent than previously assumed in OHG: 'there are far fewer incontestable examples than has been explicitly or implicitly assumed in the literature' (2007: 77). She concludes, with Reis (1901), that 'in OHG main clauses, verb-end order is rarely found'. One such example is given in (54).

(54)  min    tohter    ubilo    fon    themo    tiuuale    giuuegit    **ist**
      my     daughter  severely  by     the      devil      shaken      is
      'My daughter is severely possessed by a demon'
      (*Tatian* 273,10)

In OS, the percentage of non-conjunct main clauses with the verb later than third position is 7.5 per cent (177/2348). If, as I suggested in section 3.2, verb-third clauses are taken to be underlyingly 'verb-late' (i.e. lacking movement to the C-domain), then we need to consider the percentage of non-conjunct main clauses with the verb later than second position, which is 11.5 per cent (270/2348).

Some clauses traditionally seen as main clauses by editors may in fact be subordinate: for instance, in OHG, clauses with an anaphoric DP in the left periphery can often be analysed as internally headed relative clauses (Axel 2007: 75), as in (55) from OS:

(55)  That   ic    an    mînumu    hugi    ni    **gidar**    uuendean    mid    uuihti
      that   I     in    my        mind    NEG   dare        change      with   whit
      'I do not dare change that at all in my mind'
      OR
      'which I do not dare change at all in my mind'
      (*Heliand* 219–20)

Several other examples can be seen as subordinate clauses, contrary to the usual reading:

---

[27] (52) casts doubt on this claim, though it is possible to analyse this example as an instance of rightward movement of the participial phrase.

(56) Sie   uundradun  alle,  bihuuî  gio   sô   kindisc   man   sulica  quidi
     they  wondered    all    why     ever  so   childish  man   such    words
     mahti mid  is   mûdu  gimênean. Thar  ina   thiu  modar  **fand**
     might with his  mouth speak.INF there him   the   mother found
     'They all wondered how such a young man could speak such words. There
     his mother found him'
     OR
     '...where his mother found him'
     (*Heliand* 816–18)

(57) Thô  he   sô   hriuuig  sat,  balg        ina   an   is   briostun
     then he   so   rueful   sat   was-angry   him   in   his  breast
     'Then he sat there sadly, was angry at heart'
     OR
     'When/while he sat there sadly, he was angry at heart'
     (*Heliand* 722–3)

In (56) and (57) the second reading is supported by the fact that the words *thar, tho*, and others are ambiguous between clausal adverbs and complementizers (see also example (24)). A number of the verb-late clauses are ambiguous between main and subordinate status in this way. However, even with this proviso there are many examples that cannot be analysed away:

(58) Ic   eu    an    uuatara  **scal**  gidôpean  diurlîco
     I    you   in    water    shall    baptize   tenderly
     'I shall baptize you tenderly in water'
     (*Heliand* 882–3)

(59) Krist  im     forđ  **giuuêt**  an    Galileo       land
     Christ REFL   forth went       into  Galilee.GEN   land
     'Christ went forth into the land of Galilee'
     (*Heliand* 1134–5)

(60) Ic   is    engil  **bium**
     I    his   angel  am
     'I am his angel'
     (*Heliand* 99)

As for OE and OHG, then, verb-late was a possible pattern, though rare, in OS.

### 3.4.2 *Verb-late main clauses as an unsolved puzzle*

However frequent they may be, examples of verb-final main clauses have thus far proven problematic for all analyses that assume that the early West Germanic languages exhibited a variant of modern Continental Germanic V2. One possibility, outlined by Koopman (1995: 139–40), is to view them as simply ungrammatical. However, as Koopman notes, this position is not an attractive one, since 'it is hard to believe that different scribes made the same grammatical error throughout the period, at roughly the same percentage', and for all three languages in question this percentage is too high to simply write off.

A variant of this hypothesis is to argue that verb-late order is due to foreign influence, specifically the influence of Latin. This is the line taken by Cichosz (2010: 88–9). However, Cichosz's own data, given above, does not support this hypothesis: verb-late clauses are found more frequently in OE and OHG poetry and in OE original prose than in translated prose of either language, which is the opposite of what we would expect if the influence of Latin were the sole explanation. Similarly, Axel (2007: 72) argues that verb-late order in (54) is due to literal translation of the Latin original. Even if this is the case, it does not render the example unproblematic: can we really assume that literal translation from the source language can result in an order that is absolutely ungrammatical in the target language? For the same reason, though metre may have influenced the distribution of verb-late clauses in verse texts (see e.g. Dewey 2006: 60–6), a metrical explanation is unlikely to be fully satisfactory alone. As Lass (1997: 68) puts it, 'it is unlikely in principle... that any device used in verse will be an absolute violation of the norms of non-verse language'.

It seems necessary, then, to come up with an analysis in which these examples are accommodated. Classical asymmetric V2 analyses such as those of van Kemenade (1987) for OE, Axel (2007) for OHG, and Erickson (1997) for OS are unable to account for these examples at all if it is assumed that verb movement to $C^0$ was obligatory as in modern German. By contrast, the competing grammars analysis of Pintzuk (1999) for OE is able to, as for Pintzuk V-to-$C^0$ movement only takes place in a small subset of contexts: direct questions, verb-initial declarative and imperative clauses, and clauses with an adverb preceding the finite verb in second position (1999: 92). In all other cases, the finite verb remains in Infl, below $C^0$, which may be head-final or head-initial; cf. section 2.2.2 of this book for a discussion of the competing grammars hypothesis. However, as Koopman (1995: 142) points out, Pintzuk's analysis is unable to account for the fact that a very low proportion of main clauses are Infl-final—a problem which is ameliorated by Pintzuk and Haeberli's (2008) result that verb-final main clauses are more common than previously thought, though not solved, since this pattern is still rarer than in embedded clauses. It would be necessary to argue that one grammar was preferred over the other in main clauses but not subordinate clauses, which seems an unattractive prospect (see Fuß and Trips 2002: 211). The only analysis able to account for the data is that of Haeberli (2005), in which the verb moves to AgrS$^0$ in main clauses and T$^0$ in subordinate clauses. This allows for the headedness of AgrSP and TP to vary independently, solving the problem with

Pintzuk's (1999) analysis; however, it provides no insight into why some main clauses have head-initial AgrSP and others have final AgrSP.

It thus seems safe to conclude that verb-late main clauses are a problem for all existing accounts of early Germanic clause structure. In the next subsection I make some suggestions towards the resolution of this problem.

### 3.4.3 *An analysis*

In Mainland Scandinavian there is variation as to whether V2 is found in embedded clauses, as shown by (61) vs. (62).

(61)  Olle  sa     att    han  inte   **hade**  läst  boken
      O.    said   that   he   NEG    had    read  book.DEF

(62)  Olle  sa     att    han  **hade**  inte   läst  boken
      O.    said   that   he   had    NEG    read  book.DEF
      'Olle said that he had not read the book'
      (Swedish; Wiklund 2010: 81)

Adopting the Fox–Reinhart intuition that apparent optionality is motivated by interpretative alternations (see section 2.2), in recent years there has been substantial work on the potential interpretative differences between non-V2 (e.g. (61)) and V2 (e.g. (62)) embedded declaratives: see Julien (2007, 2009), Wiklund et al. (2009), Wiklund (2009a, 2009b, 2010).[28] In (63), a rough hypothesis about the generalization governing their distribution is stated, building on Hooper and Thompson's (1973) pioneering work on embedded main clause phenomena.

(63)  **The assertion hypothesis** (Wiklund et al. 2009: 1915)
      'The more asserted (the less presupposed) the complement is, the more compatible it is with V2 (and other root phenomena).'

Julien (2007, 2009) has defended a version of (62) in which V2 embedded clauses are asserted and non-V2 embedded clauses are not. Wiklund and co-authors, on the other hand, have defended a one-way implication: if an embedded clause is V2 then it is asserted, but not vice versa. The details are complex, and some of the judgements are disputed. Furthermore, as Wiklund et al. (2009: 1915) note, the relevant notion of assertion is not easy to define or operationalize (see also Hooper and Thompson 1973: 473). I will not go into the details here; some version of (63) seems to be correct, however, since much of the data is undisputed. For instance, sentences like (64), in which a V2 clause is embedded under a factive verb, are uncontroversially

---

[28] The intuition goes back much further, and has been applied to V2 in other Germanic languages: see Wiklund et al. (2009) and Wiklund (2010) for references.

ungrammatical, whereas their verb-late counterparts ((65)) are grammatical. This attested contrast is predicted by both Julien and Wiklund.

(64)   *Olle   ångrade   att   han   **hade**   inte   läst   boken
      O.   regretted   that   he   had   NEG   read   book.DEF

(65)   Olle   ångrade   att   han   inte   **hade**   läst   boken
      O.   regretted   that   he   NEG   had   read   book.DEF
      'Olle regretted that he had not read the book.'
      (Swedish; Wiklund 2010: 82)

The literature on assertion and presupposition within pragmatics and philosophy is extensive; see Stalnaker (1974, 1978) for one approach, and Schlenker (2010) for a recent formalization. I here assume, broadly following this approach, that a proposition is presupposed if the speaker believes that its truth belongs to the common ground, and that in asserting a proposition the speaker intends to update the common ground to include the truth of that proposition.[29] Assertion is thus an illocutionary act (Austin 1975: 98–102) with assertoric force.

Given the apparent connection between embedded V2 and assertion, examining the force of early Germanic main clauses with and without verb-movement to the C-domain suggests itself; after all, main clauses can be used for a lot more than just assertion (see Austin 1975). However, identifying the force of non-embedded clauses is not straightforward. Most of the tests proposed to distinguish asserted from presupposed content (e.g. the 'Hey, wait a minute!' test of von Fintel 2004) require native speaker judgements. Kiparsky and Kiparsky (1970) present a number of syntactic diagnostics for factive predicates (i.e. those that presuppose their complements), e.g. the ability of the complement to be preposed, and the ability of the predicate to take the noun *fact* or a gerund as its complement; unfortunately, these tests, and tests based on island constraints, are only applicable to complementation structures, not to main clauses.

The test I will use here depends on the availability of so-called speaker-oriented adverbs (Jackendoff 1972: ch. 3; Ernst 2009; Liu 2009). In modern English these include *honestly*, *probably*, *obviously*, *clearly*, and *luckily*, as in (66).[30] These adverbs have a variety of special syntactic properties: they are incompatible with interrogatives ((67))

[29] Though Julien (2007: 244; 2009: 229) suggests that some embedded clauses can be both presupposed (by the speaker) and asserted (treated as new information for the purposes of the hearer). Moreover, Hooper and Thompson (1973: 486) argue that it is possible for a clause to be neither presupposed nor asserted. The full interaction between clausal force and information packaging is too complex to be discussed here, but in the approach taken here presupposition and assertion are mutually exclusive by definition.

[30] Ernst (2009: 498) subdivides these into discourse-oriented adverbs (paraphrasable by 'I say ADV that P') and epistemic and evaluative adverbs (paraphrasable by 'It is ADJ that P'). See also Bellert (1977).

and other inversion contexts ((68)), they cannot occur in the complements of factive verbs ((69)), and they cannot occur in the scope of negation ((70)).[31]

(66)  Luckily, John was spotted by a lifeguard.
(67)  What has Charley (*luckily) discovered?
(68)  So fast did Tom (*luckily) run that he got to Texas in ten minutes.
(69)  Bill regrets that Frank (*luckily) discovered the uranium.
(70)  Karen has not (*luckily) left.

I will assume, following Bellert (1977: 342) and Liu (2009: 339), that speaker-oriented adverbs take the main proposition and construct a secondary proposition evaluating it: speaker-oriented adverb clauses are thus 'double-propositional', to use Liu's term. For (66), for instance, the main proposition is that John was spotted by a lifeguard, and the secondary proposition builds on it to express that this was a fortunate state of affairs. Crucially, the truth of the main proposition is presupposed by the secondary proposition: the evaluation in (66) presupposes that John was in fact spotted by a lifeguard.

Good candidates for speaker-oriented adverbs in OE, the early West Germanic language with the largest available corpus, include *soþlice/soðlice* 'truly' and *witodlice* 'certainly'. Little research has been done on speaker-oriented adverbs in this language, though Lenker (2010) explores their function as adverbial 'connectors',[32] and Scot (2009) and Sundmalm (2009) investigate the base-generated position of *soþlice* and *witodlice*, concluding that these are always CP-adverbs or IP-adverbs in their framework.[33]

To investigate the distribution of speaker-oriented adverbs I compared V2 clauses and V4+ clauses in the YCOE, on the assumption that these types would be likely to represent verb movement to the left periphery and the absence of such movement respectively. I considered only clauses containing three or more constituents (other than the verb), in order to avoid giving more opportunities for the adverbs to occur in V4+ clauses. The dividing line between early and late OE is 950; for more detail on this classification scheme, see Pintzuk and Taylor (2006). The results are presented in Tables 3.3 to 3.6.

In all four of the tables the hypothesis of independence can be safely rejected, with $p < 0.0001$ for each (df = 1; Yates's chi-square values: 34.297, 29.765, 98.068, and 36.813 respectively). In all four, the relative frequency of the speaker-oriented

---

[31] For me examples (67) and (68) are very marginally possible, but only with a manner reading (hence irrelevantly).

[32] Lenker (2010: 51–3) observes that Ælfric's grammar of OE (Zupitza 1880; see also Menzer 2004) discusses *soþlice* not as an adverb but under the heading of conjunctions, suggesting that its function was on the textual level.

[33] Scot (2009: 11–12) observes that *soþlice* may (rarely) have a manner reading.

TABLE 3.3. Frequency and percentage of V2 vs. V4+ declarative main clauses with and without *soþlice/soðlice* in early OE

|  | With *soþlice* | | Without *soþlice* | | Total |
|---|---|---|---|---|---|
|  | N | % | N | % | N |
| V2 | 8 | 0.1 | 5489 | 99.9 | 5497 |
| V4+ | 24 | 1.2 | 2048 | 98.8 | 2072 |
| Total | 32 | – | 7537 | – | 7569 |

TABLE 3.4. Frequency and percentage of V2 vs. V4+ declarative main clauses with and without *witodlice* in early OE

|  | With *witodlice* | | Without *witodlice* | | Total |
|---|---|---|---|---|---|
|  | N | % | N | % | N |
| V2 | 6 | 0.1 | 5491 | 99.9 | 5497 |
| V4+ | 20 | 1.0 | 2052 | 99.0 | 2072 |
| Total | 26 | – | 7543 | – | 7569 |

TABLE 3.5. Frequency and percentage of V2 vs. V4+ declarative main clauses with and without *soþlice/soðlice* in late OE

|  | With *soþlice* | | Without *soþlice* | | Total |
|---|---|---|---|---|---|
|  | N | % | N | % | N |
| V2 | 135 | 1.1 | 11631 | 98.9 | 11766 |
| V4+ | 99 | 3.9 | 2419 | 96.1 | 2518 |
| Total | 234 | – | 14050 | – | 14284 |

TABLE 3.6. Frequency and percentage of V2 vs. V4+ declarative main clauses with and without *witodlice* in late OE

|  | With *witodlice* | | Without *witodlice* | | Total |
|---|---|---|---|---|---|
|  | N | % | N | % | N |
| V2 | 56 | 0.5 | 11710 | 99.5 | 11766 |
| V4+ | 40 | 1.6 | 2478 | 98.4 | 2518 |
| Total | 96 | – | 14188 | – | 14284 |

adverb is much higher in the V4+ clauses than in the V2 clauses. Examples of verb-late clauses including *soþlice* and *witodlice* from early OE are given in (71) and (72) and examples from late OE are given in (73) and (74).

(71)  He þa      soþlice oðre       þara    flascena
      he then    truly   other.ACC the.GEN bottles.GEN
      þam      halgan    were     **brohte**
      the.DAT  holy.DAT  man.DAT  brought
      'He then truly brought one of the bottles to the holy man'
      (cogregdC,GD_2_[C]:18.141.28.1696)

(72)  Þa    witodlice æfter þæs       lichaman æriste        be
      then  certainly after the.GEN  body.GEN awakening.DAT of
      Lazares wundrum     &    mægnum       **wæs**  ætswiged
      L.GEN   wonders.DAT and  virtues.DAT  was     kept-silent
      'Then, certainly, we hear nothing of Lazarus's wonders and virtues after his body's resurrection'
      (cogregdC,GDPref_and_3_[C]:17.217.17.2929)

(73)  Zosimus  soðlice þa      eorðan   mid tearum     ofergeotende hire
      Z.       truly   the.ACC earth.ACC with tears.DAT overspilling  her.DAT
      to   **cwæð**
      to   said
      'Truly, soaking the earth with his tears, Zosimus said to her . . .'
      (comary,LS_23_[MaryofEgypt]:362.234)

(74)  ic witodlice  æghwanane      **eom**  ungesælig buton    westme
      I  certainly  in-every-way   am      unhappy   beyond   increase
      'I am truly unhappy in every way beyond increase'
      (coeust,LS_8_[Eust]:203.210)

Speaker-oriented adverbs occur in verb-late clauses with a frequency that is very clearly not due to chance, then. This is not a property of all adverbs, since the manner adverb *swiðe/swiþe* 'severely, terribly' does not pattern this way: the difference between V2 and V4+ clauses with regard to the frequency of occurrence of this adverb is not close to significance (for Table 3.7, Yates's chi-square: 0.411, $p = 0.5215$; for Table 3.8, Yates's chi-square: 0.267, $p = 0.6054$).[34]

For OS and OHG there is much less data available, and the relevant quantitative information is difficult to obtain. However, examples like (75) from OS may be

---

[34] As observed by a reviewer, there is a general difference between early and late OE, such that verb-late clauses seem to become less common over time. The association between verb-movement and assertion, then, may be one that weakened during the OE period. More research on the change is certainly needed.

TABLE 3.7. Frequency and percentage of V2 vs. V4+ declarative main clauses with and without *swiðe* in early OE

|  | With *swiðe* | | Without *swiðe* | | Total |
|---|---|---|---|---|---|
|  | N | % | N | % | N |
| V2 | 107 | 1.9 | 5390 | 98.1 | 5497 |
| V4+ | 35 | 1.7 | 2037 | 98.3 | 2072 |
| Total | 142 | – | 7427 | – | 7569 |

TABLE 3.8. Frequency and percentage of V2 vs. V4+ declarative main clauses with and without *swiðe* in late OE

|  | With *swiðe* | | Without *swiðe* | | Total |
|---|---|---|---|---|---|
|  | N | % | N | % | N |
| V2 | 79 | 0.7 | 11687 | 99.3 | 11766 |
| V4+ | 14 | 0.6 | 2504 | 99.4 | 2518 |
| Total | 93 | – | 14191 | – | 14284 |

suggestive that the asymmetry observed above holds across early West Germanic. Here the adverbial *te uuârun* 'truly, in truth' can be read as speaker-oriented.

(75)  uui    thi     te uuârun   **mugun**  ...   ûse   ârundi   ôðo   gitellien
      we    you.DAT  to truth.DAT may    ...   our   message  easily tell
      'Truly, we can happily tell you our message'
      (*Heliand* 563–4)

Another relevant observation concerns the distribution of first person subject pronouns. Since they are definitionally uttered by the speaker, it is natural to assume that first person pronouns are naturally more likely to occur in evaluatives than pronouns of other persons.

In both early and late OE, first person pronominal subjects are found with much greater frequency, relative to other personal pronouns, in V4+ clauses than in V2 clauses (once again considering only clauses with three or more constituents). The effect is significant at the $p < 0.0001$ level (Yates's chi-square, early OE (Table 3.9): 35.042; late OE (Table 3.10): 624.312). For OS, looking at Table 3.11, a similar effect appears to hold; however, the effect is not significant (Yates's chi-square: 1.623, $p = 0.2027$), so there is no evidence that the distribution we see in OS is not due to chance.

TABLE 3.9. Frequency and percentage of V2 vs. V4+ declarative main clauses with first and non-first person subject pronouns in early OE

|  | 1st | | 2nd/3rd | | Total |
|  | N | % | N | % | N |
|---|---|---|---|---|---|
| V2 | 305 | 14.0 | 1874 | 86.0 | 2179 |
| V4+ | 223 | 22.5 | 767 | 77.5 | 990 |
| Total | 528 | – | 2641 | – | 3169 |

TABLE 3.10. Frequency and percentage of V2 vs. V4+ declarative main clauses with first and non-first person subject pronouns in late OE

|  | 1st | | 2nd/3rd | | Total |
|  | N | % | N | % | N |
|---|---|---|---|---|---|
| V2 | 305 | 6.8 | 4198 | 93.2 | 4503 |
| V4+ | 397 | 33.8 | 779 | 66.2 | 1176 |
| Total | 702 | – | 4977 | – | 5679 |

TABLE 3.11. Frequency and percentage of V2 vs. V4+ declarative main clauses with first and non-first person subject pronouns in the *Heliand*

|  | 1st | | 2nd/3rd | | Total |
|  | N | % | N | % | N |
|---|---|---|---|---|---|
| V2 | 95 | 19.7 | 387 | 80.3 | 482 |
| V4+ | 29 | 25.7 | 84 | 74.3 | 113 |
| Total | 124 | – | 471 | – | 595 |

What are we to make of this, then? This data can, of course, be interpreted in many ways. However, it clearly indicates that for OE at least there was an interpretative distinction between at least some verb-late clauses and clauses in which the verb moved to the left periphery. Furthermore, it is not inconsistent with the hypothesis that verb-movement to the left periphery in declaratives was linked to the assertion of the main proposition of the clause, whereas in clauses in which the main proposition was presupposed, such as expressives/evaluatives, verb-movement did not take place.[35] Speaker-oriented adverbs, which presuppose the main proposition, and first person pronouns, which are naturally likely to occur in evaluatives, occur with greater-than-chance frequency in clauses with unmoved finite verbs.[36]

In syntactic terms we can state this in terms of $Fin^0$ lacking a $[uV]$ feature in these clauses. Since the features of the verb are then no longer a subset of the features of $Fin^0$, head-movement fails to take place. We can think of this non-verbal exponent of $Fin^0$ as a null complementizer, which, following Roberts (1996), raises to $Force^0$ for reasons to do with its clause-typing role.

An appealing offshoot of this analysis is that it may help to explain the prevalence of verb-late order in conjunct clauses, as discussed in section 3.1. It could be argued that the verb occurs late in these if and when they do not constitute part of the main assertion of the utterance in which they occur. Similarly, the approach might account for some of the variation in verb movement in early Germanic subordinate clauses. However, these extensions are beyond the scope of this chapter.

### 3.4.4 *Verb-late in Proto-Northwest Germanic*

That some form of verb-late-generating lexical items must be reconstructed for Proto-Northwest Germanic main clauses is obvious; indeed, traditional scholarship on Proto-Germanic (e.g. Fourquet 1938; Smith 1971; Lehmann 1972: 243; Antonsen 1975; Hopper 1975: 86; Kiparsky 1995: 152, 1996: 140) assumed that its basic word order was SOV. The early West Germanic languages all contain verb-late examples, as we have seen. Though ON does not, the order is prevalent in the Northwest Germanic runic inscriptions, e.g. the famous Golden Horn of Gallehus.

(76)  ek  hlewagastiz  holtijaz  horna  tawido
      I   H.           H.        horn   made
      'I, Hlewagastiz Holtijaz, made this horn.'

Eyþórsson (1995: 181) also analyses this as an unambiguous example of the lack of V-to-$C^0$ movement.[37] The Northwest Germanic runic inscriptions contain a great deal of variation with regard to the position of the finite verb, however (Antonsen 1975: 25; Ureland 1978; Braunmüller 1982: 128; Faarlund 1989, 1990: 20–9; Eyþórsson 1995), with much depending on the exact reading of individual inscriptions. It seems

---

[35] There is in fact evidence for various movements in the lower area of the clause (Fuß and Trips 2002; Haeberli and Pintzuk 2012). The crucial point here is that the verb did not move any higher than TP.

[36] Petrova (2011, 2012) shows that verb-late clauses in Middle Low German are often 'mirative', serving to highlight the unexpectedness of information. This would be compatible with the interpretation of verb-late clauses in OE outlined here: a secondary proposition built on the primary proposition expresses that the (presupposed) primary proposition is an unexpected state of affairs.

[37] Under the analysis given in this chapter, this example is actually ambiguous: it is possible to analyse it as an instance of V3, with the horn as given information in SpecFamP and the verb in $Fin^0$. In OE and OHG V3 structures, however, non-pronominal objects are rarely found in preverbal position, so this analysis is unlikely to be the correct one.

clear that examples both with and without verb-movement can be found (Eyþórsson 1995, 2011), so that 'it does not seem possible to make any statements about the absolute chronology of word order development within the language of the runic inscriptions' (Eyþórsson 2011: 40).

I have not been able to demonstrate that the division between assertive and evaluative/expressive main clauses in terms of verb-movement holds for any of the older Germanic languages except OE; the first-person-pronoun test does not yield significant results for OS, and the other early West Germanic languages have not been investigated due to the lack of parsed corpora. There is no justification for reconstructing this division for Proto-Northwest Germanic, then. The most that can be said is that the existence of some interpretatively motivated alternation between clauses with and clauses without verb-movement in the protolanguage is not implausible.

## 3.5 Main clauses in Gothic

In this section I briefly attempt to integrate the picture for early Northwest Germanic with the Gothic data. The most extensive treatment of verb position in Gothic to date is Eyþórsson (1995: 18–179), from which most of the data for this section will be drawn.

Eyþórsson notes, following Koppitz (1900, 1901) and Fourquet (1938), that when single verbs or nominals in Greek are rendered as verb plus complement in Gothic the complement normally precedes the verb: (77) and (78) are examples.

(77)  dwala              gatawida
      foolish.ACC.FEM   made.3SG
      'made foolish'
      (1 Corinthians 1: 20; Greek Majority Text: εμωρανεν)

(78)  liban      taujiþ
      live.INF   make.3SG
      'makes life'
      (John 6: 63; Greek Majority Text: ζωοποιουν)

The basic word order of Gothic is therefore assumed to be SOV.[38] However, the situation is more nuanced: object pronouns and verbal particles often follow the finite verb (Eyþórsson 1995: 29–48). Under the usual assumption that Germanic particles and pronouns cannot undergo rightward movement (Pintzuk and Haeberli 2008: 375–80), this indicates some degree of verb-movement.

---

[38] As in the Northwest Germanic languages (see section 3.3), there is a tendency towards verb-movement in negative declaratives (Eyþórsson 1995: 24–5), as well as in imperatives and interrogatives.

More interesting, however, are examples like (79) and (80), which show the relative positions of the finite verb and left-peripheral discourse particles such as *uh*.

(79) iþ    Iesus  iddj-uh   miþ   im
     but   Jesus  went-UH   with  them
     'But Jesus went with them'
     (Luke 7: 6)

(80) iþ    is   ub-uh-wopida
     but   he   PRT-UH-cried
     'but he cried'
     (Luke 18: 38)

The element *-uh* is normally enclitic to the first phonological word of the clause. However, there are fifteen cases, including (79) and (80), in which this element instead cliticizes to the finite verb, apparently ignoring the preverbal element (Eyþórsson 1995: 56–63). In all these instances, the preverbal element is a pronoun or a proper name (8× *is* 'he', 5× *Iesus*, 1× *Filippus*, 1× *eis* 'they'). When other elements are in clause-initial position, as in (81), (82), and (83), the finite verb does not precede *-uh*.

(81) þuht-uþ          þan qiþa   ni    silbins,      ak anþaris
     conscience.ACC-UH PAN say.1SG NEG self.GEN.SG  but other.GEN.SG
     'Conscience, I say, not your own, but of the other'
     (1 Corinthians 10: 29)

(82) uz-uh    þamma mela      managai   galiþun siponje    is   ibukai
     from-UH  that.DAT time.DAT many.NOM  went    disciples.GEN his  back
     'From that time many of his disciples went back'
     (John 6: 66)

(83) sumai-h   qeþun þatei  sunjeins  ist
     some-UH   said  that   good      is
     'Some said that he is good'
     (John 7: 12)

Assuming the positions of the particles *iþ* and *-uh* to be invariant,[39] Eyþórsson takes this as evidence for movement of the verb to the C-domain with definite subjects only.

---

[39] In Eyþórsson's analysis, *-uh* is base-generated in head position and attaches to the first phonological word in the same maximal projection, for him CP (see examples (80) and (82)). I will have nothing to say about this process of attachment, which I take to be morphophonological. See Eyþórsson (1995: 121–41) on cliticization in Gothic.

To analyse this data under the assumptions made here, let us consider the role and position of *iþ* and *-uh*. Following Klein (1994) and Klein and Condon (1993), Ferraresi (2005: 150) takes *iþ* to mark a shift in the discourse topic, and *-uh* to introduce a new element into the discourse. Viewing these elements in the framework of Frascarelli and Hinterhölzl (2007), *iþ* can be viewed as a lexicalization of the head of ShiftP, the phrase which hosts shifting (Givón 1983) and Aboutness (Reinhart 1981) topics. Evidence for this position is clear: *iþ* can be preceded by a topic and by subordinating conjunctions (Ferraresi 2005: 172). The enclitic *-uh*, meanwhile, can be viewed as a lexicalization of the head of FocP, the phrase which hosts foci.[40] Example (79) can then be analysed as in (84).

(84)

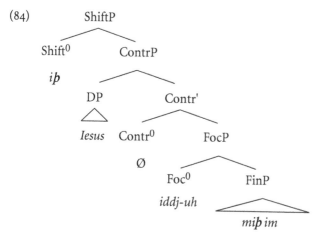

The subject is here analysed as being in SpecContrP, that is, as a contrastive topic. In terms of information structure this seems to be correct: all fifteen instances of subjects following *iþ* and preceding *-uh* are given elements active in the discourse, and involve a contrast of topic in context. The absence of objects in this position is then not remarkable: the sample is small. It also makes the right predictions with regard to the absence of sentences such as *\*iþ iddja*, with a null subject, since null subjects cannot be contrastive, and *\*iþ Iesus-uh iddja*, since the contrastive topic *Iesus* is outside FocP and hence not a legitimate target for cliticization.[41] In examples

---

[40] For Eyþórsson, *-uh* serves merely as a coordinator (1995: 53). For Ferraresi, *-uh* is in FinP, but this leaves its function as introducer of new information unexplained. One problem for the FocP hypothesis, however, is that *-uh* may introduce quantified elements (as in (83)), which are sometimes thought to be ruled out in left-peripheral (identificational) focus position (É. Kiss 1998: 252).

[41] One could then speculate that the movement of the verb to Foc[0] is a 'last-resort'-type strategy to provide a phonological host for the clitic *-uh* (cf. Eyþórsson 1995: 68–73 for a similar approach based on the need to license the subject trace), although it is not obvious that such an account can be stated in terms of the system of head-movement based on Roberts (2010b) adopted here, in which movement is a surface outcome of agreement with a defective goal. Alternatively, it could be argued that the verb moves to *-uh* because the focus is on the event itself. This approach has the advantage of accounting for the

such as (81)–(83), on the other hand, the pre-*uh* element can be analysed as in focus in SpecFocP rather than contrastive, and hence can host -*uh*.

If -*uh* is in Foc⁰, then examples such as (81)–(83) cease to present a problem for the hypothesis that the verb generally moves to Fin⁰, in the low left periphery, as I have argued for early Northwest Germanic. In (82) and similar examples, the subject can be analysed as given and in SpecFamP. In the Gospel of Matthew, 137 of the 153 non-conjunct positive indicative declarative main clauses are amenable to an analysis in which the verb is in Fin⁰, e.g. (85) and (86).

(85)  ushof        sik      jainþro
      removed      REFL     thence
      '(He) removed himself thence'
      (Matthew 11: 1; Greek Majority Text: μετεβη)

(86)  fram  saihston  þan  hveilai  warþ  riqis  ufar  allai  airþai
      from  sixth.DAT  ÞAN  hour.DAT  became  darkness  over  all.DAT  earth.DAT
      'From the sixth hour, darkness covered the whole earth'
      (Matthew 27: 45; Greek Majority Text: σκοτος εγενετο)

In (85) the verb precedes a reflexive pronoun which is not present in the Greek; in (86) *riqis* 'darkness' follows the verb, even though it is preverbal in the Greek. Only 16 of 153 examples (10.5%) resist analysis in this way, e.g. (87) and (88).

(87)  fauhons     grobos      aigun
      foxes.NOM   holes.ACC   have
      'Foxes have holes'
      (Matthew 8: 20; Greek Majority Text: αι αλωπεκες φωλεους εχουσιν)

(88)  þrutsfillai   hrainjai     wairþand
      leprous.NOM   clean.NOM    become
      'Lepers become cleansed'
      (Matthew 11: 5; Greek Majority Text: λεπροι καθαριζονται)

In these cases, the second preverbal element is new information and so cannot be treated as a SpecFamP element. Five of the 16 examples of this kind are due to the translator rendering a simple verb in Greek as a verb plus complement in Gothic, as in (88) (*hrainjai wairþand* for *kaqarizontai*). Cases such as this suggest that V-to-Fin⁰ movement cannot have been general in Gothic. On the other hand, 3 of the 137 unproblematic examples, including (85) and (86), also involve deviations

presence of -*uh* in such clauses in the first place, since it is supposed to be associated with new information.

from the Greek; recall also that the other early Germanic languages appear to lack V-to-Fin$^0$ movement in a low proportion of cases (section 3.4). Furthermore, assuming the absence of any kind of leftward verb movement in Gothic neutral declaratives would leave us with a large number of examples, including (85) and (86), which we would have to write off as completely ungrammatical. A tentative case can be made for V-to-Fin$^0$ movement in neutral declaratives even in Gothic, then, *pace* e.g. Kiparsky (1995: 162).

To sum up this section: in some contexts, there is definitive evidence for verb movement to the left periphery, as shown by Eyþórsson (1995). Furthermore, the Gothic data is largely not inconsistent with the hypothesis of V-to-Fin$^0$ movement in neutral declaratives, though it should be noted that in cases where the translator had some freedom he seems to have opted for structures in which this movement is absent.

Following Roberts (1996), Ferraresi (2005), and Axel (2007: 35–40), we might speculate that the loss of the Gothic (and presumably Proto-Germanic) system of C-domain discourse particles was related to the restricted activation of the expanded left periphery in later Northwest Germanic languages, though more research would be needed in order to substantiate such a claim.

## 3.6 Chapter summary

In this chapter I have presented an analysis of declarative main clauses in the early Germanic languages. I argued that it was likely that Proto-Northwest Germanic had an active left periphery, with verb-movement to Fin$^0$ yielding V3 and occasional V4 orders, and that generalized V2 as found in ON, OS, and later OHG was an innovation. In sections 3.3 and 3.4 I argued that V1 and verb-late were probably also structural possibilities in Proto-Northwest Germanic, with different interpretations related to different clausal forces. Section 3.5 suggested that Gothic might be amenable to an analysis along the same lines.

The reconstructions in this chapter have been limited in scope not only by difficulties of interpretation but also by the correspondence problem as discussed in Chapter 2. Nevertheless, concrete proposals have been made about the prehistory of the Germanic languages, and these can be assessed on the basis of our knowledge of the data as well as what we know about the progression of syntactic change. In addition, in the process, new facts about constituent order in the early Germanic languages have been brought to light: in particular, that OS had generalized V2 to a much higher degree than OE, comparable with late OHG, and that verb-late clauses in OE are systematically different in interpretation from verb-earlier clauses. It may be, as Lightfoot (2002a: 114) asserts, that reconstructions are 'unlikely to tell us anything new about the nature of change'. However, this chapter has shown that the close comparative work required to approach questions of reconstruction can lead us to unearth new facts about historically attested languages, and that the process of reconstruction may therefore be more fruitful than previously thought.

# 4

# The *wh*-system of early Germanic

## 4.1 Introduction

This chapter capitalizes on the intuition that syntactic reconstruction is lexical reconstruction in order to reconstruct aspects of the early Germanic *wh*-system. Lexical-phonological reconstruction has enabled us to posit forms for the early Germanic *wh*-pronouns going all the way back to Proto-Indo-European (see e.g. Ringe 2006: 289–90; Lehmann 2007: §3.4.5). The forms Ringe reconstructs for Proto-Germanic are given in Table 4.1. One separate neuter form exists, *$h^w at$* in the nominative and accusative singular; only Gothic has separate feminine forms, and these are arguably secondary developments (Prokosch 1939: 279).

In addition to these nominal interrogative pronouns 'who' and 'what', non-argumental forms, originally derived from the above paradigm, can be reconstructed for Proto-Germanic: *$h^w ar$* 'where', *$h^w ana$* 'when', *$h^w\bar{o}$* 'how'. For 'why', a form of the instrumental argumental pronoun, combined with a preposition, was used. In addition there were the forms *$h^w aþeraz$*/*$h^w eþeraz$*, discussed in section 4.4.

The task of the syntactic reconstructor is then to pair these forms, along with corresponding functional heads in the C-domain, with an appropriate syntax. Though much has been said about the syntax of interrogatives in Germanic (e.g. Kiparsky 1995; Eyþórsson 1995; Fuß 2003; Ferraresi 2005: 134–6; Axel 2007: 173–89, within the generative tradition alone), many things remain to be said. In this chapter I first give an overview and analysis of constituent order in the *wh*-system, following on from the discussion of declarative main clauses in Chapter 3. The following sections are devoted to more detailed examinations of individual *wh*-elements. Section 4.3 analyses attested cases of 'underspecification' of reflexes of *$h^w at$* in the early Germanic languages, in the sense of Munaro and Obenauer (1999); section 4.4 discusses the forms *$h^w aþeraz$*/*$h^w eþeraz$* and their reflexes in the early Germanic languages. A theme of this chapter is that comparative work on the grammars of living languages can inform work on historically attested languages and on reconstruction.

TABLE 4.1. Proto-Germanic interrogative pronouns (Ringe 2006: 290)

|  | Nom. | Acc. | Gen. | Dat. | Instr. |
|---|---|---|---|---|---|
| Masc. | *$h^{w}$as (*$h^{w}$is?) | *$h^{w}$anō̜ | *$h^{w}$es (*$h^{w}$as?) | *$h^{w}$ammai | *$h^{w}$ē, *$h^{w}$ī |
| Neut. | *$h^{w}$at | *$h^{w}$at | *$h^{w}$es (*$h^{w}$as?) | *$h^{w}$ammai | *$h^{w}$ē, *$h^{w}$ī |
| Fem. | *$h^{w}$ō̜ | *$h^{w}$ō̜ | *$h^{w}$ezōz | *$h^{w}$ezṓi (?) | *$h^{w}$ezō |

## 4.2 Word order in *wh*-interrogatives

### 4.2.1 *V2 in* wh-*interrogatives*

Direct *wh*-interrogatives in the early Germanic languages have often been held up as cases in which V-to-C$^{0}$ movement can be observed, contrary to the earlier view that Proto-Germanic was consistently verb-final. Examples (1)–(5) illustrate *wh*-V$_{fin}$ order in Gothic, ON, OE, OHG, and OS.

(1)  ƕa      skuli    þata    barn     wairþan?
     what    shall    that    child    become
     'What shall that child become?'
     (Gothic Bible, Luke 1: 66; Greek Majority Text: τι αρα το παιδιον τουτο εσται;
     Eyþórsson 1996: 110)

(2)  hverr        fell    af     láginni?
     who.MASC    fell    off    log.DEF
     'Who fell off the log?'
     (Hkr I.335.9; Faarlund 2004: 227)

(3)  Hwi     wolde     God    swa     lytles        þinges        him    forwyrnan
     why     would     God    such    small.GEN    thing.GEN    him    deny.INF
     'Why would God deny him such a small thing?'
     (cocathom1,+ACHom_I,_1:181.74.71; van Kemenade 1987: 112)

(4)  bihuuiu    uuard      christ    in    liihhi    chiboran?
     why        became     Christ    in    flesh    born
     'Why was Christ born in the flesh?'
     (*Isidor* 487; Axel 2007: 55)

(5)  huî     uuilliad    gi     sô    slâpen?
     why     want        you    so    sleep.INF
     'Why do you want to sleep so?'
     (*Heliand* 4777)

The V2 pattern with *wh*-items in the early Germanic languages is extremely robust. For Gothic, Ferraresi (2005: 45) states that 'subject-verb inversion in questions is not the rule', and that the order in which the subject precedes the verb is more common. However, Eyþórsson (1995: 24) observes that 'in *wh*-questions there is a tendency for the verb to follow the *wh*-phrase directly', even when this leads to deviations from the Greek original, as in (1). He concludes that 'verb movement to C takes place in *wh*-questions' (1995: 26). Fuß (2003) considers a number of apparent counterexamples to the V2 generalization in Gothic and argues that, since in all such examples the constituent order is identical to that of the Greek, V-to-C$^0$ movement can be said to be systematic in the grammar of this language.

For ON, Faarlund (2004: 231) takes it as given that direct *wh*-interrogatives are V2. A search of the IcePaHC corpus (Wallenberg et al. 2011) reveals that 1,151 (93.2%) of 1,235 direct *wh*-interrogatives are V2, and many of the 84 exceptions can be read as indirect *wh*-interrogatives or exclamatives.

For OE, Kiparsky (1995: 144–5) states that 'wh-questions always have verb-second order', and hence that 'wh-phrases induce verb second'. Fischer et al. (2000: 106) state that constituent questions are exceptionlessly V2. A search of the YCOE (Taylor et al. 2003) gives 2,124 (97.7%) of 2,173 direct *wh*-interrogatives as V2.[1] As with ON, many of the 49 exceptions can be read as indirect *wh*-interrogatives or exclamatives.

For early OHG, Axel (2007: 54 n. 31) reports that 22 of 25 examples of *wh*-interrogatives in the *Isidor* and all 14 instances in the Monsee Fragments are V2. She also cites Dittmer and Dittmer (1998) as investigating four chapters of the *Tatian* and finding that 10 of the 11 examples of *wh*-interrogatives found are V2. For later OHG, Axel (2007: 55 n. 32) cites Näf (1979: 161–2) as finding that all 113 examples in Notker's *Consolatio* translation are V2, often deviating from the Latin. In Williram's Song of Songs there are eight examples of *wh*-interrogatives, all of which are V2.

In the OS *Heliand*, there are 49 independent *wh*-interrogatives; 42 of these are V2. One of the remaining examples is a clause introduced by *hueđer*, which will be discussed further in section 4.4. The remaining six counterexamples all involve *te huî* or *be huî* 'why'.

The generalization that such clauses involve a species of V-to-C$^0$ movement of the finite verb (Eyþórsson 1995: 333) seems to be on firm ground, then, at least numerically speaking.[2] The remainder of this subsection is devoted to 'cleaning up' the remaining recalcitrant examples in the hope of making the generalization exceptionless. These examples may also shed light onto the precise nature of V-to-C$^0$ movement within a theory that assumes a more fine-grained C-system.

---

[1]  The 64 additional examples of non-V2 *wh*-interrogatives introduced by *hwæþer* are accounted for in section 4.4.

[2]  On even safer ground is the hypothesis that the early Germanic languages—and Proto-Germanic—were *wh*-movement languages, and not, for instance, *wh*-in-situ languages as is the case for modern Chinese (Huang, Li, and Li 2009: 260–81). I am not aware of a single counterexample.

### 4.2.2 *Particles, pronouns, topics, and the fine structure of the left periphery of* wh-*interrogatives*

The three non-V2 examples in the OHG *Isidor*, and the one non-V2 example in the *Tatian* (Dittmer and Dittmer 1998: 106), all involve elements intervening between the *wh*-pronoun and the finite verb. In addition, examples of this kind can be found in the *Tatian*. Two examples, from Axel (2007: 244–5), are given below.

(6)  uuanan  uns     sint  in  uuostinnu    so  manigu  brot?
     whence  us.DAT  are   in  desert.DAT   so  many    bread.PL
     'Where are we to get so much bread in a desert?'
     (*Tatian* 295,23)

(7)  uuer  mih  sazta      zi  duomen  oder  teilari   ubar  íuuúih
     who   me   installed  to  judge   or    divider   over  you
     'Who made me a judge or arbiter over you?'
     (*Tatian* 353,22)

This order may mimic the order of the Latin original, as in (7), but it also occurs independently, as in (6).[3] Though data is sparse, it seems to be the usual pattern when pronominal elements are present: there are two other examples like (6) in the *Isidor*, and only one in which the pronoun follows the finite verb (Axel 2007: 245).

A similar set of examples can be found in Gothic, as observed by Ferraresi (2005: 42–3) and Fuß (2003: 198–9).

(8)  duƕe  jus     mitoþ  ubila  in  hairtam      izwaraim?
     why   you.PL  think  evil   in  hearts.DAT   your.DAT
     'Why do you think evil in your hearts?'
     (Gothic Bible, Matthew 9: 4; Greek Majority Text: ινα τι υμεις ενθυμεισθε
     πονηρα εν ταις καρδιαις υμων)

(9)  ƕaiwa  þu      qiþis  þatei  frijai  wairþiþ?
     how    you.SG  say    that   free    become
     'How do you say you will become free?'
     (Gothic Bible, John 8: 33; Greek Majority Text: πως συ λεγεις οτι ελευθεροι
     γενησεσθε)

Fuß (2003: 199) observes that in these examples the word order is parallel to that of the Greek original, and concludes on this basis that they 'do not tell us anything about the syntax of Gothic'. This is problematic in that we must assume that these examples are fully ungrammatical in Gothic if we do not wish to posit this pattern as a native one. The hypothesis is also undermined by the occurrence of such examples in OHG ((6)–(7)) and also in OE, albeit very rarely, as in (10).

---

[3] This is not to deny that Latin models may lead to an increased frequency of use of a particular variant independently of direct translation; cf. Taylor (2008) on OE.

(10)  To  hwon       þu  sceole  for  owiht    þysne   man  habban...?
      to  what.INSTR  you  should  for  anything  this.ACC  man  have.INF
      'Why should you esteem this man at all?'
      (coblick,LS_32_[PeterandPaul[BlHom_15]]:179.139.2278)

Although extremely rare, such examples arguably parallel the cases of V3 in early
West Germanic declarative main clauses assessed in Chapter 3, and hence suggest
that there may have been a stage in which the left periphery of *wh*-interrogatives was
more complex than simple V2. On the other hand, this requires these examples to be
analysed as relics, and there is no secure basis for this reasoning (see Campbell 1990:
81–6 for discussion of the problem of identification of archaisms); they could equally
well be innovations, or perhaps even scribal errors or ungrammatical, as Fuß (2003:
199) suggests. However, it is at least possible that examples such as (6)–(10) indicate
that more than one constituent could move to the left periphery in early Germanic
*wh*-interrogatives. Perhaps this option, as opposed to the far more frequent V2, was
marginally available, analysed as archaic by speakers/authors, and therefore
restricted in its distribution; this would explain its occurrence in the Gothic Bible
only when corresponding exactly to the Greek original, and would save us having to
posit the existence of ungrammatical strings in this text.[4]

Another set of examples involves topics apparently preceding the *wh*-word. Such
cases can be found in Gothic, ON Eddic poetry, OE, and OHG.

(11)  izwara       huas        raihtis  wiljands  kelikn  timbrjan...?
      you.GEN.PL   who.NOM     then     wanting   tower   build
      'For which of you, wanting to build a tower, ...?'
      (Gothic Bible, Luke 14: 28; Greek Majority Text: τις γαρ εξ υμων ο θελων
      πυργον οικοδομησαι; Eyþórsson 1995: 100)

(12)  af  heilom       hvat  varð     húnom     mínom?
      of  healthy.DAT  what  became   sons.DAT  my.DAT
      'What became of my healthy sons?'
      (Vǫlundarkviða 32: 3–4; Eyþórsson 1995: 101)

(13)  Se   behydda  wisdom   and  se   bedigloda   goldhord,
      the  hidden   wisdom   and  the  concealed   gold-hoard,
      hwilc  fremu   is  ænigum   on  aðrum      þæra?
      which  benefit  is  any.DAT  in  either.DAT  them.GEN
      'The hidden wisdom and the concealed gold-hoard, what benefit does either
      of them bring?'
      (coaelhom,+AHom_9:40.1326)

---

[4] However, there are also examples of Gothic *wh*-interrogatives in which the verb occurs late on the
hypothesis that the particles involved are $C^0$-oriented (Eyþórsson 1995: 102; Fuß 2003: 200–5). I have no
account for these.

(14)   [christes  chiburt]$_i$  huuer  sia$_i$    chirahhoda?
       Christ's   birth     who   her.ACC  recounted
       'Who recounted the birth of Christ?'
       (*Isidor* 106; Axel 2007: 209)

Kiparsky (1995: 143–5) suggests that the possibility of having a topic to the left of the *wh*-phrase was general to early Germanic (see also Hale 1987a, 1987b on Vedic Sanskrit and Hittite).[5] There are other such examples in Gothic (cf. Ferraresi 2005: 44); however, Eyþórsson (1995: 99–101) stresses that (11) is the only one that does not match the Greek original, and furthermore it is possible for *izwara hʋas* in this example to be analysed as a single constituent. The cases in (13) and (14) from OE and OHG, also rare, contain resumptive elements, and hence these can be argued to involve clause-external hanging topics, not necessarily hosted in the clausal left periphery.[6] The only totally unproblematic example of a moved topic preceding the *wh*-phrase is (12), then. This is the only example in the Eddic poetry corpus, though, as Eyþórsson (1995: 101) remarks, it may be significant that it is attested in one of the oldest of the Eddic poems. In any case, I concur with Eyþórsson (1995: 99) that this single example should not be taken to indicate that this possibility was general in early Germanic, *contra* Kiparsky (1995)—the data is too sparse to draw any clear conclusions.

### 4.2.3 *Verb-late order in OE and OS wh-interrogatives*

Six examples of verb-late order can be found in the OS *Heliand*. All of these involve the wh-phrase *te huî* or *be huî* 'why', literally a preposition followed by an instrumental form of the interrogative pronoun. Two examples are given below; the remaining examples can be found on lines 3816–17, 5182, 5342, and 5967.

(15)   Bihuuî       thu hêr dôpisli  fremis undar thesumu folke...?
       to-what.INSTR  you here baptism  do     under this.DAT people.DAT
       'Why are you performing baptisms among these people?
       (*Heliand* 927–8)

---

[5] Kiparsky's own OE example involves an adverbial clause to the left of a *wh*-phrase. However, these cases are not probative, as there is evidence that such clauses were not originally integrated into the main clause in Germanic (Axel 2002, 2004; Axel and Wöllstein 2009).

[6] The classical diagnostics for left-dislocations, which are assumed to be movement-derived (Cinque 1977; Benincà and Poletto 2004), and hanging topics, which are not, are difficult to apply to these languages. Axel (2007: 209) analyses *christes chiburt* in (14) as nominative: if this were the case, then (14) would have to be analysed as a hanging topic. However, due to morphological syncretisms it could just as well be in the accusative.

(16)  fader  alomahtig  ...  te  huî          thu  mik  sô  farlieti...?
      father almighty    ...  to  what.INSTR  you  me  so  forsook
      'Almighty Father, why have you forsaken me?'
      (*Heliand* 5635–6)

Similar examples, also involving an item meaning 'why', can be found in OE.

(17)  Hwy          þu   la    Drihten   æfre   woldest  þæt   seo   wyrd
      what.INSTR   you  INTJ  Lord      ever   wanted   that  the   fate
      swa   hwyrfan     sceolde?
      so    turn        should
      'Why, o Lord, would you ever want Fate to turn thus?'
      (coboeth,Bo:4.10.17.127)

(18)  Eala, ge  eargan        & idelgeornan; hwy         ge   swa  unnytte
      INTJ  you wretched.PL  & lazy.PL        what.INSTR  you  so   useless
      sien  &  swa  aswundne?
      be    &  so   idle
      'Oh, you wretched and lazy people, why are you so useless and idle?'
      (coboeth,Bo:40.139.7.2771)

(19)  For   hwan         þu   us,   ece       god,   æfre  woldest
      for   what.INSTR   you  us    eternal   God    ever  wanted
      æt   ende  fram  þe   ahwær      drifan?
      at   end   from  you  anywhere   drive.INF
      'Why, o Lord, would you ever want to drive us from you?'
      (Paris Psalter, Psalm 73)

While from a language-internal perspective these cases may seem problematic, viewed through a cross-linguistic lens such examples are not so difficult to account for. Peculiarities with *wh*-items meaning 'why' have long led linguists to attribute a different syntactic structure to *why*-questions than to other *wh*-questions (e.g. Rizzi 1990: 46–8; Hornstein 1995: 147–50; Ko 2005; Stepanov and Tsai 2008). Questions involving 'why' have also been observed to be exceptional from an acquisitional perspective in English (Labov and Labov 1978; Crain, Goro, and Thornton 2006).[7] Most recently, Shlonsky and Soare (2011) have proposed that *why* is externally Merged in the specifier of a functional projection, ReasonP, above negation and adverbials, then undergoes movement (in its short construal) to the specifier of IntP. The cartography of the left periphery they assume follows Rizzi (2001b) and is given in (20).

(20)  ForceP > IntP > TopP > FocP > WhP > Fin(ite)P

---

[7] I am grateful to an anonymous reviewer for pointing this out.

Crucially, other *wh*-phrases, including *why* itself when it originates in a lower clause (long construal), move to SpecWhP, not SpecIntP. This difference in landing site may correlate with a difference in verb-movement.

More must be said than this, however, since both OS and OE have *why*-questions that do appear to involve movement of the finite verb to the left periphery. In OS there are 15 examples of V2 *why*-questions as opposed to 6 where the verb is in a later position. Something else needs to be said about the distribution of V2, therefore.

I suggest that the conditioning factor for verb-movement is whether the *why*-question is a 'true' question, i.e. a genuine request for information, as opposed to a 'special' question such as a rhetorical question (Obenauer 2004; see Berizzi 2010: 9–13 for discussion).[8] It has been demonstrated that 'true' and 'special' questions may differ syntactically. In those examples without movement, such as (15)–(19), the interpretation is unlikely to be as a request for information. In (15) the speakers are asserting that John the Baptist has no right to perform baptisms, since he is not one of the prophets. Examples (16), (17), and (19) are questions to God, and we can reasonably assume that the speakers are not expecting their question to be responded to (directly); a number of other examples are of this nature. Finally, in (18) the speaker is not genuinely requesting that the wretched and lazy people give reasons for their being useless and idle.

V2 *why*-questions, on the other hand, are most naturally analysable as true questions. In example (22), for instance, the disciples are asking Jesus why he wants to return to the Jews. Similarly, (23), from the OE Rule of St Benedict, is a question to ask potential monks, and (24) is a question asked of Philosophy by Boethius.

(21)  te    huî            sind   gi    sô    forhta?
      for   what.INSTR     are    you   so    afraid
      'Why are you so afraid?'
      (*Heliand* 2253)

(22)  te    huî            bist thu sô gern tharod,... fro   mîn,   te faranne?
      for   what.INSTR     are you so keen there        lord  my     to travel.INF
      'Why are you so keen to travel there, my lord?'
      (*Heliand* 3987–8)

(23)  Freond,   to    hwy            com    þu?
      friend    for   what.INSTR     come   you
      'Friend, why have you come?'
      (cobenrul,BenR:60.105.16.1090)

---

[8] Obenauer (2004) in fact identifies three types of 'special' questions: surprise/disapproval questions, rhetorical questions, and Can't-find-the-value-of-*x* questions.

(24)  Forhwi          ne      magon    hi?
      for-what.INSTR  NEG     may      they
      'Why can't they?'
      (coboeth,Bo:29.65.5.1211)

If the verb-late interrogatives in OE and OS (a) all involve *why* and (b) can all be analysed as special questions, this means that it is not necessary to weaken to a statistical generalization the claim that (genuine) interrogatives in early Germanic involve verb-movement to the left periphery: the variation can all be accounted for in a categorical manner, as is desirable given the considerations laid out in section 2.2.2. I will not here speculate on whether the 'special *why* construction' can be reconstructed for Proto-Northwest Germanic or Proto-Germanic.

## 4.3  Underspecified *h^wat?*

The OE word *hwæt* is well known within Anglo-Saxon studies as the first word of the epic poem *Beowulf*.[9] In editions of *Beowulf* this *hwæt* is often followed by a comma (e.g. Klaeber 1922; Fulk 2010) or an exclamation mark (Kemble 1835; Harrison and Sharp 1893). It is commonly held that the word can be 'used as an adv[erb]. or interj[ection]. Why, what! ah!' (Bosworth and Toller 1898, s.v. *hwæt*, 1) as well as in its normal sense, familiar from modern English, as the neuter singular of the interrogative pronoun *hwā* 'what'.

In this section I present new evidence from OE and OS constituent order which suggests that the additional punctuation after 'interjective' *hwæt* and its OS cognate *huat* is inappropriate: not only are *hwæt* and *huat* not extra-metrical, they are also unlikely to be extra-clausal in the vast majority of cases of their occurrence.[10] I argue that 'interjective' *hwæt* is not an interjection or an adverb but rather is parallel to modern English *how* as used in exclamative clauses such as *How you've changed!* In other words, it is *hwæt* combined with the clause that follows it that delivers the interpretative effect of exclamation, not *hwæt* alone.

### 4.3.1  The traditional view

As alluded to earlier, *hwæt*, as well as being the nominative/accusative neuter singular of the interrogative pronoun, was able to perform an extra role in OE, as in the first line of *Beowulf*:

---

[9]  This section to a large extent replicates material published as Walkden (2013c), though the analysis in section 4.3.3 differs from that earlier version by suggesting (*pace* Rett 2008) that exclamatives pattern syntactically with indirect questions rather than free relatives.

[10]  In the rest of this section I use *hwæt* as a cover term for both OE *hwæt* and OS *huat*, as the behaviour of the two is almost identical. Where differences exist, these will be flagged up in the text. I gloss the item simply as 'hw.' throughout.

(25) Hwæt we Gardena          in geardagum · þeodcyninga      þrym
     hw.   we Spear-Danes.GEN in year-days.DAT nation-kings.GEN power.ACC
     gefrunon hu   ða                  æþelingas     ellen     fremedon ·
     heard    how then/those.NOM princes.NOM valour    performed
     'We truly know about the might of the nation-kings in the ancient times of the
     Spear-Danes how princes then performed deeds of valour'
     (*Beowulf* 1–3; Bammesberger 2006: 3)

Bammesberger (2006) follows Stanley (2000) in suggesting that *hwæt* 'can function
more or less as an adverb' (2006: 5), and accordingly translates it as 'truly'. Other
translations include 'What ho!' (Earle 1892), 'Lo!' (Kemble 1837), 'Hear me!' (Raffel
1963), 'Yes' (Donaldson 1966), 'Attend!' (Alexander 1973), 'Indeed' (Jack 1994), 'So'
(Heaney 1999), and 'Listen!' (Liuzza 2000). The *OED* (s.v. *what*, B.11) states that *hwæt*
can be 'used to introduce or call attention to a statement' in older English, citing the
above example among others. Mitchell and Robinson (1998: 45) and Mitchell and
Irvine (2000) go so far as to analyse this instance of *hwæt* as an extra-metrical 'call to
attention', although this is far from universally accepted (see, e.g., Stanley 2000: 555;
Bammesberger 2006: 7 n. 5).

This use of *hwæt* is found not only in early OE verse but also in prose, as in the
following examples from the writings of Ælfric and the OE *Bede*:

(26) **hwæt** se    soðlice onwriið  his  fæder       scondlicnesse
     hw.   he    truly   discovers his  father.GEN nakedness.ACC
     'he certainly uncovers the nakedness of his father'
     (cobede,Bede_1:16.70.15.657)

(27) **Hwæt** ða    Eugenia  hi     gebletsode
     hw.   then  Eugenia$_i$ her$_i$ blessed
     'Then Eugenia blessed herself'
     (coaelive,+ALS_[Eugenia]:171.295)

In OS, the cognate item *huat* can be found with an apparently similar interpretation,
and in the editions this is similarly partitioned off from the clause following it by a
comma (e.g. Sievers 1878, and the *Heliand* text in Behaghel and Taeger 1996) or an
exclamation mark (e.g. the *Genesis* text in Behaghel and Taeger 1996).

(28) **Huat,** thu   thesaro   thiodo      canst       menniscan sidu
     hw.   you   this.GEN  people.GEN know.2SG human     custom.ACC
     'You know the customs of these people'
     (*Heliand* 3101–2)

(29) '**huat,** ik  iu      godes   rîki',        quað he, 'gihêt    himiles  lioht'
     hw.   I   you.DAT God's kingdom.ACC said  he promised heaven's light
     '"I promised you God's kingdom," he said, "heaven's light."'
     (*Heliand* 4572–3)

Grimm (1837: 448–51) remarked that within Germanic this use of the interrogative pronoun was specific to these two languages,[11] emphasizing that the sense was not interrogative here, since the pronoun was not followed directly by the verb as in true interrogatives; furthermore, he demonstrates that the pattern cannot be merely an artefact of translation from a Latin original, since *hwæt* in OE translations (e.g. the OE *Bede*) is often inserted even when it corresponds to nothing overt in the original. Grimm notes that it always stands at the beginning of a clause, and that it often serves to introduce speech, or even a whole poem as in the case of *Beowulf*. His conclusion is that it is 'purely an exclamation, albeit in a very moderate sense'.[12]

Brinton (1996) analyses *hwæt* as a pragmatic marker, suggesting that its function is 'very similar to that of *you know* in Modern English' (1996: 185).[13] Brinton's discussion reveals a remarkable range of functions for *hwæt*: for instance, it may serve to introduce an insulting 'verbal assault' on the addressee, but may also express deference or solidarity (1996: 188). *Hwæt* is also not uniform with respect to the status of information it introduces: it may indicate that the information to follow is common or familiar, serve to renew interest in that information and/or focus attention on its importance, but it may also precede new information (1996: 187–8). Several useful observations are made: for instance, that *hwæt* frequently (but not exceptionlessly) occurs with a first or second person pronoun (1996: 185). Brinton also discusses a potential path of grammaticalization of *hwæt* from its origins as an argumental interrogative pronoun (1996: 199–206). She suggests that it has lost its characteristics as a pronoun, e.g. its inflectional morphology and syntactic position, and undergoes 'decategorialization' to a particle or interjection. A situation of divergence, in the terminology of Hopper and Traugott (2003: 118–22), thus obtains, with *hwæt* continuing to function as an argumental interrogative in the grammar of OE. The general view of *hwæt* as having undergone grammaticalization is a cogent one, and will be adopted in what follows; however, I will argue that the data does not support the view that *hwæt* has proceeded to become a category-neutral particle or interjection.

Garley, Slade, and Terkourafi (2010) also discuss *hwæt* in relation to *Beowulf*, and their article provides a useful summary of the received wisdom regarding the word.

---

[11]  It is striking that OHG exhibits no trace of this use. Hopper (1977) speculates that *dat* 'that' in line 35b of the OHG *Hildebrandslied* may be a scribal error for *wat*, and notes that this would fill the surprising lacuna. However, his hypothesis cannot be confirmed, and given the heavy OS influence on the *Hildebrandslied* the occurrence of *wat* here would not be a reliable indication that the construction was native to OHG. In addition, Stanley (2000: 527 n. 7) refers to Cleasby and Vigfusson (1874) for some potential ON examples of *hvat* as an interjection, although states that these are 'certainly rare'. Although I have not investigated these in detail, the examples given (1874, s.v. *hvat*, B.II) do not seem parallel to those in OE and OS in which *hwæt* precedes a clause.

[12]  'ein bloßer ausruf, jedoch in sehr gemäßigtem sinn' (1837: 450).

[13]  As Brinton notes (1996: 30–1), the definitions of pragmatic markers found in the literature seem to bear little resemblance to one another. Östman (1982), for example, includes the suggestion that pragmatic particles 'tend to occur in some sense cut off from, or on a higher level than, the rest of the utterance' (1982: 149); as will be demonstrated, this is unlikely to have been the case for *hwæt*.

They take it to be a discourse-structuring formula, 'a marker employed in the representation of spoken discourse' (2010: 218). Supporting this, all 25 of the OS examples I have found in the *Heliand* occur in the speech of a character within the text. It 'signals the character's intention to begin a dialogue or a narrative' (2010: 219); eight OE poems other than *Beowulf* begin in this way (2010: 219), and 15 of the 25 OS examples initiate a character's speech, as in example (29) above. This might also explain the frequency of first and second person pronouns in clauses preceded by *hwæt* noted by Brinton. Less commonly discussed, however, are the cases in which *hwæt* cannot be assimilated to this discourse-initiating role. Garley, Slade, and Terkourafi note that it may also occur in the middle of a character's speech, as in the remaining 10 OS examples, e.g. (28) above. Even more problematic than this is its occurrence (e.g. (26), (27)) in texts such as Ælfric's *Lives of Saints*, and in particular the OE *Bede*, which are far less associated with prototypical orality and in which it therefore makes little sense to view *hwæt* as being representative of speech or functioning as a 'call to attention'. Although *hwæt* clearly had this discourse-opening function in OE and OS, then, this function alone does not suffice to characterize its meaning.[14]

### 4.3.2 *Problems with the traditional view*

Stanley (2000) provides a recent and extensive discussion of *hwæt* in OE, although without discussing clausal word order. His conclusions are much the same as Grimm's, and in addition he adduces metrical evidence to show that *hwæt* cannot have been a strong interjection: if it were stressed, then various instances of it in verse would have led to double alliteration, 'breaking a basic prosodic rule' (2000: 554). Against the Mitchell and Robinson view that *hwæt* was extra-metrical he argues that 'if an opening word were felt to be divorced from the phrase that follows we might

---

[14] For completeness it should be mentioned that in OE and OS, *hwaet* could also serve as an indefinite pronoun:

(i) | Heo | is | uoluntas, | þæt | is | wylla, | þonne | heo | **hwæt** | wyle |
| she | is | uoluntas | that | is | will | when | she | hw. | wants |

'It is *voluntas*, that is will, when it wants anything'
(coaelive, +ALS_[Christmas]:189.147)

(ii) | that | he | thar | habda | gegnungo | godcundes | huat | forsehen |
| that | he | there | had | obviously | holy.GEN | hw. | seen |

'that he had seen something holy there'
(*Heliand* 188–9)

Behaghel (1923: 366–7) suggests that in OE, and in all other older Germanic languages except OS, *hwæt* was restricted to contexts that we would now describe as licensing negative polarity items (cf. Baker 1970, Haspelmath 1997, Giannakidou 1998, and Rowlett 1998 for discussion of this concept). He argues that the use of *hwæt* in positive contexts in OS, as in (ii), must be an innovation, since only one putative example can be found in Gothic (Galatians 2: 6) while it is relatively frequent in OS. The meaning of OE *hwæt*, when used as an indefinite, was therefore presumably closer to modern English 'anything', whereas OS *huat* could additionally mean 'something'.

have expected it to be occasionally followed by a mark of punctuation, as is *hwætla* in a good Ælfric manuscript' (2000: 555). In actual fact, OE manuscripts never show punctuation between *hwæt* and a following clause (2000: 525), and the same is true of OS: no punctuation mark is ever found between *huat* and a following clause in any of the manuscripts of the *Heliand* containing a relevant example (Cotton, Munich, Straubing).[15] Furthermore, Stanley points out that Ælfric's grammar of Latin and OE[16] (edition Zupitza 1880) did not include *hwæt* as an interjection, commenting that 'Ælfric's omission is surprising seeing that this word when used to open a sentence appears to function often as an interjection' (2000: 541).

So far, then, we have seen that the traditional view of *hwæt* as an adverb or interjection (Bosworth and Toller 1898) outside the clause and potentially extra-metrical, possibly serving as a 'call to attention' (Mitchell and Robinson 1998), suffers from a number of problems, many already noted by Grimm (1837) and Stanley (2000). These are listed below for ease of reference:

(a) *Hwæt* must usually be analysed as unstressed;
(b) no punctuation between *hwæt* and the following clause is ever found;
(c) a contemporary grammarian did not analyse *hwæt* as an interjection;
(d) *hwæt* is not exclusively found in texts connected to primary orality, and does not always serve to initiate speech.

Constituent order facts are also problematic for the interjection hypothesis. Traditional philological works on syntax make little mention of constituent order in connection with *hwæt*. Behaghel (1923–32) does not mention the construction at all. Visser (1969: 1547) provides several examples of what he considers to be SV word order with initial interrogative *hwæt*, but, as Mitchell (1985: 680) points out, 'these can all be taken as non-dependent exclamations'. Hopper (1977: 483) suggests that the *hwæt*-construction is quasi-formulaic and may therefore be likely to have the 'archaic' verb-final order, but does not go into any detail on this point. Likewise, Mitchell (1985: 299–300 n. 95) suggests that interjections like *efne* 'lo!/behold!' and *hwæt* may influence word order, but does not elaborate on this. More recently, within a generative framework, Koopman (1995), in his discussion of verb-final main clauses in OE prose, observes that 'influence of style is . . . noticeable in the word order after the interjection *hwæt*' (1995: 140; see also Ohkado 2005: 246).

---

[15] The Cotton manuscript, Caligula A VII, I was able to check personally at the British Library. The other two were checked by means of digitized versions made available online by the *Bayerische Staatsbibliothek*.

[16] It has been argued (e.g. Law 1987) that Ælfric's grammar is not a grammar of OE at all, since its primary intended use is as an aid to learners of Latin. However, 'when Ælfric explains that language is made of *andgytfullic stemn*, when he shows how patronyms are formed in English, when he divides English nouns into twenty-eight categories and English adverbs into twenty-three, he is analyzing English as a grammatical entity' (Menzer 2004: 122–3).

TABLE 4.2. Frequency and percentage of V1/V2 vs. V-later *huat*-clauses vs. non-*huat* main clauses in the *Heliand*

| | V1/V2 | | V-later | | Total |
|---|---|---|---|---|---|
| | N | % | N | % | N |
| *Huat* | 9 | 36.0 | 16 | 64.0 | 25 |
| Non-*huat* (main) | 2078 | 88.5 | 270 | 11.5 | 2348 |
| Total | 2087 | – | 286 | – | 2373 |

TABLE 4.3. Frequency and percentage of V1/V2 vs. V-later *huat*-clauses vs. non-*huat* subordinate clauses in the *Heliand*

| | V1/V2 | | V-later | | Total |
|---|---|---|---|---|---|
| | N | % | N | % | N |
| *Huat* | 9 | 36.0 | 16 | 64.0 | 25 |
| Non-*huat* (sub) | 567 | 25.8 | 1629 | 74.2 | 2196 |
| Total | 576 | – | 1645 | – | 2221 |

However, the constituent-order patterns found in both OE and OS are too pervasive and significant to be ascribed to archaism or stylistic choices alone. Under the hypothesis that *huat* is an extra-clausal interjection, separated from the clause itself by a comma in writing that corresponds to a pause in speech, the null hypothesis as regards the constituent order of the following clause would be that no difference would obtain between these and other main clauses. This prediction is not, however, borne out by the data in Table 4.2.[17] Here all the non-interrogative clauses preceded by *huat* in the *Heliand* have been considered, and are compared to all the other non-conjunct main clauses in the *Heliand*. Although the number of *huat*-clauses is very small, once again, the difference between the two types of clause is clearly statistically significant ($p < 0.0001$). For anyone who takes *huat* to be clause-external, this result must surely be a mystery: if *huat* influences the constituent order of the clause that follows it, it must be a part of that clause, and hence not an 'interjection'.

Comparing clauses followed by *huat* to (non-conjunct) subordinate clauses, as in Table 4.3, is also instructive. Here the difference between the two types of clause is not statistically significant at the 0.05 level ($p = 0.2545$). This suggests that we should

[17] *hwæt* and *huat* themselves are not treated as clausal constituents in the figures given in Table 4.2 and beyond, nor is the *þa* normally collocated with *hwæt* by Ælfric, since, if the null hypothesis is that these were true extra-clausal particles, it should not be assumed that they were clausal constituents when assessing this hypothesis. Instead these elements are discounted for the purpose of counting constituents.

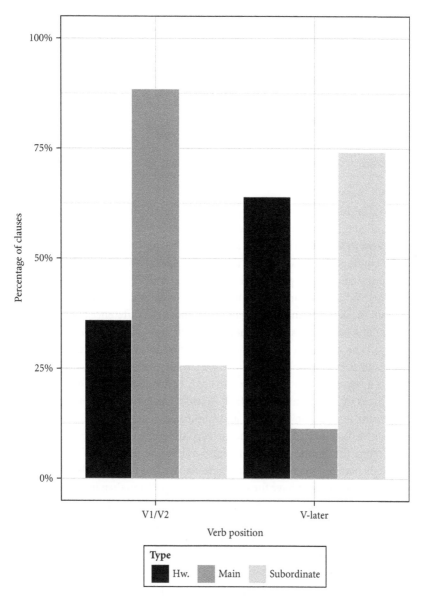

FIGURE 4.1 Percentage of V1/V2 vs. V-later *huat*-clauses vs. non-*huat* clauses in the *Heliand*

hypothesize that these two types of clause pattern together; in other words, clauses introduced by *huat* have the word order of subordinate clauses. Figure 4.1 illustrates the findings in Tables 4.2 and 4.3.

Similar results are found for OE. In the OE *Bede*, 20 of the 29 clauses preceded by *hwæt* (69.0%) have the verb in a position later than second (see Table 4.4 and

TABLE 4.4. Frequency and percentage of V1/V2 vs. V-later *hwæt*-clauses vs. non-*hwæt* clauses in the OE *Bede*

| | V1/V2 | | V-later | | Total |
|---|---|---|---|---|---|
| | N | % | N | % | N |
| Main (non-*hwæt*) | 1898 | 69.9 | 819 | 30.1 | 2717 |
| Subordinate | 1863 | 37.8 | 3067 | 62.2 | 4930 |
| *Hwæt* | 9 | 31.0 | 20 | 69.0 | 29 |
| Total | 3770 | – | 3906 | – | 7676 |

Figure 4.2). In Ælfric's *Lives of Saints*, excluding five examples of the true interjection *hwæt la* (cf. Stanley 2000), 112 clauses preceded by *hwæt* can be found, 63 of which have the verb in a position later than second (56.3%; see Table 4.5 and Figure 4.3). The results of contingency tests based on this data are clear.[18] As in the OS *Heliand*, main and subordinate clauses pattern distinctly differently in the *Historia* translation ($p < 0.0001$). While the constituent order in *hwæt*-clauses and main clauses is once again dramatically different (once again $p < 0.0001$), the difference between constituent orders in *hwæt*-clauses and in subordinate clauses falls well short of significance ($p=0.5657$). The argument for *hwæt*-clauses patterning with subordinate clauses in this text is thus even stronger than for the *huat*-clauses in the *Heliand*.

Ælfric's *Lives of Saints* is a substantial OE text dated around 996–7. Although direct sources in Latin can be identified, Ælfric's translation is generally argued (e.g. by Bethurum 1932) to be very free and idiomatic, making it a suitable object for syntactic investigations. This text has a very different range of constituent order patterns from that found in the OE *Bede*. While the position of the verb differs substantially between main and subordinate clauses ($p < 0.0001$), subordinate clauses themselves far more often have the verb in an early position than in the OE *Bede*. As a result, *hwæt*-clauses, which more frequently have the verb later, differ very significantly from both main ($p < 0.0001$) and subordinate ($p=0.0002$) clauses. Here, then, it cannot be said that *hwæt*-clauses pattern with subordinate clauses; instead they seem to follow a pattern of their own, with the verb much more likely to be later than in other clauses in general.

The fact that broadly the same results are obtained for OE and OS—a general preference for verb-later order in *hwæt*-clauses—makes it unlikely that the

---

[18] Frequency data for main and subordinate clauses in the *Historia* translation and Ælfric's *Lives of Saints* has been obtained by searching the relevant parts of the YCOE (Taylor et al. 2003) using Corpus-Search 2.0 (Randall 2005–7) and taking hit frequency counts. The queries I used to obtain these values can be obtained at <http://www.dspace.cam.ac.uk/handle/1810/226419>. Although the data is presented here in a single table for ease of exposition, for the purpose of the Fisher's exact tests I compared *hwæt*-clauses to main clauses and subordinate clauses separately.

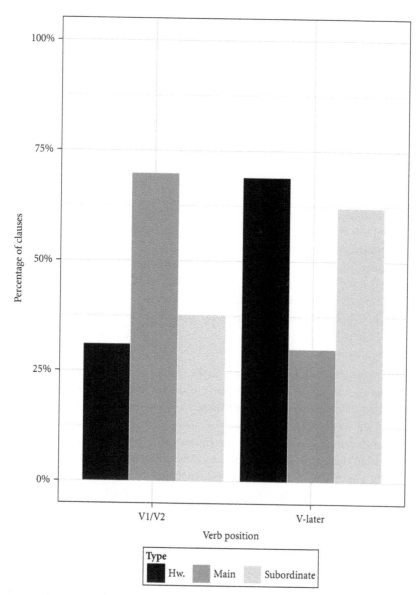

FIGURE 4.2 Percentage of V1/V2 vs. V-later *hwæt*-clauses vs. non-*hwæt* clauses in the OE *Bede*

constituent order differences between *hwæt*-clauses and other main clauses are the result of innovation in both languages; although parallel innovation (perhaps contact-facilitated) cannot be ruled out, by the criterion of diachronic parsimony it should be assumed that the verb-late pattern was the original one, and that *hwæt*-clauses patterned with subordinate clauses from their inception.

TABLE 4.5. Frequency and percentage of V1/V2 vs. V-later *hwæt*-clauses vs. non-*hwæt* clauses in Ælfric's *Lives of Saints*

|  | V1/V2 | | V-later | | Total |
|---|---|---|---|---|---|
|  | N | % | N | % | N |
| Main (non-*hwæt*) | 3204 | 76.8 | 969 | 23.2 | 4173 |
| Subordinate | 3467 | 61.5 | 2168 | 38.5 | 5635 |
| *Hwæt* | 49 | 43.7 | 63 | 56.3 | 112 |
| Total | 6720 | – | 3200 | – | 9920 |

To recapitulate: in terms of constituent order, clauses introduced by *hwæt* in OE and OS pattern statistically with subordinate clauses (including dependent questions and free relatives), rather than with main clauses as would be expected if *hwæt* were a free-standing interjection. In combination with the other issues raised by Stanley (2000) and listed in this subsection, the constituent order data therefore gives us strong reason to doubt that *hwæt* had such a syntactic role or status. In the next subsection I hypothesize as to the correct interpretation and analysis of *hwæt*-clauses.

### 4.3.3 An underspecification analysis

As a starting point for an investigation into the role of *hwæt* it is instructive to look at other languages in which the interrogative pronoun appears to exhibit polysemy. Munaro and Obenauer (1999) present three such languages: German, French, and Pagotto (a sub-variety of the northeastern Italian dialect of Bellunese). Interestingly, the sets of meanings contributed by the interrogative pronouns in these (not very closely related) languages do not appear to differ arbitrarily but instead intersect in several key ways. First, in all three of these languages the interrogative pronoun can be used non-argumentally to mean 'why' or 'how' in questions, as in examples (30) from German, (31) from French,[19] and (32) from Pagotto:

(30)  **Was**  rennst  du    so    schnell?
      what   run     you   so    fast
      'Why are you running so fast?' (Munaro and Obenauer 1999: 184)

(31)  **Que**  ne    partez-vous?
      what   NEG   leave-you
      'Why don't you leave?' (Munaro and Obenauer 1999: 208)

---

[19] The French examples are essentially only acceptable in negative contexts if at all; Munaro and Obenauer report that this use of *que* is rare in all registers.

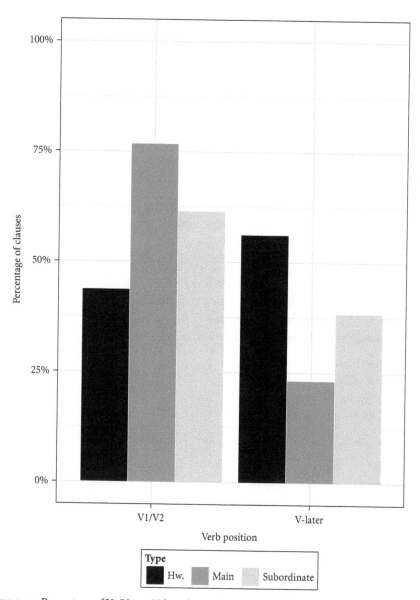

FIGURE 4.3 Percentage of V1/V2 vs. V-later *hwæt*-clauses vs. non-*hwæt* clauses in Ælfric's *Lives of Saints*

(32)  **Cossa**    zìghe-tu?
      what      shout-you
      'Why are you shouting?' (Munaro and Obenauer 1999: 191–2)

Similar examples can be found in OE ((33)) and OS ((34)), as well as in ON ((35) and (36)):

(33)  **Hwæt**  stendst  þu    her   wælhreowa  deor?
      hw.      stand    you   here  cruel      beast
      'Why are you standing here, cruel beast?'
      (coaelive,+ALS_[Martin]:1364.6872)

(34)  **huat**  uuili  thu   thes        nu    sôken  te    ûs?
      hw.       will   you   this.GEN    now   seek   to    us
      'why do you now complain about this to us?'
      (*Heliand* 5158)

(35)  **hvat**  þarftú    at   spyrja   at   nafni      minu?
      what      need-you  to   ask      to   name.DAT   mine.DAT
      'Why do you need to ask my name?'
      (Cleasby and Vigfusson 1874, s.v. *hvat*, A.I.3)

(36)  **hvat**  mun  ek  þat   vita?
      what      may  I   that  know
      'How could I know that?'
      (Cleasby and Vigfusson 1874, s.v. *hvat*, A.I.3)

Latin also permits this non-argumental use of the interrogative pronoun *quid*:

(37)  **quid**  plura    disputo?
      what      more     dispute.1SG
      'Why do I dispute at greater length?'
      (Cic. Mil. 16, 44; Lewis and Short 1879, s.v. *quis*, II.b)

(38)  **quid**  venisti?
      what      came.2SG
      'Why have you come?'
      (Plaut. Am. 1, 1, 209; Lewis and Short 1879, s.v. *quis*, II.b)

Such non-argumental uses of interrogative pronouns can also be found in Arabic (Ruba Khamam, p.c.), Ancient Greek (Brian Joseph, p.c.), Dutch, some varieties of Norwegian (Vangsnes 2008), and the early Celtic languages (Lewis and Pedersen 1937: 226–9).

Secondly, German ((39)), French ((40)), and Pagotto ((41)) also permit the interrogative pronoun to occur non-argumentally in exclamatives; German *was* and French *que* alternate in this role with the more usual *wie* and *comme* respectively.

(39)  **Was**   du    dich   verändert   hast!
     what   you   REFL   changed   have
     'How you've changed!'

(40)  **Que**   il   vous   aime!
     what   he   you   loves
     'How he loves you!' (Munaro and Obenauer 1999: 211)

(41)  **Cossa**   che'l   ghe   piaze,   al   gelato!
     what   that.CL   him   please.3SG   the   ice-cream
     'How he loves ice cream!' (Munaro and Obenauer 1999: 211)

Dutch also permits exclamatives using the interrogative pronoun *wat*, as in (40) (cf. Corver 1990):

(42)  **Wat**   ben   jij   veranderd!
     what   are   you   changed
     'How you've changed!'

Such a construction is also possible for older speakers of Afrikaans (Theresa Biberauer, p.c.). For present purposes, the important thing to note about all these examples is that certain other languages systematically exhibit a range of possible uses/meanings for their interrogative pronoun that are not possible with modern English *what*.

Munaro and Obenauer discuss two possible analyses of this state of affairs: either these *wh*-words are identical in phonological form by chance, or the two are closely and intrinsically related (1999: 185). The first view, ascribing the variety of meanings of what looks like the interrogative pronoun to accidental homophony of a variety of lexical items, cannot be ruled out, as there are many cases of such homophony throughout attested human languages: indeed, it seems plausible that this is the case with the OE adjective *hwæt* 'quick, active, vigorous, stout, bold, brave', which is generally agreed to be related in no way to the interrogative pronoun *hwæt* but instead to be derived from the verb *hwettan* 'to whet' (cf. e.g. Bosworth and Toller 1898, s.v. *hwæt*, 2). However, as Munaro and Obenauer point out (1999: 222), when the same range of meanings for the interrogative pronoun crops up in language after language it becomes increasingly unlikely that this is due to chance homophony, especially when the languages in question are not closely related.

Munaro and Obenauer instead pursue an analysis in which the relevant interrogative pronoun in German, French, and Pagotto may in each of these languages be semantically underspecified for certain features. They adduce distributional syntactic data from these languages to illustrate this. For instance, normal *wh*-words can be coordinated in German, as in (43) and (44), but this is not possible with 'why'-like *was* or 'how much'-like *was*, as illustrated in (45) and (46).

(43) Wann   und   warum   hast   du   mit   Max   gesprochen?
     when   and   why   have   you   with   M.   spoken
     'When and why did you speak to Max?'
     (Munaro and Obenauer 1999: 226)

(44) Wie   laut   und   wie   lange   er   geschrien   hat!
     how   loud   and   how   long   he   shouted   has
     'How loud and how long he shouted!'

(45) *Wann   und   **was**   hast   du   mit   Max   gesprochen?
     when   and   what   have   you   with   M.   spoken
     'When and why did you speak to Max?'

(46) ***Was**   und   wie   lange   er   geschrien   hat!
     what   and   how   long   he   shouted   has
     'How much and how long he shouted!'

These non-argumental uses of *was* are also unable to function as contrastive focus and cannot appear in truncated questions (Munaro and Obenauer 1999: 227); the same restrictions hold, *mutatis mutandis*, in French and Pagotto (1999: 229–33).

In the spirit of Cardinaletti and Starke (1999), who account for the difference between strong and weak pronouns cross-linguistically in terms of structural impoverishment, Munaro and Obenauer propose that a piece of word-internal syntactic structure is absent from the structure of underspecified *wh*-items. They do not state explicitly what the missing piece of structure is, but they suggest that it 'must be linked to the expression of argumenthood, and contain the semantic restriction... [+thing]' (1999: 236). The correct interpretation of the *wh*-item—as an argument in certain questions when fully specified, as 'why' or 'how' when underspecified and non-argumental in questions, and as 'how' or 'how much' when underspecified in exclamatives—must be vouchsafed by the particular context in which it occurs. Specifically, in its non-argumental use speakers prefer the *wh*-item to be accompanied by an expression of the speaker's attitude, particularly of surprise: this is inherently present in exclamatives, and can be expressed in e.g. German questions by use of a modal particle such as *denn*, or by a particular intonation pattern.

Jäger (2000) and Holler (2009), within Minimalist and HPSG syntactic frameworks respectively, have also argued independently that there must exist a form of *was* in German that is underspecified for [thing] and therefore non-argumental, as in examples (30) and (39) above.[20] If the underspecification logic outlined above holds in general, then it is tempting to analyse the OE and OS interrogative pronoun *hwæt* along the same lines as modern German *was*, French *que*, and Pagotto *cossa*, etc., namely as a *wh*-item which may occur non-argumentally in an underspecified form. Although it is not possible to test for contrasts such as those in (43)–(46) in OE or OS for obvious reasons, the corpus data we have is compatible with the analysis outlined above. So where does this lead us with regard to examples of clauses such as (25)–(29)? Clearly, as observed by Grimm (1837: 449), these clauses cannot be interrogative, since the word order is not that of matrix questions, *hwæt* cannot be argumental in these clauses, and no sensible interrogative interpretation is available in the contexts in which they occur. The remaining possibility is that these clauses are in fact exclamatives.

Munaro and Obenauer (1999) have little to say about the analysis of exclamatives, or how the underspecified interrogative pronoun receives its interpretation of 'how' or 'how much', speculating only that 'since it is structurally and … semantically deficient in ways parallel to "why"-like WHAT, the interpretation it eventually gets should again be construed from elements of the sentential context' (1999: 248). To pursue the matter further we must turn to analyses of exclamatives themselves, since the hypothesis that *hwæt*-clauses are exclamatives can only be tested through comparison with the properties and structures of exclamatives in general.

Current and past analyses of exclamatives have generally proposed that a key component of the interpretation of exclamatives is that their content must involve something related to degree/scalarity (e.g. Bolinger 1972; Corver 1990; D'Avis 2002; Zanuttini and Portner 2003; Sæbø 2005; Rett 2008, 2009). For simplicity's sake I will adopt here the semantic proposal of Rett (2008, 2009), who suggests the following two restrictions on the content of exclamatives:

(47)   **The Degree Restriction** (Rett 2008: 147, her (4))
       An exclamative can only be used to express surprise that the degree property which is its content holds of a particular degree.

(48)   **The Evaluativity Restriction** (Rett 2008: 155)
       The content of the exclamative must additionally be evaluative: the degrees it makes reference to are restricted such that they must exceed a contextual standard.

---

[20] Another set of data potentially supporting the underspecification analysis of German *was*, as Munaro and Obenauer (1999: 236) note, is constituted by 'expletive *wh*'-clauses such as (i).

(i)   Was      glaubst   du,    wen    Maria   getroffen   hat?
      what     believe   you    who    M.      met         has
      (Felser 2001: 5)

Since the literature on this phenomenon cross-linguistically is substantial and the correct analysis controversial (cf. Dayal 1996, Horvath 1997, and Felser 2001, 2004, *inter alia*), it will not be discussed further here.

The Degree Restriction is key for our purposes. Consider (49) (from Rett 2008: 147, her (5b)):

(49)    What languages Benny speaks!

This can be taken to express surprise at the number of languages Benny speaks, even in the absence of any overt degree morphology, for example in the context where Benny is an American and you expect him to speak only English (the 'amount reading'). Another context might be one where Benny is a Romance linguist and you expect him to speak only Romance languages, but in fact he speaks languages from other obscure/exotic language families; this is the 'gradable reading' of (49), in which surprise is being expressed at the degree to which the languages Benny speaks are exotic. Note that no overt gradable predicate 'exotic' is present in the sentence, but this interpretation is nevertheless available. Rett takes this to mean that a null gradable predicate $\mathbb{P}$, an adjective (or adverb) that receives its value from context, must be posited for the gradable reading as a 'necessary evil' (2008: 149). In a situation where you expect Benny to speak Portuguese and Romanian but discover that he instead speaks French and Italian, on the other hand, uttering (49) would be expressively incorrect. The impossibility of this 'individual reading' of (49) leads Rett to conclude that the degree reading, and hence the Degree Restriction, is an essential part of exclamativity: 'non-degree readings are *impossible* interpretations of exclamatives' (2008: 151; emphasis original).

It follows that syntactic constructions used to express *wh*-exclamatives must be able to denote a degree property (Rett 2008: 168–9). The two possible candidates are (degree) constituent questions and free relatives. The one systematic syntactic difference between these two types of construction in modern English is that subject-auxiliary inversion is required in constituent questions (contrast (50) and (51)) and impossible in free relatives ((52)–(53)); in English, subject-auxiliary inversion is impossible in traditional *wh*-exclamatives too ((54)–(55)).

(50)    How big is your car?
(51)    *How big your car is?
(52)    *I'll buy what are you selling.
(53)    I'll buy what you are selling.
(54)    *How big is your car!
(55)    How big your car is!

Questions and free relatives differ morphosyntactically in many languages other than English, and here Rett makes a stronger claim: 'in any such language I know of, exclamatives pattern in their morphosyntax with free relatives rather than with questions' (2008: 173), although she cautions that 'a thorough crosslinguistic study of these constructions is necessary to give any serious weight to this claim'.[21] In Hebrew, for instance, exclamatives and free relatives require an overt complementizer, but questions do not (2008: 175–6); in German and Icelandic, independent exclamatives typically have subordinate clause word order, lacking the full V2 present in main clauses. While Rett's semantic analysis is in principle neutral as to whether the morphosyntactic structure underlying *wh*-exclamatives is that of a question or a free relative, then, she favours the latter view.

If we assume that *hwæt*-clauses are exclamatives, the data from OS and OE casts some doubt on Rett's claim. In these languages, a *swa* wh *swa* construction is typically used for free relatives, as in (56) and (57) (Mitchell and Robinson 2007: 80).

(56)    Swa   hwær   swa   ic   beo,   hie   beoð   mid   me
        so    where   so   I   be,    he   is     with   me
        'Wherever I am, he is with me'
        (coboeth,Bo:7.17.18.274)

(57)    that   it   sô   giuuerđen   scal,   sô   huan   sô   thius   uuerold   endiod
        that   it   so   become     shall   so   when   so   this    world     ends
        'that it shall be so, when this world ends'
        (*Heliand* 4046)

As in the modern Scandinavian languages, a *wh*-element is not usually used alone to introduce a relative clause (see Berizzi 2010: 77–80 for discussion). It is only in Middle English that this modern use becomes prevalent (Mitchell and Robinson 2007: 73–4), although a few examples can be found in both OE and OS:

(58)    forðan   ic   leng     næbbe     **hwæt**   ic   on   his   lacum    aspende
        because   I   longer   NEG-have   hw.     I    on   his   service    spend
        'because I no longer have anything to spend in his service'
        (coaelive,+ALS[Lucy]:66.2205)

(59)    hie...   ne   lêt   that   manno     folc     uuitan,   **huat**   sia    uuarahtun
        he...    NEG   let   the    men.GEN   people   know     hw.    they   did
        'He did not let the people know what they were doing'
        (*Heliand* 5393–4)

---

[21] Some examples exist that are difficult to account for under this generalization. See Nye (2009) for a discussion of 'how pseudo-questions', an inversion-exhibiting construction in modern English that shares many interpretative properties with traditional *wh*-exclamatives although appearing formally identical to constituent questions at first sight:

(i)    How cool is that?!

German exclamatives can also be V2 instead of V-final, subject to some restrictions:

(ii)    Was     hast    du     dich    verändert!
        what    have   you    REFL   changed
        'How you've changed!'

However, a third possibility, not discussed by Rett, is that exclamatives pattern with *indirect* questions. Indirect questions in OE (Mitchell and Robinson 2007: 73) and OS are introduced by *wh*-words, as in examples (60) and (61).

(60) se       halga   Thomas...acsode   urne   Dryhten   hwænne
     the      holy    Thomas...asked    our    Lord      when
     Antecristes     cyme    wære
     Antichrist's    coming  were
     'St Thomas asked our Lord when the Antichrist would arrive'
     (coverhom,HomU_6_[ScraggVerc_15]:1.1850)

(61) Thô     frâgode   sie     the    hêlago   Crist,   aftar
     then    asked     them    the    holy     Christ,  after
     huemu   thiu      gelîcnessi   gilegid   uuâri
     whom    the       picture      laid      were
     'Then Jesus asked them who the picture was of'
     (*Heliand* 3825–6)

As I demonstrated in 4.3.2, *hwæt*-clauses pattern with subordinate clauses in terms of verb position. Constituent questions in OE are exceptionlessly V2 (cf. e.g. Fischer et al. 2000: 106), and the same seems to hold for OS, once a few specific classes of apparent counterexample have been properly analysed (see sections 4.2.3 and 4.4). In contrast, in indirect questions such as (60), in free relatives such as (58), as in other subordinate clauses and in *hwæt*-clauses, the verb is in a later position in OE (Fischer et al. 2000: 61) and in OS. The modified generalization thus seems to hold for OE and OS, as well as for at least modern English and German; a fuller investigation is beyond the scope of this book.[22]

What about the interpretation of these 'exclamative' *hwæt*-clauses? Consider examples (26)–(29), repeated below as (62)–(65) for ease of reference.

(62) **hwæt**   se   soðlice   onwriið   his   fæder       scondlicnesse
     hw.       he   truly     discovers his   father.GEN  nakedness.ACC
     'he certainly uncovers the nakedness of his father'
     (cobede,Bede_1:16.70.15.657)

(63) **Hwæt**   ða    Eugenia   hi     gebletsode
     hw.       then  Eugenia$_i$  her$_i$  blessed
     'Then Eugenia blessed herself'
     (coaelive,+ALS_[Eugenia]:171.295)

---

[22] Abels (2010: 141 n. 1) points out an additional difficulty for the proposal that exclamatives are free relatives: if so, they would be expected to occur only in positions that accept NPs, which does not seem to be the case. The present proposal is immune to this criticism.

(64)  **Huat**, thu thesaro thiodo     canst      menniscan sidu
      hw.   you this.GEN people.GEN know.2SG human      custom.ACC
      'You know the customs of these people'
      (*Heliand* 3101–2)

(65)  'huat, ik iu        godes  rîki',        quað he,
      hw.   I  you.DAT God's  kingdom.ACC said he
      'gihêt        himiles      lioht'
      promised   heaven's    light
      '"I promised you God's kingdom," he said, "heaven's light."'
      (*Heliand* 4572–3)

Example (62) receives a straightforward and satisfying analysis as an exclamative. According to Rett's analysis outlined in this section, underspecified *hwæt* must receive a degree reading, and a natural item for it to range over is the verb *onwrēon* 'to unbind/unwrap'. The interpretation of the clause would thus be 'How he truly uncovers the nakedness of his father!' A similar analysis can be given for the OS example in (64). If the predicate that *huat* ranges over is understood as the verb 'to know', the clause then relates to the extent of the addressee's knowledge: 'How well you know the customs of these people!'

(63) and (65) are less straightforward. At first sight it appears that there is no predicate for *huat* to range over, since the verbs 'to bless' and 'to promise' do not seem gradable in any intuitive sense. However, Rett's analysis allows for a null gradable predicate $\mathbb{P}$ which receives its value from context (recall that this null predicate is independently necessary to account for English examples such as (49) under the gradable reading). In this case we can posit a null adverb which receives a meaning 'fervently' for (63), yielding a reading 'How fervently Eugenia then blessed herself!' Likewise, (65) could be viewed as containing a null adverb 'earnestly' or 'faithfully', and receiving the reading 'How earnestly/faithfully I promised you God's kingdom!' These readings of (62)–(65) make sense not only in isolation but also in context. In (63), for instance, Eugenia is blessing herself fervently as a consequence of Melantia's attempt at temptation.

We are now in a position to revisit example (25), the first sentence of *Beowulf*. Complications other than *hwæt* mean that the correct analysis of this sentence is disputed; indeed, whole articles have been devoted to these few lines alone (e.g. Bammesberger 2006). I repeat it, without translation, as (66) below.

(66)  **Hwæt**  we  Gardena           in  geardagum
      hw.     we  Spear-Danes.GEN in  year-days
      þeodcyninga        þrym  gefrunon
      nation-kings.GEN power heard
      (*Beowulf* 1–2)

Here the verb, *frīnan* 'to learn by enquiry', can straightforwardly be read as gradable. The exclamative hypothesis suggests that this clause should be interpreted as 'How much we have heard of the might of the nation-kings of the Spear-Danes'. Of the translations so far put forward, this interpretation has the most in common with Morgan's (1952) rendering as 'How that glory remains in remembrance'.

Other well-known poetic examples are also compatible with the exclamative hypothesis. For instance, *Dream of the Rood* begins with such a clause:

(67)  **Hwæt**  ic  swefna       cyst  secgan  wylle
      hw.    I   dreams.GEN   best  tell    will
      (*Dream of the Rood* 1)

Once again, the verb 'to want' is clearly gradable, and so a reading along the lines of 'How I want to tell you of the best of dreams' is indicated by the exclamative hypothesis. Similarly (68), from the verse text *Juliana*, is neatly amenable to an exclamative analysis:

(68)  Iuliana!  **Hwæt**  þu   glæm    hafast
      J!       hw.    you  beauty  have
      (*Juliana* 167)

The gradable element here is *glæm* 'beauty', suggesting a reading of 'Juliana! How beautiful you are...'. The content of the relevant *hwæt*-clauses seems to present no problem for the hypothesis that their illocutionary force is that of exclamatives, then.

In addition, *hwæt* used in this way appears to survive sporadically into early Middle English. Brinton (1996: 201) gives some examples from Chaucer, including (69) and (70).

(69)  **What,**  welcome  be  the  cut,   a    Goddes  name!
      hw.     welcome  be  the  cut   by   God's   name
      'what, welcome be the cut, by God's name'
      (*Canterbury Tales*, prologue, 854)

(70)  Sires,  **what!**  Dun  is  in  the  myre!
      sires  hw.     dun  is  in  the  mire
      'Sirs, what! The dun-coloured horse is in the mire!'
      (*Canterbury Tales, Manciple's Tale*, 5)

Both of these examples occur in the direct speech of characters in the text, as is normal for OE *hwæt*. Each also suggests an interpretation consistent with the exclamative hypothesis. The first can be read as 'How welcome is the cut, by God's name!' The second, in which the dun-coloured horse in the mire is taken as a metaphor for events having come to a standstill, can be read as 'How things have slowed down!'

Further pieces of potential evidence for the exclamative hypothesis for OE *hwæt* come from later texts: occasional apparent degree-exclamatives with *what* are found in texts dating to as late as the sixteenth century. The *OED* (s.v. *what*, B.II.4) gives (71), from 1440:

(71)  A!   lorde,   **what**   the   wedir      is   colde!
      ah   lord    hw.     the   weather   is   cold
      'Ah! Lord, how cold the weather is!'
      (*York Mystery Plays* 14, 71)

Berizzi (2010: 140) also gives examples of 'why'-like *what* from Shakespeare. It cannot be ruled out, of course, that this pattern arose separately and is unrelated to OE *hwæt* as found in e.g. the first line of *Beowulf*. However, parsimony alone is enough to suggest that this (rare) degree-exclamative use of *what* in Middle and Early Modern English may represent not an innovation but the tail-end of a much older pattern.

Finally, the exclamative hypothesis has the merit of bringing into line a few further observations not accounted for by the traditional view. Brinton (1996: 189–91) considers, and rejects, the hypothesis (attributed to personal communication from Elizabeth Traugott, and defined only broadly) that *hwæt* functions as an 'evidential'; however, she does note that 'it does frequently precede a clause containing an evidential or an evidential-like form' (1996: 190). It is possible that the intuition is in fact not about evidentiality per se, but about presupposition. Under the exclamative hypothesis proposed here, *hwæt* introduces an exclamative clause, and it is well known that the main propositions in such clauses are presupposed (cf. e.g. Zanuttini and Portner 2003; Abels 2010). If *hwæt*-clauses involve presupposition, this explains why the intuition that *hwæt* has an epistemic element to its meaning seems to ring true; this also unifies *hwæt*-clauses with the non-asserted verb-late main clauses discussed in section 3.4. The exclamative hypothesis is also consistent with the suggestion made by Grein in his *Sprachschatz der angelsächsischen Dichter* (1912 [1864]: 367) that *hwæt* could be used with the same meaning as exclamatory *hu* 'how', and therefore that it should be distinguished from an interjection, with punctuation in editions reflecting this. As Stanley (2000: 551 n. 75) notes, Grein's suggestion was not adopted by later editors of OE and OS. However, the evidence adduced in this paper also suggests that this punctuation is superfluous, and that there is a partial parallel to be drawn between *hwæt* and exclamatory *hu* 'how'. Perhaps, then, it is time for Grein's suggestion to be rehabilitated.

A reasonable objection at this point is that the exclamative hypothesis is just one view of the reading of *hwæt*-clauses; it could turn out that there are other hypotheses consistent with the data. However, the hypothesis presented here has significant advantages over the traditional account of the function and meaning of *hwæt* as outlined in section 4.3.1: it accounts for the word order facts, it does not need to maintain that *hwæt* is an interjection (with all the concomitant problems of this stance; see section 4.3.2), and it brings the behaviour of *hwæt* into line with that of a range of other interrogative pronouns observed cross-linguistically. Furthermore, it is falsifiable: it predicts that *hwæt*-clauses must be amenable to, or at least coercible into, a degree reading. Any alternative proposal must be able to do at least as well, or better, on these counts.

### 4.3.4 *The diachrony of underspecification*

A related problem—and one that is central to this book's aim of reconstruction—is how *hwæt* came to be potentially underspecified in the first place. Was *$h^w$at* underspecified in Proto-Germanic?

Intuitively, the change toward underspecification, and the loss of the restriction [+thing] (and thus of the necessity of argument status), seems to be a 'natural' change. In studies of grammaticalization such 'semantic bleaching' has often been observed (cf. e.g. Hopper and Traugott 2003), and principles of acquisition such as 'minimize feature content' (Longobardi 2001: 294) have often been posited in the generative literature on syntactic change; see also the discussion of directionality in section 2.3.3. In OHG, for example, there are no examples of the cognate interrogative pronoun *(h)waz* in a non-argumental role (though cf. n. 11), and hence no evidence that the cognate interrogative pronoun was underspecified for the feature [thing]— and yet modern German *was* 'what' is, as illustrated in the previous section, providing another example of this change. Lass's (1997) criterion of process naturalness, discussed in 2.4.3, thus suggests a progression from argumental to non-argumental. The fact that modern English *what* may no longer be semantically underspecified in the same way, as shown by the ungrammaticality of examples such as *\*What did you do that?* and *\*What you've grown!* with intended readings of 'Why did you do that?' and 'How you've grown!' respectively, can be explained as the result of a separate change, namely the loss of underspecified *what* as a lexical item. The situation of 'divergence' that obtained in OE, with both argumental and non-argumental *hwæt* as lexical options in the language, was thus effectively counteracted.[23]

As regards the origin of this underspecification in the prehistory of the Germanic languages, the logic of language contact and the wave model may be able to help us. Among the early Germanic languages, OE, OS, and (to a lesser extent) ON

---

[23] Berizzi (2010: 139–46) in fact gives some examples of 'why'-like *what* from modern English, including (i) and (ii) (as well as some from early modern english).

(i)   Malcolm, **what** are you walking like that?
      (Malcolm in the Middle—Season 2, Ep. 17, *Surgery* (2001))

(ii)  **What** don't you go first, Andy?
      (Margot Adler, Radio Transcript, Air Date: 27 February 2006)

In my idiolect these examples are completely ungrammatical. It is unclear whether this pattern should be considered a continuation of the OE pattern via transmission or whether it represents an independent innovation. In view of the variation in provenance of these examples, the latter may be more likely.

display underspecification, while Gothic and OHG do not. If we accept the traditional family grouping discussed in section 1.4, then either way we must postulate two changes: either underspecification was innovated in Proto-Ingvaeonic and ON, or it was lost in OHG and Gothic. A criterion of economy in terms of number of changes, then—Lass's (1997) simplicity criterion discussed in section 2.4.3—does not help us here. Departing from the strict tree model, however, the change could be traced back to an early Northwest Germanic dialect continuum: we have ample evidence that considerable contact between what was to become the Ingvaeonic languages and what was to become Proto-Scandinavian must have taken place, and that there was a high degree of mutual intelligibility. One hypothesis, then, could be that the under-specification of the interrogative pronoun was an innovation diffused across the Northwest Germanic dialect continuum but which did not make it as far southeast as the pre-OHG area of Europe.

Furthermore, data exists which may help us to pin down the exact reanalysis that caused this change to happen. Interrogative examples such as (72) are occasionally found in the *Heliand*:

(72)  **huat**  uualdand  god  habit  guodes  gigereuuid
      hw.  ruling  G.  has  good.GEN  prepared
      'what good things Lord God has prepared (for us)' (*Heliand* 2533–4)

Here *huat* can still be analysed as argumental, as in essence it forms a unit with *guodes* to mean 'what of good [things]'. Such discontinuous constituents were a possibility in many early Indo-European languages: see e.g. Matthews (1981: 255) and Hale (1998: 16) on Latin, and Devine and Stephens (1999) on Greek. As the possibility of discontinuity became rarer, learners who had not acquired this possibility would require another analysis for clauses such as (72).[24] Analysis of *huat* as underspecified in such cases, specifically non-argumental and generated in the left periphery of the clause rather than extracted by *wh*-movement from a nominal constituent further down the tree, would be one solution to this problem, with *guodes* itself analysed as a genitive argument of the main verb: the clause would then receive the interpretation 'how the Lord God has prepared good things (for us)'. Once *huat* had become detached from its position in the paradigm of argumental interrogative pronouns and was able to be interpreted as underspecified 'how', it could then be extended unproblematically to exclamatives as in the construction discussed in 4.2. We thus have an argument, albeit not a watertight one, for reconstructing underspecified \*h$^w$at as a North Sea Germanic innovation.

---

[24] I have no account for the increasing rarity of discontinuity. However, if Bošković (2005, 2008, 2009) is right that languages may lack DP and that the presence of a DP is incompatible with discontinuity, then the ongoing grammaticalization of D$^0$ elements could be taken as a trigger for the loss of this property; see Lander and Haegeman (2013) for discussion in the context of ON.

To summarize section 4.3, then, I have argued that the traditional view of OE *hwæt* as an interjection meaning simply 'lo!' or 'listen!', as proposed by Grimm (1837) and assumed 'by all Anglo-Saxonists' (Stanley 2000: 541), is unsatisfactory. This is because (a) *hwæt* must usually be analysed as unstressed where it occurs in metrical texts, (b) no punctuation between *hwæt* and the following clause is ever found, (c) the contemporary grammarian Ælfric did not analyse *hwæt* as an interjection, and (d) *hwæt* is not exclusively found in texts connected to primary orality, and does not always serve to initiate speech. Most dramatically of all, clauses preceded by *hwæt* pattern with subordinate clauses, not with main clauses, with respect to the position of the verb. It is difficult to imagine how the presence of an extra-clausal interjection could have such a dramatic effect on clausal word order. Regardless of whether my own proposal is accepted, these facts must be accounted for by any satisfactory theory of *hwæt*.

According to the alternative analysis pursued in section 4.3.3, there were two variants of *hwæt* in OE: both were interrogative, but one was underspecified for the feature [thing] and thus able to assume a non-argument role. Non-interrogative clauses preceded by *hwæt* are *wh*-exclamatives parallel in interpretation to modern English *How you've changed!*; it was demonstrated that a cross-section of such clauses were amenable to this kind of interpretation. If the logic of this section is accepted, then the implications for editors and translators of OE and OS texts are significant. In section 4.3.4 it was also suggested, more tentatively, that the underspecification of *hwæt* may have originated in late Northwest Germanic through reanalysis of interrogatives containing discontinuous nominal constituents. There is thus no call to reconstruct underspecification for Proto-Germanic itself.

Note that this proposal is in no way incompatible with the view that *hwæt*, or perhaps more precisely clauses beginning with *hwæt*, were characteristic of speech, and were used to initiate discourse with particular pragmatic functions. Here we must distinguish sharply between the grammatical properties of a lexical item or clause and the way it is used by speakers of the language. It could perfectly well have been the case that it was customary among speakers of early Ingvaeonic languages, for whatever reason, to start one's speech with an exclamative; at least, this is as plausible as starting one's speech with an interjection. The 'exclamative hypothesis', then, does not quibble with the view that *hwæt* had this function; it simply argues that this function alone is insufficient to characterize the grammatical properties and interpretation of *hwæt* and clauses beginning with it.

## 4.4 Whether

Modern English *whether* has a number of strange properties as compared to other members of the *wh*-system. It cannot appear in a main clause context, with or without inversion, as shown by the ungrammaticality of (73)–(74).

(73)   *Whether did you go fishing yesterday?
(74)   *Whether you went fishing yesterday?

It is often suggested to be a subordinate clause complementizer parallel to *if* (e.g. Freidin 1992: 81; Alexopoulou and Keller 2007). However, van Gelderen (2009b: 156) and Berizzi (2010: 122) argue that *whether* cannot be analysed as a complementizer, since unlike *if* it (a) blocks *wh*-movement from a lower clause (75), (b) can be coordinated with *not* (76), and (c) can occur with prepositions (77).

(75)   Who do you wonder if/*whether I saw?
(76)   I asked whether/*if or not you had gone fishing.
(77)   It depends on whether/*if he comes.

None of these arguments is fully convincing. With regard to (a), the blocking of extraction, judgements such as those in (75) are not clear-cut for many speakers. Chung and McCloskey (1983) report extraction out of *whether*-clauses as fully grammatical; Sobin (1987) and Snyder (2000) provide experimental results indicating wildly varying judgements; Alexopoulou and Keller (2007) report results showing that *whether*-clauses and *that*-clauses pattern together as opposed to strong islands such as relative clauses. It should be noted that weak islandhood is clearly sensitive to the discourse status of the extracted element, as illustrated by (78), which is substantially more acceptable:

(78)   Which film did you wonder whether I saw?

Hofmeister and Sag (2010) have provided experimental evidence for this contrast, and a semantic explanation for it is provided by Szabolcsi and Zwarts (1993).

The coordination argument (b) is also not watertight, since *if and when* is possible; the impossibility of *if or not* may therefore be semantic, rather than syntactic, in origin. Similarly, it could be argued that occurrence with prepositions is limited to clauses that can be embedded under a null nominal, and that *whether* introduces such a clause; argument (c) would thus be without force. Rosenbaum (1967) proposed that all clauses were dominated by a nominal projection, and Kiparsky and Kiparsky (1970) propose it for factives; more recently, Adger and Quer (2001) have revived the hypothesis for certain types of clause.[25] Adger and Quer themselves analyse *whether* as a SpecCP element, but note (2001: 21 n. 15) that nothing rests on whether it is in

---

[25] However, Adger and Quer explicitly propose that *if*-clauses are embedded under a $D^0$ (2001: 119–21), on the basis of parallels with affective polarity items. This leaves the preposition-related facts mysterious, as they observe (2001: 121 n. 16).

In fact, clauses such as the supposedly ungrammatical version of (77) with *if* embedded under a preposition are in fact robustly attested in corpora: for instance, in the Corpus of Contemporary American English (COCA; Davies 2008–; accessed July 2012), 35 relevant examples of the string *depends on if* can be found, e.g. (i). This casts even more doubt on argument (c).

(i)   It all depends on if I'm healthy and if we're winning. (COCA; 2005)

SpecCP or in C⁰. In light of the above facts, I will assume that in modern English both *if* and *whether* are C⁰ heads after all, and not SpecCP elements.

Cognates in the other modern Germanic languages have different roles. For instance, German *weder* is used exclusively to form a negative disjunction ('neither'). This section will not be concerned further with the correct analysis of the modern languages: see Larson (1985), Kayne (1991: 664–6), Henry (1995), Nakajima (1996), Adger and Quer (2001), and Berizzi (2010: 122–31) for analyses of modern English *whether*, and Johannessen (2003) for an analysis of modern German *weder*. Here I will discuss reflexes of *$h^w$aþeraz/*$h^w$eþeraz in the early Germanic languages, with a view to reconstructing its properties in Proto-Germanic. It will be glossed as 'whether' throughout.

### 4.4.1 *East Germanic:* hvaþar

In Gothic, *hvaþar*, a reflex of *$h^w$aþeraz, had a completely different role from that of its modern English cognate; it served as an argumental interrogative pronoun meaning 'which of two' (Wright 1910: 129). There are six attestations of *hvaþar* in this role in the Gothic corpus, two of which are given below.

(79)  **hvaþar**   ist    raihtis   azetizo   qiþan:   afletanda   þus
     whether   is     though    easier    say.INF   be-forgiven  you.DAT
     frawaurhteis,   þau    qiþan:    urreis   jah    gagg?
     sins.NOM     or     say.INF    arise   and    go
     'Which is easier: to say "Your sins are forgiven", or to say "Arise and go"?'
     (Gothic Bible, Matthew 9: 5)

(80)  **hvaþar**   nu    þize,    qiþ,    mais   ina    frijod?
     whether   now   these.GEN   say    more   him    loves
     'Tell me: Which of these most loves him?'
     (Gothic Bible, Luke 7: 42)

It is also found as an indefinite in the *Skeireins*, as in (81). Various cognate forms are found as indefinites (often compounded) in the early Germanic languages; I will not consider these further here.

(81)  eiþan   galaubjandans   sweriþa   ju    **hvaþaramme**   usgibaima
     thus    believing       honour    now   whether.DAT     give-out.1PL
     bi    wairþidai
     by    ability
     'Thus believing we should now give out honour to each of the two according to ability'
     (*Skeireins* 5:7)

As regards constituent order, in all interrogative examples *hvaþar* is clause-initial, and in five of the six examples the verb immediately follows the pronoun. Three of these are renderings of the same utterance, (79), in different Gospels (Matthew 9: 5, Luke 5: 23, and Mark 2: 9), and one further example (Philippians 1: 22) contains only *hvaþar* and the verb; in addition, there is a V2 example in the *Skeireins* (3:3). (80) is the only verb-late example; however, it is possible for this to be analysed as an embedded interrogative selected by the verb *qiþ* 'say'. Gothic *hvaþar* thus seems to behave as a regular argumental interrogative pronoun, though, as usual with Gothic, the data is sparse.

### 4.4.2 *West Germanic:* hwæþer, hweđar, hwedar

While the OE form *hwæþer* is a reflex of *$h^w a \thetaeraz$, the OS and OHG forms *hweđar* and *hwedar* appear to be reflexes of *$h^w e \thetaeraz$. I will ignore this phonological difference here.

Allen (1980b) gives an overview of the behaviours of OE *hwæþer*. Examples (82) and (83) (from Allen 1980b: 790) show that the 'which of two' meaning could be found, as in Gothic. In this instance, fronting of the finite verb was usual, as with other *wh*-questions.[26] Example (83) shows that the pronoun could be inflected for case; genitive examples can also be found.

(82) **Hwæđer**  cweđe  we  đe  ure  đe  đæra  engla?
whether  say  we  or  ours  or  the.GEN  angels.GEN
'Which should we say: ours, or the angels'?'
(cocathom1,+ACHom_I,_15:302.95.2825)

(83) **hwæđerne**  woldes  þu  deman  wites  wyrðran?
whether.ACC  would  you  deem  punishment.GEN  worthier
'Which would you deem worthier of punishment?'
(coboeth,Bo:38.122.28.2444)

However, examples can also be found where *hwæþer* has a different meaning, as in (84) (from Allen 1980b: 789) and (85) (from van Gelderen 2009b: 143 n. 6).

---

[26] Van Gelderen (2009b: 140) suggests that an example from *Beowulf* 2530–2 (her 11c) is an exception:

(i) **hwæðer**  sel  mæge  æfter  wælræse  wunde  gedygan  uncer  twega
whether  better  may  after  bloody-storm  wounds  survive  us.GEN  two.GEN
She translates this as 'Who of us two is better at surviving wounds after the deadly battle?' However, in context this example is clearly a free relative and not a direct question, and hence the lack of verb-movement is unsurprising.

(84) **Hwæðer** ic  mote  lybban  oð   þat   ic  hine  geseo?
      whether  I   may   live   until  that  I   him   see
      'Might I live until I see him?'
      (cocathom1,+ACHom_I,_9:250.41.1601)

(85) **Hwæþer** nu   gimma   wlite   eowre  eagan  to  him  getio?
      whether  now  gems.GEN  beauty  your   eyes   to  him  attract
      'Does the beauty of gems attract your eyes to them?'
      (coboeth,Bo:13.28.27.491)

In these examples, there is no obvious sense of 'which of two': instead the semantics seem to be those of a straightforward yes/no question. Furthermore, though these examples are direct interrogatives, there is no verb fronting. Allen (1980b: 791) states that this pattern is general, with only a few counterexamples from Bede, which can be discounted on the basis that 'there are also a few examples of inversion in indirect questions in this text' (1980b: 791 n. 3). Van Gelderen (2009b: 140 n. 4) calls Allen's claim into question on the basis of examples such as (86) and (87), in which verb-movement is visible.

(86) **Hwæðer** wæs  iohannes fulluht  þe of heofonum  þe of mannum
      whether  was  John's   baptism  or of heaven.DAT  or of man.DAT
      'Which was John's baptism: of heaven, or of man?'
      (cowsgosp,Mt_[WSCp]:21.25.1438)

(87) **Hwæðer** wille ge   ðæt ic cume to eow,  ðe mid gierde  ðe
      whether  will  you  that I come to you  or with rod   or
      mid   monnðwære  gæste?
      with  gentle     spirit
      'Which do you want me to come to you with: a rod, or a gentle spirit?'
      (cocura,CP:17.117.6.784)

However, as my translations suggest, I believe that these examples are 'which of two'-questions parallel to that in (82), *pace* van Gelderen's (2009b: 142) suggestion that *hwæþer* here is an independent question marker. As such, (86) and (87) do not constitute counterexamples to Allen's generalization. The yes/no question use of *hwæþer* is rare after the Middle English period, and disappears entirely in the seventeenth century (van Gelderen 2009b: 143; Berizzi 2010: 127).

As in modern English, subordinate clauses could begin with *whether*, as in (88) and (89). (88) is conceivably an embedded 'which of two'-question; (89) is a simplex embedded interrogative.[27]

---

[27]  In addition, OE had an adverb *hwæþ(e)re* 'yet, however, nevertheless' (Bosworth and Toller 1898: 572; Mitchell and Robinson 2007: 380), which will not be further discussed here.

(88) he gecyðde **hwæðer** he mænde ðe ðæs    modes foster
he asked    whether    he    meant    or    the.GEN    spirit's    nourishment
ðe ðæs    lichoman
or the.GEN    body's
'He asked whether he meant the spirit's nourishment or the body's'
(cocura,CP:18.137.18.936)

(89) ðry    weras... axodon... **hwæðer** se    halga Petrus    þær
three men... asked...    whether the holy Peter    there
wununge hæfde
dwelling    had
'Three men asked whether Saint Peter lived there'
(coaelive,+ALS[Peter's_Chair]:109.2346)

As for the analysis of *hwæþer*, van Gelderen (2009b: 140–55) assumes that a situation of divergence obtained in OE, and that there were at least two separate items: (a) an argumental *hwæþer* with a semantic *wh*-feature, (b) *hwæþer* first Merged in a specifier of the C-domain bearing an $[iQ]$ feature, and (c) *hwæþer* as a C-domain head bearing $[uQ]$ (see also Kiparsky 1995: 142).[28] She argues that 'there is a clear tendency' for *hwæþer* to be a head, on the basis that the lack of verb-movement with *hwæþer* is indicative that it is blocking this movement much as complementizers in modern German and Dutch do under the traditional account (e.g. den Besten 1977). She suggests that evidence for it being a specifier would be provided by its co-occurring with another complementizer (2009b: 142–3), and that there are only 'a handful' of examples of this, some of which are amenable to other analyses. In subordinate clauses, diagnostic evidence is harder to come by; there are no clear cases of *hwæþer* preceding a complementizer in subordinate clauses (though there are some in Middle English; van Gelderen 2009b: 155), and verb-movement cannot serve as a diagnostic.

The arguments for head status are not watertight. Subordinate clauses are completely mute with respect to the issue, since we cannot test for OE to see whether *hwæþer* blocks extraction of another *wh*-element, and since the absence of verb-movement tells us nothing. Furthermore, we would not expect to see a complementizer in these clauses in any case, since OE embedded questions never display one even with normal *wh*-elements that are uncontroversially specifiers. In other words, whatever underlies the Doubly Filled COMP Filter (Chomsky and Lasnik 1977) for modern English already held for OE embedded questions. Berizzi (2010) also provides many examples of varieties of English in which verb-movement does not occur in direct *wh*-questions, e.g. African-American English, despite the relevant *wh*-items

---

[28] Note that van Gelderen makes a (non-standard) distinction between semantic features and interpretable features, under which both are required to participate in syntactic operations.

being in specifier position. I therefore believe it preferable to posit only two interrogative *hwæþer* items for OE: an argumental 'which of two' pronoun which moves to a specifier position in the left periphery, and a non-argumental lexicalization of an interrogative operator that is base-generated in a specifier position there.

Berizzi's own hypothesis (2010: 129–31), in order to account for the lack of verb-movement in clauses with non-argumental *hwæþer*, is that there is a silent IS IT THAT between *hwæþer* and the following clause.[29] Though highly stipulative, this analysis capitalizes on the notion that even when *hwæþer* introduces a direct question the form is that of a subordinate clause. As Fischer et al. (2000: 54) observe, this word order, along with the fact that the verb in *hwæþer*-clauses is commonly in the subjunctive, 'betrays the origin of this type of question as an indirect question'. Indeed, it seems plausible that left-peripheral operator *hwæþer* came about through reanalysis of an indirect question as a direct one. A separate reanalysis could have led to the dissociation of argumental *hwæþer* from its first-Merged position, as described in section 4.3.4 for *$h^w$at*, consistent with the Late Merge principle of directionality discussed in section 2.3.3.

In OS the picture is similar. Six examples of simplex interrogative *hwedar* can be found in the *Heliand*. (90) is a direct question parallel to the OE examples in (84) and (85), of the kind not found in Gothic, with lack of verb-movement. Although in this example two options are available, suggesting the possibility of a 'which of two' reading, in the classic OE examples from Allen (1980b) the verb in the *hwæþer*-clause is not in either of the two options, and directly follows *hwæþer*. I therefore analyse this example as an OE-style direct question. (91) and (92) are embedded *wh*- and yes/ no questions parallel to (88) and (89) respectively; two further examples like (92) can be found, on lines 3406 and 3848.[30]

---

[29] Berizzi also posits a silent IT IS THAT for *whether*-clauses in modern English, in order to explain the lack of the otherwise-available embedded verb-movement with this item in Hiberno-English. As support for the account, she gives examples where 'it is that' is lexicalized. However, the issue of when and why IT IS THAT remains unexpressed is not addressed.

[30] The remaining example presents a problem:

(i)  | **huueðer** | lêdiad | gi | uundan | gold | te | gebu |
     |-------------|--------|-----|--------|------|-----|------|
     | whether | lead | you | wound | gold | to | gift.DAT |
     | huilicun | gumuno? | | | | | |
     | which.DAT | men.GEN | | | | | |

'To whom are you taking wound gold as a gift?' (???)
(*Heliand* 554–5)

Here there are multiple *wh*-words and clear verb-movement, and the interpretation is unclear: no 'which of two' reading is evidently available. It could be that *huilicun gumuno* 'to whom?' is a separate question, and the reading could then be 'Are you taking wound gold as a gift?' But this is unsatisfactory, especially as verb-movement is involved. Perhaps an analysis as an 'expletive *wh*'-clause in the sense of Felser (2001, 2004) is available.

(90)  **hueđer**  thu    that  fan    thi    selƀumu  sprikis,
      whether  you    that  from  you    self    speak
      ...the   it    thi   ôđre  hêr    erlos   sagdun
      ...or    it    you   other here   men     told
      'Is that what you yourself say, or what others have told you?'
      (*Heliand* 5207–8)

(91)  Thuo   bigan   thie  heritogo  thia     hêri    Iudeono...  frâgoian,
      then   began   the   duke      the.ACC  people  Jews.GEN    ask.INF
      ...**hueđeron**   sia   thero   tueio   tuomian   uueldin
      ...whether.ACC  they  the.GEN  two.GEN  free.INF   would
      'Then the duke asked the Jews which of the two they wanted to free'
      (*Heliand* 5409–11)

(92)  ne    rôkead,    **huueđar**  gi   is      ênigan  thanc  antfâhan
      NEG   think.IMP  whether   you  it.GEN  any     thank  receive.INF
      'Do not think about whether you will receive any thanks for it'
      (*Heliand* 1541)

There are no examples of direct questions with 'which of two' readings; however,
I will tentatively assume with Cordes and Holthausen (1973: 248) on the basis of the
above examples that this lack is accidental, and that OS patterns with OE.

For OHG, Graff and Massmann (1838: 1217–23) provide a list of examples with
*hwedar* and related forms. (93) is a 'which of two' reading direct question parallel to
OE (80). (94) and (95) are embedded questions parallel to OE (86) and (87)
respectively.

(93)  **Uuedaran**   minnota   her   mer?
      whether.ACC  loved    he    more
      'Which of the two did he love more?'
      (*Tatian* 138,9)

(94)  Suohhemes   auur     uuir  nu     ziidh  dhera    christes   chiburdi,
      seek.1PL    however  we    now    time   the.GEN  Christ's   birth.GEN
      **huuedhar**  ir   iu       quhami   odho   uuir   noh    sculim   siin
      whether   he   already  came     or     we     still  should   his
      quhemandes       biidan
      coming           wait.INF
      'Let us now seek the time of Christ's birth, whether he already came or we
      should still be waiting for his coming'
      (*Isidor* 25,8)

(95)  **uueder**  sie  doh      machotin  ranas  unde  scinifes  unde  sanguinem
      whether  they  though  made      frogs    and    gnats    and    blood
      'whether they made frogs, gnats and blood'
      (Notker's *Psalter* 77,49)

Although suggesting that *hwedar* can function as a question particle, Graff and
Massmann (1838: 1217) give no examples of its use as such in direct questions, and
in all the examples that they do provide *hwedar*, or the constituent containing it,
immediately precedes the verb. If this absence is non-accidental, OHG *hwedar* does
not pattern with OE *hwæþer* and OS *hwedar*. Instead, as in OE, OS, and Gothic, it has
a 'which of two' reading, and additionally (as in modern English) may introduce
indirect yes/no questions. I will return to this potential difference between OHG and
the other West Germanic languages in section 4.4.4.

### 4.4.3 *North Germanic*: hvaðarr, hvárr/hvár/hvárt

The North Germanic reflexes of Proto-Germanic *$*h^waþeraz$* are *hvaðarr* and *hvárr*
(Heusler 1967: 78; Wessén 1966: 130). The latter is a contraction of the former; *hvaðarr*
occurs three times in the tenth-century poetry corpus (Cleasby and Vigfusson 1874:
298). One example is given in (96).

(96)  en  ek  veit,  at    hefr  heitit      hans  bróðir  mér    góðu
      but  I    know  that  has    promised  his    brother  me.DAT  goods
      …**hvaðarr**  tveggja
      …each        two.GEN
      'But I know that each of his brothers has promised me goods'
      (Glúmr Geirason, *Gráfeldardrápa*, 12, 5–8)

Here *hvaðarr* is used as an indefinite. The far more common form is *hvárt* (neuter),
along with its masculine form *hvárr* and its feminine form *hvár*. Examples of this
contraction in interrogatives are given in (97)–(100).

(97)  **Hvorn**        viltu        her    þiggja    teininn?
      whether.ACC  will-you  here  receive  twig.DEF
      'Which of the two twigs would you rather receive?'
      (*Haralds saga Sigurðarsonar* 23)

(98)  Eða  **hvárt**      hefir  þú    nakkvat  sét    Baldr  á    Helvegi?
      but  whether  have  you  anything  seen  Baldr  on  Hell-way
      'But have you seen anything of Baldr on the road to Hell?'
      (*Gylfaginning* 49)

(99) ok    biðr   hana   kjósa,        **hvárn**        hún   vill   eiga
     and   asks   her    choose.INF    whether.ACC     she   will   have
     'and (he) asks her to choose which of the two she will have'
     (*Hervarar Saga ok Heiðreks* 3)

(100) **hvárt**   Baldr   var   svá   ást     sæll      sem   sagt   er
      whether   Baldr   was   so    love    blessed   as    said   is
      'whether Baldr was as beloved as people said he was'
      (*Gylfaginning* 49)

All the uses of OE *hwæþer* can also be found in ON. Examples (97) and (99) are examples of the cognate pronoun with a 'which of two' reading in a main clause and in a subordinate clause respectively. Examples (98) and (100) are examples of the cognate pronoun serving as a question-introducer in a main clause and in a subordinate clause respectively, possibilities also noted by Faarlund (2004: 226–7). In modern Icelandic—uniquely among the modern Germanic languages—the 'which of two' reading for *hvort* is retained.

Unlike in OE, all these clauses have V2 word order, regardless of the reading.[31] Since the generalization of V2 is vastly more advanced in ON than it is in the other early Germanic languages, this is perhaps not surprising. Two further points need to be made about ON *hvárt*, however. First, like other *wh*-items in ON, it may occur with a complementizer, and frequently does:

(101) Hvárt    sem    hann   hét        góðu   eða   illu
      whether  that   he     promised   good   or    ill
      'Whether he promised good or ill, ...'
      (*Þorgils saga skarða* 1)

This strongly suggests that *hvárt* itself was a specifier, not a head, in this language. Second, it is often compounded with the genitive numeral *tveggja* 'of two', especially when used as an indefinite:

(102) Þetta   var    tvöfaldr    spáleikr,    því at      hvárttveggja
      that    was    twofold     prophecy     because     whether-two.GEN
      came    from   later
      kom     fram   síðan
      'That was a twofold prophecy, because the two things came to pass'
      (*Guðmundar saga*)

---

[31] Though 'embedded V2' in examples (99) and (100) is clearly not the same phenomenon as matrix V2, since, as in modern Icelandic, in embedded clauses a constituent may intervene between the interrogative pronoun and the finite verb (see e.g. Maling 1980). Smith (1971) even takes such examples as V3. Some have taken this asymmetry to indicate that the verb only moves to T in such languages, while others maintain a CP-recursion analysis: see e.g. Vikner (1995), Schwartz and Vikner (1989, 1996), and Biberauer (2002) for discussion. I will not take a position on this issue here.

TABLE 4.6. Reflexes of *$h^w$aþeraz/*$h^w$eþeraz in early Germanic

| | 'Which of two' | | Disjunctive question | | Indefinite |
|---|---|---|---|---|---|
| | Main | Sub | Main | Sub | |
| Gothic | ✓ (V2) | ✓ (V-late) | ✗ | ✗ | ✓ |
| OHG | ✓ (V2) | ✓ (V-late) | ✗? | ✓ (V-late) | ✓ |
| OE | ✓ (V2) | ✓ (V-late) | ✓ (V-late) | ✓ (V-late) | ✓ |
| OS | ? | ✓ (V-late) | ✓ (V-late) | ✓ (V-late) | ✓ |
| ON | ✓ (V2) | ✓ (V2) | ✓ (V2) | ✓ (V-to-T) | ✓ |

This indicates that the 'which of two' meaning was weakened and needed reinforcement in ON.

### 4.4.4 *The syntax of Proto-Germanic* *$h^w$aþeraz/*$h^w$eþeraz

The overall picture found in the early Germanic languages with regard to reflexes of *$h^w$aþeraz/*$h^w$eþeraz can be summarized as in Table 4.6.

As with *$h^w$at, the correspondence problem here can be resolved on lexical-phonological grounds: the different items in the five languages can be safely assumed to be cognate, reflexes of *$h^w$aþeraz/*$h^w$eþeraz.[32] Again as with *$h^w$at, a story can be told in terms of lexical split. I take the 'which of two' reading to be original and present in Proto-Germanic; this is the only reading attested in Gothic, and is supported by the availability of this reading for the cognate item in Sanskrit, *ka-tará* 'which of two', and throughout the history of Lithuanian, *katras* 'which of two' (OED; Artūras Ratkus, p.c.).

One possibility is that the disjunctive question reading was also available in Proto-Germanic. The absence of this possibility in Gothic (as well as in Sanskrit and Lithuanian) suggests that this is unlikely, however. In addition, the development of this reading can be sketched straightforwardly. At the first stage, in which only the 'which of two' reading was possible, it would also have been possible to juxtapose two independent structures in speech, as in modern English (103).

(103)    Tell me which you would prefer—that I walk, or that I cycle?

*Which* is still nominal and argumental in this example. We see this type of example in OE: for instance, (88). One of the conjuncts could then be left unexpressed, yielding the equivalent of (104).

---

[32] To be more accurate, the forms found in Gothic and ON, as well as OE *hwæþer*, are reflexes of *$h^w$aþeraz, while the forms found in OHG and OS, as well as the occasionally found alternative OE form *hweder*, are reflexes of *$h^w$eþeraz (Nielsen 1998: 78–9). I assume this phonological difference has no syntactic consequence, and that the two items behaved identically in Proto-Germanic, though this is by no means an innocent assumption.

(104)   Tell me which you would prefer—that I walk?

This type of example, however, would have been susceptible to a clause-union reanalysis in which *which* became analysed as a disjunctive question marker.[33] I hypothesize that example (94) from OHG may have involved such a marker. A third stage has indirect questions being reanalysed as direct questions; this is the stage reached by OE and OS, and accounts for the presence of verb-late order in these examples.[34]

The first reanalysis, leading from stage 1 to stage 2, is characteristic of all of Northwest Germanic. As with the reanalysis of $*h^w at$ mentioned in the previous section, the second reanalysis, leading from stage 2 to stage 3, is only attested in OE, OS, and ON. It may thus have been an innovation that was diffused across the Northwest Germanic dialect continuum at an early stage. The subsequent generalization of V2 in all types of main clauses in ON and a similar phenomenon in subordinate clauses then accounts for the presence of V2 word order with *hvárt* questions in this language.

## 4.5 Chapter summary

In this chapter, a variety of facts related to interrogatives in the early Germanic languages have been considered. It is uncontroversial that these languages all exhibit V2 (i.e. verb movement to the left periphery) in *wh*-interrogatives; section 4.2 examined some data that indicates that a slightly more nuanced view is necessary. There is some evidence from both East and West Germanic that it was possible for material (usually pronouns) to intervene between fronted *wh*-items and the finite verb under certain circumstances, suggesting that in Proto-Germanic the verb in such constructions may have moved only to $Fin^0$ and not as far as $Foc^0$ or $Int^0$. However, these examples are infrequent, and there is no independent evidence to analyse them as archaisms, so any reconstruction has to remain tentative. This is even truer of *wh*-interrogatives with a topic to the left of the *wh*-word, for which the number of examples is vanishingly small. No clear criteria of process naturalness, legality, or economy are applicable to these cases, and so no reconstruction can be reached with any certainty. This is no failing of the method outlined in Chapter 2, since it is to be expected of any reconstructive method that there will be defined circumstances under which it does not yield unequivocal results.

---

[33] Though the absence of any reflex of the complementizer or conjunction in the disjunctive questions other than *whether* itself is unaccounted for under this approach. It is also unclear why the reanalysis took place in embedded contexts, and why languages at the second stage would not immediately permit V2 questions introduced by *whether*.

[34] Diachronically, that is. Synchronically van Gelderen's (2009b) suggestion that *hwæþer* could be a head in OE provides one explanation, as does Berizzi's (2010) null structure hypothesis.

Section 4.3 examined reflexes of the word *$h^w$at* in the early Germanic languages. Certain apparently anomalous 'interjectional' uses of the word in West Germanic were analysed as well-behaved examples of exclamatives involving an underspecified *$h^w$at*; criteria of process naturalness (grammaticalization) and economy then lead us to analyse this underspecification as an innovation within West Germanic rather than reconstructing it for an earlier stage. Similar conclusions were drawn in section 4.4, where the 'which-of-two' reading is reconstructed for Proto-Germanic *$h^w$aþeraz/* *$h^w$eþeraz* and not the indirect-question marker found in some of the daughter languages.

A key finding of this chapter, then, is that syntactic reconstruction is at its most believable when dealing with the syntactic properties of those lexical items that have overt phonological forms traceable via lexical-phonological reconstruction, such as *$h^w$at* and *$h^w$aþeraz/$h^w$eþeraz*. Though much work remains to be done on the interrogative system of Proto-Germanic, I hope the narratives presented here represent progress in this direction.

# 5

## Null arguments in early Germanic

### 5.1 Introduction

In this chapter I discuss a further property of the early Germanic languages: the occurrence of null arguments. In contrast to other aspects of early Germanic syntax, such as constituent order, the details of this property have received little attention in the generative literature, although Sigurðsson (1993) on ON, van Gelderen (2000) on OE, and Axel (2007) on OHG are notable exceptions. Abraham (1991) contains some discussion of Gothic and the history of German; however, to my knowledge, the only truly comparative work on null arguments in Germanic to have appeared is Rosenkvist (2009). As Rosenkvist emphasizes, 'the resemblance between the [early Germanic] languages is quite remarkable. A possible reason why this has not been debated earlier may be that researchers have focused on one single Old Germanic language at a time' (2009: 152). However, his paper mainly reviews and summarizes the existing literature, and has a number of empirical lacunae: Gothic and OS are not mentioned at all, and the only quantitative data presented is from OHG and Old Swedish.

This chapter builds on Rosenkvist's paper, and is simultaneously broader and narrower in focus. I do not here consider the null argument property in the modern Germanic languages. In those modern Germanic varieties that do permit null arguments (e.g. Bavarian, Frisian, Övdalian), a number of differences exist that render it unlikely that the modern property is fundamentally the same phenomenon as in earlier stages of Germanic, as Rosenkvist concludes (2009: 174–5).[1] On the other hand, the scope is wider in that new quantitative data from Gothic, OE, Old Icelandic, and OS is presented. As elsewhere in this book, the ultimate aim is to

---

[1] Axel and Weiß (2011) argue that the modern null argument dialects of German inherited this property directly from OHG, based on a putative correlation with availability of agreement in $C^0$, in the form either of verb-movement or of complementizer agreement. Rosenkvist (2009) argues against such a view, on the basis that (a) some modern Germanic varieties, e.g. Zurich German, permit null subjects even in embedded clauses despite the absence of agreeing complementizers, and (b) the person split in earlier Germanic (see section 5.2 of this chapter) is not explained. In section 5.2 I provide further evidence against this hypothesis by demonstrating that even in OHG the presence of verb-movement in subordinate clauses was not relevant to the licensing of null subjects. See Table 5.12.

reconstruct the syntactic properties of unattested stages of Germanic, and so an attempt is made to unify the contrasts that appear between the attested languages in a diachronically plausible manner.

In 5.2 I present data on the occurrence of null arguments from five key early Germanic languages: Gothic, ON, OE, OHG, and OS. Section 5.3 analyses this data within a generative framework, assessing the applicability of different theories of null arguments to the data in 5.2. I argue in 5.3.1 that the theory of identification of null subjects by rich verbal agreement, as first proposed within the generative tradition by Taraldsen (1978), is not sufficient to explain the frequency and range of null arguments attested in early Germanic, especially considering the availability of null objects; in 5.3.2 I demonstrate that a traditional topic drop analysis is also ruled out. I also suggest, in 5.3.3, that the early Germanic languages were not obviously 'radical' null argument languages as argued by Huang (1984) for Mandarin Chinese, Japanese, and Korean. My proposal, in 5.3.4 and 5.3.5, links the availability of null arguments in the early Northwest Germanic languages to agreement with a topic operator in SpecShiftP, updating a proposal made by Holmberg (2010) for Finnish, and the availability of null arguments in Gothic to agreement with SpecShiftP or a left-peripheral logophoric agent ($\Lambda_A$) or logophoric patient ($\Lambda_P$) operator. Finally, in 5.4 I look at these languages from a diachronic perspective, arguing that the restriction to main clauses found in the Northwest Germanic languages is an innovation, and that we can tentatively reconstruct Proto-Germanic as a traditional null subject language, though questions remain.

## 5.2 Null arguments across the attested early Germanic languages

### 5.2.1 *Gothic*

Wright (1910: 188) remarks that subject pronouns are rare in Gothic, and in her book-length study of the syntax of Gothic, Ferraresi (2005: 47) states that 'Gothic is a null-subject language'. However, as has been emphasized in recent years by Holmberg (2010) among others, there are various different types of null subject language, and so it is necessary to look at the contexts in which null arguments can be found.

Ferraresi shows that expression of nominative pronouns in Gothic largely follows the (presumed) Greek *Vorlage*.[2] She notes that in the rare instances where there is a discrepancy between the *Vorlage* and the Gothic text it is usually (but not always) the Gothic that expresses the pronoun overtly (2005: 48); see Tables 5.1 and 5.2.

Ferraresi notes that insertion in Gothic is always preverbal, with the exception of a couple of *wh*-questions. Interestingly, 'in all the examples of embedded clauses where

---

[2] Ferraresi (2005) and Fertig (2000) both use Streitberg's reconstruction of this *Vorlage*, which may be problematic; cf. section 1.4.1 and Ratkus (2011: 28–32) for discussion.

TABLE 5.1. Subject pronouns in Gothic main clauses (Ferraresi 2005: 48, her (43))

|  | Pr V | XP Pr V | V Pr | XP V Pr |
|---|---|---|---|---|
| Gothic, not Greek | 8 | 0 | 0 | (wh) 2 |
| Greek, not Gothic | 1 | 0 | 0 | 0 |

TABLE 5.2. Subject pronouns in Gothic subordinate clauses (Ferraresi 2005: 48, her (44))

|  | C Pr V | C XP Pr V | C V Pr | C XP V Pr |
|---|---|---|---|---|
| Gothic, not Greek | 23 | 0 | 0 | 0 |
| Greek, not Gothic | 2 | 0 | 0 | 0 |

a subject pronoun has been inserted in Gothic while it is null in Greek, there is a change in the subject with respect to the main clause' (2005: 49). This tendency militates against the common picture of Wulfila as a slavish word-for-word translator, since a clear motive for inserting the subject can be identified in some cases, namely discourse clarity; at the same time, it indicates that null subjects were a native possibility in Gothic, since otherwise such insertions would be the norm and not the exception. Cf. also section 1.4.1 of this book for discussion of the degree of freedom of Wulfila's translation.

The other recent study of null subjects in Gothic, Fertig (2000), also concludes that null subjects were a native possibility. However, he notes that there are only 'a handful of cases' where the Gothic differs from Streitberg's Greek, and that they favour insertion rather than deletion. He argues against the view of Held (1903: viii), who suggests that the insertion of these pronouns was merely a stylistic preference. Fertig suggests that, if Wulfila's translation followed a strict principle of adherence to the Greek original, he would not have inserted pronouns unless virtually forced to do so by the grammar of Gothic (2000: 10). He also points out that there is no correlation between the presence of overt subject pronouns and the ambiguity of verbal endings, *pace* Streitberg (1920: 185), and speculates that the overt pronouns that we see may be just 'the tip of the iceberg' of what we would find in idiomatic Gothic (2000: 11). As regards the data itself, Fertig observes, following Schulze (1924: 96–100), that instances of non-nominative pronouns in Greek non-finite constructions often correspond to overt nominative pronominal subjects in Gothic finite clauses, but even more often correspond to null subjects; he takes this deviation from Greek to indicate that null subjects were a native possibility in Gothic, as does Schulze (1924: 107). Furthermore, Gothic pronouns tended to be inserted when the antecedent was non-topical, though

TABLE 5.3. **All subjects in Gothic finite clauses in the Gospel of Matthew**

|             | Full        | Pronominal | Null         | Total |
|-------------|-------------|------------|--------------|-------|
| Main        | 89 (32.4%)  | 15 (5.5%)  | 171 (62.2%)  | 275   |
| Subordinate | 70 (30.6%)  | 16 (7.0%)  | 143 (62.4%)  | 229   |
| Conjunct    | 105 (42.2%) | 9 (3.6%)   | 135 (54.2%)  | 249   |
| Total       | 264         | 40         | 449          | 753   |

TABLE 5.4. **Referential pronominal subjects in the Gothic Gospel of Matthew, by clause type**

|             | Overt      | Null        | Total |
|-------------|------------|-------------|-------|
| Main        | 15 (13.9%) | 93 (86.1%)  | 108   |
| Subordinate | 16 (15.4%) | 88 (84.6%)  | 104   |
| Conjunct    | 9 (15.8%)  | 48 (84.2%)  | 57    |
| Total       | 40         | 229         | 269   |

TABLE 5.5. **Referential pronominal subjects in the Gothic Gospel of Matthew, by person and number**

| Person | N      | Overt       | Null        | Total |
|--------|--------|-------------|-------------|-------|
| 1      | sg     | 11 (19.0%)  | 47 (81.0%)  | 58    |
|        | pl     | 2 (11.1%)   | 16 (88.9%)  | 18    |
| 2      | sg     | 8 (27.6%)   | 21 (72.4%)  | 29    |
|        | pl     | 8 (14.8%)   | 46 (85.2%)  | 54    |
| 3      | sg     | 4 (6.1%)    | 62 (93.9%)  | 66    |
|        | pl     | 7 (15.9%)   | 37 (84.1%)  | 44    |
|        | Totals | 40          | 229         | 269   |

were not always (2000: 13). Fertig uses this possibility to argue that Gothic occupied a different position in the typology of null subject languages from Greek, a conclusion I do not feel is necessarily warranted by the (extremely limited) data; instead I take the view of Held (1903: viii), that these deviations were merely stylistic.

For the present work I supplemented the work of Ferraresi (2005) and Fertig (2000) with an exhaustive investigation of the transmitted fragments of the Gospel of Matthew. The results are summarized in Table 5.3. The relevant subset of these, referential pronominal subjects, is presented in Table 5.4, which excludes full DP subjects as well as subjects elided under coordination, expletives, subject gaps in relative clauses, and the understood subject of imperative clauses and optative clauses with imperative force, and is ordered by clause type. Table 5.5 presents the same data by person and number. Figures 5.1 and 5.2 illustrate.

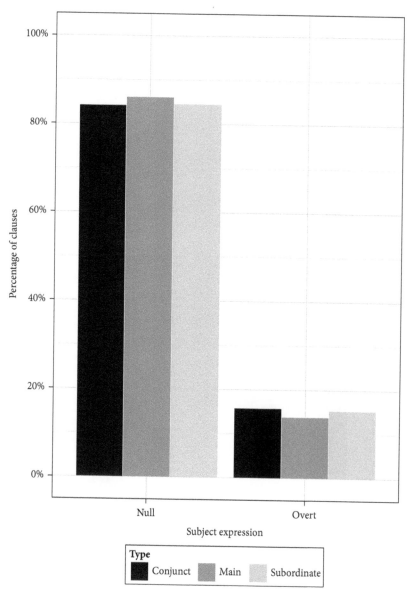

FIGURE 5.1 Referential pronominal subjects in the Gothic Gospel of Matthew, by clause type

The difference between main and subordinate clauses in Gothic in terms of occurrence of overt vs. null referential pronominal subjects is not statistically signifi-cant (p=0.8466), and neither is the effect of person and number (p=0.0807). Examples of null subjects in main and subordinate clauses respectively are given in (1) and (2).

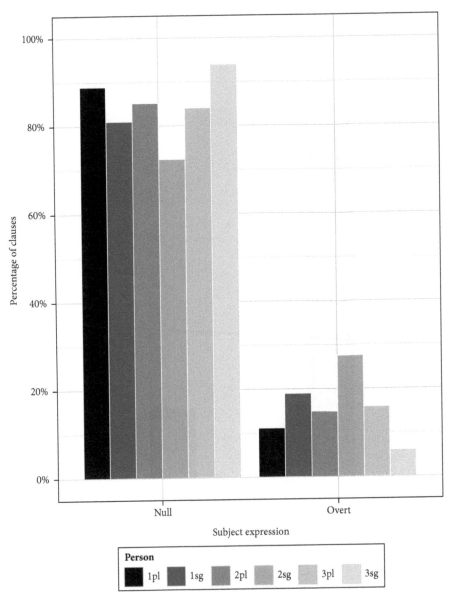

FIGURE 5.2 Referential pronominal subjects in the Gothic Gospel of Matthew, by person and number

(1)  andnemun        mizdon      seina
     take.3PL.PRET   reward.ACC  their.ACC
     'They have their reward' (Matthew 6:2)

(2)  ...ei    qemjau          gatairan     witoþ      aiþþau  praufetuns
     ...that  come.1SG.OPT    destroy.INF  law.ACC    or      prophets.ACC
     '...that I have come to destroy the law or the prophets' (Matthew 5: 17)

Ferraresi (2005: 59) also mentions that 'due to its null subject nature, Gothic does not have [overt] expletive subjects either'. An example of the absence of an overt expletive is given in (3).

(3)  Ganah          siponi        ei    wairþai           swe  laisareis    is
     suffice.3SG    disciple.ACC  that  become.3SG.OPT    as   teacher.NOM  his.NOM
     'It is enough for the disciple that he be as his master' (Matthew 10: 25)

Where subject pronouns are included, the intended interpretation is clearly as focused or contrastive, as in (4).

(4)  hausideduþ        þatei  qiþan   ist:        ni    horinos.
     heard.2PL.PRET    that   said    is.3SG      NEG   whore.2SG.OPT
     aþþan   ik    qiþa        izwis...
     but     I     say.1SG     you.DAT...
     'You have heard it said that you should not commit adultery. But I say to you...'
     (Matthew 5: 27–8)

In addition, I compared these findings to the Majority Text of the Greek New Testament (see section 1.4.1 for details). In none of the 229 instances of a null referential subject in the Gothic Gospel of Matthew does the Greek text contain a corresponding overt pronoun, a result consistent with those of Ferraresi (2005) and Fertig (2000). In 33 of the 40 cases of subject pronouns in finite clauses, the pronoun directly corresponds to a Greek pronoun (though not necessarily one that is in the nominative case). In a further six cases the pronoun corresponds to a Greek third person demonstrative o (singular) or οι (plural): this is the case in Matthew 8: 32, 9: 31, 26: 66, 26: 70, 27: 4, and 27: 66. In only one case in this sample (which is much smaller than that considered in Tables 5.1 and 5.2, from Ferraresi 2005) does the subject pronoun in Gothic correspond to nothing overt in the Majority Text: this example is given in (5).

(5)  jabai  in  Saudaumjam  waurþeina                  mahteis      þos    waurþanons
     if     in  Sodom       became.3PL.OPT.PRET        powers.NOM   those  become
     in  izwis,  aiþþau  eis   weseina                  und    hina  dag
     in  you     or      they  remain.3PL.OPT.PRET      until  this  day
     'if those great works done in you had been done in Sodom, they would have remained until this day' (Matthew 11: 23)

The expression of the pronoun here may be linked to its presence in the apodosis of a conditional, a rare construction in Gothic; the translator may have felt that the presence of the antecedent in the protasis might not have been enough to guarantee the correct interpretation.

Null objects also appear to be possible in Gothic. I have not conducted a quantitative investigation due to the difficulty of identifying which verbs require an overt object; however, clear examples can be found, as in (6) and (7).

(6)  mis      tawideduþ
     me.DAT   done.2PL.PRET
     'you have done it to me' (Matthew 25: 40)

(7)  iþ   Iesus   qaþ   du   imma:   þu    qiþis
     but  Jesus   said  to   him     you   say
     'and Jesus said to him: "So you say."' (Matthew 27: 11)

These examples follow the Greek in the omission of any object. However, as we have seen, Wulfila seems to have been capable of deviating from the *Vorlage* if he had reason to do so (cf. section 1.4.1); it is therefore not unreasonable to hypothesize that null objects were natively possible in Gothic.

### 5.2.2 *Old Norse*

Whereas in most of this book examples and data from Old Icelandic have been used to illustrate the behaviour of the older Scandinavian languages, with regard to null arguments it is Old Swedish for which the most quantitative data is available. Falk (1993), in a paper devoted mostly to non-referential null subjects in the history of Swedish, observes that Old Swedish also permitted null referential subjects, as in (8).

(8)  þer   diþi     ok    drak   miolk   af   moþor        spina
     there sucked   and   drank  milk    of   mother.GEN    teats
     'There he sucked and drank milk from his mother's teats'
     (*Tjuvabalken in Den äldre Codex af Westgöta-Lagen*, dated 1225; Falk 1993: 143, her (1a))

A thorough recent study, Håkansson (2008), also highlights the existence of such examples, although emphasizing their rarity:

(9)  þar   gierþi   kirchiu   aþra
     there built    church    other
     'There they built another church'
     (*Guta Saga*; Håkansson 2008: 14, his (1.3))

Håkansson (2008: 101) also concludes that referential null subjects are most frequently found in main clauses. Of the 540 main clauses investigated, 31 (5.7%) had null subjects, as opposed to only 12 of 513 subordinate clauses (2.3%). Furthermore, whereas 44 of 765 third person referential subjects (5.8%) are null, this is the case for only 3 of 164 first person subjects (1.8%) and 0 of 132 second person subjects (Håkansson 2008: 115). As noted by Rosenkvist (2009: 158), these patterns appear to be similar to those found in OHG (section 5.2.4).

A number of works have addressed the situation in Old Icelandic. The possibility of null arguments was investigated by Nygaard (1894, 1906), and the most extensive discussion in terms of generative syntactic theory is that of Sigurðsson (1993), building on empirical work by Hjartardóttir (1987). Here I will limit myself to discussing the data; Sigurðsson's theoretical approach will be discussed in section 5.3. Faarlund (2004: 221) also discusses the issue briefly, arguing that 'Old Norse is not a regular "*pro*-drop" language' and that 'deletion of a specified subject is rare' (2004: 223; cf. also Faarlund 1994: 56, Rögnvaldsson 1990). However, as Rosenkvist (2009: 157) laments, there appear to be no quantitative studies of null subjects comparable to those carried out for e.g. OHG. Hróarsdóttir (1996: 130) reports that she found thirteen examples of referential null subjects in her sample of Icelandic between 1730 and 1750, but the numbers given are absolute, and hence there is no way of comparing this to the number of overt subjects in the sample; clausal context (main or subordinate) is also not mentioned.

Null non-referential subjects are the norm in Old Icelandic, as pointed out by Faarlund (2004: 220) and illustrated by (10) (his (68)a).

(10)  var    þá    myrkt   af   nátt
      was   then   dark   at   night
      'Then it was dark at night'

However, referential subjects and objects may also be null, as in (11) and (12) from Sigurðsson (1993) (fourteenth century; his (1) and (2)).

(11)  ok   kom   hann   þangat,   ok   var   Hoskuldr uti,          er     reið  í    tún
      and  came  he     there     and  was   H.             outdoors when  rode into field
      'And he$_i$ came there, and Hoskuldr was outside when he$_i$ rode into the field'

(12)  dvergrinn   mælti,   at   sa    baugr   skyldi   vera   hverjum
      dwarf.DEF   said     that  the   ring    should   be     anyone.DAT
      hofuðsbani,   er   átti
      headbane   that  possessed
      'The dwarf said that the ring would bring death to anyone who possessed it'

A quantitative investigation of null subjects in Old Icelandic is now possible, due to the availability of a pre-final version of the IcePaHC corpus of historical Icelandic (version 0.9.1; Wallenberg et al. 2011). Using this corpus I have investigated the frequency of null vs. overt pronominal subjects in texts from the twelfth and

TABLE 5.6. Referential pronominal subjects in Old Icelandic finite clauses in IcePaHC 0.9.1, by text and clause type

| Text | Clause type | Overt | Null | Total |
|---|---|---|---|---|
| *First Grammatical Treatise* (1150.FIRSTGRAMMAR.SCI-LIN) | Main | 55 (96.5%) | 2 (3.5%) | 57 |
| | Subordinate | 102 (80.3%) | 25 (19.7%) | 127 |
| | Conjunct | 25 (92.6%) | 2 (7.4%) | 27 |
| | Total | 182 (86.3%) | 29 (13.7%) | 211 |
| *Íslensk hómilíubók* (1150.HOMILIUBOK.REL-SER) | Main | 610 (98.9%) | 7 (1.1%) | 617 |
| | Subordinate | 1120 (98.2%) | 20 (1.8%) | 1140 |
| | Conjunct | 239 (95.6%) | 11 (4.4%) | 250 |
| | Total | 1969 (98.1%) | 38 (1.9%) | 2007 |
| *Jarteinabók* (1210.JARTEIN.REL-SAG) | Main | 126 (99.2%) | 1 (0.8%) | 127 |
| | Subordinate | 228 (87.7%) | 32 (12.3%) | 260 |
| | Conjunct | 144 (94.7%) | 8 (5.3%) | 152 |
| | Total | 498 (92.4%) | 41 (7.6%) | 539 |
| *Þorláks saga helga* (1210.THORLAKUR.REL-SAG) | Main | 149 (100.0%) | 0 (0.0%) | 149 |
| | Subordinate | 312 (97.8%) | 7 (2.2%) | 319 |
| | Conjunct | 117 (95.1%) | 6 (4.9%) | 123 |
| | Total | 578 (97.8%) | 13 (2.2%) | 591 |
| *Íslendinga saga* (1250.STURLUNGA.NAR-SAG) | Main | 497 (99.4%) | 3 (0.6%) | 500 |
| | Subordinate | 358 (97.0%) | 11 (3.0%) | 369 |
| | Conjunct | 248 (93.9%) | 16 (6.1%) | 264 |
| | Total | 1103 (97.4%) | 30 (2.6%) | 1133 |
| *Egils saga* (Theta manuscript; 1250.THETUBROT.NAR-SAG) | Main | 65 (98.5%) | 1 (1.5%) | 66 |
| | Subordinate | 94 (98.9%) | 1 (1.1%) | 95 |
| | Conjunct | 26 (96.3%) | 1 (3.7%) | 27 |
| | Total | 185 (98.4%) | 3 (1.6%) | 188 |
| *Jómsvíkinga saga* (1260.JOMSVIKINGAR.NAR-SAG) | Main | 263 (99.2%) | 2 (0.8%) | 265 |
| | Subordinate | 542 (97.5%) | 14 (2.5%) | 556 |
| | Conjunct | 344 (95.8%) | 15 (4.2%) | 359 |
| | Total | 1149 (97.4%) | 31 (2.6%) | 1180 |
| *Grey Goose Laws* (*Grágás*; 1270.GRAGAS.LAW-LAW) | Main | 68 (94.4%) | 4 (5.6%) | 72 |
| | Subordinate | 171 (85.1%) | 30 (14.9%) | 201 |
| | Conjunct | 58 (95.1%) | 3 (4.9%) | 61 |
| | Total | 297 (88.9%) | 37 (11.1%) | 334 |
| *Morkinskinna* (1275.MORKIN.NAR-HIS) | Main | 428 (93.4%) | 30 (6.6%) | 458 |
| | Subordinate | 508 (95.3%) | 25 (4.7%) | 533 |
| | Conjunct | 355 (90.8%) | 36 (9.2%) | 391 |
| | Total | 1291 (93.4%) | 91 (6.6%) | 1382 |

thirteenth centuries. In the IcePaHC, referential null subjects (*pro*) are tagged distinctly from subjects elided under coordination (*con*) and null expletives (*exp*), using *pro* only when an analysis in terms of one of the other two is impossible. This makes the search for relevant examples relatively simple. The results are presented in Table 5.6 and Figure 5.3.

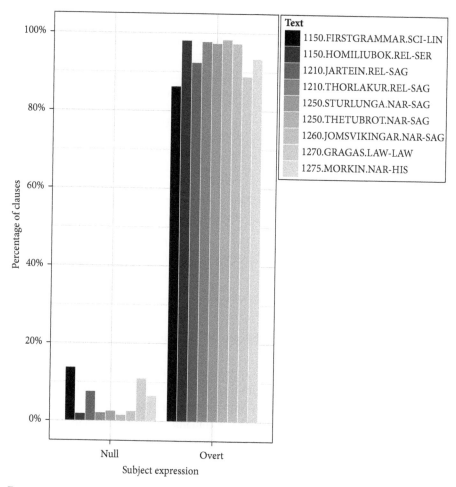

FIGURE 5.3 Referential pronominal subjects in Old Icelandic finite clauses in IcePaHC 0.9.1, by text

In contrast to Gothic, the proportions of null subjects in these texts are uniformly low, and never above 20 per cent. Some texts provide better evidence of a null subject property in Old Icelandic than others: while the *Íslensk hómilíubók* and the *Egils saga* manuscript contain few unambiguous examples, for instance, the *First Grammatical Treatise* and *Morkinskinna* contain a robust number. The effect of clause type (main vs. subordinate) is significant only for the *First Grammatical Treatise* (p = 0.0031), *Jarteinabók* (p < 0.0001), *Íslendinga saga* (p = 0.0111), and the *Grey Goose Laws* (p = 0.0390). The effect in these texts—null subjects are more common in subordinate clauses than in main clauses—is the opposite of that found by Håkansson (2008)

TABLE 5.7. Referential pronominal subjects in finite clauses in the *First Grammatical Treatise* and *Morkinskinna*, by person and number

| Text | Person | N | Overt | Null | Total |
|------|--------|---|-------|------|-------|
| *First Grammatical Treatise* | 1 | sg | 78 (100.0%) | 0 (0.0%) | 78 |
| | | pl | 6 (100.0%) | 0 (0.0%) | 6 |
| | 2 | sg | 14 (100.0%) | 0 (0.0%) | 14 |
| | | pl | 0 | 0 | 0 |
| | 3 | sg | 63 (71.6%) | 25 (28.4%) | 88 |
| | | pl | 21 (84.0%) | 4 (16.0%) | 25 |
| | | Totals | 182 | 29 | 211 |
| *Morkinskinna* | 1 | sg | 269 (99.3%) | 2 (0.7%) | 271 |
| | | pl | 79 (95.2%) | 4 (4.8%) | 83 |
| | 2 | sg | 185 (99.5%) | 1 (0.5%) | 186 |
| | | pl | 13 (100.0%) | 0 (0.0%) | 13 |
| | 3 | sg | 562 (90.1%) | 62 (9.9%) | 624 |
| | | pl | 183 (89.3%) | 22 (10.7%) | 205 |
| | | Totals | 1291 | 91 | 1382 |

for Old Swedish and that found in the early West Germanic languages (for which see sections 5.2.3–5).[3]

Person also has a strong effect on expression (see Table 5.7 and Figures 5.4 and 5.5), and in this respect my data agrees with that of Nygaard (1906: 8–9) and Hjartardóttir (1987) for Old Icelandic as well as with that of Håkansson (2008: 106) for Old Swedish.[4] The *First Grammatical Treatise* contains no first or second person null subjects at all, and for both texts investigated the effect of first vs. non-first person is statistically significant ($p < 0.0001$ for both; cf. the discussion of the early West Germanic languages in sections 5.2.3–5). The effect of number in the third person is not significant (*First Grammatical Treatise*, $p = 0.3005$; *Morkinskinna*, $p = 0.7897$).

A problematic factor that must be noted is the potential availability of 'quirky' or 'oblique' subjects, i.e. subjects in a case other than the nominative, in Old Icelandic. Opinions vary on whether this property, widely acknowledged to hold for modern Icelandic, also held for Old Icelandic, or whether the relevant elements are objects; Rögnvaldsson (1991, 1995), Haugan (1998), Barðdal (2000, 2009), and Barðdal and Eyþórsson (2005, 2012) argue that they are subjects, whereas Faarlund (2001, 2004: 194–5) argues against this on the basis that non-subjects other than predicate

[3] A reviewer suggests that null subjects in subordinate clauses in Old Icelandic might be analysable as (null) long-distance reflexives, and that this difference between Old Icelandic and the other Northwest Germanic languages could then be reduced to an independent property, namely the availability of long-distance reflexivization in this language. This intriguing suggestion warrants further investigation.

[4] Dual pronouns are treated as plural for the purposes of Table 5.7.

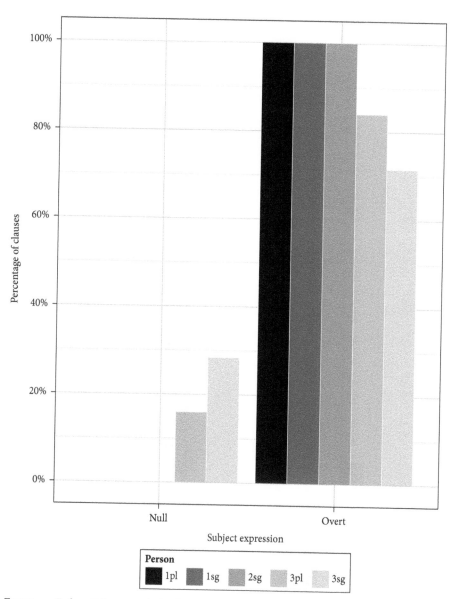

FIGURE 5.4 Referential pronominal subjects in finite clauses in the *First Grammatical Treatise*, by person and number

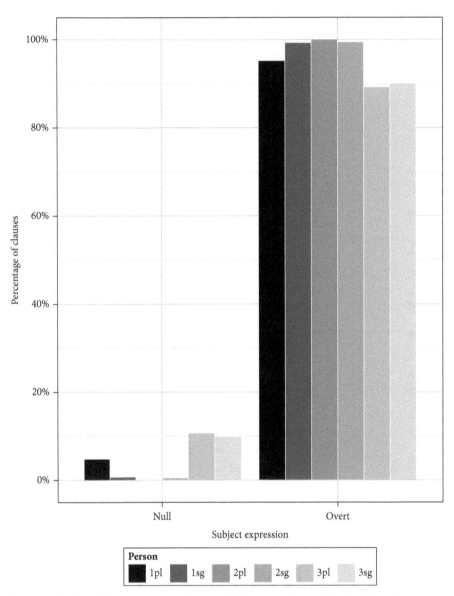

FIGURE 5.5 Referential pronominal subjects in finite clauses in the *Morkinskinna*, by person and number

complements otherwise never occur in the nominative in Old Icelandic. Since the IcePaHC corpus takes the former view and tags as subjects constituents that may be in the dative or the genitive, I have followed their annotation scheme and assumed that these constituents are indeed subjects.[5] This is important to note when comparing the data for Old Icelandic to that for other older Germanic languages. My assumption for these is that all subjects take nominative case and that non-nominative arguments cannot be subjects, which is not uncontroversial (see Harris 1973; Allen 1995; Barðdal and Eyþórsson 2005) but is made largely for ease of quantitative investigation. Though it affects the classification of the data, this assumption in fact has minimal bearing on the analysis presented in section 5.3, for which the grammatical relations involved are irrelevant.

Null objects are also found in early Icelandic texts such as the *First Grammatical Treatise*, e.g. (13).

(13)  leka  myndi  húsið,    ef   eigi  mændi    smiðurinn
      leak  may    house.DEF if   not  roof.SBJV smith.DEF
      'A house may leak if a craftsman does not roof it'
      (1150.FIRSTGRAMMAR.SCI-LIN,.71)

Finally, Kinn (2013) has looked at null arguments in Old Norwegian. She finds that, as in Old Swedish and the West Germanic languages, null subjects are more common in main than subordinate clauses. This indicates an early difference between Old Icelandic and what were to become the Mainland Scandinavian languages. A further finding of Kinn (2013) is that, as in other early Northwest Germanic languages, null subjects in the first and second person are extremely rare. As in the other languages, examples of null objects in Old Norwegian can also be found.

### 5.2.3 *Old English*

Compared to e.g. clausal constituent order, the availability of null arguments in OE has been little investigated, and the literature contains conflicting claims.[6] Hulk and van Kemenade (1995: 245) state that 'the phenomenon of referential *pro*-drop does not exist in Old English'; van Gelderen (2000: 137), on the other hand, claims that 'Old English has pro-drop' (cf. also van Gelderen 2013). Mitchell (1985: 633) apparently takes a middle ground, suggesting that the possibility of leaving arguments unexpressed 'occurs (or survives) only spasmodically' in OE. In this section I will show that there is an element of truth in all three suggestions. The availability of the

---

[5] This decision taken by the annotators is intended to ease retrieval rather than as a theoretical statement, though Wallenberg, Sigurðsson, and Ingason (2011) argue that there are good reasons to analyse Old Icelandic this way.

[6] The data in this section was first reported in Walkden (2013b).

YCOE (Taylor et al. 2003) makes it possible to conduct a quantitative investigation of null arguments on a larger scale than carried out before.

It is not a new observation that OE contains examples of referential null subjects. Pogatscher (1901) provides a large number of examples, which Visser (1963–73) and Mitchell (1985) take into account in their overview works on English historical syntax. Pogatscher's data must be used with caution, since he conflates all examples of subject omission, including those which would be grammatical in modern English, such as coordination reduction as found in (14) (van Gelderen 2000: 124). However, many of Pogatcher's examples can only be analysed as true null referential subjects; (15) is of this kind.

(14)    The king went to Normandy and met the bishop.

(15)    Nu     scylun   hergan   hefaenricaes                    uard
        now    must     praise   heavenly-kingdom.GEN   guard
        'Now we must praise the lord of the heavenly kingdom'
        (*Caedmon's Hymn*, Cambridge University Library MS M, line 1; van Gelderen
        2000: 126, her (16))

Example (15) is from the eighth-century Northumbrian version of *Caedmon's Hymn*. In other versions transmitted in different manuscripts, the subject is expressed as a pronoun. Example (16) is of this kind.

(16)    Nu we sculan herian heofonrices Weard.
        (Bodleian Library MS T$_1$, line 1; van Gelderen 2000: 126, her (17))

Corpus Christi Oxford MS 279 (MS O) contains interesting palaeographical evidence with regard to this sentence: it seems as if the scribe initially copied *Nu sculan* 'Now must' but then inserted the pronoun, yielding *Nu we sculan* 'Now we must' (see Kiernan 1990: 164 for discussion of this variability). This leads to a concern, also voiced by Pogatscher (1901: 277): if subject omission became rarer and rarer through the diachrony of English, scribes may have made 'intelligent revisions' (Kiernan 1990: 164) to fill in omitted subjects, and this could skew our data in the direction of over-representation of pronouns, particularly in texts that only survive in late manuscripts. A similar problem is caused by the insertion of pronouns by modern editors of OE texts (Pogatscher 1901: 275–6). As the YCOE (Taylor et al. 2003) is based on critical editions, this could also lead to over-representation of pronouns in the data reported here. In what follows it is important to bear in mind that null subjects may have been more frequent in actual OE usage than this section suggests.

As in the IcePaHC, referential null subjects have their own tag (*pro*) in the YCOE, distinct from cases of coordination reduction (*con*) and null expletives (*exp*). The principle guiding annotation is that *pro* is only used when *con* and *exp* are independently ruled out. Searching for relevant examples is therefore relatively simple. Nevertheless, a pilot search for all instances of *pro* uncovered two broad classes of examples which would be dubious as support for a prototypical referential null subject analysis.

First, in a number of cases, the verbal mood is subjunctive and the clause delivers an order or recipe, as in (17).[7]

(17)  gemenge   wið   buteran
      mix.SBJV   with   butter
      'Mix with butter'
      (colaece,Lch_II_[1]:3.8.2.406)

Although the force is that of an instruction, much like imperatives, the form of the verb itself is clearly subjunctive; *(ge)mengan* is a class Ib weak verb, and the expected imperative form here would be *(ge)meng*. The impossibility of an imperative analysis presumably underpins the annotation decision in the YCOE to include *pro* in the syntactic parse of these sentences. Since this 'jussive' or 'hortative' *pro* is extremely common (in the *Benedictine Rule*, 29 of 30 examples of *pro* in main clauses are of this type, and 48 of 52 in the *Heptateuch*), I decided to exclude all clauses containing a subjunctive finite verb from my analysis.

The second category of *pro* that occurs with unexpected frequency is the type illustrated in (18), involving the verb *hatan* 'to be called'. Such examples could be analysed as involving a special type of asyndetic (subject-gap) contact relative clause rather than a true null referential subject; see Mitchell (1985: 186), Dekeyser (1986: 108), and Poppe (2006: 197–201).[8]

(18)  Ualens   wæs   gelæred   from   anum   Arrianiscan   biscepe,
      Valens   was   taught   from   an   Arian   bishop
      Eudoxius   wæs   haten
      Eudoxius   was   called
      'Valens was taught by an Arian bishop called Euxodius.'
      (coorosiu,Or_6:33.151.22.3215)

The pilot search yielded a higher percentage of *pro* in main clauses in *Orosius* than in other texts, at 6.4 per cent (34 examples). However, 27 of these 34 examples involve the verb *hatan*, and all but one of the other seven are cases of 'jussive' *pro* of the type discussed above. The OE *Bede* also contains a number of such examples. The search was therefore refined in order to find and exclude these cases. Results are presented in Table 5.8 and Figure 5.6.

---

[7] Interestingly, (17) also lacks an object, perhaps due to 'recipe drop' (cf. Culy 1996 and Bender 1999).
[8] This construction is available in older stages of German as well (Gärtner 1981; Poppe 2006: 200). Dekeyser (1986: 112–13) in fact argues that it is an 'offshoot' of earlier optionality in the expression of the subject pronoun.

I investigated all texts of over 15,000 words in the corpus in their entirety, as well as *Beowulf*, which can be found in the YCOEP corpus of poetry (Pintzuk and Plug 2001). These larger texts were selected on the basis that their size would make quantitative results less likely to be accidental. Table 5.8 for OE can thus be considered equivalent to Tables 5.4 for Gothic, 5.6 for Old Icelandic, 5.11 for OHG, and

TABLE 5.8. Referential pronominal subjects in OE finite indicative clauses in the YCOE and YCOEP, by text and clause type

| Text | Clause type | Overt | Null | Total |
|---|---|---|---|---|
| *Ælfric's Homilies Supplemental* (coaelhom.03) | Main | 585 (99.8%) | 1 (0.2%) | 586 |
| | Subordinate | 871 (99.8%) | 2 (0.2%) | 873 |
| | Conjunct | 501 (99.4%) | 3 (0.6%) | 504 |
| | Total | 1957 (99.7%) | 6 (0.3%) | 1963 |
| *Ælfric's Lives of Saints* (coaelive.03) | Main | 789 (99.2%) | 6 (0.8%) | 795 |
| | Subordinate | 1137 (99.4%) | 7 (0.6%) | 1144 |
| | Conjunct | 532 (96.4%) | 20 (3.6%) | 552 |
| | Total | 2458 (98.7%) | 33 (1.3%) | 2491 |
| *Bede's History of the English Church* (cobede.02) | Main | 719 (96.6%) | 25 (3.4%) | 744 |
| | Subordinate | 1038 (98.0%) | 21 (2.0%) | 1059 |
| | Conjunct | 377 (92.6%) | 30 (7.4%) | 407 |
| | Total | 2134 (96.6%) | 76 (3.4%) | 2210 |
| *Benedictine Rule* (cobenrul.03) | Main | 144 (99.3%) | 1 (0.7%) | 145 |
| | Subordinate | 177 (98.3%) | 3 (1.7%) | 180 |
| | Conjunct | 29 (100.0%) | 0 (0.0%) | 29 |
| | Total | 350 (98.9%) | 4 (1.1%) | 354 |
| *Beowulf* (cobeowul; from YCOE Poetry) | Main | 190 (78.2%) | 53 (21.8%) | 243 |
| | Subordinate | 139 (93.3%) | 10 (6.7%) | 149 |
| | Conjunct | 24 (92.3%) | 2 (7.7%) | 26 |
| | Total | 353 (84.4%) | 65 (15.6%) | 418 |
| *Blickling Homilies* (coblick.023) | Main | 436 (99.5%) | 2 (0.5%) | 438 |
| | Subordinate | 582 (99.1%) | 5 (0.9%) | 587 |
| | Conjunct | 345 (98.9%) | 4 (1.1%) | 349 |
| | Total | 1363 (99.2%) | 11 (0.8%) | 1374 |
| *Boethius, Consolation of Philosophy* (coboeth.02) | Main | 902 (99.4%) | 5 (0.6%) | 907 |
| | Subordinate | 1095 (99.6%) | 4 (0.4%) | 1099 |
| | Conjunct | 260 (98.5%) | 4 (1.5%) | 264 |
| | Total | 2257 (99.4%) | 13 (0.6%) | 2270 |
| *Ælfric's Catholic Homilies I* (cocathom1.03) | Main | 1271 (99.9%) | 1 (0.1%) | 1272 |
| | Subordinate | 1507 (99.7%) | 4 (0.3%) | 1511 |
| | Conjunct | 648 (99.1%) | 6 (0.9%) | 654 |
| | Total | 3426 (99.7%) | 11 (0.3%) | 3437 |
| *Ælfric's Catholic Homilies II* (cocathom2.03) | Main | 1071 (99.9%) | 1 (0.1%) | 1072 |
| | Subordinate | 1191 (99.7%) | 4 (0.3%) | 1195 |
| | Conjunct | 547 (98.7%) | 7 (1.3%) | 554 |
| | Total | 2809 (99.6%) | 12 (0.4%) | 2821 |

| | | | | |
|---|---|---|---|---|
| *Chrodegang of Metz* (cochdrul) | Main | 83 (97.6%) | 2 (2.4%) | 85 |
| | Subordinate | 168 (100.0%) | 0 (0.0%) | 168 |
| | Conjunct | 43 (97.7%) | 1 (2.3%) | 44 |
| | Total | 294 (99.0%) | 3 (1.0%) | 297 |
| *Anglo-Saxon Chronicle C* (cochronC) | Main | 51 (94.4%) | 3 (5.6%) | 54 |
| | Subordinate | 165 (100.0%) | 0 (0.0%) | 165 |
| | Conjunct | 199 (89.6%) | 23 (10.4%) | 222 |
| | Total | 415 (94.1%) | 26 (5.9%) | 441 |
| *Anglo-Saxon Chronicle D* (cochronD) | Main | 66 (88.0%) | 9 (12.0%) | 75 |
| | Subordinate | 197 (99.0%) | 2 (1.0%) | 199 |
| | Conjunct | 213 (88.4%) | 28 (11.6%) | 241 |
| | Total | 476 (92.4%) | 39 (7.6%) | 515 |
| *Anglo-Saxon Chronicle E* (cochronE.034) | Main | 115 (95.0%) | 6 (5.0%) | 121 |
| | Subordinate | 246 (98.8%) | 3 (1.2%) | 249 |
| | Conjunct | 238 (93.3%) | 17 (6.7%) | 255 |
| | Total | 599 | 26 | 625 |
| *Cura Pastoralis* (cocura.02, cocuraC) | Main | 722 (99.6%) | 3 (0.4%) | 725 |
| | Subordinate | 1504 (99.7%) | 5 (0.3%) | 1509 |
| | Conjunct | 339 (99.4%) | 2 (0.6%) | 341 |
| | Total | 2565 (99.6%) | 10 (0.4%) | 2575 |
| *Gregory's Dialogues C* (cogregdC.024) | Main | 747 (99.7%) | 2 (0.3%) | 749 |
| | Subordinate | 1409 (99.7%) | 4 (0.3%) | 1413 |
| | Conjunct | 651 (99.7%) | 2 (0.3%) | 653 |
| | Total | 2807 (99.7%) | 8 (0.3%) | 2815 |
| *Gregory's Dialogues H* (cogregdH.023) | Main | 240 (100.0%) | 0 (0.0%) | 240 |
| | Subordinate | 424 (100.0%) | 0 (0.0%) | 424 |
| | Conjunct | 117 (99.2%) | 1 (0.8%) | 118 |
| | Total | 781 (99.9%) | 1 (0.1%) | 782 |
| *Herbarium* (coherbar) | Main | 451 (100.0%) | 0 (0.0%) | 451 |
| | Subordinate | 119 (100.0%) | 0 (0.0%) | 119 |
| | Conjunct | 162 (100.0%) | 0 (0.0%) | 162 |
| | Total | 732 (100.0%) | 0 (0.0%) | 732 |
| *Bald's Leechbook* (colaece.02) | Main | 90 (76.3%) | 28 (23.7%) | 118 |
| | Subordinate | 94 (94.0%) | 6 (6.0%) | 100 |
| | Conjunct | 23 (65.7%) | 12 (34.3%) | 35 |
| | Total | 207 (81.8%) | 46 (18.2%) | 253 |
| *Martyrology* (comart3.023) | Main | 182 (99.5%) | 1 (0.5%) | 183 |
| | Subordinate | 242 (98.8%) | 3 (1.2%) | 245 |
| | Conjunct | 206 (98.1%) | 4 (1.9%) | 210 |
| | Total | 630 (98.7%) | 8 (1.3%) | 638 |
| *Orosius* (coorosiu.02) | Main | 344 (99.7%) | 1 (0.3%) | 345 |
| | Subordinate | 707 (99.3%) | 5 (0.7%) | 712 |
| | Conjunct | 299 (93.1%) | 22 (6.9%) | 321 |
| | Total | 1350 (98.0%) | 28 (2.0%) | 1378 |

*(continued)*

TABLE 5.8. **Continued**

| Text | Clause type | Overt | Null | Total |
|------|-------------|-------|------|-------|
| *Heptateuch* (cootest.03) | Main | 748 (99.9%) | 1 (0.1%) | 749 |
| | Subordinate | 804 (99.9%) | 1 (0.1%) | 805 |
| | Conjunct | 450 (98.9%) | 5 (1.1%) | 455 |
| | Total | 2002 (99.7%) | 7 (0.3%) | 2009 |
| *St Augustine's Soliloquies* (cosolilo) | Main | 393 (100.0%) | 0 (0.0%) | 749 |
| | Subordinate | 411 (100.0%) | 0 (0.0%) | 805 |
| | Conjunct | 64 (100.0%) | 0 (0.0%) | 455 |
| | Total | 868 (100.0%) | 0 (0.0%) | 868 |
| *Vercelli Homilies* (coverhom) | Main | 464 (98.9%) | 5 (1.1%) | 469 |
| | Subordinate | 609 (99.3%) | 4 (0.7%) | 613 |
| | Conjunct | 393 (98.3%) | 7 (1.8%) | 400 |
| | Total | 1466 (98.9%) | 16 (1.1%) | 1482 |
| *West-Saxon Gospels* (cowsgosp.03) | Main | 1411 (99.7%) | 4 (0.3%) | 1415 |
| | Subordinate | 1139 (99.7%) | 3 (0.3%) | 1142 |
| | Conjunct | 820 (99.4%) | 5 (0.6%) | 825 |
| | Total | 3370 (99.6%) | 12 (0.4%) | 3382 |
| *The Homilies of Wulfstan* (cowulf.034) | Main | 128 (100.0%) | 0 (0.0%) | 128 |
| | Subordinate | 351 (100.0%) | 0 (0.0%) | 351 |
| | Conjunct | 181 (100.0%) | 0 (0.0%) | 181 |
| | Total | 660 (100.0%) | 0 (0.0%) | 660 |

5.15 for OS, in that it leaves out of consideration other types of null subject such as expletives, subjects elided under coordination, relative clause subject gaps, and imperatives. From Table 5.8 we see that, in the majority of classical OE texts, examples of null referential arguments are so rare as to be potentially considered entirely ungrammatical. However, in certain other texts the phenomenon occurs with a frequency and distribution that cannot be attributed entirely to performance errors.

Many of these texts, including Ælfric's *Catholic Homilies* and *Homilies Supplemental*, as well as the *Benedictine Rule*, *Blickling Homilies*, *Chrodegang of Metz*, the translation of Boethius' *Consolation of Philosophy*, the *Cura Pastoralis*, both manuscripts of *Gregory's Dialogues*, the *Martyrology*, the *Heptateuch*, St Augustine's *Soliloquies*, the *West-Saxon Gospels*, and Wulfstan's *Homilies*, show a frequency of overt pronouns of 98–100 per cent in all clause types. This arguably lends weight to Hulk and van Kemenade's (1995) claim, since one approach to such low figures is to consider these examples ungrammatical; at any rate it is easy to see why such a claim would have been made.

In Ælfric's *Lives of Saints* and *Orosius*, null subjects are found at a substantial frequency only in conjunct clauses. Why this should be the case is unclear, especially

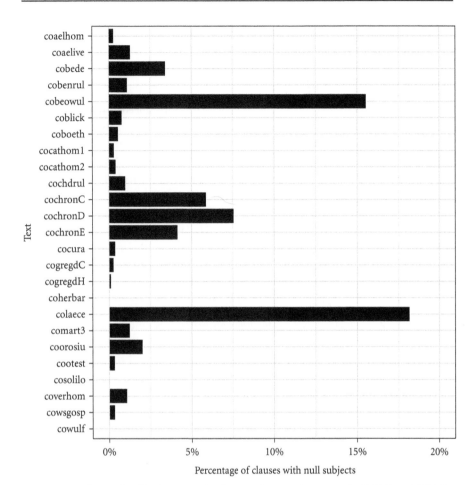

FIGURE 5.6 Referential null subjects in OE finite indicative clauses in the YCOE and YCOEP, by text

for Ælfric, in whose other writings null subjects in general are extremely rare. Perhaps the systems underlying these texts are characterized by a rule of conjunction reduction in which arguments can be shared across conjuncts 'regardless of case or grammatical function', as suggested by Faarlund (1990: 104) for ON. In any case, I will leave these two texts out of consideration in what follows.

The remaining texts are Bede's *History of the English Church*, *Beowulf*, *Bald's Leechbook*, and the C, D, and E manuscripts of the Anglo-Saxon Chronicle. All of these texts exhibit null subjects to a greater extent. Some examples are given below.

(19)  Wæs  ærest  læded  to  Bretta        biscopum
      was   first   led    to  Britons.GEN  bishops
      'He was first led to the priests of the Britons'
      (cobede,Bede_2:2.100.3.926)

(20)  þonne  bið  on  hreþre  under  helm  drepen  biteran  stræle
      then   is   in  heart   under  helm  hit     bitter   dart
      'Then he is hit in the heart, under the helmet, by the bitter dart'
      (cobeowul,54.1745.1443)

In (19) the understood subject is a blind man, who was introduced as the direct object of the previous clause. In (20) it is an unspecified king. Note that this example and others like it preclude a 'pronoun zap' analysis of OE null arguments *à la* Ross (1982) and Huang (1984) on German (see section 5.3.2), since *þonne* 'then' is in initial preverbal position. For more examples of OE null subjects, particularly from *Beowulf*, see van Gelderen (2000: 126–9) and Visser (1963: 4ff.).

In all of these texts, including *Beowulf*, null subjects are more common in main clauses than in subordinate clauses. The effect of clause type in *Beowulf* (main vs. subordinate, as conjunct clauses in general are rare in this text), for instance, is clearly significant ($p < 0.0001$). This result is similar to that found by Håkansson (2008) for Old Swedish, and by Eggenberger (1961) and Axel (2007) for OHG. (21) and (22) are examples of null subjects in subordinate clauses.

(21)  þætte  oft   þæt  wiðerworde  yfel  abeorende  &    ældend      bewereð
      that   often that noxious      evil  enduring   and  concealing  prevents
      'that she (the Church) often suppresses that noxious evil through endurance and connivance'
      (cobede,Bede_1:16.70.33.666)

(22)  þæt  þone  hilderæs      hæl   gedigeð
      that the   battle-charge hale  endure
      'that they will survive the assault unharmed'
      (cobeowul,11.293.236)

This result enables us to fill a hole in Rosenkvist's (2009) table 4. Null subjects in OE were sensitive to clausal status as in OHG and Old Swedish, though not in any absolute way, such that Pogatscher (1901: 261) is correct to state that it is possible for subjects to remain unexpressed both in main and subordinate clauses. Note that in both examples (21) and (22) the verb is in final position. This would be problematic for an attempt to extend to OE Axel's (2007) approach to OHG, which seeks to explain the restricted occurrence of null subjects in subordinate clauses by correlating it with V2 word order in such clauses; cf. section 5.2.4 for discussion. Six of the ten examples of null subjects in indicative subordinate clauses in *Beowulf*, and two of the six examples in *Bald's Leechbook*, cannot be analysed as involving verb-movement to the left periphery.

As in Old Icelandic (section 5.2.2) and OHG (section 5.2.4), person has a statistically significant effect on the expression vs. non-expression of subjects. Van Gelderen (2000: 132–6) makes this into a crucial part of her analysis. Table 5.9 summarizes the data, taken from a study by Berndt (1956); Figure 5.7 illustrates.

TABLE 5.9. Referential pronominal subjects in finite indicative clauses in the *Lindisfarne Gospels* and *Rushworth Glosses*, by person and number (based on Berndt 1956: 65–8; cf. van Gelderen 2000: 133, her table 3.1)

| Text | Person | N | Overt | Null | Total |
|---|---|---|---|---|---|
| *Rushworth Glosses*, part 1 | 1 | sg | 191 (97.0%) | 6 (3.0%) | 197 |
| | | pl | 44 (97.8%) | 1 (2.2%) | 45 |
| | 2 | sg | 90 (88.2%) | 12 (11.8%) | 102 |
| | | pl | 168 (89.4%) | 20 (10.6%) | 188 |
| | 3 | sg | 246 (58.2%) | 177 (41.8%) | 423 |
| | | pl | 141 (58.0%) | 102 (42.0%) | 243 |
| | | Totals | 880 | 318 | 1198 |
| *Lindisfarne Gospels*, part 1 | 1 | sg | 212 (96.4%) | 8 (3.6%) | 220 |
| | | pl | 53 (100.0%) | 0 (0.0%) | 53 |
| | 2 | sg | 103 (87.3%) | 15 (12.7%) | 118 |
| | | pl | 206 (95.8%) | 9 (4.2%) | 215 |
| | 3 | sg | 116 (26.3%) | 325 (73.7%) | 441 |
| | | pl | 108 (36.9%) | 185 (63.1%) | 293 |
| | | Totals | 798 | 542 | 1340 |
| *Lindisfarne Gospels*, part 2 | 1 | sg | 656 (98.6%) | 9 (1.4%) | 665 |
| | | pl | 120 (99.2%) | 1 (0.8%) | 121 |
| | 2 | sg | 308 (93.3%) | 22 (6.7%) | 330 |
| | | pl | 428 (95.7%) | 19 (4.3%) | 447 |
| | 3 | sg | 225 (18.3%) | 1003 (81.7%) | 1228 |
| | | pl | 154 (24.5%) | 475 (75.5%) | 629 |
| | | Totals | 1891 | 1529 | 3420 |
| *Rushworth Glosses*, part 2 | 1 | sg | 528 (96.5%) | 19 (3.5%) | 547 |
| | | pl | 100 (98.0%) | 2 (2.0%) | 102 |
| | 2 | sg | 226 (91.1%) | 22 (8.9%) | 248 |
| | | pl | 302 (83.7%) | 59 (16.3%) | 361 |
| | 3 | sg | 186 (19.0%) | 795 (81.0%) | 981 |
| | | pl | 124 (22.8%) | 420 (77.2%) | 544 |
| | | Totals | 1466 | 1317 | 2783 |

Though in his own tables (1956: 65–8) Berndt distinguishes between subjects elided under coordination and other null referential subjects (1956: 75 n. 1), van Gelderen conflates the two categories in her figures for null subjects in table 3.1. In Table 5.9 I have excluded Berndt's cases of subjects elided under coordination in order to ensure comparability with Table 5.10 and others.

Berndt investigates two texts, the *Lindisfarne Gospels* (Northumbrian) and the *Rushworth Glosses* (of which the first part is Mercian and the second Northumbrian). The effect of third vs. non-third person is significant ($p < 0.0001$) in both parts of each text, as van Gelderen (2000: 132 n. 6) also shows. There is also an effect of number in the third person, with overt subjects preferred for plurals, although the effect is only statistically significant in the *Lindisfarne Gospels* (part 1: $p = 0.0025$, part 2: $p = 0.0023$), not in the *Rushworth Glosses* (part 1: $p = 1$, part 2: $p = 0.0841$). Number has no effect in

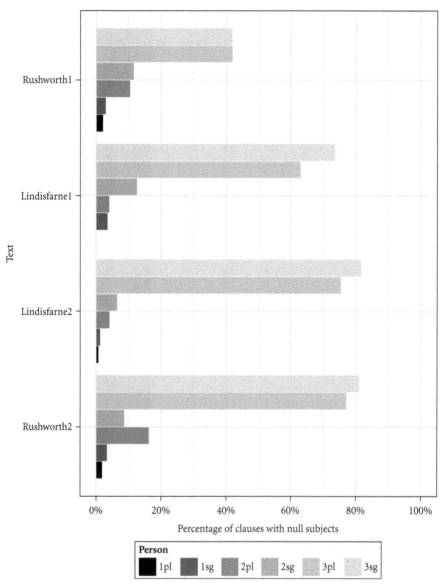

FIGURE 5.7 Referential null subjects in finite indicative clauses in the *Lindisfarne Gospels* and *Rushworth Glosses*, by person and number

TABLE 5.10. Referential pronominal subjects in finite indicative clauses in *Beowulf*, *Bald's Leechbook*, *Bede*, and MS E of the *Chronicle*, by person and number

| Text | Person | N | Overt | Null | Total |
|---|---|---|---|---|---|
| *Beowulf* | 1 | sg | 75 (97.4%) | 2 (2.6%) | 77 |
| | | pl | 21 (100.0%) | 0 (0.0%) | 21 |
| | 2 | sg | 26 (96.3%) | 1 (3.7%) | 27 |
| | | pl | 10 (100.0%) | 0 (0.0%) | 10 |
| | 3 | sg | 172 (80.4%) | 42 (19.6%) | 214 |
| | | pl | 49 (71.0%) | 20 (29.0%) | 69 |
| | | Totals | 353 | 65 | 418 |
| *Bald's Leechbook* | 1 | sg | 1 (100.0%) | 0 (0.0%) | 1 |
| | | pl | 11 (100.0%) | 0 (0.0%) | 11 |
| | 2 | sg | 52 (100.0%) | 0 (0.0%) | 52 |
| | | pl | 0 | 0 | 0 |
| | 3 | sg | 108 (77.1%) | 32 (22.9%) | 140 |
| | | pl | 35 (71.4%) | 14 (28.6%) | 49 |
| | | Totals | 207 | 46 | 253 |
| *Bede* | 1 | sg | 129 (100.0%) | 0 (0.0%) | 129 |
| | | pl | 171 (98.8%) | 2 (1.2%) | 173 |
| | 2 | sg | 69 (100.0%) | 0 (0.0%) | 69 |
| | | pl | 25 (96.2%) | 1 (3.8%) | 26 |
| | 3 | sg | 1504 (97.2%) | 44 (2.8%) | 1548 |
| | | pl | 236 (89.1%) | 29 (10.9%) | 265 |
| | | Totals | 2134 | 76 | 2210 |
| *Chronicle* MS E | 1 | sg | 3 (100.0%) | 0 (0.0%) | 3 |
| | | pl | 18 (100.0%) | 0 (0.0%) | 18 |
| | 2 | sg | 3 (100.0%) | 0 (0.0%) | 3 |
| | | pl | 3 (100.0%) | 0 (0.0%) | 3 |
| | 3 | sg | 297 (97.1%) | 9 (2.9%) | 306 |
| | | pl | 275 (94.2%) | 17 (5.8%) | 292 |
| | | Totals | 599 | 26 | 625 |

the first person (Lindisfarne part 1: $p = 0.3612$, part 2: $p = 0.6570$; Rushworth part 1: $p = 1$, part 2: $p = 0.5558$) and no consistent effect in the second person (Lindisfarne part 1: $p = 0.0067$, part 2: $p = 0.1464$; Rushworth part 1: $p = 0.8449$, part 2: $p = 0.0076$). Similar facts hold for four YCOE texts exhibiting null subjects *Beowulf*, *Bald's Leechbook*, the OE *Bede*, and the *Chronicle* MS E, as shown in Table 5.10 and Figure 5.8, though the proportions of null subjects in general in these texts is much lower.

In both texts the effect of third vs. non-third person is statistically significant ($p < 0.0001$ for both).[9] The effect of number in the third person is not statistically

---

[9] First and second person dual pronouns in *Beowulf* have been treated as plural.

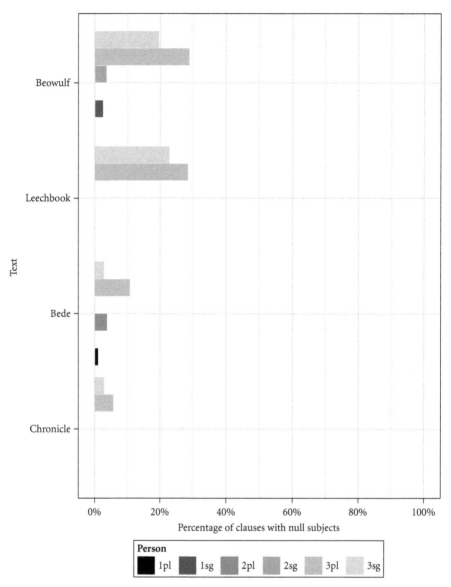

FIGURE 5.8 Referential null subjects in finite indicative clauses in *Beowulf, Bald's Leechbook, Bede,* and MS E of the *Chronicle,* by person and number

significant in any of the texts except *Bede* at p < 0.0001 (*Beowulf:* p = 0.1311; *Bald's Leechbook:* p = 0.4427; *Chronicle* MS E: p = 0.1080).

Among other things, van Gelderen takes this systematicity to show that the null argument property of at least some OE texts cannot be attributed solely to Latin influence: since in Latin overt pronouns are almost never present, if the absence of pronouns in OE resulted entirely from isolated instances of over-literal translation we would expect a random distribution of null subjects across persons and numbers, which is not the case (2000: 133). I concur; furthermore, such a hypothesis would be problematic when dealing with autochthonous texts such as *Beowulf* which display many null arguments despite being universally acknowledged as having no Latin original and displaying little Latin influence.

Likewise, the null argument property of OE cannot be attributed solely to metrical considerations in texts such as *Beowulf*, because this would not account for the greater frequency of null subjects in the third person than in the first and second: all three types of personal pronoun are unstressed monosyllables in OE. Furthermore, such a hypothesis would be problematic when dealing with prose texts such as *Bald's Leechbook*, for which no metrical explanation is available. If translation from Latin and/or metrical considerations played a role in favouring null subjects at all in OE texts, then, it could only have led to a slight general quantitative preference, as neither of these factors is able to account for the person and clause-type asymmetries in OE or the range of texts in which null subjects are found.

Was OE a null subject language, then? The answer appears to be that there is variation. The texts I have investigated that display null subjects robustly have in common with those investigated by Berndt (1956) that they are Anglian (Northumbrian or Mercian) or exhibit Anglian features. Berndt (1956: 59–60) demonstrates this for the *Lindisfarne Gospels* and the *Rushworth Glosses*, in the process noting that they exhibit null subjects where the West Saxon Corpus MS of the Gospels virtually never does (1956: 78–82). Fulk (2009: 96) notes that the OE *Bede* and *Bald's Leechbook* and the D and E manuscripts of the Anglo-Saxon Chronicle, though traditionally assigned to West Saxon, display Anglian features.[10] Though it is agreed that *Bald's Leechbook* in its transmitted form was composed in Winchester (Meaney 1984: 236), Wenisch (1979: 54) argues on a lexical basis that an Anglian (probably Mercian) original must have existed. As for *Beowulf*, Fulk (1992: 309–25) notes a number of Anglian lexical and morphological features. If null subjects can be considered an Anglian feature on the basis of their distribution across texts, it seems fair to suggest, tentatively, that both van Gelderen (2000) and Hulk and van Kemenade (1995) are correct: referential null subjects were not grammatical in classical OE (West Saxon), as exemplified by e.g. the works of Ælfric, but were available, subject to certain restrictions, in Anglian dialects. The key to resolving the apparent contradiction lies

---

[10] The only possible exception is MS C of the Chronicle. Swanton (1996: xxiv) notes that it was produced at Abingdon 'on the border between Wessex and Mercia'. If Mercian influence can be suggested on this basis, then the (few) examples of null subjects in this text cease to present a problem for my hypothesis.

in dispelling the illusion of OE as a monolithic entity: the texts provide evidence for diatopic and diachronic variation.[11]

Finally, null objects can also be found in OE: Ohlander (1943), van der Wurff (1997), and van Gelderen (2000) provide a number of examples, including (23) and (24).

(23) se    here...   gesæt    þæt  lond  and  gedælde
     the   army     invaded  the  land  and  divided
     'The army...invaded the country and divided it up'
     (cochronC,ChronC_[Rositzke]:881.1.762)

(24) hie...  leton  holm  beran /  geafon  on  garsecg
     they   let    sea   bear    gave    on  ocean
     'They let the sea bear him, gave him to the ocean'
     (cobeowul,4.47.41–2)

Van Gelderen (2000: 149) claims that this is expected under her analysis, insofar as all cases are of third person. However, this does not obviously follow, given that she adopts 'a Taraldsen/Platzack [account]' of *pro*-licensing (2000: 125): such accounts predict that a null argument may occur where the verb bears agreement for that element, and OE verbs never agree with their object. See section 5.3.1 for further discussion.

### 5.2.4 Old High German

Null subjects are also possible in OHG, as illustrated by (25) and (26).

(25) Sume      hahet       in cruci
     some-ACC  hang-2PL    to cross
     'Some of them you will crucify'
     (Monsee Fragments XVIII.17; Matthew 23: 34; Axel 2007: 293)

(26) steih       tho   in    skifilin
     stepped.3SG then  into  boat
     'He then stepped into the boat'
     (*Tatian* 193.1; Axel 2007: 293)

The situation for OHG is different from that of the other older Germanic languages in that recent work by Axel (2005, 2007: ch. 6; Axel and Weiß 2011) has brought the language's null subject property to the attention of linguists. Axel presents

---

[11] Berndt (1956: 82–5) considers but rejects the hypothesis of dialectal variation, instead suggesting that the relevant criterion is closeness to the West Saxon 'standard'. However, his argument rests on the claim (justified on functional grounds) that the systematic use of first and second person pronouns was an innovation in colloquial OE; as comparative data from the other early Northwest Germanic languages shows, this is unlikely to have been the case.

TABLE 5.11. Referential pronominal subjects in OHG finite clauses, by text and clause type (based on Axel 2007: 310, her table 2; data from Eggenberger 1961)

| Text | Clause type | Overt | Null | Total |
|------|-------------|-------|------|-------|
| *Isidor* | Main | 61 (56.0%) | 48 (44.0%) | 109 |
| | Subordinate | 85 (91.4%) | 8 (8.6%) | 93 |
| | Total | 146 | 56 | 202 |
| Monsee Fragments | Main | 48 (36.4%) | 84 (63.6%) | 132 |
| | Subordinate | 73 (84.9%) | 13 (15.1%) | 86 |
| | Total | 121 | 97 | 218 |
| *Tatian* | Main | 1434 (59.9%) | 960 (40.1%) | 2394 |
| | Subordinate | 1180 (92.5%) | 95 (7.5%) | 1275 |
| | Total | 2614 | 1055 | 3669 |

quantitative data based on the exhaustive survey of null subjects in OHG texts in Eggenberger (1961: 128, 124–6, 84–6). Table 5.11 (her table 2) is calculated on the basis of this data, and includes only referential pronouns/null subjects and arbitrary pronouns/null subjects. These texts are all early prose texts; in later OHG, such as the writings of Notker, null subjects are basically no longer attested (Axel 2007: 298). Eggenberger does not separate conjunct clauses from other clause types for this purpose. Figure 5.9 illustrates.

Within each text, the effect of clause type is statistically significant ($p < 0.0001$ in all cases). Specifically, as Axel remarks (2007: 309), null subjects are clearly rarer in subordinate clauses than in main clauses. Axel interprets this as evidence that null subjects must follow the finite verb (2007: 311), as proposed by Adams (1987b) for Old French. She argues that (27) (her (27)), for instance, can be analysed as verb-second.

(27)  uuanta    sehente    nigisehent
      because   seeing     NEG-see.3PL
      'because seeing they do not see'
      (*Tatian* 235.15)

Like van Gelderen (2000) for OE, Axel argues that null subjects in OHG cannot be explained away as loan syntax from Latin (2007: 306), since the main/subordinate clause asymmetry has no explanation if null referential subjects were not a grammatical feature of OHG itself. Furthermore, she notes that the *Hildebrandslied*, an autochthonous text, features five instances of null subjects as opposed to 29 overt pronouns. However, Axel resorts to the loan-syntax hypothesis to explain the existence of examples of referential null subjects occurring in unambiguously verb-late clauses in the *Tatian* and Monsee Fragments, since these pose a problem for her hypothesis that such subjects are only licensed when they follow the finite verb

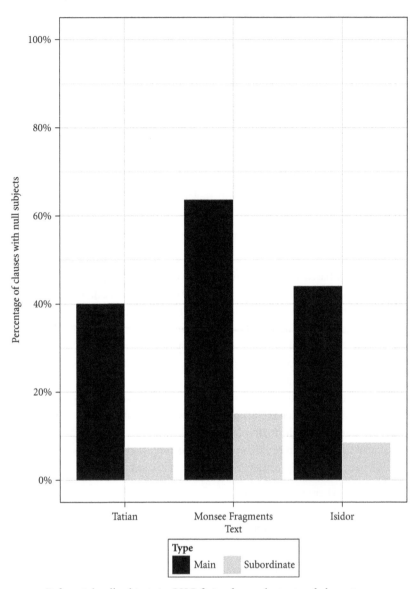

FIGURE 5.9  Referential null subjects in OHG finite clauses, by text and clause type

(2007: 311), suggesting that Latin 'may have had a minor impact' here. Schlachter (2010: 161–3) finds this unconvincing, and gives several examples where Latin influence is unlikely. Furthermore, an analysis of the constituent order patterns in the examples of pronominals in subordinate clauses in the *Isidor* given by Eggenberger (1961: 128) reveals that four of the eight examples of null pronominals cannot be

TABLE 5.12. Referential pronominal subjects in subordinate clauses in *Isidor* by possibility of verb-movement

| V-movement possible? | Overt | Null | Total |
|---|---|---|---|
| Yes | 26 (30.6%) | 4 (50.0%) | 30 |
| No | 59 (69.4%) | 4 (50.0%) | 63 |
| Total | 85 | 8 | 93 |

analysed as involving verb-movement to the left periphery under Axel's assumptions.[12] The distribution is illustrated in Table 5.12.

The difference in verb position between clauses with overt pronominals and clauses with null pronominals is not significant ($p = 0.2666$). This text thus provides no support for the hypothesis that null subjects are licensed only postfinitely in OHG. (28) is one of the four counterexamples.

(28) nibu      fona    zuuem    chiboran    uuerdhe
     NEG-if    from    two      born        become-3SG.SBJV
     'if he is not born of two people'
     (*Isidor* 3.15)

Person also seems to have influenced the availability of null referential subjects, as in Old Swedish, Old Icelandic, and OE. Axel (2007: 315, her table 3) illustrates this once more using data from Eggenberger (1961), reproduced here in Table 5.13 and Figure 5.10.

For each text, third person null referential subjects occur at a higher rate than first or second person null referential subjects ($p < 0.0001$ in all cases).

Much as for the ON and OE texts I have investigated, the effect of number within the third person is not statistically significant for any text: for *Isidor*, $p = 0.7544$; for the Monsee Fragments, $p = 1.0000$; for *Tatian*, $p = 0.0918$. I therefore conclude, provisionally, that number has no effect on the possibility of null subjects in OHG, and that plural and singular referential subjects were equally likely to be null.[13]

---

[12] Clauses were analysed as potentially involving verb-movement to the left periphery if the finite verb was preceded by 0 or 1 constituents or by an XP-SubjPron sequence, in accordance with Axel's own assumptions (see Chapter 3).

[13] Axel also observes (2007: 317) that the choice between the two first person plural endings available in OHG, the shorter -*n*/-*m* vs. the longer -*mēs*, appeared to influence the availability of postverbal null subjects (cf. also Dieter 1900; Harbert 1999). Schlachter (2010: 168–9) is sceptical as to whether this is relevant to the overall system of OHG, suggesting that these clauses can be analysed as adhortatives. Since Axel does not provide quantitative evidence on this point, and since the origins and analysis of the longer ending are debatable (cf. Shields 1996; Jóhannsson 2009), I leave this issue aside here.

TABLE 5.13. Referential pronominal subjects in main clauses in *Isidor*, the Monsee Fragments, and the *Tatian*, by person and number (based on Axel 2007: 315, her table 3; data from Eggenberger 1961)

| Text | Person | N | Overt | Null | Total |
|---|---|---|---|---|---|
| *Isidor* | 1 | sg | 36 (94.7%) | 2 (5.3%) | 38 |
| | | pl | 2 (40.0%) | 3 (60.0%) | 5 |
| | 2 | sg | 3 (60.0%) | 2 (40.0%) | 5 |
| | | pl | 1 (100.0%) | 0 (0.0%) | 1 |
| | 3 | sg | 15 (34.1%) | 29 (65.9%) | 44 |
| | | pl | 4 (25.0%) | 12 (75.0%) | 16 |
| | | Totals | 61 | 48 | 109 |
| Monsee Fragments | 1 | sg | 10 (66.7%) | 5 (33.3%) | 15 |
| | | pl | 2 (66.7%) | 1 (33.3%) | 3 |
| | 2 | sg | 5 (62.5%) | 3 (37.5%) | 8 |
| | | pl | 16 (61.5%) | 10 (38.5%) | 26 |
| | 3 | sg | 12 (18.8%) | 52 (81.3%) | 64 |
| | | pl | 3 (18.8%) | 13 (81.3%) | 16 |
| | | Totals | 48 | 84 | 132 |
| *Tatian* | 1 | sg | 415 (80.1%) | 103 (19.9%) | 518 |
| | | pl | 62 (69.7%) | 27 (30.3%) | 89 |
| | 2 | sg | 131 (60.9%) | 84 (39.1%) | 215 |
| | | pl | 262 (86.2%) | 42 (13.8%) | 304 |
| | 3 | sg | 394 (46.1%) | 460 (53.9%) | 854 |
| | | pl | 170 (41.1%) | 244 (58.9%) | 414 |
| | | Totals | 1434 | 960 | 2394 |

Axel (2007: 299) acknowledges that OHG does not pattern with canonical full null-subject languages such as modern Italian, since overt subjects do not appear to be necessarily emphatic or contrastive. She also argues against a 'topic drop' analysis of OHG null arguments (see section 5.3.2) on the basis of cases such as (25) where the subject is null and a non-subject has been topicalized. She further observes that the cases of null arguments almost exclusively involve subjects, unlike in modern German, for example, in which objects may also be null when topicalized. In general, Axel (2007) does not consider null objects, commenting, for example, that this possibility 'has hardly been discussed in the literature' (2007: 182). Nevertheless, examples can be found, such as (29).

(29)  denne   varant      engilâ    uper   dio   marhâ,   wechant   deotâ,
      then    travel.3PL   angels    over   the   lands    wake.3PL   people
      wîssant   ze   dinge
      lead.3PL   to   judgement
      'Then angels fly over the lands, wake the people, lead them to the judgement'
      (*Muspilli* 79–80; Lockwood 1968: 215)

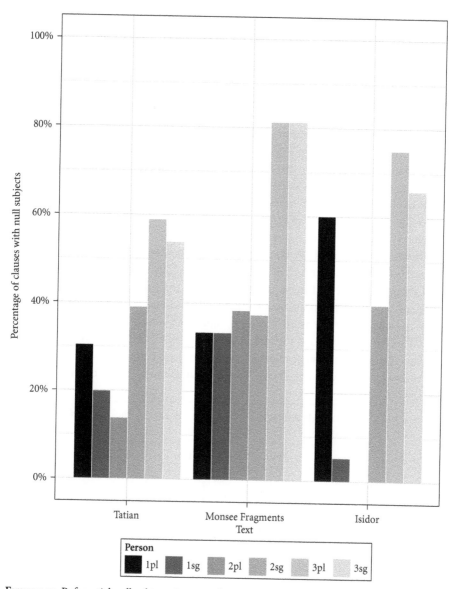

FIGURE 5.10 Referential null subjects in main clauses in OHG, by person and number

Krisch (2009: 211) also gives an example from the Strasbourg Oaths. Such examples would not be expected to occur *at all* under the hypothesis that the possibility of early OHG null subjects was conditioned by rich agreement, since the language lacks object agreement entirely (see section 5.3.1). With this in mind it is difficult to see how Axel's approach, which links the possibility of null arguments to post-finite position, could account for them. Although I accept that topic drop is not a suitable explanation for the OHG facts, then, the existence of examples such as (29) casts doubt on Axel's own analysis.

### 5.2.5  *Old Saxon*

The possibility for subjects to remain unexpressed in OS has occasionally been remarked upon in the literature. Pogatscher (1901: 276–7) mentions it in passing, his main sources being Heyne (1873) and Behaghel (1897), neither of whom devotes more than a few pages to the topic (Heyne 1873: 212, 297; Behaghel 1897: 298). Behrmann (1879) has a more thorough discussion, observing that pronouns can be omitted when there is no nominative antecedent.

At first glance, the *Heliand* appears to contain a relatively high proportion of unexpressed subjects: the figures for the whole text are provided in Table 5.14. However, the style in which the text is written involves a considerable amount of paratactic repetition by means of clauses which could be analysed as conjoined by a null element. As a result, most of these unexpressed subjects could potentially be analysed as cases of conjunction reduction. Once these as well as null expletive subjects, subject gaps in relative clauses, and unexpressed subjects in imperatives are taken out of the picture, the figures are as in Table 5.15 (Figure 5.11).

These figures for null subjects are a lower bound: it is entirely possible that some of the cases I have analysed as conjunction reduction are in fact cases of referential null

TABLE 5.14. **All subjects in OS finite clauses in the *Heliand*, by clause type**

|  | Full | Pronominal | Null | Total |
|---|---|---|---|---|
| Main | 1295 (50.5%) | 969 (37.8%) | 301 (11.7%) | 2565 |
| Subordinate | 636 (28.6%) | 1277 (57.5%) | 307 (13.8%) | 2220 |
| Conjunct | 146 (10.1%) | 97 (6.7%) | 1201 (83.2%) | 1444 |
| Total | 2077 | 2343 | 1809 | 6229 |

TABLE 5.15. **Referential pronominal subjects in the OS *Heliand*, by clause type**

|  | Overt | Null | Total |
|---|---|---|---|
| Main | 969 (93.4%) | 68 (6.6%) | 1037 |
| Subordinate | 1277 (99.4%) | 8 (0.6%) | 1285 |
| Conjunct | 97 (74.6%) | 33 (25.4%) | 130 |
| Total | 2343 | 109 | 2452 |

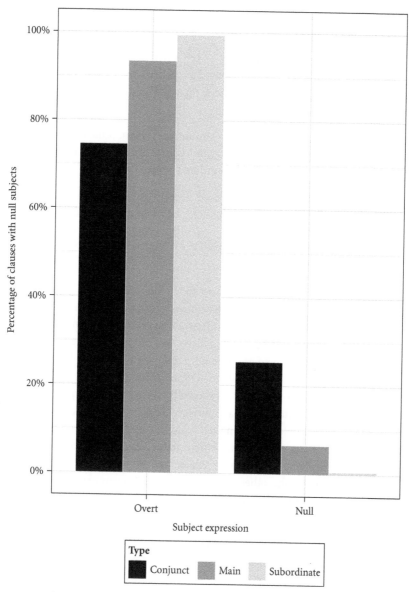

FIGURE 5.11 Referential pronominal subjects in the OS *Heliand*, by clause type

subjects in non-conjunct clauses. Some examples of true referential null subjects I have found are given in (30)–(32) below.

(30) Giuuitun    im          thô    eft    te    Hierusalem    iro    sunu    sôkean
      went.3PL    REFL.DAT    then   after   to    Jerusalem     their   son     seek.INF
      'They then went to Jerusalem to seek their son'
      (*Heliand* 806–7)

(31) gisâhun    iro    barn       biforan,   kindiunge      man,   qualmu      sueltan
      saw.3PL    their   children   before      child-young   men    murder.INSTR   die.INF
      'They saw their young children murdered before them'
      (*Heliand* 749–51)

(32) lîbes        uueldi    ina    bilôsien,   of    he    mahti    gilêstien    sô
      life.GEN    would    him    take        if    he    could    achieve      so
      'he$_i$ would take his$_j$ life if he$_i$ could'
      (*Heliand* 1442)

In all of these cases there is no antecedent in the nominative that is present in the immediately preceding clauses, thus excluding an analysis involving conjunction reduction. In (30), for example, the understood subject is 'Joseph and Mary', yet Joseph is not mentioned in the preceding discourse. In (31) the understood subject is 'the women of Bethlehem', who are present in the preceding clause but in the dative case. Finally, (32) excludes an analysis for OS involving traditional 'topic drop': the verb has moved to the left periphery, as shown by the fact that it precedes the object pronoun, and yet a fronted item (a genitive object) is also present, in preverbal position; cf. Axel's example (25) from OHG and section 5.3.2.

In addition to the 109 examples in which neither manuscript contains an overt subject, there are also 30 examples in which one of the two main manuscripts contains a pronoun but the other does not. Two such examples are given in (33) and (34), here using the parallel edition provided by Sievers (1878).

(33) M: Oc    scal    ic    iu    te    uuarun    seggean
      C: Oc    scal          iu    te    uuaron    seggean
          also   shall   (I)    you   to    truth      say.INF
          'I will also truly tell you…'
          (*Heliand* 1628; Sievers 1878: 114–15)

(34) M: Ac    than           uuillean    te    iuuuomo    herron   helpono   biddean
      C: Ac    than    gi    uuellean    te    iuuuon       herron   helpono   biddean
          but    when   (you)   want.2PL    to    your         lord      help       request.INF
          'But when you want to ask for help from your lord,…'
          (*Heliand* 1573–4; Sievers 1878: 112–13)

In eight of these cases, e.g. (34), it is manuscript M that omits the pronoun; in the other twenty-two it is manuscript C, e.g. (33). It is tempting to speculate, with Pogatscher (1901: 277), that in the manuscripts in which the pronoun is present it represents an addition by a scribe of a later period and that the original contained no pronoun. However, for the purposes of the numbers in Tables 5.14 and 5.15 I have erred on the side of caution and treated all such examples as cases of overt pronouns.

There is a clear effect of clause type (cf. Behrmann 1879: 19): leaving second conjunct clauses out of consideration, the effect of clause type (main vs. subordinate) is statistically significant ($p < 0.0001$). I found only eight examples in the *Heliand* of subordinate clauses that unambiguously contained a referential null subject. (35) is one of these.

(35)  that   brôđer      brûd       an   is   bed   nâmi
      that   brother.GEN  bride.ACC  to   his  bed   take.SBJV
      '...that he takes his brother's bride to his bed'
      (*Heliand* 2713)

It is therefore safe to conclude that null subjects were strongly dispreferred in subordinate clauses, if not universally disallowed; this ties in with findings for Old Swedish (5.2.2), OE (5.2.3), and OHG (5.2.4).

Next let us consider the effect of person and number on the occurrence of referential null subjects in OS. Table 5.16 and Figure 5.12 present the data.

All but four examples of null referential subjects found were third person, though a few examples where the manuscripts differ would be counterexamples if original: (33) and (34) are of this type, involving first person singular and second person plural subjects respectively. There is also a statistically significant effect of third vs. non-third person ($p < 0.0001$). Within the third person, the percentage of plural referential pronominal subjects that are null is higher than that of singular referential pronominal subjects. This is the opposite tendency to that found by van Gelderen (2000) based on Berndt's (1956) data, although the effect is not quite as clear-cut as the others found in this section ($p = 0.0275$).

TABLE 5.16. Referential pronominal subjects in the OS *Heliand*, by person and number

| Person | N | Overt | Null | Total |
|---|---|---|---|---|
| 1 | sg | 262 (100.0%) | 0 (0.0%) | 262 |
|   | pl | 61 (100.0%) | 0 (0.0%) | 61 |
| 2 | sg | 247 (99.2%) | 2 (0.8%) | 249 |
|   | pl | 230 (99.1%) | 2 (0.9%) | 232 |
| 3 | sg | 1089 (94.5%) | 63 (5.5%) | 1152 |
|   | pl | 454 (91.5%) | 42 (8.5%) | 496 |
|   | Totals | 2343 | 109 | 2452 |

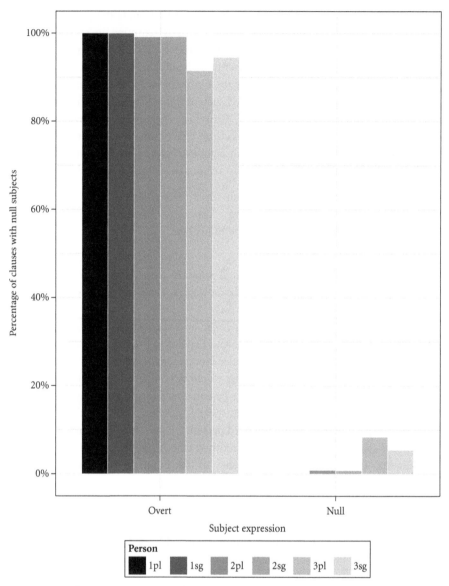

FIGURE 5.12 Referential pronominal subjects in the OS *Heliand*, by person and number

As argued by van Gelderen (2000: 133) for OE and Axel (2007: 306) for OHG, I take it that the non-random distribution of null subjects in this text, as illustrated by Tables 5.15 and 5.16, militates against the argument that their presence is due simply to Latin influence; 'pure' translation can be ruled out, since, although the *Heliand* definitely had Latin sources, primarily Tatian's *Diatessaron* (cf. Sievers 1878: xli and

Haferland 2001, 2004 for discussion), the Germanicized content and alliterative style demonstrate that it represents a substantial piece of original verse composition. These distributional considerations also suggest that a purely prosodic/metrical analysis is likely to be insufficient to explain the data, all other things being equal.

Finally, as in all the other early Germanic languages under discussion, null objects can also be found in the OS *Heliand*, as illustrated by the following section of discourse explaining why not to amass a hoard of earthly treasures.

(36)  huuand   it   rotat   hîr   an   roste,   endi   regintheoƀos   farstelad,
      because   it   rusts   here   to   rust   and   thieves       steal
      uurmi   auuardiad...
      worms   spoil
      'because it rusts away, thieves steal (it), worms spoil (it)...'
      (*Heliand* 1644–5)

### 5.2.6 *Summary: distribution of null arguments in early Germanic*

In Gothic, null referential pronominal subjects are the norm in all persons, numbers, and clause types. Referential pronominal objects may also be null.

In the Northwest Germanic languages the distribution of referential null arguments is very similar (cf. Rosenkvist 2009). In all of these languages, referential null subjects are not obligatory and are outnumbered by overt pronominal subjects. The proportion of third person null referential subjects in these languages is considerably higher than that of first and second person null referential subjects.[14] Null subjects of all types are rarer in subordinate clauses than they are in main clauses (except in Old Icelandic). Finally, null objects are allowed in all of these languages.

These facts may cast doubt on Hopper's (1975: 31) assertion that 'in the early Germanic languages the use of a pronominal subject was probably usual', depending on how 'usual' is understood. These are the facts I will be attempting to account for in the next section.

## 5.3  Analysis of null arguments in early Germanic

### 5.3.1 *Null arguments conditioned by rich agreement?*

The traditional account of the Null Subject Parameter associated the possibility of null subject properties with rich verbal agreement, following Taraldsen (1978).[15]

---

[14] Rosenkvist (2009: 159) cites de Smet (1970) as making this claim also for Old Dutch.

[15] Although Taraldsen was the first to formalize the intuition, this idea itself did not originate with him: indeed, it has a long tradition within Indo-European philology whose origins are not easy to trace. Wright (1910: 121) applies it to Gothic directly, stating that nominative pronouns were 'rarely used except to express emphasis', because the relevant features were 'sufficiently indicated by the personal endings of the verb'; cf. also Grimm (1837: 203), and Lockwood (1968: 64), who claims that this was the case for Common

Some connection between rich agreement, as manifested morphologically, and the possibility of null arguments in certain languages has since been assumed by many authors, including Chomsky (1981), Rizzi (1982), McCloskey and Hale (1984), Adams (1987a, 1987b), Platzack (1987), Jaeggli and Safir (1989), Falk (1993), Roberts (1993), Barbosa (1995, 2009), Rohrbacher (1999), Müller (2005, 2008), Alexiadou (2006), Koeneman (2006), Poletto (2006), Cole (2009, 2010), Roberts (2010a), and Biberauer and Roberts (2010). These authors bring to bear data from various languages, including modern Hebrew, Basque, Breton, Pashto, and dialects of Arabic and Italian. For early Germanic languages the connection is assumed by van Gelderen (2000) and Axel (2007).

Although the rich agreement connection has proved difficult to formalize, as noted by e.g. Roberts (1993), Huang (2000: 57–9), Müller (2005), and Cole (2009), the intuition is clearly too relevant to be simply abandoned. For one thing, it may apply within languages as well as across them. Sigurðsson (1993: 275) reports that in Övdalian, a Scandinavian language spoken in Sweden, null subjects may only occur in the first and second person plural, which happen to be the only two clearly distinct forms in the verbal paradigm of this language (cf. also Rosenkvist 2010). In Hebrew, subjects may only be null in tenses with rich agreement (Borer 1989). Huang (1984: 535–6) furthermore reports that in Pashto both null subjects and null objects are found. Verbs agree with the subject except in transitive clauses expressing past events, in which case they agree with the object. Crucially, objects may only be null if object agreement is present on the verb, in which case subjects may not be, and vice versa. Abandoning any attempt to link rich agreement to null arguments, then, equates to throwing the baby out with the bathwater.[16] I will assume that in 'Italian-style' languages such as these, in which rich verbal agreement plays a role in allowing null arguments, the relevant arguments are in fact contained inside the verb. This 'I-subject' approach (or potentially 'I-object' in cases such as Pashto) is due originally to Borer (1986), and has been adopted more recently by Barbosa (1995, 2009), Alexiadou and Anagnostopoulou (1998), Platzack (2004), Müller (2005), Alexiadou (2006), Holmberg (2010), and Sigurðsson (2011).[17]

---

Germanic. Householder (1981) cites Apollonius Dyscolus as making a similar claim for Ancient Greek in the second century AD.

[16] Holmberg (2005: 560), while acknowledging the existence of such a connection, suggests that it should be captured at the level of processing and not as part of syntax; cf. also Ackema and Neeleman (2007). An alternative, which remains to be explored but which is consistent with the approach to typological generalizations proposed in section 2.2, is that the correlation may be at least partially explicable diachronically rather than as a hard-wired universal. The grammaticalization of subject pronouns as clitics and then agreement affixes is a well-known phenomenon that seems to be ongoing in modern French, and other such cases are reasonably common; cf. Fuß (2004: 167–204), Koeneman (2006: 90). Of course, an account of the derivation of the facts synchronically would still be required for each language.

[17] Roberts (2010a) argues against the I-subject approach (at least in Narrow Syntax) on the basis of evidence from Holmberg (2005) that *pro* can occupy SpecTP in Finnish: *pro* and the overt expletive *sitä* are

In order to approach the question of whether null arguments in the early Germanic languages were connected to rich agreement, however, the notion of rich agreement needs to be operationalized. One recent and comprehensive proposal to this effect is that of Müller (2005, 2008), also adopted by Roberts (2010a), and is given in (37).

(37)  **Pro Generalization:**
      An argumental *pro* DP cannot undergo Agree with a functional head α if α has been subjected (perhaps vacuously) to φ-feature neutralizing impoverishment in the numeration.

Impoverishment is identified through the occurrence of system-wide syncretisms. The Germanic language family plays a key role in motivating this generalization. As Fertig (2000: 6) notes, earlier proposals, such as those of Rohrbacher (1999) and Jaeggli and Safir (1989), had the disadvantage of making rich agreement into a necessary but not sufficient condition for the occurrence of null arguments (cf. also Poletto 2006: 159), since there exist languages with generally rich agreement, such as German, Icelandic, and Faroese, which do not permit Italian-style null arguments. Müller (2005) argues that this problem does not arise for his analysis: modern German, for instance, has a system-defining syncretism in its verbal paradigm for first and third person plural in all tenses, modern Icelandic has a system-defining syncretism for second and third person singular in the present tense, and both modern German and modern Icelandic have syncretic first and third person singular forms in the past tense.[18]

Let us now see how this account fares when faced with verbal agreement in the earlier Germanic languages. Tables 5.17–5.21 provide sample verbal paradigms for Gothic, Old Icelandic, OE, OHG, and OS weak verbs, abstracting away from much detail (see the references given for each language).

Apparent syncretisms can be recognized in all of these paradigms. In Müller's (2005) terms, the Ingvaeonic languages OE and OS, for example, are both characterized by the

---

in complementary distribution. However, this does not rule out the approach in other languages where it appears to be warranted; Barbosa (2009) argues this forcefully, and Holmberg (2010: 117) retracts his earlier view on this point. The Italian data from Cardinaletti (1997, 2004) presented by Roberts (2010a: 71–2), as well as the arguments of Cardinaletti and Starke (1999: 175–6), are mute with respect to the issue of whether '*pro*' is a clitic or a weak pronoun.

[18] It is unclear, however, how Müller's system would permit partial null subject phenomena such as those found in Bavarian and Övdalian; see Rosenkvist (2010: 256–8) for discussion of these varieties. It is also not clear what (37) follows from, if anything, as Müller (2008: n. 2) notes, though cf. Roberts (2010a: 82) for a suggestion. Cole's (2009) concept of language-specific 'morphological maximality' may fare better in this regard, although this account must stipulate the facts for Arabic, as Cole recognizes (2009: 579). Furthermore, Cole's account has no obvious way of capturing purely syntactic asymmetries in null argument distribution, such as the virtual absence of null arguments in subordinate clauses in Old French and the early Northwest Germanic languages (cf. section 5.4.2).

TABLE 5.17. Verb paradigm for the simple present and past tenses in Gothic: *nasjan* ('to save') (Wright 1910: 150–1)

| N | Person | Present ind. | Past ind.[19] | Present subj. | Past subj. |
|---|---|---|---|---|---|
| sg | 1 | nasj-a | nasi-d-a | nasj-áu | nasi-dēd-jáu |
| | 2 | nasj-is | nasi-d-ēs | nasj-áis | nasi-dēd-eis |
| | 3 | nasj-iþ | nasi-d-a | nasj-ái | nasi-dēd-i |
| du | 1 | nasj-ōs | nasi-dēd-u | nasj-áiwa | nasi-dēd-eiwa |
| | 2 | nasj-ats | nasi-dēd-uts | nasj-áits | nasi-dēd-eits |
| pl | 1 | nasj-am | nasi-dēd-um | nasj-áima | nasi-dēd-eima |
| | 2 | nasj-iþ | nasi-dēd-uþ | nasj-áiþ | nasi-dēd-eiþ |
| | 3 | nasj-and | nasi-dēd-un | nasj-áina | nasi-dēd-eina |

TABLE 5.18. Verb paradigm for the simple present and past tenses in Old Icelandic: *telja* ('to tell') (Faarlund 2004: 49–53)

| N | Person | Present ind. | Past ind. | Present subj. | Past subj. |
|---|---|---|---|---|---|
| sg | 1 | tel | tal-d-a | tel-ja | tel-d-i |
| | 2 | tel-r | tal-d-ir | tel-ir | tel-d-ir |
| | 3 | | tal-d-i | tel-i | tel-d-i |
| pl | 1 | tel-jum | töl-d-um | tel-im | tel-d-im |
| | 2 | tel-ið | töl-d-uð | tel-ið | tel-d-ið |
| | 3 | tel-ja | töl-d-u | tel-i | tel-d-i |

TABLE 5.19. Verb paradigm for the simple present and past tenses in OE: *nerian* ('to save') (Mitchell and Robinson 2007: 46)

| N | Person | Present ind. | Past ind. | Present subj. | Past subj. |
|---|---|---|---|---|---|
| sg | 1 | ner-ie | ner-ed-e | ner-ie | ner-ed-e |
| | 2 | ner-est | ner-ed-est | | |
| | 3 | ner-eþ | ner-ed-eþ | | |
| pl | | ner-iaþ | ner-ed-on | ner-ien | ner-ed-en |

impoverishment rule in (38): plural forms are never distinguished for person. OE, in addition, is characterized by (39): forms in the subjunctive are also never distinguished for person. OHG and OS, similarly but less drastically, do not distinguish between third and first person singular forms in the subjunctive ((40)).

---

[19] The morphological segmentation of these Gothic 'long form' preterites of weak verbs is tricky, but for my purposes nothing rests on it. For overviews of the historical issues see Ball (1968), Ringe (2006: 167–8), and especially Tops (1974).

TABLE 5.20. Verb paradigm for the simple present and past tenses in OHG: *nerien* ('to save') (Braune and Eggers 1975: 256)

| N | Person | Present ind. | Past ind. | Present subj. | Past subj. |
|---|---|---|---|---|---|
| sg | 1 | neri-e | neri-t-a | neri-e | neri-t-i |
| | 2 | neri-s(t) | neri-t-ōs(t) | neri-ēs(t) | neri-t-īs(t) |
| | 3 | neri-t | neri-t-a | neri-e | neri-t-i |
| pl | 1 | neri-emēs | neri-t-um | neri-ēm | neri-t-īm |
| | 2 | neri-et | neri-t-ut | neri-ēt | neri-t-īt |
| | 3 | neri-ent | neri-t-un | neri-ēn | neri-t-īn |

TABLE 5.21. Verb paradigm for the simple present and past tenses in OS: *nērian* ('to save') (Cordes and Holthausen 1973: 109–11)

| N | Person | Present ind. | Past ind. | Present subj. | Past subj. |
|---|---|---|---|---|---|
| sg | 1 | nēri-u | nēri-d-a | nēri-e | nēri-d-i |
| | 2 | nēri-s | nēri-d-es | nēri-es | nēri-d-is |
| | 3 | nēri-ēd | nēri-d-a | nēri-e | nēri-d-i |
| pl | | nēri-ad | nēri-d-un | nēri-en | nēri-d-in |

(38)  $[\pm 1, \pm 2] \rightarrow \emptyset/[+\text{pl}]$ ___        (OE, OS)

(39)  $[\pm 1, \pm 2] \rightarrow \emptyset/[+\text{subjunctive}]$ ___        (OE)

(40)  $[\pm 1] \rightarrow \emptyset/[-2, \text{pl}, +\text{subjunctive}]$ ___        (OHG, OS)

This rules out all three of the West Germanic languages as languages with rich agreement in Müller's sense. A different impoverishment rule is in play in Old Icelandic, namely (41), which Müller (2005: 107) notes is also operational in modern Icelandic. This results in identity between second and third person present forms.

(41)  $[\pm 2] \rightarrow \emptyset/[-1, \text{pl}, -\text{past}]$    (Old Icelandic)

Finally, all five of these languages exhibit some form of syncretism between first and third person singular past forms. For Old Icelandic and OE, this is solely in the subjunctive, as in (42); for Gothic, only in the indicative, as in (43); and for OS and OHG, in all singular past forms, as in (44).

(42)  $[\pm 1] \rightarrow \emptyset/[-2, \text{pl}, +\text{subjunctive}, +\text{past}]$ ___        (OE, Old Icelandic)

(43)  $[\pm 1] \rightarrow \emptyset/[-2, \text{pl}, -\text{subjunctive}, +\text{past}]$ ___        (Gothic)

(44)  $[\pm 1] \rightarrow \emptyset/[-2, \text{pl}, +\text{past}]$ ___        (OHG, OS)

Counting up impoverishment rules, then, OE and OS are in the lead, with three apiece, followed by OHG and Old Icelandic with two, while Gothic has only one.[20] Even one should be enough to rule out the occurrence of null arguments under Müller's generalization in (37), however. Müller is in fact aware of some of the older Germanic facts (2005: 107), suggesting either that rich agreement does not license *pro* in one or more of these languages or that 'the general nature of the 1./3.SG.PAST syncretism has not yet become manifest in a system-defining impoverishment rule'. Sigurðsson (1993), Rosenkvist (2009), and Schlachter (2010) also conclude that the distribution of referential null subjects in these languages does not depend on rich agreement.

There are independent reasons to think that rich agreement cannot account for all the patterns of null arguments found in the early Germanic languages. First, all of these languages have been shown to permit null referential objects as well as null subjects, e.g. (6) and (7) from Gothic, (13) from Old Icelandic, (23) and (24) from OE, (29) from OHG, and (36) from OS. Since no Germanic language exhibits object agreement morphology on the verb, this would be unexpected under the rich agreement approach, *pace* van Gelderen (2000).[21]

Secondly, in Italian-style null subject languages where rich agreement is implicated, overt pronouns are generally only permitted in finite clauses when they have an 'emphatic' interpretation; in all the languages examined in section 5.2 except Gothic, however, overt pronouns outnumber null subjects. Furthermore, in Italian-style languages an overt subject pronoun in a subordinate adverbial clause cannot be coreferential with the matrix subject. This obviation effect is illustrated by the Spanish example in (45), from Larson and Luján (1989), and the Italian example in (46), from Holmberg and Roberts (2010: 7).

(45)  *Cuando  él$_i$  trabaja,   Juan$_i$  no   bebe
       when     he    work.3SG   Juan    NEG  drink.3SG
      'When he$_i$ works, Juan$_i$ doesn't drink.'

(46)  *Il  professore$_i$  ha   parlato  dopo   che   lui$_i$  è   arrivato
       the  professor     has  spoken   after  that  he      is  arrived
      'The professor$_i$ spoke after he$_i$ arrived.'

However, in all of the early West Germanic languages examined in section 5.2, the opposite effect can clearly be found: null subjects are strongly disfavoured in

---

[20] The eagle-eyed reader may have spotted another syncretism in Gothic, between the third singular and second plural present indicative forms. However, these combinations of features do not form a natural class under Müller's (2005) system, and hence this syncretism cannot be formulated as an impoverishment rule.

[21] In van der Wurff (1997: 352), following Kortlandt (1983), it is suggested that the thematic vowel of Proto-Indo-European verbs may have originated as an object marker, thus sanctioning null referential objects in PIE. This analysis cannot reasonably be extended to the attested stages of Germanic, however.

subordinate clauses. (47), from OS, is an example of the lack of obviation effects in these languages.

(47)  Thô   he$_i$ thanan   scolda...   sôkien     lioht ôđar,
      when  he  thence     should.3SG seek.INF   light other
      thô   he$_i$ im      iungron    hêt                  gangan    nâhor
      then  he  REFL disciples   commanded.3SG        go.INF   nearer
      'When he$_i$ was about to die, he$_i$ told his disciples to gather round'
      (*Heliand* 576–9)

Gothic, on the other hand, appears to allow overt subject pronouns only exceptionally, as demonstrated in 5.2.1. Furthermore, it may have displayed obviation effects to an extent; recall Ferraresi's (2005: 49) observation that insertion of subject pronouns in Wulfila's translation occurred only where there was a change of subject with respect to the main clause. Of the older Germanic languages, then, only Gothic seems to pattern with Italian-style languages. This suggests that rich agreement may be relevant in the case of Gothic. It may, then, be possible to analyse the syncretism between first and third person singular past indicative verb forms as a 'family resemblance' effect (e.g. Pinker and Prince 1988; cf. Neeleman and Szendrői 2007: 692–3) rather than as a global impoverishment rule, following Müller's (2005: 107) suggestion. However, even in Gothic not all null arguments can be accounted for in terms of rich agreement, as null referential objects are found. This suggests that Gothic may have had two strategies for identifying null arguments, as Rosenkvist (2010) argues for Övdalian.

   To summarize this subsection: it has been argued that rich agreement is unlikely to have played a role in allowing null arguments in any of the early Germanic languages, with the possible exception of Gothic. This is because (a) verbal agreement is not rich enough in these languages, according to Müller's (2005) criterion; (b) null objects may occur in these languages, which is not predicted by the rich agreement approach; and (c) these languages (again with the possible exception of Gothic) do not display the same properties as Italian-style null subject languages with regard to the distribution of null and overt pronominal subjects. Another account for the early Germanic data must be found, then.

### 5.3.2  Topic drop?

Another hypothesis that could be advanced is that some or all of the null argument phenomena in early Germanic are due to topic drop or 'pronoun zap'. This process, discussed by Ross (1982) for modern German and Huang (1984: 546–8), Sigurðsson (1989), and Rizzi (1994) more broadly, allows a topic in SpecCP to be null, as in (48) and (49).

(48) Hab'  ihn   schon     gesehen.
     have   him    already   seen
     'I have seen him already.'

(49) Hab'  ich    schon     gesehen.
     have   I       already   seen
     'I have seen him/her/it/them already.'

Topic drop may affect objects as well as subjects, as (49) shows, and is unconnected to verbal agreement. It is restricted to elements that are in SpecCP, and as a result there can only be one null argument per clause under topic drop. Analyses of topic drop generally posit either a null operator in SpecCP binding the null argument or a DP moved to SpecCP and deleted there (Sigurðsson 2011).

   Alone, however, topic drop is inadequate to account for the early Germanic facts, as argued by Sigurðsson (1993) for Old Icelandic, Axel (2007) for OHG, and van Gelderen (2013: 275) for OE. Sigurðsson (1993: 262) presents cases such as (50) in which an overt topic in SpecCP (here *áðr* 'before') co-occurs with a null subject.

(50) þá    skar   Rognvaldr  hár   hans,  en    áðr     var   úskorit
     then   cut     R.            hair   his     but    before   was   uncut
     'Then Rognvaldr cut his hair, but it had been uncut before'
     (Nygaard 1906: 10)

Axel (2007: 304–5) presents similar cases from OHG (e.g. (25) above), as well as examples involving yes/no interrogatives, such as (51). Since overt pronouns are never clause-initial in this clause type, there is no reason to assume a null argument or topic operator in SpecCP, as pointed out by Trutkowski (2011: 208); indeed, topic drop in questions is ungrammatical in modern German.[22]

(51) quidis   zi    uns    thesa    parabola
     say.2SG   to    us      this      parable
     'Are you telling this parable to us?'
     (*Tatian* 529.2; Axel 2007: 308, her (25a))

OS also exhibited null arguments in overt topicalization contexts (e.g. (32) above), as did OE, as illustrated by (52).

---

[22] Examples such as (25), and its equivalents in OE such as (52), do not constitute decisive evidence against a pure topic drop analysis, since OHG and OE displayed a split CP structure in which familiar topics could occupy a left-peripheral preverbal position, as argued in Chapter 3. But OS and Old Icelandic did not allow this possibility, and so I assume that classical German-style topic drop alone is insufficient across the early Germanic languages, for simplicity's sake.

(52)  Nearwe      genyddon    on    norðwegas
      anxiously    hastened    on    north-ways
      'Anxiously they hastened north.'
      (*Exodus* 68; van Gelderen 2000: 129, her (34))

Evidence for Gothic is a little more difficult to come by due to the greater uncertainty about verb-movement in this language (see section 3.5). However, the interrogative clitic -*u*, which has no equivalent in the Greek *Vorlage*, is generally assumed to be in $C^0$ (Eyþórsson 1995: 104), and yes/no interrogatives are verb-initial in Gothic, with no element in SpecCP (Eyþórsson 1995: 105).[23] This being the case, under an analysis in which all null arguments in Gothic were due to topic drop we would predict overt subjects to be obligatory in yes/no interrogatives. This prediction is not borne out, as can be seen from (53).

(53)  niu          hauseis      hvan    filu      ana      þuk    weitwodjand
      NEG.PRT    hear.2SG    how    much    against    you    testify.3PL
      'Do you not hear how many things they testify against you?'
      (Matthew 27: 13)

A topic drop analysis predicts that only one argument may be null in a given clause, as observed in modern German (Huang 1984: 548). This is certainly false for Gothic, as shown by (6) in section 5.2.1. Finally, a topic drop analysis predicts that null arguments may not occur in subordinate clauses, as in modern German (Sigurðsson 1993: 263); as we have seen, however, all the early Germanic languages permit these, albeit at a lower frequency than in main clauses. In sum, then, in none of the five languages surveyed can a topic drop analysis alone account for all cases of null arguments found in the texts.[24]

### 5.3.3 *Radical null argument languages?*

A further major subtype is the 'radical' (or 'discourse') null argument language, typically exemplified by East Asian languages such as Japanese, Korean, Thai, and Mandarin Chinese but also including Imbabura Quechua and arguably Brazilian Portuguese and Övdalian (Huang 1984: 533–4; Cole 1987: 597–8; Roberts and

---

[23] -*u* is enclitic to the leftmost overt head in the complex that moves to $C^0$, presumably by some morphophonological process. In example (53) this is the negation particle *ni*; see Eyþórsson (1995: 135–40) for discussion.

[24] Another potential analysis that can safely be rejected is one in which apparent null subjects arise via 'SLF-coordination' (Höhle 1983; Heycock and Kroch 1994) of the kind needed to account for modern German examples like (i).

(i)  Das    Gepäck    ließ    er    fallen    und    rannte    zum      Hinterausgang
    the    baggage    let    he    fall      and    ran      to-the    rear-exit
    'He dropped the baggage and ran to the rear exit.'

This is because not all of the cases of null subjects arise in conjunct clauses.

Holmberg 2010: 8–10; Rosenkvist 2010: 244–7; Sigurðsson 2011). Huang (1984) argued from the start that topic drop as discussed in 5.3.2 alone could not account for the distribution of null subjects in these languages, and Cole (1987) argues that topic drop cannot account for the distribution of null objects at least in Imbabura Quechua, Korean, and Thai; cf. also Neeleman and Szendrői (2007: 674–5). It is therefore necessary to assume a process, distinct from topic drop, by which certain discourse-given arguments may come to be phonologically null.

Within and outside Minimalist theorizing, radical null arguments have received a wide range of analyses. Huang (1984) presents an analysis of null subjects in terms of control: null pronouns must be controlled in their control domain. Agr-in-Infl$^0$ is a potential controller in languages with subject-verb agreement; if this agreement is rich enough, as in Italian, Agr serves as controller. However, if this agreement is too weak, as in English, then Agr will fail to control the null pronoun. In Mandarin Chinese, Infl$^0$ does not contain Agr at all, and the control domain for null pronouns is therefore larger. Cole (1987: 611) proposes that Huang's Generalized Control Rule, which requires that an empty pronominal be coindexed with the closest nominal element, be parameterized as to whether it holds for *pro*: if it does, then referential object *pro* will be excluded, as in Mandarin Chinese, Italian, and English; if not, then referential object *pro* will be permitted, as in Imbabura Quechua, Thai, and Korean.

Sigurðsson (1993: 250) proposes a further identification strategy for use in Old Icelandic: free discourse indexing, by which subject and object *pro* could be identified under free coindexing with an NP in preceding discourse. He proposes that this is not the same strategy as topic drop, which in Old Icelandic allows null arguments that are not coindexed with any NP in preceding discourse, adducing data from Hjartardóttir (1987) and Nygaard (1906) to illustrate this point: null arguments without a coreferential antecedent are only possible in verb-initial main clauses (1993: 258). As it is difficult to investigate quantitatively, I have not considered the nature of the antecedent in this chapter (see Rusten 2010 for OE). However, such an approach, taking into account the distinction between syntactically conditioned and discourse-conditioned null arguments drawn by Luraghi (2003), is a desideratum for further work on null arguments in early Germanic. In any case, Sigurðsson's (1993) analysis will also be put aside, since, as with Cole's (1987) analysis, it is unclear how to formulate the parametrization of identification, particularly free discourse indexing, which involves 'free coindexing at LF with a construed clause-external topic' (1993: 260), in terms of lexical features; Sigurðsson's (1993) analysis has also been superseded by Sigurðsson (2011).

Some approaches to radical null arguments make the absence of verbal agreement a necessary condition: this is true of the analyses in Huang (1984), Jaeggli and Safir (1989), Speas (1994, 2006), and Saito (2007); Müller (2005) makes a similar suggestion. Null arguments, according to this theory, are only blocked when agreement exists but is impoverished. However, it is not true that impoverished agreement entails the absence of null arguments, as pointed out by O'Grady (1997: 87), Butt (2001), and Neeleman and Szendrői (2007: 676): one counterexample mentioned by Neeleman and Szendrői is the Oceanic language Kokota, described by Palmer (1999), in which richness of agreement differs across paradigms but all arguments can be dropped. I will therefore assume that richness of verbal agreement is tangential to the radical null argument property or properties.

Tomioka (2003: 336) argues that radical pro-drop arises from the deletion of NPs, which is only possible in languages that do not have obligatory determiners, since otherwise these determiners would be stranded: all languages that allow radical pro-drop are thus predicted to allow (robust) bare NP arguments. Neeleman and Szendrői (2007: 678) observe that standard Japanese and Korean have obligatory case-marking, however, and so this analysis predicts, wrongly, that case particles should be stranded by NP-deletion in these languages. In addition, the Oceanic language Cheke Holo has obligatory determiners but nevertheless allows radical null arguments, providing a counterexample to the generalization that emerges from Tomioka's (2003) work.

A recent and influential proposal by Neeleman and Szendrői (2007, 2008) attempts to support and motivate the generalization in (54).

(54)  **Radical-Pro-Drop Generalization**
      Radical pro-drop requires agglutinating morphology on pronouns.

The generalization is derived by three key assumptions, given in (55), in a framework not unlike that of Distributed Morphology.

(55)  **Assumptions** (Neeleman and Szendrői 2007: 679–87)
      (a)  Null arguments are ordinary DPs that fail to be spelled out at PF
      (b)  Spell-out rules may target non-terminal, non-head nodes
      (c)  The Elsewhere Principle regulates spell-out rules

The Elsewhere Principle blocks the zero spell-out rule that gives rise to null pronouns in languages with fusional pronominal morphology, since it is only one rule targeting KP (Case Phrase) and is blocked by more specific rules for spell-out of individual pronouns (e.g. first singular nominative), which also target KP. In languages with agglutinative pronominal morphology, spell-out rules for (parts of) pronouns target subparts of the KP and thus do not stand in an elsewhere relation to the zero spell-out rule (2007: 687–9).[25]

---

[25] Assumption (a) is potentially problematic. Neeleman and Szendrői's approach provides no rationale for the fact that it is the zero spell-out rule that is the most general one in radical null argument languages, nor for the fact that this general rule spells out as zero. All else being equal, the approach therefore predicts the existence of unattested varieties, such as 'pro-*elephant*' languages, in which discourse-given pronouns of all specifications are spelled out as *elephant*, and 'pro-add' languages in which all and only pronouns that are discourse-new are spelled out as zero. Of course, there could be a functional or Gricean explanation for the non-existence of such varieties.

The observation, based on the fact that pronouns in Japanese and Chinese exhibit agglutinating morphology for case and number respectively, is supported by a typological survey of the *World Atlas of Language Structures* (Haspelmath et al. 2005), which reveals no clear counterexamples.[26] The stronger claim that the relation is biconditional, i.e. that a language has radical pro-drop iff it has agglutinating morphology on pronouns, is considered (2007: 705–6), but tentatively rejected on the basis of Finnish. Neeleman and Szendrői's analysis also does not attempt to address the pragmatic conditions under which arguments may be null, suggesting that the Accessibility Theory of Ariel (1990) might be an appropriate candidate (cf. also Ackema and Neeleman 2007; Cole 2009, 2010).

Let us now assess whether early Germanic can be said to have agglutinating pronominal morphology. The pronominal paradigms of the early Germanic languages are presented in Tables 5.22–6. A few notes are in order on these paradigms. Forms preceded by an asterisk in Table 5.22 are unattested forms reconstructed for Gothic by analogy. The Old Icelandic third person forms in Table 5.23 are original distal demonstratives that have taken on the role of personal pronouns. OHG, unlike the other early Germanic languages, has lost its dual pronominal forms. Finally, it has been argued for OE that the genitive pronouns are not simplex pronouns but are inherently adjectival, since they take adjectival agreement (Caha 2009: 273–6); if so, they should be excluded from consideration when looking at Table 5.24.

TABLE 5.22. **Gothic pronouns (Wright 1910: 120)**

|  | Nominative | | Accusative | Dative | Genitive |
|---|---|---|---|---|---|
| 1 SG | ik | | mik | mis | meina |
| 2 SG | þu | | þuk | þus | þeina |
| 3 SG M | is | | ina | imma | is |
| 3 SG N | | ita | | | |
| 3 SG F | si | | ija | izái | izōs |
| 1 DU | wit | | ugkis | | *ugkara |
| 2 DU | *jut | | igqis | | igqara |
| 1 PL | weis | | uns, unsis | | unsara |
| 2 PL | jus | | izwis | | izwara |
| 3 PL M | eis | | ins | izē | |
| 3 PL N | ija | | *ija | *izē | im |
| 3 PL F | *ijōs | | ijōs | izō | |

---

[26] Cole (2009: 562–3) suggests that Vietnamese, Aiton, and Lao are counterexamples, though it should be noted that at least Vietnamese and Lao have agglutinative marking for number in at least some forms. Sato and Kim (2012) also propose that Colloquial Singapore English is a radical null argument variety without agglutinating pronominal morphology.

TABLE 5.23. **Old Icelandic pronouns (Faarlund 2004: 33–6)**

|        | Nominative | Accusative | Dative | Genitive |
|--------|------------|------------|--------|----------|
| 1 SG   | ek         | mik        | mér    | mín      |
| 2 SG   | þú         | þik        | þér    | þín      |
| 3 SG M | hann       |            | honum  | hans     |
| 3 SG N | þat        |            | því    | þess     |
| 3 SG F | hon        | hana       | henni  | hennar   |
| 1 DU   | vit        | okkr       |        | okkar    |
| 2 DU   | it         | ykkr       |        | ykkar    |
| 1 PL   | vér        | oss        |        | vár      |
| 2 PL   | ér         | yðr        |        | yðar     |
| 3 PL M | þeir       | þá         |        |          |
| 3 PL N | þau        |            | þeim   | þeira    |
| 3 PL F | þær        |            |        |          |

TABLE 5.24. **OE pronouns (Mitchell and Robinson 2007: 18–19)**

|        | Nominative | Accusative | Dative    | Genitive                     |
|--------|------------|------------|-----------|------------------------------|
| 1 SG   | ić         | mē, meć    | mē        | mín                          |
| 2 SG   | þū         | þē, þeć    | þē        | þín                          |
| 3 SG M | hē         | hine       |           |                              |
| 3 SG N | hit        |            | him       | his                          |
| 3 SG F | hēo, hīo   | hīe, hī    | hire      |                              |
| 1 DU   | wit        | unc        |           | uncer                        |
| 2 DU   | ġit        | inc        |           | incer                        |
| 1 PL   | wē         | ūs, ūsic   | ūs        | ūre                          |
| 2 PL   | ġē         | ēow, ēowic | ēow       | ēower                        |
| 3 PL M |            |            |           |                              |
| 3 PL N | hīe, hī    |            | him, heom | hira, hiera, heora, hiora    |
| 3 PL F |            |            |           |                              |

It is unclear from these paradigms whether early Germanic pronouns in fact were agglutinating for case or number. The presence of dual forms in all but OHG, with their characteristic -*t* endings in the nominative, indicates a degree of agglutination for number, and agglutination for case may appear to be present in the accusative, genitive, and dative of the first and second persons singular. However, numerous portmanteau fusional forms are found, especially in the nominative case, and none of these fusional patterns stretches across the full paradigm in any of these languages,

TABLE 5.25. OHG pronouns (Braune and Eggers 1975: 238–9)

|        | Nominative  | Accusative | Dative    | Genitive      |
|--------|-------------|------------|-----------|---------------|
| 1 SG   | ih          | mih        | mir       | mīn           |
| 2 SG   | dū, du      | dih        | dir       | dīn           |
| 3 SG M | ër          | inan, in   | imu, imo  | sīn           |
| 3 SG N | iʒ          |            |           | ës, is        |
| 3 SG F | siu, sī, si | sia, sie   | iru, iro  | ira, iru, iro |
| 1 PL   | wir         | unsih      | uns       | unsēr         |
| 2 PL   | it          | iuwih      | iu        | iuwēr         |
| 3 PL M | sie         |            |           |               |
| 3 PL N | siu         |            | im, in    | iro           |
| 3 PL F | sio         |            |           |               |

TABLE 5.26. OS pronouns (Cordes and Holthausen 1973: 104–5)

|        | Nominative | Accusative | Dative | Genitive |
|--------|------------|------------|--------|----------|
| 1 SG   | ik         | mik        | mī     | mīn      |
| 2 SG   | thū        | thik       | thī    | thīn     |
| 3 SG M | hiē        | ina        | imu    | is       |
| 3 SG N | it         |            |        |          |
| 3 SG F | siu        | sia        | iru    | ira      |
| 1 DU   | wit        | unk        |        | unkar    |
| 2 DU   | git        | ink        |        | inkar    |
| 1 PL   | wī         | ūnsik      | ūs     | ūsar     |
| 2 PL   | gī         | iuwik      | iu     | iuwar    |
| 3 PL M | sia        |            |        |          |
| 3 PL N | siu        |            | im     | iro      |
| 3 PL F | sia        |            |        |          |

i.e. there is no feature value or combination of feature values such that they define a non-singleton set of forms in which all members share phonetic material (cf. Neeleman and Szendrői 2007: 706). Furthermore, all five languages exhibit numerous syncretisms. It is therefore unclear whether we are dealing with true agglutination in any of these cases or rather 'family resemblance' in the sense of Pinker and Prince (1988). Neeleman and Szendrői (2007: 692–4) examine three modern Germanic languages, Dutch, Swedish, and Afrikaans, and conclude that their paradigms are not in fact agglutinative. The personal pronouns of these languages do not have dual or dative forms; however, they are otherwise very similar to those of the older Germanic languages. Though modern German is not considered, Neeleman and Szendrői (2007: 692) claim that pronominal paradigms are fusional 'in all Germanic languages'. Although the case is not clear-cut, then, assuming that Neeleman and Szendrői's (2007, 2008) proposal in (54) is a robust generalization about the distribution of radical null arguments, it does not seem promising to analyse the early Germanic languages as radical null argument languages.

### 5.3.4 *A partial null argument analysis*

The early Germanic languages do not seem to fit very well into any of the traditional categories of null argument language, then. However, they are not alone in this. Finnish and Hebrew both allow referential null arguments under certain conditions (Borer 1989; Vainikka and Levy 1999; Holmberg 2005, 2010). It has been argued that these languages, as well as others such as Icelandic, Russian, Marathi, and Brazilian Portuguese, should be classed as 'a separate type of null-argument language' (Holmberg and Roberts 2010: 10–11); modern Irish might also fall into this category (cf. McCloskey and Hale 1984).[27] In formal and written Finnish, for example, first and second person pronouns can always be left unexpressed in finite contexts, and third person pronouns can be left unexpressed when 'bound by a higher argument, under conditions that are rather poorly understood' (Holmberg 2005: 539). Referential objects may also be unexpressed in similar contexts (Huang 2000: 85–6; Frascarelli 2007: 723). Hebrew has a similar pattern in the past and future tenses, which have person marking; in the present tense, which does not, subject pronouns are obligatory (Vainikka and Levy 1999: 615). While it is not altogether clear that these languages form a coherent class (as opposed to a 'dustbin category'; indeed, Holmberg (2010: 122) argues that Finnish and Icelandic do not in fact form a group), the analytic tools developed to approach them will be useful in analysing the early Germanic languages, even though these languages may display null arguments in all persons and tenses. In particular, I here follow an approach based on Holmberg (2010), arguing that the early Germanic languages were in a sense the mirror image of languages such as modern formal Finnish.

In Holmberg's analysis, referential null subjects in partial null subject languages are DPs that bear a full set of φ-features but whose D-feature is uninterpretable ($[uD]$). $T^0$, which bears $[u\varphi]$-features associated with an EPP-feature, Agrees with the subject and attracts it to be second-Merged in SpecTP, thereby valuing $T^0$'s $[u\varphi]$-features as well as the $[u\text{Case}]$ feature of the subject DP. In consistent null subject languages, $T^0$ (together with an incorporated φP pronoun) has a $[uD]$ feature which can be valued by Agree with a null Aboutness topic in the C-domain. In partial null subject languages, since $T^0$ does not bear a $[uD]$ feature, the incorporation of a φP pronoun into $T^0$ with a referential interpretation is not available. Finnish then has

---

[27] Although the conditions on null arguments in Finnish appear to be discourse-based, Neeleman and Szendrői (2007: 705) state categorically that Finnish is not a radical null argument language in their view, as the distribution of null arguments is asymmetrical across persons.

two ways of valuing the [*u*D] feature on the subject DP. In the case of first and second person null subjects, it is valued by agreement with a speaker or addressee operator in the left periphery (local logophoric agent or patient, $\Lambda_A$ or $\Lambda_P$, in the sense of Sigurðsson 2004: 227). In the case of third person referential null subjects, it is valued through a structurally defined control relation with a DP antecedent (Holmberg 2010: 101–4; cf. also Holmberg, Nayudu, and Sheehan 2009; Holmberg and Sheehan 2010). The nullness of the pronoun is then due to an extended version of chain reduction. The relevant derivation is illustrated for Finnish in (56); solid lines indicate head-movement.

(56)

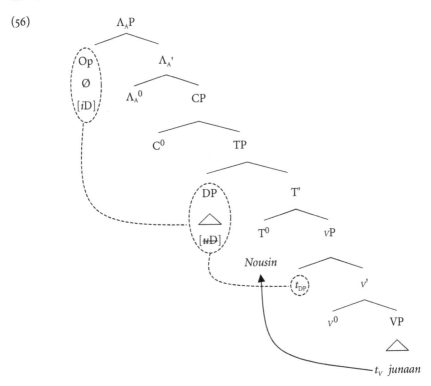

Nousin     junaan
boarded    train
'I boarded the train'

One immediate question is why a null Aboutness topic cannot control a null subject in SpecTP directly. Holmberg (2010: n. 11) speculates on this point, but it is clear that it cannot straightforwardly be the case for Finnish main clauses, since null referential third person subjects are not allowed in this context (e.g. Vainikka and Levy 1999: 614). An analysis involving a null Aboutness topic would make the prediction that this topic could be present in main clauses in Finnish as it is in consistent null subject languages such as Italian and could thus value the $[uD]$ feature of the null subject pronoun.

A related question is how the Agree relation between left-peripheral speech features, or Aboutness topics in the case of consistent null subject languages, and $T^0$ or the subject pronoun in SpecTP comes to hold. The purpose of this Agree relation in Holmberg's (2010) system is to value the $[uD]$ feature of $T^0$ or the subject pronoun. To achieve this the left-peripheral category must bear a valued D-feature. In Chomsky's (2000, 2001) Agree system, however, it is the higher category that probes, and it may only do so if it bears an uninterpretable feature itself.

Both problems can be solved at once if it is hypothesized that the ability of these left-peripheral categories to probe is itself parameterized. Specifically, in a given language, operators in $Spec\Lambda_AP$, $Spec\Lambda_PP$, and SpecShiftP may each independently bear an uninterpretable feature—$[uAnaphor]$ or $[u\varphi]$ (see section 5.3.5)—alongside their valued D feature, and it is this that gives them the ability to probe and thus enter into an Agree relation with SpecTP or $T^0$, valuing the latter's $[uD]$ feature as a by-product of this.[28] Assuming for the moment that the logophoric operators in $Spec\Lambda_AP$ and $Spec\Lambda_PP$ pattern together in whether they bear $[uAnaphor]/[u\varphi]$-features or not, this gives us a four-way typology, as illustrated in Table 5.27, which cross-cuts previous typologies of null argument languages.

I would like to propose that option (d) in Table 5.27 is the one instantiated by the early Northwest Germanic languages (putting Gothic aside for the moment). As observed by Sigurðsson (1993) for Old Icelandic, van Gelderen (2000) for OE, Axel (2007) for OHG, Håkansson (2008) for Old Swedish, and in section 5.2 above, first

TABLE 5.27. **Typology of null-argument context-linking**

| | | $[uAnaphor]/$ $[u\varphi]$ in $\Lambda_A$, $\Lambda_P$ | $[uAnaphor]/$ $[u\varphi]$ in ShiftP | Examples |
|---|---|---|---|---|
| (a) | | Yes | Yes | Greek, Italian, Japanese |
| (b) | | Yes | No | Finnish, Hebrew, Marathi |
| (c) | | No | No | French, Bambara (H. Koopman 1992) |
| (d) | | No | Yes | Shipibo (Camacho and Elías-Ulloa 2010), early Northwest Germanic languages |

[28] Landau's (2000, 2004) theory of control, followed by Holmberg (2010), employs a $[-R]$ feature with a similar function to the $[uAnaphor]$ feature proposed here, though he follows the approach to Agree taken by Pesetsky and Torrego (2001) in which interpretability and valuedness are distinct. Landau himself proposes that since checked features are not deleted until sent to Spellout they can probe twice (2004: 843); I do not adopt this here. The difference between $[uAnaphor]$-probing and $[u\varphi]$-probing is elaborated upon in section 5.3.5.

and second person null arguments are comparatively rare. As Sigurðsson (1993: 254) observes, this is expected if null arguments are required to have discourse topicality: Sigurðsson argues that, while it is not impossible for first and second person arguments to be Aboutness topics, this type of topicality is not easily established in direct speech. I therefore assume that $\Lambda_A$ and $\Lambda_P$ operators lacked the ability to probe in the early Northwest Germanic languages, and that the [*u*D] feature of a null argument could therefore only be valued by agreement with an Aboutness topic operator in SpecShiftP.

The derivation of a clause containing a null subject would proceed as follows. The subject pronoun, a DP bearing a [*u*D] feature, would first be Merged in Spec*v*P, and could subsequently be displaced to SpecTP or SpecFinP (I remain agnostic concerning the traditional EPP in these languages). Upon merger of the operator in SpecShiftP, the [*u*Anaphor]-feature of this operator would probe downwards, being satisfied by the first anaphoric element it encountered, typically the null DP subject. The [*u*Anaphor]-feature of the operator would thus be valued, as well as the [*u*D] feature of the null subject as a by-product. The derivation is illustrated in (57).

(57)

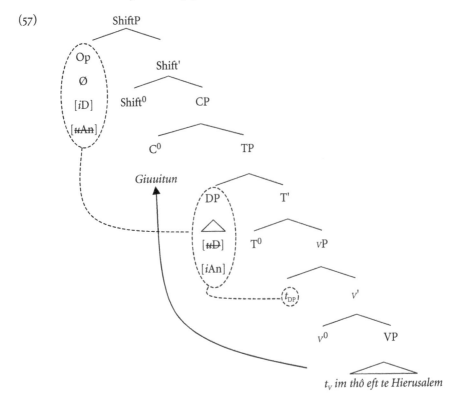

| Giuuitun | im | thô | eft | te | Hierusalem |
|----------|-----|------|-------|-----|------------|
| went.3PL | REFL.DAT | then | after | to | Jerusalem |

'Then they went to Jerusalem'

Null objects would be derived in a similar way. I have assumed that $Fin^0$ in these languages always bears an Edge Feature associated with the movement-triggering feature ^ , which requires that it project a specifier but does not mind what category fills it; see Chapter 3 for details. Crucially, since this movement is not Agree-based, intervention locality conditions do not apply to it, and hence the object can be moved over the subject. Then when the Aboutness topic operator is Merged and probes, the first [uAnaphor]-bearing element it encounters will be the object rather than the subject. All partial null argument languages I am aware of allow null objects as well as null subjects: see Huang (2000: 85–6) and Frascarelli (2007: 723) on Finnish, Farrell (1990) on Brazilian Portuguese, and Taube (2012) on Hebrew.[29]

As was additionally established in 5.2, all the Northwest Germanic languages except ON furthermore show an asymmetry between main and subordinate clauses with regard to the frequency of null arguments: null arguments are substantially rarer in subordinate clauses, once again displaying the mirror image of the behaviour of Finnish. This is captured if subordinate finite clauses in these languages are strong phases and do not always project their own ShiftP. If ShiftP is present in a subordinate clause, the Aboutness topic operator probes for a valued [Anaphor]-feature and may identify a null argument. If it is not present, null arguments may not be identified, since topic operators in a higher finite clause may not probe across a phase boundary. One could speculate that the presence or absence of the information-structural layer of the CP may be linked to the referentiality of the clause in the sense of Haegeman and Ürögdi (2010), or to (non-)assertiveness in the sense of Hooper and Thompson (1973), Truckenbrodt (2006), Wiklund (2010), and Sheehan and Hinzen (2012); Haegeman (2003) in fact makes just such a proposal. The presence or absence of the information-structural layer of the CP may or may not be connected to the possibility of movement of the verb into the C-domain in subordinate clauses in the West Germanic languages; I would suggest that the connection is at best indirect, however, as a number of examples of subordinate clause null subjects without verb movement can be found in OHG, as shown by Schlachter (2010: 161–3).[30]

---

[29] Extending the typology of partial null subject languages to allow for grammars in which only third person subjects may be null entails a loss in predictive power. Indeed, Vainikka and Levy (1999: 623) explicitly predict that such languages cannot exist: 'it cannot be the case that only third person subject pronouns may be omitted, while first/second pronouns must be retained'. However, other languages of a similar type have (occasionally) been noted in the literature: Shipibo, an indigenous American (Panoan) language, for instance (Camacho and Elías-Ulloa 2010), as well as potentially Old North Russian (Kwon 2009) and several Austronesian languages of the Philippines (Laurie Reid, p.c.). Deal (2005: 95) also comes to the conclusion that '1st/2nd person *pro*-drop and 3rd person *pro*-drop are independently available UG options'.

[30] The status of Old Icelandic as an exception to the generalization that null subjects are rarer in subordinate clauses than in main clauses in early Northwest Germanic may be connected to the prevalence of subordinate clause V2 in this language, which is not shared by the other early Germanic languages. There is some evidence that this property is an innovation (see Eyþórsson 1995, Gade 1995: 213, and Þorgeirsson 2012 on the absence of subordinate clause V2 in older verse).

Since there is only one ShiftP per clause (Frascarelli and Hinterhölzl 2007), it follows that in these languages only one null argument should be licensed per clause. There are only a few apparent counterexamples to this in the early Northwest Germanic languages; Gothic will be discussed in the next section.[31]

Null arguments in partial null argument languages never seem to be obligatory, unlike in Italian and Spanish, for instance, in which obviation effects are found. This can be captured if we assume a principle of Minimize Structure like that of Cardinaletti and Starke (1999: 198), according to which the smallest structure possible is always chosen.[32] Since $\varphi$P is smaller than DP, in canonical null subject languages $\varphi$P pronominals (null) will always be chosen over DP pronominals (overt) unless the smaller structure is independently ruled out (e.g. by a contrastivity requirement). In partial null argument languages, on the other hand, the choice is between [$i$D] and [$u$D] DPs, which are of equal size, and thus neither is preferred over the other. More needs to be said than this to explain the differences in frequency between the individual Germanic languages, but this is a start.

A final important feature of partial null subject languages, according to Holmberg (2005: 540) and Holmberg, Nayudu, and Sheehan (2009: 60), is that they permit generic null subjects, unlike consistent null subject languages.[33] This is so because $\varphi$P pronouns in partial null subject languages, lacking [$u$D], may not incorporate into $T^0$ in these languages and receive a referential interpretation, since $T^0$ also lacks [$u$D], hence if they are incorporated into $T^0$ they may only be interpreted as generic null subjects. Generic null subjects with no antecedent are certainly possible in Old Icelandic, as illustrated by (58) (see also Faarlund 2004: 220), in OHG, as illustrated by (59) (see also Axel 2007: 300–3), and in OE, as illustrated by (60), though in the West Germanic languages the use of *man/mon* is more common (cf. Hopper 1975: 81).

(58)  en    heyrði    til    hǫDo,    þá    er    þór    bar    hverinn
      but   heard.3SG to    handle.GEN when that Thor   carried kettle.DEF.ACC
      'But you could hear the handle rattle when Thor carried the kettle'
      (1150.FIRSTGRAMMAR.SCI-LIN,.170)

(59)  Gebet,    thanne    gibit    íu
      give.2PL, then     give.3SG  you.PL.DAT
      'Give, and it shall be given to you'
      (*Otfrid* 39,3; Eggenberger 1961: 102)

---

[31]  Van Gelderen (2013: 279–83) argues independently that null subjects in OE were Aboutness topics. However, Rusten (2010: 95) provides examples in which an analysis in terms of Aboutness-topicality seems inadequate; Kinn (2013) also gives examples from Old Norwegian in which more than one argument seems to be null.

[32]  Though this type of constraint is suspect, as it appears to require comparison of derivations.

[33]  As Cole (2010: 275) points out, Övdalian seems to be a counterexample to this insofar as it is a partial null subject language.

(60) Wiþ   þæs   magan   springe   þonne   þurh   muð   bitere
       for   the   maw.GEN   sore.DAT   when   through   mouth   bitterly
       hræcð   oþþe   bealcet
       retches   or   belches
       'For sores of the mouth when the patient retches or belches bitterly through the mouth'
       (colaece,Lch_II_[2]:15.1.1.2296)

It thus seems that there is a plausible case to be made for the earlier Northwest Germanic languages as partial null argument languages.

### 5.3.5 *Cross-linguistic reach of the proposal*

In this section I briefly illustrate how the analysis and typology of null subjects in the previous section extends to other null argument languages beyond early Germanic; in the process I will return to Gothic.

I have suggested that the appropriate probing feature on left-peripheral operators may be [$u$Anaphor] or [$u$φ], and that in early Northwest Germanic the topic operator in SpecShiftP bore [$u$Anaphor]. The two possibilities make differing empirical predictions. In particular, when the probing feature is [$u$φ], a much larger class of elements count as potential 'defective interveners' in the sense of Chomsky (2000: 123), most notably the φ-feature-bearing finite verb, which I argued in Chapter 3 generally moves to Fin$^0$ in main clauses: an instance of agreement between a left-peripheral operator and an element below the C-domain in any of these languages would therefore violate Relativized Minimality (Rizzi 1990, 2001a). Furthermore, if topicalized/focalized elements must pass through SpecFinP in V2 languages, as I likewise argued in Chapter 3, such elements would also act as interveners in these languages, predicting the incompatibility of overt topicalization/focalization with null arguments of any kind. The question that then presents itself is whether there are any languages that differ minimally from the early Northwest Germanic languages in probing for φ-features rather than for [$i$Anaphor].

Modern German appears to be such a language. As discussed in 5.3.2, modern German displays a process of topic drop by which only arguments in the left periphery may be null. Since modern German is a V2 language, this leads to verb-initial clauses, and only one argument per clause may be null. Under the account given above, we can see how this happens. When the topic operator is Merged, it probes for a φ-feature-bearing element. In the normal case, the first such element it will encounter will be either the subject or some argumental element that is stopping off in SpecFinP on its way up to a left-peripheral topic/focus position. Then if the derivation contains a DP bearing a [$u$D] feature in a position below Fin$^0$, this [$u$D] feature will be unable to be valued by the [$i$D] feature on the topic operator, and so the derivation will crash. The only way for this [$u$D] feature to be valued is for the

DP-pronoun to move to SpecFinP itself, precluding topicalization and focalization of any other element.

Topic drop is also ungrammatical in subordinate clauses, which is what we would expect given that the German finite complementizer *dass* is usually analysed as being in complementary distribution with the verb in $C^0$/$Fin^0$ (since at least den Besten 1977; cf. Vikner 1995 for extensive discussion of embedded main clause phenomena in modern Germanic). If subordinate clauses in German are FinPs, then we would not expect to find null arguments in these clauses.

This property is not the only null-argument-related difference between modern German and the early Northwest Germanic languages. Consider again (48) and (49), repeated below.

(48)  Hab'  ihn    schon     gesehen.
      have  him    already   seen
      'I have seen him already.'

(49)  Hab'  ich    schon     gesehen.
      have  I      already   seen
      'I have seen him/her/it/them already.'

In early Northwest Germanic, as I have shown in section 5.2, there is an asymmetry between third person and first and second person pronominal arguments in that the latter are much less likely to be null. This does not appear to be the case in modern German, where all persons can be freely omitted. Fortunately, there are independent reasons to believe that the difference between [*u*Anaphor]-probing and [*u*φ]-probing is not the only difference at work here. Trutkowski (2011) observes that examples such as (48) and (49) are not exactly parallel: while (48) is appropriate in any context, (49) may only be used in contexts where an antecedent is present in the discourse. Trutkowski takes this to indicate that a process of *out-of-the-blue drop*, affecting first and second person subjects, must be active in German in addition to topic drop, and connects this to verbal agreement. However, since this phenomenon appears remarkably similar to the contrasts in binding between 'This paper was written by Ann and myself' and '*This paper was written by Ann and himself', noted by Ross (1970: 228), I will assume that these processes can be accounted for by assuming that $\Lambda_A$ and $\Lambda_P$, the logophoric agent and patient operators in the clausal left periphery (Sigurðsson 2004, 2011), are also [*u*φ]-probes in this language, without making reference to verbal agreement.

What about traditional (Italian-style) null subject languages? Holmberg (2010) proposes that in these languages [*u*D] is present on $T^0$ rather than on the pronoun itself, and must be valued through agreement with a left-peripheral null topic just as the [*u*D] feature on the pronoun must in partial null subject languages. The pronoun itself is a φP rather than a DP, however, and incorporates into $T^0$ following an approach to head-movement based on Roberts (2010b): $T^0$ bears $[u\varphi]$-features and establishes an Agree relation with the subject, and since the features of the $\varphi$P pronoun are a subset of those of $T^0$ it is not spelled out. This derivation is illustrated in (61).

(61)

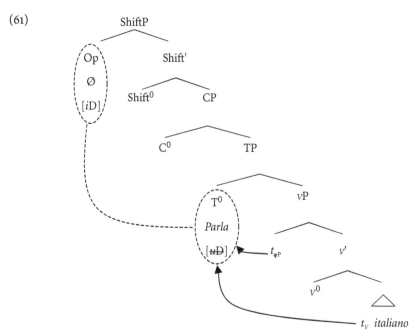

Parla      italiano
speak.3SG    Italian
'He/she/it speaks Italian'

Crucially, for this to be possible it must bear no features that $T^0$ does not also bear. If a [*i*Anaphor] feature is present in the derivation, then, it must be on $T^0$. It seems more plausible and restrictive to assume that Aboutness operators (and $\Lambda_A$ and $\Lambda_P$ operators) in Italian and other consistent null subject languages bear $[u\varphi]$ rather than [*u*Anaphor] (cf. Frascarelli 2007: 718). Since for Italian there is no need to posit an EF on Fin$^0$ requiring that its specifier be filled, there is no way for the object to intervene between the topic operator and $T^0$, and hence no way to derive referential null objects in Italian; a correct position, since only null objects with arbitrary reference are allowed in this language (Rizzi 1986).

The proposal is equally extensible to the original partial null argument languages discussed by Holmberg (2010), the crucial difference with early Northwest Germanic being that in these languages it is $\Lambda_A$ and $\Lambda_P$ operators, rather than Aboutness topic operators, that may bear [*u*Anaphor].[34] In these languages, as in early Northwest Germanic, but not in consistent null subject languages, null referential objects may be found.

Radical null argument languages are straightforward to account for under this proposal: they simply instantiate the possibility under which all three types of left-peripheral operator bear [*i*D] and [*u*Anaphor], and thus any argument may in principle be null in any position.[35]

Finally, it might be objected that nothing in the present account prevents English from displaying partial null argument properties in principle. However, there exist varieties of English that do permit null arguments: colloquial spoken varieties and 'diary drop', which work in a similar (though not identical) way to German topic drop (cf. Haegeman 1990; Haegeman and Ihsane 1999; Weir 2008), and potentially Colloquial Singapore English (Sato and Kim 2012). Space precludes more extensive discussion of these varieties in this context, but I take it as a desirable consequence of the present account that the possibility or impossibility of null arguments in 'weak-agreement' languages such as English is simply a matter of parametric variation.

We are now in a position to return to Gothic. In section 5.3.1 it was argued that Gothic, unlike the other early Germanic languages, displayed some of the characteristics of a consistent null subject language. This possibility is compatible with Müller's (2005) theory of morphological richness if it is assumed that the first–third singular syncretism was actually an accidental homophony, despite being system-wide. This can in fact be made to fall out of a system similar to Müller's if an alternative feature system is adopted: rather than the person features [±1] and [±2] we might choose to adopt Harbour's (2006) theory of person features, based on [±author], [±participant], and [hearer] (cf. also Noyer 1992). I assume that [hearer] is not active in the early Germanic languages (since it is needed only to capture languages in which a distinction between inclusive and exclusive first person is made). First person then is [+author, +participant]; second person is [−author, +participant]; third person is [−author, −participant]. There is no way under this system of characterizing first and third persons only without also including second person: a rule referring to [±author], [±participant] would be too permissive, and any other specification of environment would be too restrictive. It follows that syncretism rules collapsing first and third person forms cannot be stated, and so

---

[34] A complication arises with respect to the original cases of control into embedded finite clauses discussed by Holmberg (2010) and Holmberg and Sheehan (2010), since it is not desirable to stipulate that any DP may bear [*u*Anaphor]. I have no solution to this problem at present.

[35] Though the present account predicts that only one null argument per clause is possible, due to (defective) intervention, a prediction that is clearly false. Positional restrictions such as those reported by Huang (1984: 538) for Chinese must also be investigated in more detail.

cannot exist. As regards the morphological component, then, there would be no syncretisms at all in Gothic.[36]

Null objects are also found in Gothic, however. This indicates that Gothic is a language that has two means of licensing null arguments at its disposal. First of all, φP pronouns may be incorporated into $T^0$, which then has its $[uD]$ feature valued by agreement with an operator, which bears $[iD]$ and may have $[u\varphi]$-probes. Secondly, DP pronouns bearing $[uD]$ may occur. They cannot appear in subject position, since they would then act as interveners blocking the valuation of $T^0$'s own $[uD]$ feature. If present in object position, however, their $[uD]$ feature may be valued by agreement with a left-peripheral operator bearing a $[u$Anaphor$]$-probe (for which a φP pronominal subject does not count as an intervener). It is thus possible for both referential subjects and referential objects to remain phonologically null, and this is the norm for subjects. This account predicts that generic inclusive subjects cannot be null in Gothic, since φP subjects inevitably incorporate into $T^0$ and receive a definite interpretation; I have not found any counterexamples, though the generic inclusive subject construction is rare and potential cases all seem to follow the Greek, as in (62).

(62)  ni    bi    hlaib   ainana   libaid       manna
      NEG   by    bread   alone    live.3SG     man
      'Man does not live by bread alone'
      (Luke 4: 4; Greek Majority Text: ουκ επ αρτω μονω ζησεται [ο] ανθρωπος)

This account of Gothic, together with the account of early Northwest Germanic in section 5.3.4, sets the stage for a discussion of the diachronic development of the early Germanic languages, including the question of what to reconstruct for Proto-Germanic. This will be the focus of section 5.4.

## 5.4 Null arguments across the history of Germanic

### 5.4.1 *Diachronic trajectories*

I have argued that the situation in the individual early Northwest Germanic languages with regard to null arguments was the same or at least very similar, with Gothic differing from the others essentially only in being a language with $[uD]$ in $T^0$. In this section I briefly discuss possible diachronic trajectories of the individual languages. Since the 'middle' stages of these languages are outside the focus of the present study, the discussion will necessarily remain speculative.

---

[36] There would also no longer be any syncretisms at all in OHG, predicting that this language too would be a consistent null subject language. Such a solution, although convenient for Gothic, is therefore not ideal.

Gothic can be set aside immediately; the available Gothic documents do not permit us to get a diachronic cross-section of the language, which is now extinct.

Modern Icelandic and modern (Low and High) German are all topic drop languages. In addition, Icelandic has been a symmetric V2 language essentially throughout its recorded history (see Þráinsson 2007 on the modern language, and Faarlund 2004 on earlier stages). Hróarsdóttir (1996) reports that referential null subjects were lost during the eighteenth and nineteenth centuries.[37] As discussed in Chapter 3, the only OHG texts that robustly exhibit V3 are the *Isidor* translation and the Monsee Fragments, with other texts displaying predominantly V2 order in main clauses; null subjects, on the other hand, persisted through the eighth and ninth centuries (e.g. in the V2 *Tatian*) and are essentially no longer found in later OHG such as that of Notker (Axel 2007: 298). The OS *Heliand* is also V2 with null arguments.

As discussed in the previous section, what differentiates a topic drop language from a partial null argument language syntactically is the probing feature on the $[iD]$-bearing left-peripheral operator, specifically whether it is $[u\varphi]$ or $[u\text{Anaphor}]$. Now in a V2 language, all else being kept constant, a grammar in which the left-peripheral operator bears $[u\text{Anaphor}]$ will generate a set of sentences that is a superset of that generated by a grammar in which the left-peripheral operator bears $[u\varphi]$. Specifically, clauses such as (32) from OS, repeated below, with a fronted element preverbally as well as a null argument, can be generated by the $[u\text{Anaphor}]$ grammar but not by the $[u\varphi]$ grammar, due to intervention.

(32)  lîbes      uueldi   ina     bilôsien,   of   he   mahti   gilêstien   sô
      life.GEN   would    him     take        if   he   could   achieve     so
      'he$_i$ would take his$_j$ life if he$_i$ could'
      (*Heliand* 1442)

The Subset Principle of Berwick (1985), as stated in (63), comes into play here.

(63)  **The Subset Principle**
      The learner must guess the smallest possible language compatible with the input at each stage of the learning procedure.
      (Clark and Roberts 1993: 304–5)

---

[37] Icelandic, and to a lesser extent also German, is thus problematic for Yang's claim that 'the combination of *pro*-drop and V2 is intrinsically unstable and necessarily gives away to an SVO (plus *pro*-drop) grammar' (2000: 243–4). Earlier Icelandic permitted null arguments for at least half a millennium despite being a V2 language, and when a change did occur it was a reduction in the possibilities for null arguments, not the loss of V2. These indicate that Yang's claim must be made more specific or else abandoned. Kashmiri, which is also V2 with null arguments of various kinds (Wali and Koul 1997: 119), may also present a problem for Yang's hypothesis insofar as it is not imminently losing either.

(63) follows from the assumption (disputable; see Clark and Lappin 2011 for discussion) that acquirers during the critical period do not make use of negative evidence. Since they therefore have no way to retreat from hypotheses of feature specifications that are too permissive, they must make use of a strategy to avoid such 'superset traps'.[38] The Subset Principle can be viewed as a third-factor-motivated part of the learning algorithm rather than as part of grammar as such; cf. Biberauer and Roberts (2009) for discussion of this principle in the context of syntactic change.

If clauses such as (32) are not robustly represented in the primary linguistic data, then, the acquirer will default to $[u\varphi]$-probing rather than $[u\text{Anaphor}]$-probing by the Subset Principle. Such clauses do seem to be rare in the languages investigated: in my OS data (32) was the only unambiguous example. Chance fluctuation could therefore have led to their absence in a given set of PLD. We thus have a rationale for the change from partial null argument language to 'topic drop' language in the histories of Icelandic and German, though the picture needs to be investigated in more detail.[39]

This leaves English, in which, at least in the standard variety, all forms of referential null argument are ungrammatical in finite clauses. As observed in section 5.2.3, even most OE (West Saxon) texts do not appear to contain referential null arguments in any robust way, leading to Hulk and van Kemenade's (1995: 245) statement that 'the phenomenon of referential *pro*-drop does not exist in Old English'. Assuming that earlier stages of Northwest Germanic did allow referential null arguments (see section 5.4.2), this property must have been lost in these dialects during and before the time that our very earliest texts were being produced. Why did this occur in OE but not in the other early Northwest Germanic varieties?

I suggest that the loss of null arguments in these varieties was due to the language contact situation in the British Isles during the relevant time period, specifically the substantial substratum of speakers of Brythonic Celtic and British Latin. Tristram (2004: 94–9) outlines the prevalence of these speakers in Wessex and elsewhere in the OE-speaking area, arguing that the social situation was one which was likely to produce imperfect second language learning of OE by subjected Britons. This type of social situation may lead to 'imposition' of features from Brythonic Celtic onto OE, in the terminology of Winford (2005); see section 3.2.4 for discussion. Tristram (2004) argues that this was the case for loss of the inflectional endings in the OE NP (cf. also Trudgill 2011: ch. 1), and for the rise of verbal aspect. However, Lucas's (2009: 145) notion of 'restructuring' may be more relevant for the loss of null arguments. Bini (1993) has shown that speakers of Spanish (a consistent null subject

---

[38] For a fuller discussion of the status of the Subset Principle in syntactic acquisition and learnability theory, see Fodor and Sakas (2005) and Clark and Lappin 2011.

[39] This change equates to the 'loss of free discourse indexing as an identification strategy for null-arguments' suggested by Sigurðsson (1993: 277) for Icelandic.

language) learning Italian (another consistent null subject language) as an L2, up to an intermediate proficiency level, systematically overproduce 'redundant' overt pronouns. Bini's study supplemented existing studies that showed that L2 learners of Italian with English as an L1 also overproduced overt pronouns—unsurprisingly, since imposition can be invoked in these cases. The literature on L2 acquisition of null subject languages is substantial (see Sorace et al. 2009 for a recent overview), but the relevant point for our purposes is that L2 learners of *any* null subject language appear to 'use overt subject pronouns as a compensatory "default" strategy' (Sorace et al. 2009: 464), regardless of the structure of their L1. Thus, although Brythonic Celtic probably allowed subject pronouns to be omitted, in common with many other early Indo-European varieties (Koch 1991: 24), it is not implausible to suppose that the overgeneralization of overt pronouns by L2 learners of OE, primarily speakers of Brythonic Celtic and British Latin, was responsible for the loss of the possibility of null arguments in West Saxon and in later varieties of English.[40]

### 5.4.2 *The main clause constraint: innovation or retention?*

Assuming once again that the distribution of null arguments in Proto-Northwest Germanic was the same as that of its early North and West Germanic descendants (see section 5.4.3), one striking property to be accounted for is the rarity of null arguments in subordinate clauses. How might this be accounted for?

Recall that under the analysis given in 5.3.4, this rarity was accounted for on the basis of features that had nothing to do with null arguments as such: it was proposed that subordinate clauses in the early Northwest Germanic languages were (a) usually FinPs lacking a higher information-structural layer, and (b) inaccessible for agreement with elements in higher clauses. The rarity of null arguments in subordinate clauses thus falls out from an interaction with an independent property of the grammar of these languages.

However, a very similar constraint has been observed in older Romance languages, especially Old French (Thurneysen 1892; Foulet 1919; Vanelli, Renzi, and Benincà 1986: 169–72; Adams 1987a, 1987b; Roberts 1993: 208; Vance 1997). In the relevant subset of the medieval Romance languages, specifically Old French, some dialects of Occitan, Franco-Provençal, Northern Italian dialects, and Florentine (Vanelli, Renzi, and Benincà 1986: 163), null arguments were generally unavailable in subordinate clauses except where these clauses were V2. The similarity between these languages and the early Northwest Germanic languages in this respect has occasionally been

---

[40] Note that under the 'restructuring' logic given above, this conclusion holds regardless of whether Brythonic Celtic or British Latin were themselves null argument languages.

remarked upon (e.g. by Axel 2007: 323).[41] It is, in my view, unlikely that this is due to chance. If so, then the direction of contact influence must be established.

Fortunately this is made simple both by the geographical distribution of the main clause constraint and by the probable language contact situation. As regards the former, the subset of the old Romance varieties that do not freely allow null subjects in subordinate clauses covers a geographically contiguous area. The same cannot be said for the complement of this subset, which includes the Iberian peninsula, southern and central Italian varieties, and Romanian (Vanelli, Renzi, and Beninca 1986: 163); this area is divided at least by a wedge of main clause constraint varieties stretching down to the Mediterranean coast at the base of the Alps. Classic dialect geography suggests that the contiguous area should be viewed as the area of an innovation that has spread, whereas the non-contiguous area should be viewed as preserving older forms (e.g. Chambers and Trudgill 1998: 94). Furthermore, the area in which the main clause constraint is found in Medieval Romance corresponds roughly to the area controlled by Frankish tribes in the sixth–eighth centuries; see Figure 5.13.

The light grey area in Figure 5.13 represents the area controlled by the Frankish empire as of AD 814 (see Shepherd 1926: 53). The dark grey area, which is fully contained within this area, represents the extent of the early Romance languages in which the main clause constraint for null subjects is in operation; this area is estimated based on the geographical extent of the corresponding modern Romance languages as depicted in Harris and Vincent (1988: 481–3).

It thus seems plausible that the main clause constraint, in the medieval Romance varieties that exhibit it, is of West Germanic origin. By contrast, if the main clause constraint had originated in Romance and spread to Germanic via contact, its presence in Old Norwegian and Old Swedish would be surprising, although diffusion across the Germanic dialect continuum cannot completely be ruled out. This reverse theory also leaves unexplained the absence of the main clause constraint in those Romance varieties that have *not* undergone heavy contact with West Germanic.

Considerations of language contact type also militate against the reverse theory. It is known that, ultimately, the Frankish language failed to prevail in France (cf. e.g. Rickard 1993: 8). Pre-Old French remained the socially dominant language, meaning that Frankish L1 speakers would have had to learn it as an L2: precisely the sort of sociolinguistic situation that can lead to imposition of linguistic material under source language agentivity in the sense of Winford (2005). A plausible psycholinguistic mechanism for the transfer of the main clause constraint from West Germanic to northern Romance varieties thus exists, and we have an explanation for the origin of this constraint in Romance, something I believe has not been attempted

---

[41] Since the main clause constraint is characteristic of all the early Northwest Germanic languages, this property can be added to Mathieu's (2009) list of the 'Germanic properties of Old French'.

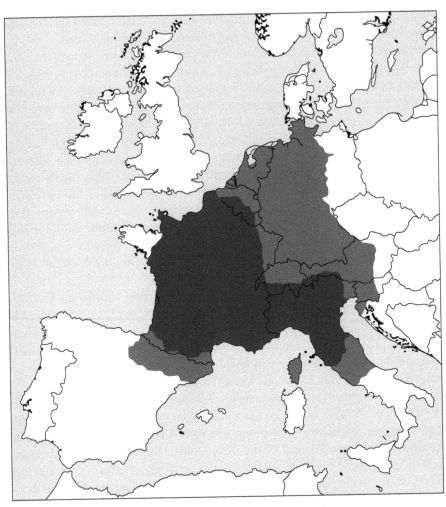

FIGURE 5.13 Frankish dominance and the main clause constraint in Romance

before in the literature. Since Latin clearly did not have this restriction, this is a positive step. In addition, the main clause constraint must already have been present in West Germanic in order to be borrowed from it into Romance; the simplest hypothesis for its presence in both North and West Germanic is that it was a retention in both.

### 5.4.3 *Proto-Germanic as a null argument language*

To recap: I have argued in section 5.3.4 that the early Northwest Germanic languages displayed a system in which null referential pronouns are DPs bearing [*u*D] and [*i*Anaphor], finite $T^0$ does not bear a [*u*D] feature, and a left-peripheral Aboutness topic operator may bear [*i*D] and [*u*Anaphor]. Furthermore, subordinate clauses in these languages may lack the information-structural layer containing Aboutness topics. Classical OE is the only exception to these generalizations, and I have argued in section 5.4.1 that a contact-based explanation is plausible for the change that took place in this language; northern OE varieties, and the early stage of OE represented by *Beowulf*, clearly exhibit null arguments, as shown by Berndt (1956) and van Gelderen (2000), with a similar distribution to those of the other early Northwest Germanic varieties.

As far as I have been able to determine, then, the syntactic situation across the early Northwest Germanic languages is one of identity.[42] Lass's (1997) 'oddity condition', discussed in section 2.3.4, requires that rare systems require more evidence to reconstruct, and languages in which null subjects occur systematically in the third person do seem to be rare. However, the evidence from the attested daughter languages in this case is unequivocal, and so the reconstruction of the same pattern for Proto-West Germanic and Proto-Northwest Germanic should therefore be uncontroversial; as we have seen, even sceptics like Lightfoot accept reconstruction in cases of identity (e.g. 2002a: 120). The runic evidence is not inconsistent with this picture. For instance, of fourteen complete inscriptions containing first person singular verbs, two contain no corresponding pronoun (Antonsen 2002: 188–9): the Trollhättan bracteate, *tawo laþodu* '(I) make invocation', and the Sievern bracteate, *r writu* '(I) write runes' (Antonsen 2002: 213, 216). Elsewhere, full pronouns are found, either *ek* or the enclitic *-eka/-ika*. This sort of distribution is to be expected if it was possible but rare for first and second person pronouns to be null in Northwest Germanic. Unfortunately, but unsurprisingly, contexts for second and third person subject pronouns are entirely unattested in the corpus of early runic inscriptions.

In section 5.3.5 I argued that the system in Gothic was extremely similar to that found in early Northwest Germanic, with one key difference: finite $T^0$ in Gothic was able to bear a [*u*D] feature. This enabled φP pronouns to incorporate into $T^0$, receiving their 'referential index' via agreement with [*i*D] on a left-peripheral operator. More minor differences were that in Gothic the logophoric agent and patient operators $\Lambda_A^0$ and $\Lambda_P^0$ were able to probe in addition to the topic operator, and the probing feature on all three was [*u*φ].

What, then, can we reconstruct for Proto-Germanic? To claim that this language was a null subject language would not be novel. Grimm (1837: 203) makes the suggestion, as do Paul (1919: 22), Lockwood (1968: 64), and Fertig (2000: 8).

---

[42] Further differences between the languages almost certainly exist. For instance, underlying the quantitative differences between the West Germanic languages presented in section 5.2 there are probably qualitative differences that I have been unable to discover. Future research will hopefully be able to shed light on these.

Hopper (1975) is more tentative, suggesting that expletive and quasi-argumental subjects are reconstructable for Proto-Germanic (1975: 80) and drawing no firm conclusion about referential pronominal subjects (1975: 31–2). Meillet (1909: 89) and Behaghel (1928: 443) are similarly cautious. In any case, studies of null subject languages within the Principles & Parameters framework have shown us nothing if not that there are multiple types of languages omitting referential null arguments (cf. e.g. Roberts and Holmberg 2010). It is thus necessary to be more specific than this.

Proto-Germanic would clearly count as a null subject language under either the Gothic system or the Northwest Germanic system; the question, then, is which type was closer to the original. Any suggestion must be tentative given the equivocal nature of the Gothic evidence. However, all partial null argument languages for which we have written history seem to exhibit an earlier stage of being a full null subject language. Brazilian Portuguese was once such a language (Roberts 2011), like modern European Portuguese. Marathi is descended from Sanskrit, another typical null subject language (Kiparsky 2009: 55); likewise for Old Church Slavonic (Eckhoff and Meyer 2011), which is likely to be similar to the Common Slavonic ancestor of modern Russian. Though the generalization is in need of further testing, it seems that partial null argument languages occupy a late position in a 'null argument cycle', developing out of canonical null subject languages. If this is how partial null argument systems arise, then it may be the case that the Northwest Germanic system represents an innovation, and that the Gothic system is the one that should be reconstructed for Proto-Germanic.

# 6

## Conclusion

### 6.1 Summary of results

This book has focused on the problem of 'reconstructing' the syntax of unattested stages of linguistic family trees. As laid out in Chapter 1, we know that the Germanic languages are related by descent from a common ancestor, and a natural question to ask is: what was this language like? While comparative-reconstructive linguistics has had great success in reconstructing ancestral sound systems, it has not always accorded a central place to syntax. This book approached the question of syntactic reconstruction via a detailed examination of aspects of the syntax of the early Germanic languages with a view to reconstruction of Proto-Germanic. The plausibility of these case studies was used to argue that, given an appropriate theoretical framework, the reconstruction of syntax is possible and worthwhile.

The rationale, as laid out in Chapter 2, runs as follows. In certain current theories of syntax, all syntactic variation is attributed to properties of lexical items themselves, with the assembly of sentences in the mind guided by instructions attached to the lexical items being assembled. This view of variation suggests an analogy with traditional methods of reconstructing words and sounds, which depend on establishing diachronic relatedness ('cognacy') between individual sounds at different stages as well as between individual lexical items. Where in traditional reconstruction we compare a lower level unit, sounds, through their context of appearance as part of a higher level unit, the word, in syntactic reconstruction we can compare a lower level unit, lexical items, through their context of appearance in sentences. In both cases we can establish diachronic relatedness between individual items and thus proceed to reconstruction. However, the parallel only runs so far: unlike lexical items, sentences are not transmitted across generations but instead are constructed anew by each speaker. In section 2.4 I argued that this limitation, the 'correspondence problem', prevents wholesale importation of the methods of traditional reconstruction into syntax; however, I also argued that this problem is not fatal to syntactic reconstruction, as other ways of establishing correspondences can be sought.

The following three chapters applied this line of thinking to several concrete problems in the prehistory of the Germanic language family, building on research into the earliest attested languages—Old English, Old Saxon, Old High German, Old Icelandic, and Gothic—that made use of electronic parsed and tagged corpora and statistical tests where available.

Chapter 3 dealt with topicalization and the position of the verb in the clause structure of early Northwest Germanic. I argued that both verb-second and verb-third patterns can be reconstructed for neutral declarative main clauses, and (following Bech 1998, 2001; Westergaard 2005; and Speyer 2008, 2010) that the distribution of these patterns is conditioned by information-structural factors such as given vs. new information status of constituents. This is in contrast to an earlier hypothesis, widely accepted, that verb-third clauses occur only when pronominal subjects are present; following Bech (2001), Haeberli (2002), and Speyer (2008, 2010), I adduced data from OE to show that this claim is false. By contrast, a new quantitative study of OS showed that this language did not mimic OE as previously assumed, and that the verb-third pattern of OE and OHG is not present in this language. Another suggestive finding was that 'verb-late' main clauses, which have often been considered either ungrammatical or in free variation with V2 and V3 clauses in OE, contain higher proportions of speaker-oriented adverbs and first person pronouns than other main clauses. I tentatively linked this to their double-propositional semantics, though I was not able to demonstrate that the finding generalizes to other early Germanic languages.

Chapter 4 concerned *wh*-elements (*who*, *what*, etc.) and the syntax of interrogatives in early Germanic. It was observed that *wh*-interrogatives in these languages are predominantly verb-second (Eyþórsson 1995), and that the apparent exceptions to this pattern can receive a principled account. I outlined an empirical discovery about word order in OE and OS clauses preceded by the word *hwæt*, namely that the finite verb occurs consistently later in the clause than in normal declarative clauses. I argued that *hwæt* is not clause-external or extrametrical as traditionally assumed, but rather serves as part of the clause, introducing an exclamative clause parallel to modern English *How you've changed!* or colloquial modern German *Was du dich verändert hast!* This led me to propose a new reading of the first line of *Beowulf*, among other things. Finally I discussed reflexes of Proto-Germanic *$h^w$aþeraz/ *$h^w$eþeraz, arguing that these items were originally nominal interrogative pronouns meaning 'which of two', and that the alternative use of this pronoun as a marker of disjunctive questions was an innovation within Northwest Germanic.

Chapter 5 addressed the conditions under which it was possible to leave subjects (and objects) unexpressed in early Germanic. New quantitative studies of all five of the early Germanic languages under consideration revealed features that have previously gone unnoticed: for instance, in the West Germanic languages, as well as in Old Swedish, subject pronouns are almost never left unexpressed in subordinate clauses (in contrast to main clauses). In addition, object pronouns can be unexpressed in all the early North and West Germanic languages. I argued that Proto-Northwest Germanic was probably unlike either English or Italian with regard to this property, instead behaving more like modern Finnish or Hebrew as a 'partial null argument language', building on a proposal by Holmberg (2010). More tentatively, it was suggested that Proto-Germanic may have been a more canonical Italian-style null subject language.

## 6.2 Beyond Germanic

In this section I compare my hypotheses about Proto-Germanic to those voiced for other daughters of Proto-Indo-European.[1] As discussed in section 1.4, the choice of a relatively shallow time-depth family like Germanic was intentional: the relevant data, though diverse, is much more manageable than attempting to take into account all early Indo-European languages. In the case of Germanic, it is at least in principle possible for a single scholar to be familiar with all of the relevant languages, and the subgrouping is relatively well understood. In the case of Indo-European, syntactic reconstructionists have (rightly) been criticized for putting too much emphasis on particular languages at the expense of others: for instance, Lehmann (1974) focuses heavily on Vedic Sanskrit, and Friedrich (1975) focuses on Homeric Greek. Even Delbrück's celebrated work lacks reference to Albanian, Armenian, and Celtic, as he notes (1893: 88). Watkins (1976: 310) wryly refers to this inevitable bias as 'Teeter's Law: the language of the family you know best always turns out to be the most archaic'. What follows should therefore not be understood as a serious attempt to reconstruct syntactic properties of Proto-Indo-European, but rather as preliminary observations of similarities between reconstructions of subfamilies: I will not discuss the feature contents of individual lexical items.

Word order research on the older Germanic languages has a long pedigree, going back at least to Delbrück (1893). In Chapter 3 I took no firm stance on the position of the verb in Proto-Germanic. It is revealing, however, that all studies addressing the word order of the early Indo-European languages within a generative framework have argued for the need to posit more than just a single CP at the clausal left periphery. This is true even for those studies, like Hale (1987a, 1987b), Garrett (1990), and Kiparsky (1995), that pre-date Rizzi's (1997) influential split-CP proposal.[2] Vedic Sanskrit is analysed by Hale (1987b) as requiring two pragmatically driven specifier positions, on the basis that topical elements can precede *wh*-words. Garrett (1990) finds the same for Hittite. Fortson (2004) and Ledgeway (2012: chapter 5) argue for a large number of pragmatically driven left-peripheral positions for Latin.[3] The

---

[1] I'd like to thank Ian Roberts for encouraging me to write this section.

[2] Strictly speaking, Kiparsky (1995) argues that there is no CP in Proto-Indo-European. However, he does posit multiple information-structurally active positions in the clausal left periphery.

[3] Ledgeway (2012: chapter 4) outlines a different view, according to which the very earliest stages of Latin were completely non-configurational, i.e. exhibiting flat structure. Given the syntactic assumptions made in chapter 1, including binary Merge, this alternative is not available to me.

findings of Dik (1995) and Matić (2003) for Ancient Greek are also interpretable in terms of a split CP domain, as Newton (2006: 124–5) notes. Newton argues (2006: 141) that for Old Irish there is no evidence for a split CP, though Roberts (2005) and Adger (2006b) suggest otherwise. The left periphery in the early Celtic languages is agreed to have been innovative (Watkins 1976; Newton 2006: 140–55), with the initial placement of the verb in these languages being the result of a reanalysis of an earlier pragmatically driven movement.

As for Germanic, even if the position of the verb remains unclear, I have argued in section 3.2.4 that at least two left-peripheral specifier positions are required for Proto-Northwest Germanic main clauses. Ferraresi (2005) provides evidence for a rigidly ordered hierarchy of left-peripheral particles, as discussed in section 3.5, interspersed with specifier positions; this can be interpreted in our terms as clear evidence for a split CP.

The studies discussed here make various different theoretical assumptions and are based on data collected in various ways. However, the fact that all the languages investigated (with the possible exception of early Celtic) have an active left periphery is strongly indicative that Proto-Indo-European did too.

With regard to interrogatives as discussed in Chapter 4, the situation in relation to verb movement is clear in Germanic (there was movement to the left periphery; cf. also Eyþórsson 1995), but not so clear in other early Indo-European languages. An alternative claim—that *wh*-movement took place in all these languages—derives immediate support from the references given above, though. Some daughter languages contain *wh*-in-situ, e.g. Hindi and varieties of French, but the attested history of these languages shows that these are clearly innovations.

Finally, null subjects of some type were almost certainly a property of Proto-Indo-European. As Hale (2013: 7 n. 4) puts it, 'null subjects are confidently reconstructed by all practicing Indo-Europeanists for the protolanguage, on the basis of the overwhelmingly clear evidence of the most archaic daughters'. Of course, since null subjects are not a unitary phenomenon, this sort of pretheoretical claim only serves to narrow down the hypothesis space. Proto-Germanic had relatively rich subject agreement morphology on verbs, and because of this and the Gothic situation I suggested in section 5.4.3 that it was an Italian-style null subject language. As noted there, Sanskrit and Old Church Slavonic were also null subject languages, as were Latin, Ancient Greek, and Hittite. Problematic for an Italian-style null subject account of Proto-Indo-European is, however, the frequent occurrence of referential null objects in the early daughters (see Krisch 2009; Luraghi 2010). This includes all the early Germanic languages, as shown in section 5.2; Luraghi (2010) also gives examples from Vedic Sanskrit, Latin, and Ancient Greek, and Krisch (2009) presents a few examples from Hittite. Since the early Indo-European languages did not display object agreement, presumably neither did Proto-Indo-European (though see Kortlandt 1983). This opens up two further possibilities: either Proto-Indo-European was a radical null argument language in the sense of Neeleman and Szendrői (2007, 2008), or it had multiple strategies at its disposal for licensing null arguments. The former is not unreasonable, since the personal pronouns of Proto-Indo-European as reconstructed by Beekes (1995: 207–11) can be analysed as agglutinative without too much special pleading.

In this brief section, I have compared some of the results mentioned in section 6.1 with results reached elsewhere in the literature. Several points emerge. First, it is difficult to compare the results of studies making differing theoretical assumptions and using different methodologies; secondly, the hypotheses defended here suggest that Proto-Germanic was not wildly dissimilar from other daughters of Proto-Indo-European; thirdly, that a reconstruction of Proto-Indo-European itself might not be out of reach, although it will inevitably be less certain than any hypothesis about the reconstruction of its daughters, since it must build on such hypotheses.

## 6.3  Reconstructing grammars

When we reconstruct syntax, what is it that we are reconstructing? Could a speaker of Proto-Germanic, at some point in history, at least potentially have uttered a sentence that looked at least somewhat like (1) when discussing his exploits (cf. Watkins 1995)?

(1)  *Ek   slōh    wurmi
    I       killed  dragon.ACC
    'I slew a dragon.'

The question is difficult to evaluate. I have argued, in Chapter 3, that V2 involving verb-movement to $Fin^0$ was probably a possibility for neutral declarative main clauses in early Northwest Germanic, and perhaps available in Gothic and Proto-Germanic as well. If so, the word order of (1) is unproblematic. But much depends on the information-structure and interpretation. Since the object (the dragon) is post-verbal, we have to assume that it is not given information (i.e. not in SpecFamP). If the clause is non-assertive, it might lack verb-movement, as suggested in section 3.4 for OE; a more expected string might then be (2).

(2)  *Ek   wurmi      slōh
    I       dragon.ACC  killed
    'I slew a dragon.'

As suggested in section 4.3, lack of verb-movement may also have been more likely in an exclamative, as in (3).

(3)  *H$^w$at   ek   wurmi       slōh
    hw.      I     dragon.ACC  killed
    'How (impressively) I slew a dragon!'

If Proto-Germanic was a canonical null subject language, as I have suggested in Chapter 5, then it might have been more usual to leave the subject out, as in (4), unless a contrastive interpretation was intended ('It was I').

(4)    Wurmi        slōh
       dragon.ACC   killed
       'I killed a dragon.'

A large number of other assumptions would also be made in claiming that (1) was a grammatical sentence of Proto-Germanic, including assumptions about verbal valency, complementation, and case assignment. And even if verb-movement to the left periphery were unavailable in Proto-Germanic, a string such as (1) might be derivable through another process, for instance 'rightward movement' of the object *wurmi* under presentational focus (on which see Wallenberg 2009: 202–46 and Taylor and Pintzuk 2009, 2012). A string like (4) might have been grammatical, but not felicitous in all contexts.

All this means that it is not very meaningful to talk about the reconstruction of sentences for Proto-Germanic (or any other language). As a result, I disagree with Klein's (2010: 721) claim that we should eschew the 'stultifying search for I-language'. As the above should make clear, when reconstructing syntax, fragments of grammar—of I-language—are realistically all that we can hope to construct.

In other respects, the view espoused by this book is not too dissimilar to that of Klein (2010), as well as other recent work such as Harris (2008), Willis (2011), and Barðdal and Eyþórsson (2012). The reconstructions proposed here, as in these works, have been 'item-based'—making existential rather than universal claims about the grammatical inventories of protolanguages, unlike the much-criticized typological reconstructions of the 1970s. I agree with Klein that 'the closer we link our reconstructions to formal cognation, the greater our prospects of success become' (2010: 721). When cognacy can be established independently on lexical-phonological grounds, as outlined in section 2.4.2, and common directional tendencies can be employed in reconstructing a proto-form, we are on the safest ground. Conversely, when the cognacy of two syntactic lexical items has to be established on grounds of formal similarity and distributional complementarity alone, and when less is known about tendencies of directionality—as with the reconstructions to do with word order in Chapter 3, for instance—our conclusions are inevitably less firm. Still, given the nature of all reconstruction (and all historical linguistics—see Chapter 1) as a process of competitive myth-construction, this should not be a cause for despair.

## 6.4 Afterword

> A whole life cannot be spent upon syntax and etymology, and ... even a whole life would not be sufficient. (Johnson 1755: preface)

On the specific side, this book has aimed to provide a better idea of what the syntax of Proto-Germanic may have been like. More generally, the book is an extended argument for the feasibility of syntactic reconstruction, and tries to show that the hybrid approach to syntactic change outlined in Chapter 2, drawing on history, philology, and evolutionary biology as well as the mentalist approach to linguistics, can be both powerful and revealing.

I haven't had a whole life to work on this book, only the three years of a Ph.D. project, and I'm not Dr Johnson. That doesn't excuse any errors or omissions in this book, of course, but it might make them more understandable. In the spirit of myth-making, however, I hope that the reader is encouraged to improve on the proposals made here, and to come up with better ideas, rather than rejecting the enterprise out of hand.

# References

## Texts, dictionaries, editions, and corpora

Alexander, Michael (1973). *Beowulf: a verse translation*. Harmondsworth: Penguin.

Behaghel, Otto, and Burkhard Taeger (1996). *Heliand und Genesis*. 10th edn. Halle: Max Niemeyer.

Bierce, Ambrose G. (1911). *The Devil's dictionary*. New York: Neale.

Bosworth, Joseph, and T. Northcote Toller (1898). *An Anglo-Saxon dictionary*. Oxford: Clarendon.

Cleasby, Richard, and Gudbrand Vigfusson (1874). *An Icelandic–English dictionary*. Oxford: Clarendon.

Davies, Mark (2008–). The Corpus of Contemporary American English: 425 million words, 1990–present.

Donaldson, E. Talbot (1966). *Beowulf: a new prose translation*. New York: Norton.

Earle, John (1892). *The Deeds of Beowulf*. Oxford: Clarendon.

Fulk, Robert D. (2010). *The Beowulf manuscript: complete texts and the Fight at Finnsburg*. Cambridge, Mass.: Harvard University Press.

Graff, Eberhard Gottlieb, and Hans Ferdinand Massmann (1838). *Althochdeutscher Sprachschatz; oder: Wörterbuch der althochdeutschen Sprache*, vol. iv. Berlin: Nikolaischen Buchhandlung.

Harrison, James, and Robert Sharp (eds.) (1893). *Beówulf: an Anglo-Saxon Poem*. 4th edn. Boston and New York: Ginn.

Heaney, Seamus (1999). *Beowulf: a new verse translation*. London: Faber and Faber.

Heyne, Moritz (1873). *Hêliand: mit ausführlichem Glossar*. 2nd edn. Paderborn: Ferdinand Schöninghausen.

Jack, George B. (1994). *Beowulf: a student edition*. Oxford: Clarendon.

Kemble, John (ed.) (1835). *The Anglo-Saxon poems of Beowulf*. 2nd edn. London: Pickering.

Kemble, John (1837). *A translation of the Anglo-Saxon poem of Beowulf*. London: Pickering.

Klaeber, Friedrich (ed.) (1922). *Beowulf and the Fight at Finnsburg*. Boston and New York: Heath.

Lewis, Charlton T., and Charles Short (1879). *A Latin dictionary*. Oxford: Clarendon.

Liuzza, Roy (2000). *Beowulf: a new verse translation*. Peterborough, Ontario: Broadview Press.

Mitchell, Bruce, and Susan Irvine (eds.) (2000). 'Beowulf repunctuated', *Old English Newsletter Subsidia* 29.

Mitchell, Bruce, and Fred Robinson (eds.) (1998). *Beowulf: an edition with relevant shorter texts*. Oxford: Blackwell.

Morgan, Edwin (1952). *Beowulf: a verse translation into Modern English*. Aldington: Hand and Flower Press.

Nestle, Eberhard, Erwin Nestle, Barbara Aland, and Kurt Aland (2001). *Novum Testamentum Graece*. 27th edn. Stuttgart: Deutsche Bibelgesellschaft.

*Oxford English Dictionary Online* (2012). Oxford: Oxford University Press.

Pintzuk, Susan, and Leendert Plug (2001). The York–Helsinki Parsed Corpus of Old English Poetry.

Raffel, Burton (1963). *Beowulf.* New York: New American Library.

Randall, Beth (2005–7). CorpusSearch 2.

Robinson, Maurice A., and William G. Pierpont (2005). *The New Testament in the original Greek: Byzantine Textform.* Southborough, Mass.: Chilton.

Sievers, Eduard (1878). *Heliand.* Halle: Verlag der Buchhandlung des Waisenhauses.

Streitberg, Wilhelm (ed.) (1919). *Der gotische Bibel: der gotische Text und seine griechische Vorlage, mit Einleitung, Lesarten und Quellennachweisen sowie den kleineren Denkmälern als Anhang.* Heidelberg: Carl Winter.

Taylor, Ann, Anthony Warner, Susan Pintzuk, and Frank Beths (2003). York–Toronto–Helsinki Parsed Corpus of Old English Prose.

Trask, Robert Lawrence (1996a). *A dictionary of phonetics and phonology.* London: Routledge.

Wallenberg, Joel C., Anton Karl Ingason, Einar Freyr Sigurðsson, and Eiríkur Rögnvaldsson (2011). *Icelandic Parsed Historical Corpus (IcePaHC).* Version 0.9.1.

## Secondary literature

Abels, Klaus (2003). *Successive cyclicity, anti-locality, and adposition stranding.* Ph.D. dissertation. University of Connecticut, Storrs.

Abels, Klaus (2010). 'Factivity in exclamatives is a presupposition', *Studia Linguistica* 64: 141–57.

Aboh, Enoch (2010). 'Information structuring begins with the numeration', *Iberia* 2: 12–42.

Abraham, Werner (1991). 'Null subjects: from Gothic, Old High German and Middle High German to Modern German. From pro-drop to semi-pro-drop', *Groninger Arbeiten zur germanistischen Linguistik* 34: 1–28.

Ackema, Peter, and Ad Neeleman (2007). 'Restricted pro drop in Early Modern Dutch', *Journal of Comparative Germanic Linguistics* 10: 81–107.

Adams, Marianne (1987a). *Old French, null subjects and verb second phenomena.* Ph.D. dissertation. UCLA.

Adams, Marianne (1987b). 'From Old French to the theory of pro-drop', *Natural Language and Linguistic Theory* 5: 1–32.

Adger, David (2003). *Core syntax: a Minimalist approach.* Oxford: Oxford University Press.

Adger, David (2006a). 'Combinatorial variability', *Journal of Linguistics* 42: 503–30.

Adger, David (2006b). 'Post-syntactic movement and the Old Irish verb', *Natural Language and Linguistic Theory* 24: 605–54.

Adger, David (2010). 'A Minimalist theory of feature structure', in Anna Kibort and Greville G. Corbett (eds.), *Features: perspectives on a key notion in linguistics.* Oxford: Oxford University Press, 185–218.

Adger, David, and Josep Quer (2001). 'The syntax and semantics of unselected embedded questions', *Language* 77: 107–33.

Adger, David, and Jennifer Smith (2005). 'Variation and the Minimalist Program', in Leonie Cornips and Karen Corrigan (eds.), *Syntax and variation: reconciling the biological and the social*. Amsterdam: John Benjamins, 148–75.

Aikhenvald, Alexandra Y. (2006). 'Grammars in contact: a cross-linguistic perspective', in Alexandra Y. Aikhenvald (ed.), *Grammars in contact: a cross-linguistic typology*. Oxford: Oxford University Press, 1–66.

Alexiadou, Artemis (2006). 'Uniform and non-uniform aspects of pro-drop', in Peter Ackema, Patrick Brandt, Maaike Schoorlemmer, and Fred Weerman (eds.), *Arguments and Agreement*. Oxford: Oxford University Press, 127–58.

Alexiadou, Artemis, and Elena Anagnostopoulou (1998). 'Parametrizing AGR: word order, V-movement and EPP checking', *Natural Language and Linguistic Theory* 16: 491–539.

Alexopoulou, Theodora, and Frank Keller (2007). 'Locality, cyclicity and resumption: at the interface between the grammar and the human sentence processor', *Language* 83: 110–60.

Allen, Cynthia L. (1977). *Topics in diachronic English syntax*. Ph.D. dissertation. University of Massachusetts.

Allen, Cynthia L. (1980a). 'Movement and deletion in Old English', *Linguistic Inquiry* 11: 261–325.

Allen, Cynthia L. (1980b). '*Whether* in Old English', *Linguistic Inquiry* 11: 789–93.

Allen, Cynthia L. (1990). 'Review of van Kemenade (1987)', *Language* 66: 146–52.

Allen, Cynthia L. (1995). *Case marking and reanalysis: grammatical relations from Old to Modern English*. Oxford: Oxford University Press.

Andersen, Henning (1973). 'Abductive and deductive change', *Language* 49: 765–93.

Anderson, John M. (2006). 'Structural analogy and universal grammar', *Lingua* 116: 601–33.

Andrew, Samuel O. (1940). *Syntax and style in Old English*. Cambridge: Cambridge University Press.

Angantýsson, Ásgrímur (2007). 'Verb-third in embedded clauses in Icelandic', *Studia Linguistica* 61: 237–60.

Antonsen, Elmer H. (1975). *A concise grammar of the older Runic inscriptions*. Tübingen: Max Niemeyer.

Antonsen, Elmer H. (2002). *Runes and Germanic linguistics*. Berlin: Mouton de Gruyter.

Ariel, Mira (1990). *Accessing noun-phrase antecedents*. New York: Routledge.

Aronoff, Mark (1976). *Word formation in generative grammar*. Cambridge, Mass.: MIT Press.

Austin, J. L. (1975). *How to do things with words*. 2nd edn. Oxford: Oxford University Press.

Axel, Katrin (2002). 'Zur diachronen Entwicklung der syntaktischen Integration linksperipherer Adverbialsätze im Deutschen: ein Beispiel für syntaktischen Wandel?', *Beiträge zur Geschichte der deutschen Sprache und Literatur* 124: 1–43.

Axel, Katrin (2004). 'The syntactic integration of preposed adverbial clauses on the German left periphery: a diachronic perspective', in Horst Lohnstein and Susanne Trissler (eds.), *The syntax and semantics of the left periphery*. Berlin: Mouton de Gruyter, 23–58.

Axel, Katrin (2005). 'Null subjects and verb placement in Old High German', in Stephan Kepser and Marga Reis (eds.), *Linguistic evidence: empirical, theoretical and computational perspectives*. Berlin: Mouton de Gruyter, 27–48.

Axel, Katrin (2007). *Studies on Old High German syntax: left sentence periphery, verb placement and verb-second*. Amsterdam: John Benjamins.

Axel, Katrin, and Helmut Weiß (2011). '*Pro*-drop in the history of German from Old High German to the modern dialects', in Melani Wratil and Peter Gallmann (eds.), *Null pronouns*. Berlin: Mouton de Gruyter, 21–52.

Axel, Katrin, and Angelika Wöllstein (2009). 'German verb-first conditionals as unintegrated clauses: a case study in converging synchronic and diachronic evidence', in Sam Featherston and Susanne Winkler (eds.), *The fruits of empirical linguistics*, vol. ii: *Product*. Berlin: Mouton de Gruyter, 1–36.

Bailey, Charles-James N. (1973). *Variation and linguistic theory*. Washington, DC: Center for Applied Linguistics.

Bailey, Charles-James N. (1996). *Essays on time-based linguistic analysis*. Oxford: Clarendon.

Baker, C. Lee (1970). 'Double negatives', *Linguistic Inquiry* 1: 169–86.

Baker, Mark (1996). *The polysynthesis parameter*. Oxford: Oxford University Press.

Baker, Mark (2001). *The atoms of language*. Oxford: Oxford University Press.

Baker, Mark (2008). 'The macroparameter in a microparametric world', in Theresa Biberauer (ed.), *The limits of syntactic variation*. Amsterdam: John Benjamins, 351–73.

Baker, Mark (2009). 'Language universals: abstract but not mythological', *Behavioural and Brain Sciences* 32: 448–9.

Ball, C. J. E. (1968). 'The Germanic dental preterite', *Transactions of the Philological Society* 67: 162–88.

Bammesberger, Alfred (2006). 'The syntactic analysis of the opening verses in Beowulf', *ANQ* 19: 3–7.

Barbosa, Maria do Pilar Pereira (1995). *Null subjects*. Ph.D. dissertation. MIT.

Barbosa, Maria do Pilar Pereira (2001). 'On inversion in *wh*-questions in Romance', in Aafke Hulk and Jean-Yves Pollock (eds.), *Subject inversion in Romance and the theory of Universal Grammar*. Oxford: Oxford University Press, 20–59.

Barbosa, Maria do Pilar Pereira (2009). 'Two kinds of subject *pro*', *Studia Linguistica* 63: 2–58.

Barnes, Michael (2004). *A new introduction to Old Norse. Part I: Grammar*. 2nd edn. Exeter: Short Run Press.

Barðdal, Jóhanna (2001). 'Oblique subjects in Old Scandinavian', *NOWELE* 37: 25–51.

Barðdal, Jóhanna (2009). 'The development of case in Germanic', in Jóhanna Barðdal and Shobhana Lakshmi Chelliah (eds.), *The role of semantic, pragmatic, and discourse factors in the development of case*. Amsterdam: John Benjamins, 123–59.

Barðdal, Jóhanna (2013). 'Construction-based historical-comparative reconstruction', in Graeme Trousdale and Thomas Hoffmann (eds.), *The Oxford handbook of Construction Grammar*. Oxford: Oxford University Press, 438–57.

Barðdal, Jóhanna, and Þórhallur Eyþórsson (2005). 'Oblique subjects: a common Germanic inheritance', *Language* 81: 824–81.

Barðdal, Jóhanna, and Þórhallur Eyþórsson (2012). 'Reconstructing syntax: Construction Grammar and the comparative method', in Hans C. Boas and Ivan Sag (eds.), *Sign-based construction grammar*. Stanford, Calif.: CSLI Publications, 257–308.

Baxter, William H. (2002). 'Where does the "comparative method" come from?', in Fabrice Cavoto (ed.), *The linguist's linguist: a collection of papers in honour of Alexis Manaster Ramer*, vol. i. Munich: Lincom Europa, 33–52.

Bean, Marian (1983). *The development of word order patterns in Old English*. London: Croom Helm.

Bech, Kristin (1998). 'Pragmatic factors in language change: XVS and XSV clauses in Old and Middle English', *Folia Linguistica Historica* 19: 79–102.

Bech, Kristin (2001). *Word order patterns in Old and Middle English: a syntactic and pragmatic study*. Ph.D. dissertation. University of Bergen.

Beekes, Robert S. P. (1995). *Comparative Indo-European linguistics: an introduction*. Amsterdam: John Benjamins.

Behaghel, Otto (1897). *Die Syntax des Heliand*. Vienna: Tempsky.

Behaghel, Otto (1923–32). *Deutsche Syntax: eine geschichtliche Darstellung*. 4 vols. Heidelberg: Carl Winter.

Behrmann, Adolf (1879). *Die pronomina personalia und ihr Gebrauch im Hêliand*. Marburg: C. L. Pfeil.

Bellert, Irene (1977). 'On semantic and distributional properties of sentential adverbs', *Linguistic Inquiry* 8: 337–51.

Bender, Emily (1999). 'Constituting context: null objects in English recipes revisited', *University of Pennsylvania Working Papers in Linguistics* 6: 53–68.

Benincà, Paola, and Cecilia Poletto (2004). 'Topic, focus and V2: defining the CP sublayers', in Luigi Rizzi (ed.), *The cartography of syntactic structures*, vol. ii: *The structure of CP and IP*. Oxford: Oxford University Press, 52–75.

Bennett, William H. (1980). *An introduction to the Gothic language*. New York: Modern Language Association of America.

Berard, Stephen A. (1993). 'Biblical Gothic and the configurationality parameter', *American Journal of Germanic Linguistics and Literatures* 5: 111–62.

Bergen, Linda van (2003). *Pronouns and word order in Old English, with particular reference to the indefinite pronoun man*. London: Routledge.

Berizzi, Mariachiara (2010). *Interrogatives and relatives in some varieties of English*. Ph.D. dissertation. Università degli Studi di Padova.

Berndt, Rolf (1956). *Form und Funktion des Verbums im nördlichen Spätaltenglischen*. Halle: Max Niemeyer.

Berwick, Robert (1985). *The acquisition of syntactic knowledge*. Cambridge, Mass.: MIT Press.

Berwick, Robert, and Noam Chomsky (2011). 'The biolinguistic program: the current state of its evolution and development', in Ana Maria Di Sciullo and Cedric Boeckx (eds.), *The biolinguistic enterprise: new perspectives on the evolution and nature of the human language faculty*. Oxford: Oxford University Press, 19–41.

Besten, Hans den (1977). *On the interaction of root transformations and lexical deletive verbs*. MS. University of Amsterdam.

Bethurum, Dorothy (1932). 'The form of Ælfric's Lives of Saints', *Studies in Philology* 29: 515–33.

Biberauer, Theresa (2002). 'Reconsidering embedded verb second: How "real" is this phenomenon?', *Working Papers in English and Applied Linguistics* 8: 25–60.

Biberauer, Theresa (2008). 'A "third factor"-imposed typology of (dis)harmonic languages?', paper presented at the Cambridge-Delhi-Hyderabad-Nanzan Workshop, Hyderabad, India.

Biberauer, Theresa, Anders Holmberg, and Ian Roberts (2010). *A syntactic universal and its consequences*. MS. University of Cambridge.

Biberauer, Theresa, and Marc Richards (2006). 'True optionality: when the grammar doesn't mind', in Cedric Boeckx (ed.), *Minimalist essays*. Amsterdam: John Benjamins, 35–67.

Biberauer, Theresa, and Ian Roberts (2004). 'Evidence that V2 involves two movements: a reply to Müller', *Cambridge Occasional Papers in Linguistics* 1: 100–20.

Biberauer, Theresa, and Ian Roberts (2005). 'Changing EPP parameters in the history of English: accounting for variation and change', *English Language and Linguistics* 9: 5–46.

Biberauer, Theresa, and Ian Roberts (2008). 'Cascading parameter changes: internally-driven change in Middle and Early Modern English', in Þórhallur Eyþórsson (ed.), *Grammatical change and linguistic theory: the Rosendal papers*. Amsterdam: John Benjamins, 79–114.

Biberauer, Theresa, and Ian Roberts (2009). 'The return of the Subset Principle: a diachronic perspective', in Paola Crisma and Giuseppe Longobardi (eds.), *Historical syntax and linguistic theory*. Oxford: Oxford University Press, 58–74.

Biberauer, Theresa, and Ian Roberts (2010). 'Subjects, tense and verb-movement', in Theresa Biberauer, Anders Holmberg, Ian Roberts, and Michelle Sheehan (eds.), *Parametric variation: null subjects in Minimalist theory*. Cambridge: Cambridge University Press, 263–302.

Bini, Milena (1993). 'La adquisición del italiano: más allá de las propiedades sintácticas del parámetro pro-drop', in J. M. Liceras (ed.), *La lingüística y el análisis de los sistemas no nativos*. Ottawa: Dovehouse, 126–39.

Blevins, Juliette (2004). *Evolutionary phonology: the emergence of sound patterns*. Cambridge: Cambridge University Press.

Boeckx, Cedric (2010). *What Principles and Parameters got wrong*. MS. ICREA/UAB.

Boeckx, Cedric (2011). 'Approaching parameters from below', in Ana Maria Di Sciullo and Cedric Boeckx (eds.), *The biolinguistic enterprise: new perspectives on the evolution and nature of the human language faculty*. Oxford: Oxford University Press, 205–21.

Bolinger, Dwight (1972). *Degree words*. Paris: Mouton.

Bopp, Franz (1816). *Über das Conjugationssystem der Sanskritsprache in Vergleichung mit jenem der griechischen, lateinischen, persischen und germanischen Sprachen*. Frankfurt am Main: Andreä.

Borer, Hagit (1984). *Parametric syntax*. Dordrecht: Foris.

Borer, Hagit (1986). 'I-subjects', *Linguistic Inquiry* 17: 375–416.

Borer, Hagit (1989). 'Anaphoric Agr', in Osvaldo Jaeggli and Kenneth J. Safir (eds.), *The null subject parameter*. Dordrecht: Kluwer, 69–109.

Borer, Hagit, and Kenneth Wexler (1992). 'Bi-unique relations and the maturation of grammatical principles', *Natural Language and Linguistic Theory* 10: 147–89.

Bošković, Željko (2005). 'On the locality of left branch extraction and the structure of NP', *Studia Linguistica* 59: 1–45.

Bošković, Željko (2008). 'What will you have, DP or NP?', *Proceedings of NELS* 37: 101–14.

Bošković, Željko (2009). 'More on the no-DP analysis of article-less languages', *Studia Linguistica* 63: 187–204.

Bowern, Claire (2008). 'Syntactic change and syntactic borrowing in generative grammar', in Gisella Ferraresi and Maria Goldbach (eds.), *Principles of syntactic reconstruction*. Amsterdam: John Benjamins, 187–216.

Branigan, Phil (1996). 'Verb second and the A-bar status of subjects', *Studia Linguistica* 50: 354–80.

Braune, Wilhelm, and Hans Eggers (1975). *Althochdeutsche Grammatik*. 13th edn. Tübingen: Max Niemeyer.

Braunmüller, Kurt (1982). *Syntaxtypologische Studien zum Germanischen*. Tübingen: Narr.

Breitbarth, Anne (2009). 'A hybrid approach to Jespersen's Cycle in West Germanic', *Journal of Comparative Germanic Linguistics* 12: 81–114.

Brentari, Diane (1998). *A prosodic model of sign language phonology*. Cambridge, Mass.: MIT Press.

Bresnan, Joan, and Ashwini Deo (2001). *Grammatical constraints on variation: 'Be' in the survey of English dialects and (stochastic) Optimality Theory*. MS. Stanford University.

Brinton, Laurel J. (1996). *Pragmatic markers in English: grammaticalization and discourse functions*. Berlin: Mouton de Gruyter.

Bromberger, Sylvain, and Morris Halle (1989). 'Why phonology is different', *Linguistic Inquiry* 20: 51–70.

Brugmann, Karl (1904). *Kurze vergleichende Grammatik der indogermanischen Sprachen*. Strasbourg: Karl J. Trübner.

Butt, Miriam (2001). 'Case, agreement, pronoun incorporation and pro-drop in South Asian languages', paper presented at the Workshop on the Role of Agreement in Argument Structure, Utrecht University.

Buttery, Paula (2006). *Computational models for first language acquisition*. Technical Report 675, University of Cambridge Computer Laboratory.

Caha, Pavel (2009). *The nanosyntax of case*. Ph.D. dissertation. University of Tromsø.

Camacho, José, and José Elías-Ulloa (2010). 'Null subjects in Shipibo switch-reference systems', in José Camacho, Rodrigo Gutiérrez-Bravo, and Liliana Sánchez (eds.), *Information structure in indigenous languages of the Americas: syntactic approaches*. Berlin: Mouton de Gruyter, 65–85.

Campbell, Alistair (1970). 'Verse influences in Old English prose', in James L. Rosier (ed.), *Philological essays: studies in Old and Middle English language and literature in honour of Herbert Dean Merritt*. The Hague: Mouton de Gruyter, 93–8.

Campbell, Lyle (1990). 'Syntactic reconstruction and Finno-Ugric', in Henning Andersen and Konrad Körner (eds.), *Historical Linguistics 1987: papers from the 8th International Conference on Historical Linguistics*. Amsterdam: John Benjamins, 51–94.

Campbell, Lyle (2001). 'What's wrong with grammaticalization?', *Language Sciences* 23: 113–61.

Campbell, Lyle (2013). *Historical linguistics: an introduction*. 3rd edn. Edinburgh: Edinburgh University Press.

Campbell, Lyle, and Alice C. Harris (2002). 'Syntactic reconstruction and demythologizing "Myths and the prehistory of grammars"', *Journal of Linguistics* 38: 599–618.

Campbell, Lyle, and Marianne Mithun (1981). 'Syntactic reconstruction: priorities and pitfalls', *Folia Linguistica Historica* 1: 19–40.

Campbell, Lyle, and William J. Poser (2008). *Language classification: history and method*. Cambridge: Cambridge University Press.

Campbell-Kibler, Kathryn (2010). 'The sociolinguistic variable as a carrier of social meaning', *Language Variation and Change* 22: 423–41.

Cardinaletti, Anna (1997). 'Subjects and clause structure', in Liliane Haegeman (ed.), *The new comparative syntax*. London: Longman, 33–63.

Cardinaletti, Anna (2004). 'Toward a cartography of subject positions', in Luigi Rizzi (ed.), *The cartography of syntactic structures*, vol. ii: *The structure of CP and IP*. Oxford: Oxford University Press, 115–65.

Cardinaletti, Anna, and Michal Starke (1999). 'The typology of structural deficiency: a case study of the three classes of pronouns', in Henk van Riemsdijk (ed.), *Clitics in the languages of Europe*. Berlin: Mouton de Gruyter, 145–235.

Castillo, Juan Carlos, John E. Drury, and Kleanthes K. Grohmann (2009). 'Merge over Move and the Extended Projection Principle: MOM and the EPP revisited', *Iberia* 1: 53–114.

Chambers, J. K., and Peter Trudgill (1998). *Dialectology*. 2nd edn. Cambridge: Cambridge University Press.

Chirikba, Viacheslav A. (2008). 'The problem of the Caucasian Sprachbund', in Pieter Muysken (ed.), *From linguistic areas to areal linguistics*. Amsterdam: John Benjamins, 25–93.

Chomsky, Noam (1957). *Syntactic structures*. The Hague: Mouton.

Chomsky, Noam (1980). *Rules and representations*. Oxford: Blackwell.

Chomsky, Noam (1981). *Lectures on Government and Binding*. Dordrecht: Foris.

Chomsky, Noam (1986a). *Barriers*. Cambridge, Mass.: MIT Press.

Chomsky, Noam (1986b). *Knowledge of language*. New York: Praeger.

Chomsky, Noam (1995). *The Minimalist Program*. Cambridge, Mass.: MIT Press.

Chomsky, Noam (2000). 'Minimalist inquiries: the framework', in Roger Martin, David Michaels, and Juan Uriagereka (eds.), *Step by step: essays on Minimalist syntax in honor of Howard Lasnik*. Cambridge, Mass.: MIT Press, 89–156.

Chomsky, Noam (2001). 'Derivation by phase', in Michael Kenstowicz (ed.), *Ken Hale: a life in language*. Cambridge, Mass.: MIT Press, 1–53.

Chomsky, Noam (2004). *The generative enterprise revisited: discussions with Riny Huybregts, Henk van Riemsdijk, Naoki Fukui and Mihoko Zushi*. Berlin: Mouton de Gruyter.

Chomsky, Noam (2005). 'Three factors in language design', *Linguistic Inquiry* 36: 1–22.

Chomsky, Noam, and Howard Lasnik (1977). 'Filters and Control', *Linguistic Inquiry* 8: 425–504.

Chung, Sandra, and James McCloskey (1983). 'On the interpretation of certain island effects in GPSG', *Linguistic Inquiry* 14: 704–13.

Cichosz, Anna (2010). *The influence of text type on word order of old Germanic languages: a corpus-based contrastive study of Old English and Old High German*. Frankfurt: Peter Lang.

Cinque, Guglielmo (1977). 'The movement nature of left dislocation', *Linguistic Inquiry* 8: 397–412.

Cinque, Guglielmo (1999). *Adverbs and functional heads: a cross-linguistic perspective*. Oxford: Oxford University Press.

Cinque, Guglielmo, and Luigi Rizzi (2010). 'The cartography of syntactic structures', in Bernd Heine and Heiko Narrog (eds.), *The Oxford handbook of linguistic analysis*. Oxford: Oxford University Press, 51–65.

Clackson, James (2007). *Indo-European linguistics*. Cambridge: Cambridge University Press.

Clahsen, Harold, and Pieter Muysken (1986). 'The availability of universal grammar to adult and child learners: a study of the acquisition of German word order', *Second Language Research* 2: 93–119.

Clark, Alexander, and Shalom Lappin (2011). *Linguistic nativism and the poverty of the stimulus*. New York: John Wiley and Sons.

Clark, Brady Z. (2004). *A Stochastic Optimality Theory approach to language change*. Ph.D. dissertation. Stanford University.

Clark, Robin (1992). 'The selection of syntactic knowledge', *Language Acquisition* 2: 83–149.

Clark, Robin, and Ian Roberts (1993). 'A computational approach to language learnability and language change', *Linguistic Inquiry* 24: 299–345.

Coetsem, Frans van (1988). *Loan phonology and the two transfer types in language contact*. Dordrecht: Foris.

Cole, Melvyn (2009). 'Null subjects: a reanalysis of the data', *Linguistics* 47: 559–87.

Cole, Melvyn (2010). 'Thematic null subjects and accessibility', *Studia Linguistica* 64: 271–320.

Cole, Peter (1987). 'Null objects in Universal Grammar', *Linguistic Inquiry* 18: 597–612.

Cordes, Gerhard, and Ferdinand Holthausen (1973). *Altniederdeutsches Elementarbuch*. Heidelberg: Carl Winter.

Corver, Norbert (1990). *The syntax of left-branch extractions*. Ph.D. dissertation. Katholieke Universiteit Brabant.

Costello, John R. (1983). *Syntactic change and syntactic reconstruction: a tagmemic approach*. Dallas: Summer Institute of Linguistics.

Crain, Stephen, Takuya Goro, and Rosalind Thornton (2006). 'Language acquisition is language change', *Journal of Psycholinguistic Research* 35: 31–49.

Cranenbroeck, Jeroen van, and Liliane Haegeman (2007). 'The derivation of subject-initial V2', *Linguistic Inquiry* 38: 167–78.

Crisma, Paola, and Giuseppe Longobardi (2009). 'Introduction: change, relatedness and inertia in historical syntax', in Paola Crisma and Giuseppe Longobardi (eds.), *Historical syntax and linguistic theory*. Oxford: Oxford University Press, 1–13.

Croft, William (2001). *Explaining language change: an evolutionary approach*. Oxford: Oxford University Press.

Cruschina, Silvio (2009). 'The syntactic role of discourse-related features', *Cambridge Occasional Papers in Linguistics* 5: 15–30.

Culbertson, Jennifer, Paul Smolensky, and Géraldine Legendre (2012). 'Learning biases predict a word order universal', *Cognition* 122: 306–29.

Culy, Christopher (1996). 'Null objects in English recipes', *Language Variation and Change* 8: 91–124.

Curme, George O. (1911). 'Is the Gothic Bible Gothic?', *Journal of English and Germanic Philology* 10: 151–90, 335–77.

Dąbrowska, Ewa (2012). 'Different speakers, different grammars: individual differences in native language attainment', *Linguistic Approaches to Bilingualism* 2: 219–53.

Dahl, Östen (2004). *The growth and maintenance of linguistic complexity*. Amsterdam: John Benjamins.

D'Avis, Franz-Josef (2002). 'On the interpretation of *wh*-clauses in exclamative environments', *Theoretical Linguistics* 28: 5–31.

Davis, Graeme, and Karl Bernhardt (2002). *Syntax of West Germanic: the syntax of Old English and Old High German*. Göppingen: Kümmerle.

Dayal, Veneeta (1996). *Locality in* wh-*quantification: questions and relative clauses in Hindi.* Dordrecht: Kluwer.

Deal, Amy Rose (2005). '*Pro*-drop and subject (non-)recoverability: the case of Nez Perce', *Generative Grammar @ Geneva* 4: 93–111.

Dekeyser, Xavier (1986). 'English contact clauses revisited: a diachronic approach', *Folia Linguistica Historica* 7: 107–20.

Delbrück, Berthold (1893–1900). *Vergleichende Syntax der indogermanischen Sprachen.* 3 vols. Strasbourg: Karl J. Trübner.

Derbyshire, Desmond C. (1979). *Hixkaryana.* Amsterdam: North-Holland.

Deutscher, Guy (2002). 'On the misuse of the notion of "abduction" in linguistics', *Journal of Linguistics* 38: 469–85.

Devine, Andrew, and Laurence Stephens (1999). *Discontinuous syntax: hyperbaton in Greek.* Oxford: Oxford University Press.

Dewey, Tonya Kim (2006). *The origins and development of Germanic V2.* Ph.D. dissertation. UC Berkeley.

Dewey, Tonya Kim, and Yasmin Syed (2009). 'Case variation in Gothic absolute constructions', in Jóhanna Barðdal and Shobhana Lakshmi Chelliah (eds.), *The role of semantic, pragmatic, and discourse factors in the development of case.* Amsterdam: John Benjamins, 3–21.

Diesing, Molly (1988). 'Word order and the subject position in Yiddish', in James Blevins and Judi Carter (eds.), *Proceedings of NELS 18*, vol. i. Amherst, Mass.: University of Massachusetts, 124–40.

Diesing, Molly (1990). 'Verb movement and the subject position in Yiddish', *Natural Language and Linguistic Theory* 8: 41–79.

Diesing, Molly (1992). *Indefinites.* Cambridge, Mass.: MIT Press.

Diesing, Molly (1997). 'Yiddish VP order and the typology of object movement in Germanic', *Natural Language and Linguistic Theory* 15: 369–427.

Dieter, Ferdinand (1900). *Laut- und Formenlehre der altgermanischen Dialekte*, vol. ii. Leipzig: Reisland.

Dik, Helma (1995). *Word order in Ancient Greek: a pragmatic account of word order variation in Herodotus.* Amsterdam: J. C. Gieben.

Dittmer, Arne, and Ernst Dittmer (1998). *Studien zur Wortstellung: Satzgliedstellung in der althochdeutschen Tatianübersetzung.* Göttingen: Vandenhoeck and Ruprecht.

Dressler, Wolfgang (1971). 'Über die Rekonstruktion der indogermanischen Syntax', *Zeitschrift für vergleichende Sprachforschung* 85: 5–22.

Dryer, Matthew (1992). 'The Greenbergian word order correlations', *Language* 68: 81–138.

Dudley, Karen (1997). *Giant pandas.* Calgary: Weigl.

Dunn, Michael, Stephen C. Levinson, Eva Lindström, Ger Reesink, and Angela Terrill (2008). 'Structural phylogeny in historical linguistics: methodological explorations applied in Island Melanesia', *Language* 84: 710–59.

Ebbinghaus, Ernst A. (1997). 'The Gothic documents: their provenance and age', *NOWELE* 31/2: 101–3.

Eckhoff, Hanne, and Roland Meyer (2011). 'Conditions on null subjects in Old Church Slavonic: a contrastive view', paper presented at the Workshop on the Diachrony of Referential Null Arguments, 20th International Conference on Historical Linguistics, Osaka.

Eggenberger, Jakob (1961). *Das Subjektpronomen im Althochdeutschen: ein syntaktischer Beitrag zur Frühgeschichte des deutschen Schrifttums.* Grabs: self-published.

Ellegård, Alvar (1953). *The auxiliary* do: *the establishment and regulation of its use in English.* Stockholm: Almqvist and Wiskell.

Elton, Geoffrey Rudolph (1967). *The practice of history.* London: Fontana.

Emeneau, Murray B. (1956). 'India as a linguistic area', *Language* 32: 3–16.

Erickson, Jon (1997). 'Some observations on word order in Old Saxon', in Christa Dürscheid, Karl Heinz Ramers, and Monika Schwarz (eds.), *Sprache im Fokus: Festschrift für Heinz Vater zum 65. Geburtstag.* Tübingen: Max Niemeyer, 95–105.

Ernst, Thomas (2009). 'Speaker-oriented adverbs', *Natural Language and Linguistic Theory* 27: 497–544.

Erschler, David (2009). 'Possession marking in Ossetic: arguing for Caucasian influence', *Linguistic Typology* 13: 417–50.

Evans, Nicholas, and Stephen C. Levinson (2009). 'The myth of language universals: language diversity and its importance for cognitive science', *Behavioural and Brain Sciences* 32: 429–48.

Evers, Arnold (1981). 'Verb-second movement rules', *Wiener Linguistische Gazette* 26: 15–34.

Evers, Arnold (1982). 'Twee functionele principes voor de regel "Verschuif het Werkwoord"', *Glot* 1: 11–30.

Eyþórsson, Þórhallur (1995). *Verbal syntax in the early Germanic languages.* Ph.D. dissertation. Cornell University.

Eyþórsson, Þórhallur (1996). 'Functional categories, cliticization, and verb movement in the Early Germanic languages', in Höskuldur Þráinsson, Samuel D. Epstein, and Steve Peter (eds.), *Studies in comparative Germanic syntax*, vol. ii. Dordrecht: Kluwer, 109–39.

Eyþórsson, Þórhallur (2011). 'Variation in the syntax of the older Runic inscriptions', *Futhark: International Journal of Runic Studies* 2: 27–49.

Faarlund, Jan Terje (1989). 'Syntactic and pragmatic principles as arguments in the interpretation of runic inscriptions', in Jacek Fisiak (ed.), *Historical linguistics and philology.* Berlin: Mouton de Gruyter, 165–86.

Faarlund, Jan Terje (1990). *Syntactic change: towards a theory of historical syntax.* Berlin: Mouton de Gruyter.

Faarlund, Jan Terje (1994). 'Old and Middle Scandinavian', in Ekkehard König and Johan van der Auwera (eds.), *The Germanic languages.* London: Routledge, 38–71.

Faarlund, Jan Terje (2001). 'The notion of oblique subject and its status in the history of Icelandic', in Jan Terje Faarlund (ed.), *Grammatical relations in change.* Amsterdam: John Benjamins, 99–135.

Faarlund, Jan Terje (2004). *The syntax of Old Norse.* Oxford: Oxford University Press.

Falk, Cecilia (1993). 'Non-referential subjects and agreement in the history of Swedish', *Lingua* 89: 143–80.

Fanselow, Gisbert (2003). 'Münchhausen-style head movement and the analysis of verb-second', in Anoop Mahajan (ed.), *Syntax at sunset: head movement and syntactic theory.* UCLA Working Papers in Linguistics, 40–76.

Farrar, Kimberley, and Mari C. Jones (2002). 'Introduction', in Mari C. Jones and Edith Esch (eds.), *Language change: the interplay of internal, external, and extra-linguistic factors*. Berlin: Mouton de Gruyter, 1–16.

Farrell, Patrick (1990). 'Null objects in Brazilian Portuguese', *Natural Language and Linguistic Theory* 8: 325–46.

Felser, Claudia (2001). '*Wh*-expletives and secondary predication: German partial *wh*-movement reconsidered', *Journal of Germanic Linguistics* 13: 5–38.

Felser, Claudia (2004). '*Wh*-copying, phases, and successive cyclicity', *Lingua* 114: 543–74.

Ferguson, Charles (1959). 'Diglossia', *Word* 15: 325–40.

Ferraresi, Gisella (2005). *Word order and phrase structure in Gothic*. Leuven: Peeters.

Ferraresi, Gisella, and Maria Goldbach (eds.) (2008). *Principles of syntactic reconstruction*. Amsterdam: John Benjamins.

Fertig, David (2000). 'Null subjects in Gothic', *American Journal of Germanic Linguistics and Literatures* 12: 3–21.

Filppula, Markku (2010). 'Contact and the early history of English', in Raymond Hickey (ed.), *The handbook of language contact*. Oxford: Oxford University Press, 432–53.

Finazzi, Rosa B., and Paola Tornaghi (2013). 'Gothica Bononiensia: analisi linguistica e filologia di un nuovo documento', *Aevum* 87: 113–55.

Fintel, Kai von (2004). 'Would you believe it? The King of France is back! Presuppositions and truth-value intuitions', in Marga Reimer and Anne Bezuidenhout (eds.), *Descriptions and beyond: an interdisciplinary collection of essays on definite and indefinite descriptions and other related phenomena*. Oxford: Oxford University Press, 315–41.

Fischer, Olga, Ans van Kemenade, Willem Koopman, and Wim van der Wurff (2000). *The syntax of early English*. Cambridge: Cambridge University Press.

Fisher, Ronald A. (1922). 'On the interpretation of $\chi^2$ from contingency tables, and the calculation of P', *Journal of the Royal Statistical Society* 85: 87–94.

Flood, Christopher G. (2002). *Political myth*. London: Routledge.

Fodor, Janet Dean (1998). 'Unambiguous triggers', *Linguistic Inquiry* 29: 1–36.

Fodor, Janet Dean, and William G. Sakas (2005). 'The Subset Principle in syntax: costs of compliance', *Journal of Linguistics* 41: 513–69.

Fortson, Benjamin W. (2004). *Indo-European language and culture*. Oxford: Blackwell.

Foulet, Lucien (1919). *Petite syntaxe de l'ancien français*. Paris: Champion.

Fourquet, Jean (1938). *L'ordre des éléments de la phrase en germanique ancien: étude de syntaxe de position*. Strasbourg: Les belles lettres.

Fox, Anthony (1995). *Linguistic reconstruction: an introduction to theory and method*. Oxford: Oxford University Press.

Fox, Danny (2000). *Economy and semantic interpretation*. Cambridge, Mass.: MIT Press.

Frampton, John, and Sam Gutmann (2002). 'Crash-proof syntax', in Samuel David Epstein and T. Daniel Seely (eds.), *Derivation and explanation in the Minimalist Program*. Oxford: Blackwell, 90–105.

Frascarelli, Mara (2007). 'Subjects, topics and the interpretation of referential pro: an interface approach to the linking of (null) pronouns', *Natural Language and Linguistic Theory* 25: 691–734.

Frascarelli, Mara, and Roland Hinterhölzl (2007). 'Types of topics in German and Italian', in Kerstin Schwabe and Susanne Winkler (eds.), *On information structure, meaning and form: generalizations across languages.* Amsterdam: John Benjamins, 87–116.

Freidin, Robert (1992). *Foundations of generative syntax.* Cambridge, Mass.: MIT Press.

Frey, Werner (2000). 'Über die syntaktische Position des Satztopiks im Deutschen', *ZAS Papers in Linguistics* 20: 137–72.

Frey, Werner (2004). 'The grammar–pragmatics interface and the German prefield', *Sprache und Pragmatik* 52: 1–39.

Friedrich, Paul (1975). *Proto-Indo-European syntax: the order of meaningful elements.* Journal of Indo-European Studies Monograph 1. Butte, Mont.

Fulk, Robert D. (1992). *A history of Old English meter.* Philadelphia: University of Pennsylvania Press.

Fulk, Robert D. (2009). 'Anglian dialect features in Old English anonymous homiletic literature: a survey, with preliminary findings', in Susan Fitzmaurice and Donka Minkova (eds.), *Studies in the history of the English language,* vol. iv: *Empirical and analytical advances in the study of English language change.* Berlin: Mouton de Gruyter, 81–100.

Fuß, Eric (2003). 'On the historical core of V2 in Germanic', *Nordic Journal of Linguistics* 26: 195–231.

Fuß, Eric (2004). *The rise of agreement: a formal approach to the syntax and grammaticalization of verbal inflection.* Ph.D. dissertation. Johann-Wolfgang-Goethe Universität zu Frankfurt am Main.

Fuß, Eric, and Carola Trips (2002). 'Variation and change in Old and Middle English: on the validity of the Double Base Hypothesis', *Journal of Comparative Germanic Linguistics* 4: 171–224.

Gade, Kari Ellen (1995). *The structure of Old Norse dróttkvætt poetry.* Ithaca, NY: Cornell University Press.

Gallée, Johan Hendrik, and Ingrid Tiefenbach (1993). *Altsächsische Grammatik.* Tübingen: Max Niemeyer.

García, Erica C. (1990). 'Renalysing actualization, and actualizing reanalysis', in Henning Andersen and Konrad Körner (eds.), *Historical Linguistics 1987: papers from the 8th International Conference on Historical Linguistics.* Amsterdam: John Benjamins, 141–59.

Garley, Matthew, Benjamin Slade, and Marina Terkourafi (2010). 'A text in speech's clothing: discovering specific functions of formulaic expressions in Beowulf and blogs', in David Wood (ed.), *Perspectives on formulaic language: acquisition and communication.* London: Continuum, 213–33.

Garrett, Andrew (1990). *The syntax of Anatolian pronominal clitics.* Ph.D. dissertation. Harvard University.

Gärtner, Kurt (1981). 'Asyndetische Relativsätze in der Geschichte der Deutschen', *Zeitschrift für germanistische Linguistik* 9: 152–63.

Gelderen, Elly van (2000). *A history of English reflexive pronouns: person, self, and interpretability.* Amsterdam: John Benjamins.

Gelderen, Elly van (2004). *Grammaticalization as economy.* Amsterdam: John Benjamins.

Gelderen, Elly van (2009a). 'Feature economy in the Linguistic Cycle', in Paola Crisma and Giuseppe Longobardi (eds.), *Historical syntax and linguistic theory*. Oxford: Oxford University Press, 93–109.

Gelderen, Elly van (2009b). 'Renewal in the left periphery: economy and the complementiser layer', *Transactions of the Philological Society* 107: 131–95.

Gelderen, Elly van (2011). *The linguistic cycle: language change and the language faculty.* Oxford: Oxford University Press.

Gelderen, Elly van (2013). 'Null subjects in Old English', *Linguistic Inquiry* 44: 271–85.

Giannakidou, Anastasia (1998). *Polarity sensitivity as (non)veridical dependency.* Amsterdam: John Benjamins.

Gibson, Edward, and Kenneth Wexler (1994). 'Triggers', *Linguistic Inquiry* 25: 407–54.

Gildea, Spike (ed.) (1999). *Reconstructing grammar: comparative linguistics and grammaticalization.* Amsterdam: John Benjamins.

Givón, Talmy (1971). 'Historical syntax and synchronic morphology: an archaeologist's field trip', *Chicago Linguistic Society* 7: 394–415.

Givón, Talmy (1983). 'Topic continuity in discourse: an introduction', in Talmy Givón (ed.), *Topic continuity in discourse: a quantitative crosslanguage study.* Amsterdam: John Benjamins, 5–41.

Givón, Talmy (1999). 'Internal reconstruction: as method, as theory', in Spike Gildea (ed.), *Reconstructing grammar: comparative linguistics and grammaticalization.* Amsterdam: John Benjamins, 107–59.

Gordon, Eric V. (1927). *An introduction to Old Norse.* Oxford: Clarendon.

Grein, Christian W. M., Ferdinand Holthausen, and Johann J. Köhler (eds.) (1912 [1864]). *Sprachschatz der angelsächsischen Dichter.* Heidelberg: Carl Winter.

Grimm, Jacob (1837). *Deutsche Grammatik, iv: Syntax.* Göttingen: Dieterichsche Buchhandlung.

Haan, Germen J. de (2001). 'Why Old Frisian is really Middle Frisian', *Studia Linguistica Historica* 22: 179–206.

Haeberli, Eric (1999a). *Features, categories and the syntax of A-positions.* Ph.D. dissertation. University of Geneva.

Haeberli, Eric (1999b). 'On the word order "XP-subject" in the Germanic languages', *Journal of Comparative Germanic Linguistics* 3: 1–36.

Haeberli, Eric (2002). 'Inflectional morphology and the loss of V2 in English', in David Lightfoot (ed.), *Syntactic effects of morphological change.* Oxford: Oxford University Press, 88–106.

Haeberli, Eric (2005). 'Clause type asymmetries in Old English and the syntax of verb movement', in Montserrat Batllori, Maria-Lluïsa Hernanz, Carme Picallo, and Francesc Roca (eds.), *Grammaticalization and parametric variation.* Oxford: Oxford University Press, 267–83.

Haeberli, Eric, and Susan Pintzuk (2012). 'Revisiting verb (projection) raising in Old English', in Dianne Jonas, John Whitman, and Andrew Garrett (eds.), *Grammatical change: origins, nature, outcomes.* Oxford: Oxford University Press, 219–38.

Haegeman, Liliane (1990). 'Understood subjects in English diaries', *Multilingua* 9: 157–99.

Haegeman, Liliane (2001). 'Antisymmetry and verb-final order in West Flemish', *Journal of Comparative Germanic Linguistics* 3: 207–32.

Haegeman, Liliane (2003). 'Conditional clauses: external and internal syntax', *Mind and Language* 18: 317–39.

Haegeman, Liliane, and Tabea Ihsane (1999). 'Subject ellipsis in embedded clauses in English', *English Language and Linguistics* 3: 117–45.

Haegeman, Liliane, and Barbara Ürögdi (2010). 'Referential CPs and DPs: an operator-movement account', *Theoretical Linguistics* 36: 111–52.

Haferland, Harald (2001). 'Der Haß der Feinde: Germanische Heldendichtung und die Erzählkonzeption des Heliand', *Euphorion* 95: 237–56.

Haferland, Harald (2004). *Mündlichkeit, Gedächtnis und Medialität: Heldendichtung im deutschen Mittelalter*. Göttingen: Vandenhoeck and Ruprecht.

Håkansson, David (2008). *Syntaktisk variation och förändring. En studie av subjektslösa satser i fornsvenska*. Ph.D. dissertation. University of Lund.

Håkansson, Gisela, Manfred Pienemann, and Susan Sayehli (2002). 'Transfer and typological proximity in the context of second language processing', *Second Language Research* 18: 250–73.

Hale, Mark (1987a). *Studies in the comparative syntax of the oldest Indo-Iranian languages*. Ph.D. dissertation. Harvard University.

Hale, Mark (1987b). 'Notes on Wackernagel's law in the language of the Rigveda', in Calvert Watkins (ed.), *Studies in memory of Warren Cowgill*. Berlin: Mouton de Gruyter, 38–50.

Hale, Mark (1998). 'Diachronic syntax', *Syntax* 1: 1–18.

Hale, Mark (2007). *Historical linguistics: theory and method*. Oxford: Blackwell.

Hale, Mark (2013). 'What changes in syntactic change? Some implications for syntactic reconstruction', paper presented at the LSA Summer Institute's Workshop on Diachronic Syntax, Ann Arbor.

Hale, Mark, and Charles Reiss (2008). *The phonological enterprise*. Oxford: Oxford University Press.

Harbert, Wayne (1992). 'Gothic relative clauses and syntactic theory', in Irmengard Rauch, Gerald F. Carr, and Robert L. Kyes (eds.), *On Germanic linguistics: issues and methods*. Berlin: Mouton de Gruyter, 109–46.

Harbert, Wayne (1999). 'Erino portun ih firchnussu', in Gerald F. Carr, Wayne Harbert, and Lihua Zhang (eds), *Interdigitations: essays for Irmengard Rauch*. New York: Peter Lang, 257–68.

Harbert, Wayne (2007). *The Germanic languages*. Cambridge: Cambridge University Press.

Harbour, Daniel (2006). 'Person hierarchies and geometry without hierarchies or geometries', *Queen Mary's Occasional Papers Advancing Linguistics* 6.

Harbour, Daniel (2010). 'Mythomania? Methods and morals from "The Myth of Language Universals"', *Queen Mary's Occasional Papers Advancing Linguistics* 20.

Harris, Alice C. (1973). 'Psychological predicates in Middle English', paper presented at the Annual Meeting of the Linguistic Society of America, San Diego.

Harris, Alice C. (1985). *Diachronic syntax: the Kartvelian case*. New York: Academic Press.

Harris, Alice C. (2008). 'Reconstruction in syntax: reconstruction of patterns', in Gisella Ferraresi and Maria Goldbach (eds.), *Principles of syntactic reconstruction*. Amsterdam: John Benjamins, 73–95.

Harris, Alice C., and Lyle Campbell (1995). *Historical syntax in cross-linguistic perspective*. Cambridge: Cambridge University Press.

Harris, Martin, and Nigel Vincent (1988). *The Romance languages*. London: Croom Helm.

Harrison, Shelly P. (2003). 'On the limits of the comparative method', in Brian D. Joseph and Richard D. Janda (eds.), *The handbook of historical linguistics*. Oxford: Blackwell, 213–43.

Haspelmath, Martin (1997). *Indefinite pronouns*. Oxford: Clarendon.

Haspelmath, Martin, Matthew S. Dryer, David Gil, and Bernard Comrie (eds.) (2005). *The world atlas of language structures*. Oxford: Oxford University Press.

Haugan, Jens (1998). 'Passiv av norrøne dobbelt objekt-konstruksjonar og subjektspørsmålet', *Norsk Lingvistik Tidsskrift* 16: 157–84.

Hauser, Marc, Noam Chomsky, and W. Tecumseh Fitch (2002). 'The faculty of language: what is it, who has it, and how did it evolve?', *Science* 298: 1569–79.

Hawkins, John A. (1983). *Word order universals*. New York: Academic Press.

Hawkins, John A. (1990). 'A parsing theory of word order universals', *Linguistic Inquiry* 21: 223–61.

Hawkins, Roger (2001). *Second language syntax: a generative introduction*. Oxford: Blackwell.

Heine, Bernd, and Tania Kuteva (2002). *World lexicon of grammaticalization*. Cambridge: Cambridge University Press.

Held, Karl (1903). *Das Verbum ohne pronominales Subjekt in der älteren deutschen Sprache*. Berlin: Mayer and Müller.

Henry, Alison (1995). *Belfast English and Standard English: dialect variation and parameter setting*. Oxford: Oxford University Press.

Henry, Alison (2002). 'Variation and syntactic theory', in J. K. Chambers, Peter Trudgill, and Natalie Schilling-Estes (eds.), *The handbook of language variation and change*. Oxford: Blackwell, 267–82.

Heusler, Andreas (1967). *Altisländisches Elementarbuch*. 7th edn. Heidelberg: Carl Winter.

Heycock, Caroline, and Anthony Kroch (1994). 'Verb movement and coordination in a dynamic theory of licensing', *Linguistic Review* 11: 257–83.

Hinterhölzl, Roland, and Svetlana Petrova (2009). 'From V1 to V2 in West Germanic', *Lingua* 120: 315–28.

Hjartardóttir, Thóra Björk (1987). *Getið í eyðurnar*. MA dissertation. University of Iceland.

Hjelmslev, Louis (1943). *Omkring Sprogteoriens Grundlæggelse*. Copenhagen: Ejnar Munksgaard.

Hobsbawm, Eric (1997). *On history*. London: Weidenfeld and Nicolson.

Hock, Hans Henrich (1985). 'Yes, Virginia, syntactic reconstruction is possible', *Studies in the Linguistic Sciences* 15: 49–60.

Hock, Hans Henrich (1996). 'Subversion or convergence? The issue of pre-Vedic retroflexion reconsidered', *Studies in the Linguistic Sciences* 23: 73–115.

Hockett, Charles F. (1960). 'The origin of speech', *Scientific American* 203: 89–97.

Hofmeister, Philip, and Ivan A. Sag (2010). 'Cognitive constraints and island effects', *Language* 86: 366–415.

Höhle, Tilman (1983). *Subjektlücken in Koordinationen*. MS. Universität Köln.

Holler, Anke (2009). 'Towards an analysis of the adverbial use of German *was* ("what")', in Stefan Müller (ed.), *Proceedings of the 16th International Conference on Head-Driven Phrase Structure Grammar*. Stanford, Calif.: CSLI Publications, 131–49.

Holmberg, Anders (2005). 'Is there a little *pro*? Evidence from Finnish', *Linguistic Inquiry* 36: 533–64.

Holmberg, Anders (2010). 'Null subject parameters', in Theresa Biberauer, Anders Holmberg, Ian Roberts, and Michelle Sheehan (eds.), *Parametric variation: null subjects in Minimalist theory*. Cambridge: Cambridge University Press, 88–124.

Holmberg, Anders, Aarti Nayudu, and Michelle Sheehan (2009). 'Three partial null-subject languages: a comparison of Brazilian Portuguese, Finnish and Marathi', *Studia Linguistica* 63: 59–97.

Holmberg, Anders, and Ian Roberts (2010). 'Introduction: parameters in Minimalist theory', in Theresa Biberauer, Anders Holmberg, Ian Roberts, and Michelle Sheehan (eds.), *Parametric variation: null subjects in Minimalist theory*. Cambridge: Cambridge University Press, 1–57.

Holmberg, Anders, and Michelle Sheehan (2010). 'Control into finite clauses in partial null-subject languages', in Theresa Biberauer, Anders Holmberg, Ian Roberts, and Michelle Sheehan (eds.), *Parametric variation: null subjects in Minimalist theory*. Cambridge: Cambridge University Press, 125–52.

Honeybone, Patrick (2011). 'History and historical linguistics: two types of cognitive reconstruction', in Nils Langer, Steffan Davies, and Wim Vandenbussche (eds.), *Language and history, linguistics and historiography: interdisciplinary approaches*. Bern: Peter Lang, 15–48.

Hooper, Joan, and Sandra Thompson (1973). 'On the applicability of root transformations', *Linguistic Inquiry* 4: 465–97.

Hopper, Paul J. (1975). *The syntax of the simple sentence in Proto-Germanic*. The Hague: Mouton.

Hopper, Paul J. (1977). 'Hildebrandslied 35b: *Dat ih dir it nu bi huldi gibu*', in Paul J. Hopper (ed.), *Studies in descriptive and historical linguistics: Festschrift for Winfred P. Lehmann*. Amsterdam: John Benjamins, 481–5.

Hopper, Paul J. (1991). 'On some principles of grammaticization', in Elizabeth Closs Traugott and Bernd Heine (eds.), *Approaches to grammaticalization*, vol. i. Amsterdam: John Benjamins, 37–80.

Hopper, Paul J., and Elizabeth Closs Traugott (2003). *Grammaticalization*. 2nd edn. Cambridge: Cambridge University Press.

Hornstein, Norbert (1995). *Logical form: from GB to Minimalism*. Oxford: Blackwell.

Horvath, Julia (1997). 'The status of "*wh*-expletives" and the partial *wh*-movement construction of Hungarian', *Natural Language and Linguistic Theory* 15: 509–72.

Householder, Fred W. (1981). *Syntax of Apollonius Dyscolus*. Amsterdam: John Benjamins.

Hróarsdóttir, Þorbjörg (1996). 'The decline of OV word order in the Icelandic VP: a diachronic study', *Working Papers in Scandinavian Syntax* 57: 92–141.

Huang, C.-T. James (1984). 'On the distribution and reference of empty pronouns', *Linguistic Inquiry* 15: 531–74.

Huang, C.-T. James, Y.-H. Audrey Li, and Yafei Li (2009). *The syntax of Chinese*. Cambridge: Cambridge University Press.

Huang, Yan (2000). *Anaphora: a cross-linguistic study*. Oxford: Oxford University Press.

Hudson, Richard A. (1996). *Sociolinguistics*. 2nd edn. Cambridge: Cambridge University Press.

Hulk, Aafke, and Ans van Kemenade (1995). 'V2, *pro*-drop, functional projections and language change', in Adrian Battye and Ian Roberts (eds.), *Clause structure and language change*. Oxford: Oxford University Press, 227–56.

Hulst, Harry van der (2005). 'Why phonology is the same', in Hans Broekhuis, Norbert Corver, Martin Everaert, and Jan Koster (eds.), *Organizing grammar: linguistic studies in honor of Henk van Riemsdijk*. Berlin: Mouton de Gruyter, 252–62.

Isac, Daniela, and Charles Reiss (2008). *I-language: an introduction to linguistics as cognitive science*. Oxford: Oxford University Press.

Itkonen, Esa (2002). 'Grammaticalization as an analogue of hypothetic-deductive thinking', in Ilse Wischer and Gabriele Diewald (eds.), *New reflections on grammaticalization*. Amsterdam: John Benjamins, 413–22.

Jackendoff, Ray S. (1972). *Semantic interpretation in generative grammar*. Cambridge, Mass.: MIT Press.

Jaeggli, Osvaldo, and Kenneth J. Safir (1989). 'The null subject parameter and parametric theory', in Osvaldo Jaeggli and Kenneth J. Safir (eds.), *The null subject parameter*. Dordrecht: Kluwer, 1–44.

Jäger, Agnes (2000). *Unterspezifikation am Beispiel des Pronomens* was. *Zur Grammatik eines* w-*Elements*. MA dissertation. University of Jena.

Janda, Richard D. (2001). 'Beyond "pathways" and "unidirectionality": on the discontinuity of language transmission and the counterability of grammaticalization', *Language Sciences* 23: 265–340.

Jarrick, Arne (2004). 'God historia är mer än goda historier', *Folkvett* 3: 6–26.

Jasanoff, Jay H. (2004). 'Gothic', in Roger D. Woodard (ed.), *Encyclopedia of the world's ancient languages*. Cambridge: Cambridge University Press, 881–906.

Jeffers, Robert J. (1976). 'Syntactic change and syntactic reconstruction', in W. M. Christie, Jr. (ed.), *Current progress in historical linguistics: proceedings of the 2nd International Conference on Historical Linguistics*. Amsterdam: North-Holland, 1–15.

Jenkins, Keith (1991). *Re-thinking history*. London: Routledge.

Johannessen, Janne Bondi (2003). 'Correlative adverbs in Germanic languages', *Nordlyd* 31: 165–86.

Jóhannsson, Ellert Thor (2009). *Old High German 1st person plural ending* -mes *and Cod. Sang. 916*. Ph.D. dissertation. Cornell University.

Johnson, Samuel (1755). *Dictionary of the English language*. London: Dodsley, Longman et al.

Jucquois, Guy (1976). *La Reconstruction linquistique: application à l'indo-européen*. 2nd edn. Leuven: Peeters.

Julien, Marit (2007). 'Embedded V2 in Norwegian and Swedish', *Working Papers in Scandinavian Syntax* 80: 103–61.

Julien, Marit (2009). 'The force of the argument', *Working Papers in Scandinavian Syntax* 84: 225–32.

Kayne, Richard S. (1975). *French syntax: the transformational cycle*. Cambridge, Mass.: MIT Press.

Kayne, Richard S. (1991). 'Romance clitics, verb movement, and PRO', *Linguistic Inquiry* 22: 647–86.

Kayne, Richard S. (1994). *The antisymmetry of syntax*. Cambridge, Mass.: MIT Press.

Kayne, Richard S. (2005). 'Some notes on comparative syntax, with special reference to English and French', in Guglielmo Cinque and Richard Kayne (eds.), *The Oxford handbook of comparative syntax*. Oxford: Oxford University Press, 3–69.

Keenan, Edward L. (2003). 'An historical explanation of some binding-theoretic facts in English', in John Moore and Maria Polinsky (eds.), *The nature of explanation in linguistics*. Stanford, Calif.: CSLI Publications, 153–89.

Kegl, Judy, Ann Senghas, and Marie Coppola (1999). 'Creation through contact: sign language emergence and sign language change in Nicaragua', in Michel DeGraff (ed.), *Language creation and language change: creolization, diachrony, and development*. Cambridge, Mass.: MIT Press, 179–238.

Keidan, Artemio (2006). '"Kal'kirovannyj arxaizm" gotskogo jazyka', *Materialy čtenij pamjati I. M. Tronskogo* 10: 149–55.

Kemenade, Ans van (1987). *Syntactic case and morphological case in the history of English*. Dordrecht: Foris.

Kemenade, Ans van (2007). 'Formal syntax and language change: developments and outlook', *Diachronica* 24: 155–69.

Kemenade, Ans van, and Bettelou Los (2006). 'Discourse adverbs and clausal syntax in Old and Middle English', in Ans van Kemenade and Bettelou Los (eds.), *The handbook of the history of English*. Malden, Mass., and Oxford: Blackwell, 224–48.

Kiernan, Kevin (1990). 'Reading Caedmon's "Hymn" with someone else's glosses', *Representations* 32: 157–74.

Kinn, Kari (2013). 'Null arguments in Old Norwegian in an early Germanic perspective', paper presented at the 21st International Conference on Historical Linguistics, Oslo.

Kiparsky, Paul (1975). 'What are phonological theories about?', in David Cohen and Jessica R. Wirth (eds.), *Testing linguistic hypotheses*. Washington, DC: Hemisphere Publishing Corp, 187–210.

Kiparsky, Paul (1988). 'Phonological change', in Frederick J. Newmeyer (ed.), *Linguistics: the Cambridge survey*, vol. i. Cambridge: Cambridge University Press, 363–415.

Kiparsky, Paul (1995). 'Indo-European origins of Germanic syntax', in Adrian Battye and Ian Roberts (eds.), *Clause structure and language change*. Oxford: Oxford University Press, 140–69.

Kiparsky, Paul (1996). 'The shift to head-initial VP in Germanic', in Höskuldur Þráinsson, Samuel D. Epstein, and Steve Peter (eds.), *Studies in comparative Germanic syntax*, vol. ii. Dordrecht: Kluwer, 140–79.

Kiparsky, Paul (2009). 'On the architecture of Pāṇini's grammar', in Gérard Huet, Amba Kulkarni, and Peter Scharf (eds.), *Sanskrit computational linguistics*. Berlin: Springer, 33–94.

Kiparsky, Paul, and Carol Kiparsky (1970). 'Fact', in Manfred Bierwisch and Karl Erich Heidolph (eds.), *Progress in linguistics*. The Hague: Mouton, 143–73.

Kiss, Katalin É. (1998). 'Identificational focus vs. information focus', *Language* 74: 245–73.

Klein, Jared S. (1994). 'Gothic *þaruh, þanuh* and *-(u)h þan*', *Indogermanische Forschungen* 99: 253–76.

Klein, Jared S. (2010). 'Review of Ferraresi and Goldbach (2008)', *Language* 86: 720–6.

Klein, Jared S., and Nancy L. Condon (1993). 'Gothic *-uh*: a synchronic and comparative study', *Transactions of the Philological Society* 91: 1–62.

Ko, Heejeong (2005). 'Syntax of why-in-situ: Merge into [SPEC,CP] in the overt syntax', *Natural Language and Linguistic Theory* 23: 867–916.

Koch, John T. (1991). 'On the prehistory of Brittonic syntax', in James Fife and Erich Poppe (eds.), *Studies in Brythonic word order*. Amsterdam: John Benjamins, 1–43.

Koeneman, Olaf (2006). 'Deriving the difference between full and partial *pro*-drop', in Peter Ackema, Patrick Brandt, Maaike Schoorlemmer, and Fred Weerman (eds.), *Arguments and agreement*. Oxford: Oxford University Press, 76–100.

Kohonen, Viljo (1978). *On the development of English word order in religious prose around 1000 and 1200 A.D: a quantitative study of word order in context*. Åbo: Åbo Akademi.

König, Werner (2005). *dtv-Atlas Deutsche Sprache*. 15th edn. Munich: Deutscher Taschenbuch Verlag.

Koopman, Hilda (1992). 'On the absence of Case chains in Bambara', *Natural Language and Linguistic Theory* 10: 555–94.

Koopman, Willem (1985). 'Verb and particle combinations in Old and Middle English', in Roger Eaton, Olga Fischer, Willem Koopman, and Frederike van der Leek (eds.), *Papers from the 4th International Conference on English Historical Linguistics*. Amsterdam: John Benjamins, 109–21.

Koopman, Willem (1992). 'Old English clitic pronouns: some remarks', in Fran Colman (ed.), *Evidence for Old English*. Edinburgh: John Donald, 44–87.

Koopman, Willem (1995). 'Verb-final main clauses in Old English prose', *Studia Neophilologica* 67: 129–44.

Koopman, Willem (1996). 'Evidence for clitic adverbs in Old English: an evaluation', in Derek Britton (ed.), *English Historical Linguistics 1994*. Amsterdam: John Benjamins, 223–45.

Koopman, Willem (1997). 'Another look at clitics in Old English', *Transactions of the Philological Society* 95: 73–93.

Koopman, Willem (1998). 'Inversion after single and multiple topics in Old English', in Jacek Fisiak and Marcin Krygier (eds.), *Advances in English historical linguistics*. Berlin: Mouton de Gruyter, 135–49.

Koppitz, Alfred (1900). 'Gotische Wortstellung', *Zeitschrift für deutsche Philologie* 32: 433–63.

Koppitz, Alfred (1901). 'Gotische Wortstellung', *Zeitschrift für deutsche Philologie* 33: 7–44.

Kortlandt, Frederik (1983). 'Proto-Indo-European verbal syntax', *Journal of Indo-European Studies* 11: 307–24.

Krahe, Hans, and Wolfgang Meid (1969). *Germanische Sprachwissenschaft*. Berlin: Sammlung Göschen.

Krisch, Thomas (2009). 'On the "syntax of silence" in Proto-Indo-European', in Roland Hinterhölzl and Svetlana Petrova (eds.), *Information structure and language change: new approaches to word order variation in Germanic*. Berlin: Mouton de Gruyter, 191–220.

Kroch, Anthony (1989). 'Reflexes of grammar in patterns of language change', *Language Variation and Change* 1: 199–244.

Kroch, Anthony (1994). 'Morphosyntactic variation', in Katherine Beals (ed.), *Proceedings of the 30th annual meeting of the Chicago Linguistic Society*. Chicago: Chicago Linguistic Society, 180–201.

Kroch, Anthony (2001). 'Syntactic change', in Mark Baltin and Chris Collins (eds.), *The handbook of contemporary syntactic theory*. Malden, Mass.: Blackwell, 699–729.

Kroch, Anthony, and Ann Taylor (1997). 'Verb movement in Old and Middle English: dialect variation and language contact', in Ans van Kemenade and Nigel Vincent (eds.), *Parameters of morphosyntactic change*. Cambridge: Cambridge University Press, 297–325.

Kuhn, Hans (1933). 'Zur Wortstellung und-betonung im Altgermanischen', *Beiträge zur Geschichte der deutschen Sprache und Literatur* 57: 1–109.

Kwon, Kyongjoon (2009). 'The subject cycle of pronominal auxiliaries in Old North Russian', in Elly van Gelderen (ed.), *Cyclical change*. Amsterdam: John Benjamins, 157–84.

Labov, William (1994). *Principles of linguistic change*, vol. i: *Internal factors*. Oxford: Blackwell.

Labov, William (2001). *Principles of linguistic change*, vol. ii: *Social factors*. Oxford: Blackwell.

Labov, William (2007). 'Transmission and diffusion', *Language* 83: 344–87.

Labov, William (2010). *Principles of linguistic change*, vol. iii: *Cognitive and cultural factors*. Oxford: Wiley-Blackwell.

Labov, William, and Teresa Labov (1978). 'Learning the syntax of questions', in Robin N. Campbell and Philip T. Smith (eds.), *Recent advances in the psychology of language*, vol. iii. New York: Plenum Press, 1–44.

Landau, Idan (2000). *Elements of control: structure and meaning in infinitival constructions*. Dordrecht: Kluwer.

Landau, Idan (2004). 'The scale of finiteness and the calculus of control', *Natural Language and Linguistic Theory* 22: 811–77.

Lander, Eric T., and Liliane Haegeman (2013). 'Old Norse as an NP language: with observations on the Common Norse and Northwest Germanic runic inscriptions', *Transactions of the Philological Society*, published online (Early View).

Langacker, Ronald W. (1977). 'Syntactic reanalysis', in Charles N. Li (ed.), *Mechanisms of syntactic change*. Austin: University of Texas Press, 57–139.

Larson, Richard (1985). 'On the syntax of disjunction scope', *Natural Language and Linguistic Theory* 3: 217–64.

Larson, Richard, and Maria Lujàn (1989). *Emphatic pronouns*. MS. Stony Brook University.

Lasch, Agathe (1914). *Mittelniederdeutsche Grammatik*. Halle: Max Niemeyer.

Lass, Roger (1980). *On explaining language change*. Cambridge: Cambridge University Press.

Lass, Roger (1993). 'How real(ist) are reconstructions?', in Charles Jones (ed.), *Historical linguistics: problems and perspectives*. London: Longman, 156–89.

Lass, Roger (1997). *Historical linguistics and language change*. Cambridge: Cambridge University Press.

Law, Vivien (1987). 'Anglo-Saxon England: Ælfric's Exceptiones de arte grammatica anglice', *Histoire Épistémologie Langage* 9: 47–71.

Ledgeway, Adam (2012). *From Latin to Romance: morphosyntactic typology and change*. Oxford: Oxford University Press.

Lehmann, Winfred P. (1972). 'Proto-Germanic syntax', in Frans van Coetsem and Herbert Kufner (eds.), *Toward a grammar of Proto-Germanic*. Tübingen: Max Niemeyer, 239–68.

Lehmann, Winfred P. (1973). 'A structural principle of language and its implications', *Language* 49: 47–66.

Lehmann, Winfred P. (1974). *Proto-Indo-European syntax*. Austin: University of Texas Press.

Lehmann, Winfred P. (1994). 'Gothic and the reconstruction of Proto-Germanic', in Ekkehard König and Johan van der Auwera (eds.), *The Germanic languages*. London: Routledge, 19–37.

Lehmann, Winfred P. (2007). *A grammar of Proto-Germanic*. University of Texas at Austin: Linguistics Research Center.

Lenerz, Jürgen (1984). *Syntaktischer Wandel und Grammatiktheorie: eine Untersuchung an Beispielen aus der Sprachgeschichte des Deutschen*. Tübingen: Max Niemeyer.

Lenerz, Jürgen (1993). 'Zu Syntax und Semantik deutscher Personalpronomina', in Marga Reis (ed.), *Wortstellung und Informationsstruktur*. Tübingen: Max Niemeyer, 117–53.

Lenker, Ursula (2010). *Argument and rhetoric: adverbial connectors in the history of English*. Berlin: Mouton de Gruyter.

Lenneberg, Eric (1967). *Biological foundations of language*. New York: John Wiley and Sons.

Lewis, Henry, and Holger Pedersen (1937). *A concise comparative Celtic grammar*. Göttingen: Vandenhoeck and Ruprecht.

Lightfoot, David (1979). *Principles of diachronic syntax*. Cambridge: Cambridge University Press.

Lightfoot, David (1980). 'On reconstructing a proto-syntax', in Paolo Ramat (ed.), *Linguistic reconstruction and Indo-European syntax: proceedings of the colloquium of the 'Indogermanische Gesellschaft'*. Amsterdam: John Benjamins, 27–45.

Lightfoot, David (1991). *How to set parameters*. Cambridge, Mass.: MIT Press.

Lightfoot, David (1997). 'Shifting triggers and diachronic reanalyses', in Ans van Kemenade and Nigel Vincent (eds.), *Parameters of morphosyntactic change*. Cambridge: Cambridge University Press, 253–72.

Lightfoot, David (1999). *The development of language: acquisition, change, and evolution*. Oxford: Blackwell.

Lightfoot, David (2002a). 'Myths and the prehistory of grammars', *Journal of Linguistics* 38: 113–36.

Lightfoot, David (2002b). 'More myths', *Journal of Linguistics* 38: 619–26.

Lightfoot, David (2006). *How new languages emerge*. Cambridge: Cambridge University Press.

Lightfoot, David, and Marit Westergaard (2007). 'Language acquisition and language change: inter-relationships', *Language and Linguistics Compass* 1: 396–416.

Linde, Sonja (2009). 'Aspects of word order and information structure in Old Saxon', in Roland Hinterhölzl and Svetlana Petrova (eds.), *Information structure and language change: new approaches to word order variation in Germanic*. Berlin: Mouton de Gruyter, 367–89.

Lippert, Jörg (1974). *Beiträge zur Technik und Syntax althochdeutscher Übersetzungen unter besonderer Berücksichtigung der Isidorgruppe und des althochdeutschen Tatian*. Munich: Fink.

Liu, Mingya (2009). 'Speaker-oriented adverbs of the German -*weise* sort', in Arndt Riester and Torgrim Solstad (eds.), *Proceedings of Sinn und Bedeutung 13*. Stuttgart: Universität Stuttgart, 333–45.

Lockwood, William B. (1968). *Historical German syntax*. Oxford: Clarendon.

Longobardi, Giuseppe (2001). 'Formal syntax, diachronic Minimalism, and etymology: the history of French *chez*', *Linguistic Inquiry* 32: 275–302.

Longobardi, Giuseppe (2003). 'Methods in parametric linguistics and cognitive history', *Linguistic Variation Yearbook* 3: 101–8.

Longobardi, Giuseppe (2005). 'A minimalist program for parametric linguistics?', in Hans Broekhuis, Norbert Corver, Martin Everaert, and Jan Koster (eds.), *Organizing grammar: linguistic studies in honor of Henk van Riemsdijk*. Berlin: Mouton de Gruyter, 407–14.

Longobardi, Giuseppe, and Cristina Guardiano (2009). 'Evidence for syntax as a sign of historical relatedness', *Lingua* 119: 1679–706.

Longobardi, Giuseppe, and Ian Roberts (2010). 'Universals, diversity and change in the science of language: reaction to "The Myth of Language Universals and Cognitive Science"', *Lingua* 120: 2699–703.

Lucas, Christopher (2009). *The development of negation in Arabic and Afro-Asiatic*. Ph.D. dissertation. University of Cambridge.

Luraghi, Silvia (2003). 'Null objects in Latin and Greek and the relevance of linguistic typology for language reconstruction', in Karlene Jones-Bley, Martin E. Huld, Angela Della Volpe, and Miriam Robbins Dexter (eds.), *Proceedings of the 15th Annual UCLA Indo-European Conference*. Washington, DC: Institute for the Study of Man, 234–56.

Luraghi, Silvia (2010). 'The rise (and possible downfall) of configurationality', in Silvia Luraghi and Vit Bubenik (eds.), *The Continuum Companion to Historical Linguistics*. London: Continuum, 212–29.

McCloskey, James, and Ken Hale (1984). 'On the syntax of person-number inflection in modern Irish', *Natural Language and Linguistic Theory* 1: 487–533.

McDaniels, Todd (2003). 'What's wrong with reanalysis?', *Toronto Working Papers in Linguistics* 21: 81–8.

McMahon, April M. S. (1994). *Understanding language change*. Cambridge: Cambridge University Press.

Maling, Joan (1980). 'Inversion in embedded clauses in Modern Icelandic', *Íslenskt mál og almenn málfræði* 2: 175–93.

Manzini, Maria Rita, and Kenneth Wexler (1987). 'Parameters, binding theory, and learnability', *Linguistic Inquiry* 18: 413–44.

Mardale, Alexandru (2011). 'Prepositions as a semilexical category', *Bucharest Working Papers in Linguistics* 13: 35–50.

Mathieu, Eric (2009). 'On the Germanic properties of Old French', in Paola Crisma and Giuseppe Longobardi (eds.), *Historical syntax and linguistic theory*. Oxford: Oxford University Press, 344–57.

Matić, Dejan (2003). 'Topic, focus, and discourse structure: Ancient Greek word order', *Studies in Language* 27: 573–633.

Matthews, Peter H. (1981). *Syntax*. Cambridge: Cambridge University Press.

Meaney, Audrey L. (1984). 'Variant versions of Old English medical remedies and the compilation of Bald's *Leechbook*', *Anglo-Saxon England* 13: 235–68.

Meillet, Antoine (1909). 'Notes sur quelques faits gotiques', *Mémoires de la Société de Linguistique de Paris* 15: 73–103.

Meillet, Antoine (1954). *La Méthode comparative en linguistique historique*. 6th edn. Paris: Champion.

Meisel, Jürgen M. (2011). 'Bilingual acquisition and theories of diachronic change: bilingualism as cause and effect of grammatical change', *Bilingualism: Language and Cognition* 14: 121–45.

Mengden, Ferdinand von (2008). 'Reconstructing complex structures: a typological perspective', in Gisella Ferraresi and Maria Goldbach (eds.), *Principles of syntactic reconstruction*. Amsterdam: John Benjamins, 97–119.

Menzer, Melissa (2004). 'Ælfric's English grammar', *Journal of English and Germanic Philology* 103: 106–24.

Metlen, Michael (1932). *Does the Gothic Bible represent idiomatic Gothic?* Ph.D. dissertation. Northwestern University.

Meyerhoff, Miriam (2006). *Introducing sociolinguistics*. London: Taylor & Francis.

Michaelis, Laura A. (2012). 'Making the case for Construction Grammar', in Hans C. Boas and Ivan Sag (eds.), *Sign-Based Construction Grammar*. Stanford, Calif.: CSLI Publications, 31–69.

Mielke, Jeff (2008). *The emergence of distinctive features*. Oxford: Oxford University Press.

Miller, D. Gary (1975). 'Proto-Indo-European: VSO, SOV, SVO or all three?', *Lingua* 37: 31–52.

Milroy, Lesley (1987). *Language and social networks*. 2nd edn. Oxford: Blackwell.

Mitchell, Bruce (1985). *Old English syntax*. 2 vols. Oxford: Clarendon.

Mitchell, Bruce, Christopher Ball, and Angus Cameron (1975). 'Short titles of Old English texts', *Anglo-Saxon England* 4: 207–21.

Mitchell, Bruce, Christopher Ball, and Angus Cameron (1979). 'Short titles of Old English texts: addenda and corrigenda', *Anglo-Saxon England* 8: 331–3.

Mitchell, Bruce, and Fred Robinson (2007). *A guide to Old English*. 7th edn. Oxford: Blackwell.

Mobbs, Iain (2008). *'Functionalism', the design of the language faculty, and (disharmonic) typology*. M.Phil. dissertation. University of Cambridge.

Mohr, Sabine (2009). 'V2 as a single-edge phenomenon', in Kleanthes K. Grohmann and Phoevos Panagiotidis (eds.), *Selected papers from the 2006 Cyprus Syntaxfest*. Newcastle-upon-Tyne: Cambridge Scholars Publishing, 141–58.

Morpurgo Davies, Anna (1998). *History of linguistics*, vol. iv: *Nineteenth-century linguistics*. London: Longman.

Motut, Alexandra (2010). 'Merge over Move and the empirical force of economy in Minimalism', *Toronto Working Papers in Linguistics* 33: 1–54.

Müller, Gereon (2004). 'Verb-second as vP-first', *Journal of Comparative Germanic Linguistics* 7: 179–234.

Müller, Gereon (2005). 'Pro-drop and impoverishment', in Patrick Brandt and Eric Fuß (eds.), *Form, structure and grammar: a festschrift presented to Günther Grewendorf on the occasion of his 60th birthday*. Tübingen: Narr, 93–115.

Müller, Gereon (2008). 'Some consequences of an impoverishment-based approach to morphological richness and pro-drop', in Jacek Witkós and Gisbert Fanselow (eds.), *Elements of Slavic and Germanic grammars: a comparative view*. Frankfurt: Peter Lang, 125–45.

Munaro, Nicola, and Hans-Georg Obenauer (1999). 'On underspecified *wh*-elements in pseudo-interrogatives', *University of Venice Working Papers in Linguistics* 9: 181–253.

Näf, Anton (1979). *Die Wortstellung in Notkers Consolatio: Untersuchungen zur Syntax und Übersetzungstechnik*. Berlin: de Gruyter.

Nakajima, Heizo (1996). 'Complementizer selection', *Linguistic Review* 13: 143–64.

Neeleman, Ad, and Kriszta Szendrői (2007). 'Radical pro drop and the morphology of pronouns', *Linguistic Inquiry* 38: 671–714.

Neeleman, Ad, and Kriszta Szendrői (2008). 'Case morphology and radical *pro*-drop', in Theresa Biberauer (ed.), *The limits of syntactic variation*. Amsterdam: John Benjamins, 331–48.

Newmeyer, Frederick J. (1998). *Language form and language function*. Cambridge, Mass.: MIT Press.

Newmeyer, Frederick J. (2000). 'On the reconstruction of Proto-World word order', in Chris Knight, Michael Studdert-Kennedy, and James R. Hurford (eds.), *The evolutionary emergence of language*. Cambridge: Cambridge University Press, 372–88.

Newmeyer, Frederick J. (2004). 'Against a parameter-setting approach to typological variation', *Linguistic Variation Yearbook* 4: 181–234.

Newmeyer, Frederick J. (2005). *Possible and probable languages*. Oxford: Oxford University Press.

Newmeyer, Frederick J. (2006). *A rejoinder to 'On the role of parameters in Universal Grammar: a reply to Newmeyer' by Ian Roberts and Anders Holmberg*. MS. University of Washington.

Newton, Glenda (2006). *The development and loss of the Old Irish double system of verbal inflection*. Ph.D. dissertation. University of Cambridge.

Nichols, Johanna (2003). 'Diversity and stability in language', in Brian D. Joseph and Richard D. Janda (eds.), *The handbook of historical linguistics*. Oxford: Blackwell, 283–310.

Nielsen, Hans Frede (1998). *The continental backgrounds of English and its insular development until 1154*. Odense: Odense University Press.

Nielsen, Hans Frede (2000a). *The early Runic language of Scandinavia. Studies in Germanic dialect geography*. Heidelberg: Carl Winter.

Nielsen, Hans Frede (2000b). 'Ingwäonisch', in Johannes Hoops, Heinrich Beck, Dieter Geuenich, and Heiko Steuer (eds.), *Reallexikon der germanischen Altertumskunde*, 2nd edn., vol. xv. Berlin: Mouton de Gruyter, 432–8.

Nilsen, Øystein (2003). *Eliminating positions: syntax and semantics of sentence modification*. Ph.D. dissertation. Universiteit Utrecht.

Niyogi, Partha (2006). *The computational nature of language learning and evolution*. Cambridge, Mass.: MIT Press.

Niyogi, Partha, and Robert Berwick (1995). *The logical problem of language change*. MIT Artificial Intelligence Laboratory Memo No. 1516. Cambridge, Mass.

Niyogi, Partha, and Robert Berwick (2009). 'The proper treatment of language acquisition and change in a population setting', *PNAS* 109: 10124–9.

Norde, Muriel (2001). 'Deflexion as a counterdirectional factor in grammatical change', *Language Sciences* 23: 231–64.

Norde, Muriel (2009). *Degrammaticalization*. Oxford: Oxford University Press.

Noyer, Rolf (1992). *Features, positions and affixes in autonomous morphological structure*. Ph.D. dissertation. MIT.

Nübling, Damaris (1992). *Klitika im Deutschen. Schriftsprache, Umgangssprache, alemannische Dialekte*. Tübingen: Narr.

Nye, Rachel (2009). How *pseudo questions and the interpretation of* wh-*clauses in English*. MA dissertation. University of Essex.

Nygaard, Marius (1894). 'Udeladelse av subject: "Subjektlöse" sætninger i det norröne sprog (den klassiske sagastil)', *Arkiv för nordisk filologi* 10: 1–25.

Nygaard, Marius (1906). *Norrøn syntax*. Kristiania: Aschehough.

Obenauer, Hans-Georg (2004). 'Nonstandard *wh*-questions and alternative checkers in Pagotto', in Horst Lohnstein and Susanne Trissler (eds.), *The syntax and semantics of the left periphery*. Berlin: Mouton de Gruyter, 343–84.

O'Grady, William (1997). *Syntactic development*. Chicago: University of Chicago Press.

Ohala, John J. (1981). 'The listener as a source of sound change', in Carrie S. Masek, Robert A. Hendrick, and Mary F. Miller (eds.), *Papers from the parasession on language and behavior, Chicago Linguistic Society*. Chicago: Chicago Linguistic Society, 178–203.

Ohkado, Masayuki (2005). *Clause structure in Old English*. Ph.D. dissertation. University of Amsterdam.

Ohlander, Urban (1943). 'Omission of the object in English', *Studia Neophilologica* 16: 105–27.

Önnerfors, Olaf (1997). *Verb-erst-Deklarativsätze: Grammatik und Pragmatik*. Stockholm: Almqvist and Wiskell International.

Ortony, Andrew (1979). 'Metaphor: a multidimensional problem', in Andrew Ortony (ed.), *Metaphor and thought*. Cambridge: Cambridge University Press, 1–18.

Osgood, Charles, and Thomas Sebeok (1954). 'Psycholinguistics: a survey of theory and research problems', *Journal of Abnormal and Social Psychology* 49: 1–203.

Osthoff, Hermann, and Karl Brugmann (1878). *Morphologische Untersuchungen auf dem Gebiet der indogermanischen Sprachen*, vol. i. Leipzig: Hirzel.

Östman, Jan-Ola (1982). 'The symbiotic relationship between pragmatic particles and impromptu speech', in Nils Erik Enkvist (ed.), *Impromptu speech: a symposium*. Åbo: Åbo Akademi, 147–77.

Ottósson, Kjartan (1992). *The Icelandic middle voice: the morphological and phonological development*. Ph.D. dissertation. University of Lund.

Ottosson, Kjartan (2008). 'The Old Nordic middle voice in the pre-literary period', in Folke Josephson and Ingmar Söhrman (eds.), *Interdependence of diachronic and synchronic analyses*. Amsterdam: John Benjamins, 185–219.

Ottosson, Kjartan (2009). *The anticausative and related categories in the Old Germanic languages*. MS. University of Oslo.

Palander-Collin, Minna (1997). 'A medieval case of grammaticalization, *methinks*', in Matti Rissanen, Merja Kytö, and Kirsi Heikkonen (eds.), *Grammaticalization at work: studies of long-term developments in English*. Berlin: Mouton de Gruyter, 371–403.

Palmer, Bill (1999). *A grammar of the Kokota language, Santa Isabel, Solomon Islands*. Ph.D. dissertation. University of Sydney.

Paolillo, John C. (2000). 'Formalizing formality: an analysis of register variation in Sinhala', *Journal of Linguistics* 36: 215–59.

Paul, Hermann (1880). *Prinzipien der Sprachgeschichte*. 1st edn. Halle: Max Niemeyer.

Paul, Hermann (1919). *Deutsche Grammatik, Teil IV: Syntax*, vol. iii. Tübingen: Niemeyer.

Pesetsky, David, and Esther Torrego (2001). 'T-to-C movement: causes and consequences', in Michael Kenstowicz (ed.), *Ken Hale: a life in language*. Cambridge, Mass.: MIT Press, 355–426.

Pesetsky, David, and Esther Torrego (2004). 'Tense, case, and the nature of syntactic categories', in Jacqueline Guéron and Jacqueline Lecarme (eds.), *The syntax of time*. Cambridge, Mass.: MIT Press, 495–538.

Petrova, Svetlana (2011). 'Information structure and syntactic variation in root declaratives in Middle Low German', paper presented at the Workshop on Information Structure Annotation in Historical Corpora, Oslo.

Petrova, Svetlana (2012). 'Multiple XP-fronting in Middle Low German root clauses', *Journal of Comparative Germanic Linguistics* 15: 157–88.

Pica, Pierre (2001). 'Introduction', *Linguistic Variation Yearbook* 1: v–xii.

Pinker, Steven, and Alan Prince (1988). 'On language and connectionism: analysis of a parallel distributed processing model of language acquisition', *Cognition* 28: 73–93.

Pintzuk, Susan (1993). 'Verb seconding in Old English: verb movement to Infl', *Linguistic Review* 10: 5–35.

Pintzuk, Susan (1999). *Phrase structures in competition: variation and change in Old English word order*. New York: Garland.

Pintzuk, Susan (2005). 'Arguments against a universal base: evidence from Old English', *English Language and Linguistics* 9: 115–38.

Pintzuk, Susan, and Eric Haeberli (2008). 'Structural variation in Old English root clauses', *Language Variation and Change* 20: 367–407.

Pintzuk, Susan, and Anthony Kroch (1989). 'The rightward movement of complements and adjuncts in the Old English of Beowulf', *Language Variation and Change* 1: 115–43.

Pintzuk, Susan, and Ann Taylor (2006). 'The loss of OV order in the history of English', in Ans van Kemenade and Bettelou Los (eds.), *The handbook of the history of English*. Malden, Mass., and Oxford: Blackwell, 249–78.

Pires, Acrisio, and Sarah G. Thomason (2008). 'How much syntactic reconstruction is possible?', in Gisella Ferraresi and Maria Goldbach (eds.), *Principles of syntactic reconstruction*. Amsterdam: John Benjamins, 27–72.

Plaster, Keith, and Maria Polinsky (2010). 'Features in categorization, or a new look at an old problem', in Anna Kibort and Greville G. Corbett (eds.), *Features: perspectives on a key notion in linguistics*. Oxford: Oxford University Press, 109–42.

Platzack, Christer (1987). 'The Scandinavian languages and the null-subject parameter', *Natural Language and Linguistic Theory* 5: 377–401.

Platzack, Christer (2004). 'Agreement and the person phrase hypothesis', *Working Papers in Scandinavian Syntax* 73: 83–112.

Pogatscher, Alois (1901). 'Unausgedrücktes Subject im Altenglischen', *Anglia* 23: 261–301.

Poletto, Cecilia (2006). 'Asymmetrical pro-drop in northern Italian dialects', in Peter Ackema, Patrick Brandt, Maaike Schoorlemmer, and Fred Weerman (eds.), *Arguments and agreement*. Oxford: Oxford University Press, 159–91.

Poppe, Erich (2006). 'Celtic influence on Old English relative clauses?', in Hildegard Tristram (ed.), *The Celtic Englishes*, vol. iv. Potsdam: Universitätsverlag Potsdam, 191–211.

Pratt, Lynda, and David Denison (2000). 'The language of the Southey–Coleridge circle', *Language Sciences* 22: 401–22.

Prokosch, Eduard (1939). *A comparative Germanic grammar*. Philadelphia: Linguistic Society of America.

Puhvel, Jaan (1987). *Comparative mythology*. Baltimore: Johns Hopkins University Press.

Pulgram, Ernst (1959). 'Proto-Indo-European reality and reconstruction', *Language* 35: 421–6.

Radford, Andrew (1997). *Syntax: a Minimalist introduction*. Cambridge: Cambridge University Press.

Ratkus, Artūras (2011). *The adjective inflection in Gothic and early Germanic: structure and development*. Ph.D. dissertation. University of Cambridge.

Rauch, Irmengard (1992). *The Old Saxon language: grammar, epic narrative, linguistic interference*. New York: Peter Lang.

Reinhart, Tanya (1981). 'Pragmatics and linguistics: an analysis of sentence topics', *Philosophica* 27: 53–94.

Reinhart, Tanya (1995). 'Interface strategies', *OTS Working Papers in Linguistics*, Utrecht.

Reis, Hans (1901). 'Über althochdeutsche Wortfolge', *Zeitschrift für deutsche Philologie* 33: 212–38, 330–49.

Reis, Marga (2000a). 'Anmerkung zu Verb-erst-Satz-Typen im Deutschen', in Rolf Thieroff, Matthias Tamrat, Nanna Furhop, and Oliver Teuber (eds.), *Deutscher Grammatik in Theorie und Praxis*. Tübingen: Max Niemeyer, 215–27.

Reis, Marga (2000b). 'Review of O. Önnerfors: Verb-erst-Deklarativsätze. Grammatik und Pragmatik', *Studia Linguistica* 54: 90–100.

Rett, Jessica (2008). *Degree modification in natural language*. Ph.D. dissertation. Rutgers University.

Rett, Jessica (2009). 'A degree account of exclamatives', in Tova Friedman and Satoshi Ito (eds.), *Proceedings of SALT XVIII*. Ithaca, NY: Cornell University Press.

Rickard, Peter (1993). *A history of the French language*. 2nd edn. London: Routledge.

Ries, John (1880). *Die Stellung von Subject und Prädicatsverbum im Hêliand*. Strasbourg and London: Karl J. Trübner.

Ringe, Donald (2006). *A linguistic history of English*, vol. i: *From Proto-Indo-European to Proto-Germanic*. Oxford: Oxford University Press.

Ringe, Donald, Tandy Warnow, and Ann Taylor (2003). 'Indo-European and computational cladistics', *Transactions of the Philological Society* 100: 59–129.

Rizzi, Luigi (1978). 'Violations of the *wh*-island condition in Italian and the subjacency condition', *Montreal Working Papers in Linguistics* 11: 155–90.

Rizzi, Luigi (1982). *Issues in Italian syntax*. Dordrecht: Foris.

Rizzi, Luigi (1986). 'Null objects in Italian and the theory of *pro*', *Linguistic Inquiry* 17: 501–57.

Rizzi, Luigi (1990). *Relativized Minimality*. Cambridge, Mass.: MIT Press.

Rizzi, Luigi (1994). 'Early null subjects and root null subjects', in Teun Hoekstra and Bonnie D. Schwartz (eds.), *Language acquisition studies in generative grammar: papers in honour of Kenneth Wexler from the 1991 GLOW workshops*. Amsterdam: John Benjamins, 151–76.

Rizzi, Luigi (1997). 'The fine structure of the left periphery', in Liliane Haegeman (ed.), *Elements of grammar*. Dordrecht: Kluwer, 281–337.

Rizzi, Luigi (2001a). 'Relativized Minimality effects', in Mark Baltin and Chris Collins (eds.), *The handbook of contemporary syntactic theory*. Oxford: Blackwell, 89–110.

Rizzi, Luigi (2001b). 'On the position "int(errogative)" in the left periphery of the clause', in Guglielmo Cinque and Giampaolo Salvi (eds.), *Current studies in Italian syntax: essays offered to Lorenzo Renzi*. Amsterdam: Elsevier, 267–96.

Rizzi, Luigi (2006). 'Grammatically-based target-inconsistencies in child language', in Kamil Ud Deen, Jun Nomura, Barbara Schulz, and Bonnie D. Schwartz (eds.), *Proceedings of the Inaugural Conference on Generative Approaches to Language Acquisition—North America (GALANA)*, vol. iv. Cambridge, Mass.: University of Connecticut Occasional Papers in Linguistics, 19–49.

Roberts, Ian (1993). *Verbs and diachronic syntax*. Dordrecht: Kluwer.

Roberts, Ian (1996). 'Remarks on the Old English C-system and the diachrony of V2', in Ellen Brandner and Gisella Ferraresi (eds.), *Language change and generative grammar. Linguistische Berichte*, Sonderheft 7. Opladen: Westdeutscher Verlag, 154–64.

Roberts, Ian (1998). 'Review of Harris and Campbell (1995)', *Romance Philology* 51: 363–70.

Roberts, Ian (2004). 'The C-system in Brythonic Celtic languages, V2, and the EPP', in Luigi Rizzi (ed.), *The cartography of syntactic structures*, vol. ii: *The structure of CP and IP*. Oxford: Oxford University Press, 297–328.

Roberts, Ian (2005). *Principles and parameters in a VSO language: a case study in Welsh*. Oxford: Oxford University Press.

Roberts, Ian (2007). *Diachronic syntax*. Oxford: Oxford University Press.

Roberts, Ian (2010a). 'A deletion analysis of null subjects', in Theresa Biberauer, Anders Holmberg, Ian Roberts, and Michelle Sheehan (eds.), *Parametric variation: null subjects in Minimalist theory*. Cambridge: Cambridge University Press, 58–87.

Roberts, Ian (2010b). *Agreement and head movement: clitics, incorporation and defective goals*. Cambridge, Mass.: MIT Press.

Roberts, Ian (2011). 'Taraldsen's Generalization and diachronic syntax: two ways to lose null subjects', in Peter Svenonius (ed.), *Festschrift for Tarald Taraldsen*. Oxford: Oxford University Press.

Roberts, Ian, and Anders Holmberg (2005). 'On the role of parameters in Universal Grammar: a reply to Newmeyer', in Hans Broekhuis, Norbert Corver, Martin Everaert, and Jan Koster (eds.), *Organizing grammar: linguistic studies in honor of Henk van Riemsdijk*. Berlin: Mouton de Gruyter, 538–53.

Roberts, Ian, and Anna Roussou (1999). 'A formal approach to "grammaticalization"', *Linguistics* 37: 1011–41.

Roberts, Ian, and Anna Roussou (2002). 'The Extended Projection Principle as a condition on the tense dependency', in Peter Svenonius (ed.), *Subjects, expletives, and the EPP*. Oxford: Oxford University Press, 125–56.

Roberts, Ian, and Anna Roussou (2003). *Syntactic change: a Minimalist approach to grammaticalization*. Cambridge: Cambridge University Press.

Robinson, Orrin W. (1992). *Old English and its closest relatives*. London: Routledge.

Robinson, Orrin W. (1997). *Clause subordination and verb placement in the Old High German Isidor translation*. Heidelberg: Carl Winter.

Rögnvaldsson, Eiríkur (1990). 'Null objects in Icelandic', in Joan Maling and Annie Zaenen (eds.), *Modern Icelandic syntax*. San Diego: Academic Press, 367–79.

Rögnvaldsson, Eiríkur (1991). 'Quirky subjects in Old Icelandic', in Halldór Ármann Sigurðsson (ed.), *Papers from the twelfth Scandinavian conference of linguistics*. Reykjavik: University of Iceland, 369–78.

Rögnvaldsson, Eiríkur (1995). 'Old Icelandic: a non-configurational language?', *NOWELE* 26: 3–29.

Rögnvaldsson, Eiríkur, and Höskuldur Þráinsson (1990). 'On Icelandic word order once more', in Joan Maling and Annie Zaenen (eds.), *Modern Icelandic syntax*. San Diego: Academic Press, 3–40.

Rohrbacher, Bernhard (1999). *Morphology-driven syntax: a theory of V-to-I raising and pro-drop*. Amsterdam: John Benjamins.

Rosenbaum, Peter (1967). *The grammar of English predicate complement constructions*. Cambridge, Mass.: MIT Press.

Rosenkvist, Henrik (2009). 'Referential null subjects in Germanic: an overview', *Working Papers in Scandinavian Syntax* 84: 151–80.

Rosenkvist, Henrik (2010). 'Null referential subjects in Övdalian', *Nordic Journal of Linguistics* 33: 231–67.

Ross, John Robert (1970). 'On declarative sentences', in Roderick Jacobs and Peter Rosenbaum (eds.), *Readings in English Transformational Grammar*. Waltham, Mass.: Ginn and Co, 222–77.

Ross, John Robert (1982). 'Pronoun-deleting processes in German', paper presented at the annual meeting of the Linguistic Society of America, San Diego, Calif.

Round, Erich R. (2010). 'Syntactic reconstruction by phonology: Edge Aligned Reconstruction and its application to Tangkic truncation', in Rachel Hendery and Jennifer Hendriks (eds.), *Grammatical change: theory and description*. Canberra: Pacific Linguistics, 65–82.

Rowlett, Paul (1998). *Sentential negation in French*. Oxford: Oxford University Press.

Rusten, Kristian A. (2010). *A study of empty referential pronominal subjects in Old English*. M.Phil. dissertation. University of Bergen.

Sæbø, Kjell Johan (2005). 'Explaining clausal exclamatives', paper presented at the JSM05, Paris.

Saito, Mamoru (2007). 'Notes on East Asian argument ellipsis', *Language Research* 43: 203–27.

Samuels, Bridget (2009). *The structure of phonological theory*. Ph.D. dissertation. Harvard University.

Samuels, Bridget (2011). 'A minimalist program for phonology', in Cedric Boeckx (ed.), *The Oxford handbook of linguistic minimalism*. Oxford: Oxford University Press, 574–94.

Samuels, Bridget, and Cedric Boeckx (2009). 'What emerges from Merge in phonology?', paper presented at the 6th Old World Conference on Phonology, Edinburgh.

Sankoff, Gillian, and Hélène Blondeau (2007). 'Language change across the lifespan: /r/ in Montreal French', *Language* 83: 560–88.

Santorini, Beatrice (1994). 'Some similarities and differences between Icelandic and Yiddish', in David Lightfoot and Norbert Hornstein (eds.), *Verb movement*. Cambridge: Cambridge University Press, 87–106.

Sapir, Edward (1921). *Language*. New York: Harcourt Brace.

Sato, Yosuke, and Chonghyuck Kim (2012). 'Radical pro drop and the role of syntactic agreement in Colloquial Singapore English', *Lingua* 122: 858–73.

Schäferdiek, Knut (1981). 'Die Fragmente der "Skeireins" und der Johanneskommentar des Theodor von Herakleia', *Zeitschrift für deutsches Altertum und deutsche Literatur* 110: 175–93.

Schlachter, Eva (2010). *Syntax und Informationsstruktur im Althochdeutschen: Untersuchungen am Beispiel der Isidor-Gruppe*. Ph.D. dissertation. Humboldt-Universität zu Berlin.

Schleicher, August (1853). 'Die ersten Spaltungen des indogermanischen Urvolkes', *Allgemeine Monatsschrift für Wissenschaft und Literatur* 1853: 786–7.

Schleicher, August (1861/2). *Compendium der vergleichenden Grammatik der indogermanischen Sprache*. 2 vols. Weimar: Hermann Böhlau.

Schleicher, August (1863). *Die darwinsche Theorie und die Sprachwissenschaft*. Weimar: Hermann Böhlau.

Schlenker, Philippe (2010). 'Presuppositions and local contexts', *Mind* 119: 377–91.

Schulze, Wilhelm (1924). 'Personalpronomen und Subjektausdruck im Gotischen', in Wilhelm Horn (ed.), *Beiträge zur germanischen Sprachwissenschaft: Festschrift für Otto Behaghel*. Heidelberg: Carl Winter, 92–109.

Schwartz, Bonnie D., and Sten Vikner (1989). 'All verb second clauses are CPs', *Working Papers in Scandinavian Syntax* 43: 27–49.

Schwartz, Bonnie D., and Sten Vikner (1996). 'The verb always leaves IP in V2 clauses', in Adriana Belletti and Luigi Rizzi (eds.), *Parameters and functional heads*. Oxford: Oxford University Press, 11–63.

Scot, Sky (2009). *An investigation concerning the base generation of four Old English conjunct and disjunct adverbials within the structure of Old English clauses*. Undergraduate dissertation, University of Stockholm.

Seppänen, Aimo (1985). 'On the use of the dual in Gothic', *Zeitschrift für deutsches Altertum und deutsche Literatur* 114: 1–41.

Sheehan, Michelle, and Wolfram Hinzen (2012). 'Moving towards the edge', *Linguistic Analysis* 37: 405–58.

Shepherd, William R. (1926). *Historical Atlas*. 3rd edn. New York: Henry Holt and Company.

Shields, Kenneth (1996). 'Old High German 1st plural *mês*', *International Journal for Germanic Linguistics and Semiotic Analysis* 1: 283–92.

Shlonsky, Ur, and Gabriela Soare (2011). 'Where's "Why"?', *Linguistic Inquiry* 42: 651–69.

Sigurðsson, Halldór Ármann (1989). *Verbal syntax and case in Icelandic*. Ph.D. dissertation. University of Lund.

Sigurðsson, Halldór Ármann (1993). 'Argument drop in Old Icelandic', *Lingua* 89: 247–80.

Sigurðsson, Halldór Ármann (2004). 'The syntax of Person, Tense, and speech features', *Italian Journal of Linguistics* 16: 219–51.

Sigurðsson, Halldór Ármann (2011). 'Conditions on argument drop', *Linguistic Inquiry* 42: 267–304.

Smet, Gilbert de (1970). 'Het subjectspronomen in de oudnederfrankische psalmfragmenten', *Studia Germanica Gandensia* 12: 145–58.

Smet, Hendrik de (2009). 'Analysing reanalysis', *Lingua* 119: 1728–55.

Smith, Jesse R. (1971). *Word order in the older Germanic dialects*. Ph.D. dissertation. University of Illinois at Urbana-Champaign.

Smith, Neil V., and Ann Law (2009). 'On parametric (and non-parametric) variation', *Biolinguistics* 3: 332–43.

Snyder, William (2000). 'An experimental investigation of syntactic satiation effects', *Linguistic Inquiry* 31: 575–82.

Sobin, Nicholas (1987). 'The variable status of COMP-trace phenomena', *Natural Language and Linguistic Theory* 5: 33–60.

Sokal, Alan (2008). *Beyond the hoax*. Oxford: Oxford University Press.

Sonderegger, Stefan (2003). *Althochdeutsche Sprache und Literatur: eine Einführung in das älteste Deutsch. Darstellung und Grammatik*. 3rd edn. Berlin: de Gruyter.

Sorace, Antonella, Ludovica Serratrice, Francesca Filiaci, and Michela Baldo (2009). 'Discourse conditions on subject pronoun realization: testing the linguistic intuitions of older bilingual children', *Lingua* 119: 460–77.

Speas, Margaret (1994). 'Null arguments in a theory of economy of projection', in Elena Benedicto and Jeffrey Runner (eds.), *University of Massachusetts occasional papers in linguistics*. Amherst: University of Massachusetts, GLSA, 179–208.

Speas, Margaret (2006). 'Economy, agreement and the representation of null arguments', in Peter Ackema, Patrick Brandt, Maaike Schoorlemmer, and Fred Weerman (eds.), *Arguments and agreement*. Oxford: Oxford University Press, 35–75.

Speyer, Augustin (2008). *Topicalization and clash avoidance: on the interaction of prosody and syntax in the history of English with a few glimpses at German*. Ph.D. dissertation. University of Pennsylvania.

Speyer, Augustin (2010). *Topicalization and stress clash avoidance in the history of English*. Berlin: Mouton de Gruyter.

Stalnaker, Robert (1974). 'Pragmatic Presuppositions', in Milton K. Munitz and Peter Unger (eds.), *Semantics and Philosophy*. New York: New York University Press, 197–214.

Stalnaker, Robert (1978). 'Assertion', *Syntax and Semantics* 9: 315–32.

Stanley, Eric (2000). '*Hwæt*', in Jane Roberts and Janet Nelson (eds.), *Essays on Anglo-Saxon and related themes in memory of Lynne Grundy*. London: King's College Centre for Late Antique and Medieval Studies, 525–56.

Stepanov, Arthur, and Wei-Tien Dylan Tsai (2008). 'Cartography and licensing of *wh*-adjuncts: a crosslinguistic perspective', *Natural Language and Linguistic Theory* 26: 589–638.

Stockwell, Robert P., and Donka Minkova (1990). 'Verb phrase conjunction in Old English', in Henning Andersen and Konrad Körner (eds.), *Historical linguistics 1987: papers from the 8th International Conference on Historical Linguistics*. Amsterdam: John Benjamins, 499–515.

Streitberg, Wilhelm (1920). *Gotisches Elementarbuch*. 6th edn. Heidelberg: Carl Winter.

Sundmalm, Sara Maria (2009). *The syntactic origin of Old English sentence adverbials*. Undergraduate dissertation, Stockholm University.

Svenonius, Peter (2003). *On the edge*. MS. University of Tromsø.

Swan, Toril (1994). 'Old English and Old Norse initial adverbials and word order', in Toril Swan, Endre Mørck, and Olaf Janse Westvik (eds.), *Language change and language structure: older Germanic languages in comparative perspective*. Berlin: Mouton de Gruyter, 233–70.

Swanton, Michael (1996). *The Anglo-Saxon Chronicle*. New York: Routledge.

Szabolcsi, Anna, and Frans Zwarts (1993). 'Weak islands and an algebraic semantics for scope-taking', *Natural Language Semantics* 1: 235–84.

Szemerényi, Oswald (1996). *Introduction to Indo-European linguistics*. Oxford: Clarendon.

Taraldsen, Knut Tarald (1978). *On the NIC, vacuous application, and the that-t filter*. MS. Massachusetts Institute of Technology.

Taube, Sharon (2012). 'The mystery of the missing argument: Hebrew object drop', in Balázs Surányi and Diána Varga (eds.), *Proceedings of the First Central European Conference in Linguistics for Postgraduate Students*. Budapest: Pázmány Péter Catholic University, 318–31.

Taylor, Ann (2008). 'Contact effects of translation: distinguishing two kinds of influence in Old English', *Language Variation and Change* 20: 341–65.

Taylor, Ann, and Susan Pintzuk (2009). 'Information structure and the syntax of objects in Old English: a corpus study', paper presented at the Workshop on Corpus-based Advances in Historical Linguistics, University of York.

Taylor, Ann, and Susan Pintzuk (2012). 'Verb order, object position and information status in Old English', *York Papers in Linguistics* 2: 29–52.

te Velde, John R. (2010). 'Towards an account of adverbials in the *Vor-Vorfeld*: Beyond V2-syntax', *Tampa Journal of Linguistics* 1: 62–86.

Thomason, Olga (2006). *Prepositional systems in Biblical Greek, Gothic, Classical Armenian, and Old Church Slavic*. Ph.D. dissertation. University of Georgia.

Thomason, Sarah Grey, and Terrence Kaufman (1988). *Language contact, creolization, and genetic linguistics*. Berkeley and Los Angeles: University of California Press.

Þorgeirsson, Haukur (2012). 'Late placement of the finite verb in Old Norse *fornyrðislag* meter', *Journal of Germanic Linguistics* 24: 233–69.

Þráinsson, Höskuldur (2007). *The syntax of Icelandic*. Cambridge: Cambridge University Press.

Thurneysen, Rudolf (1892). 'Zur Stellung des Verbums im Altfranzösischen', *Zeitschrift für Romanische Philologie* 16: 289–307.

Timberlake, Alan (1977). 'Reanalysis and actualization in syntactic change', in Charles N. Li (ed.), *Mechanisms of syntactic change*. Austin: University of Texas Press, 141–77.

Tindall, George B. (1989). 'Mythology: a new frontier in Southern History', in Patrick Gerster and Nicholas Cords (eds.), *Myth and Southern History*, vol. i: *The Old South*. 2nd edn. Chicago: University of Illinois Press, 1–16.

Tomaselli, Alessandra (1986). 'Das unpersönliche *es*: eine Analyse im Rahmen der Generativen Grammatik', *Linguistische Berichte* 102: 171–90.

Tomaselli, Alessandra (1995). 'Cases of verb third in Old High German', in Adrian Battye and Ian Roberts (eds.), *Clause structure and language change*. Oxford: Oxford University Press, 345–69.

Tomioka, Satoshi (2003). 'The semantics of Japanese null pronouns and its cross-linguistic implications', in Kerstin Schwabe and Susanne Winkler (eds.), *The interfaces: deriving and interpreting omitted structures*. Amsterdam: John Benjamins, 321–39.

Tops, Guy A. J. (1974). *The origin of the Germanic dental preterit: a critical research history since 1912*. Leiden: Brill.

Trask, Robert Lawrence (1996b). *Historical linguistics*. London: Arnold.

Trask, Robert Lawrence (1999). *Key concepts in language and linguistics*. London: Routledge.

Travis, Lisa de Mena (1984). *Parameters and effects of word order variation*. Ph.D. dissertation. MIT.

Travis, Lisa de Mena (1991). 'Parameters of phrase structure and verb-second phenomena', in Robert Freidin (ed.), *Principles and parameters in comparative grammar*. Cambridge, Mass.: MIT Press, 339–64.

Tristram, Hildegard (2004). 'Diglossia in Anglo-Saxon England, or what was spoken Old English like?', *Studia Anglica Posnaniensia* 40: 87–110.

Trudgill, Peter (1989). 'Language contact and simplification', *Nordlyd* 15: 113–21.

Trudgill, Peter (1996). 'Dual-source pidgins and reverse creoloids: northern perspectives on language contact', in Ernst Håkon Jahr and Ingvild Broch (eds.), *Language contact in the Arctic: northern pidgins and contact languages*. Berlin: Mouton de Gruyter, 5–14.

Trudgill, Peter (2011). *Sociolinguistic typology: social determinants of linguistic complexity*. Oxford: Oxford University Press.

Trutkowski, Ewa (2011). 'Referential null subjects in German', in Chris Cummins, Chi-Hé Elder, Thomas Godard, Morgan Macleod, Elaine Schmidt, and George Walkden (eds.), *Proceedings of the Sixth Cambridge Postgraduate Conference in Linguistics (CamLing)*. Cambridge: Cambridge Institute for Language Research, 206–17.

Twaddell, W. Freeman (1948). 'The prehistoric Germanic short syllabics', *Language* 24: 139–51.

Ureland, P. Sture (1978). 'Typological, diachronic, and areal linguistic perspectives of North Germanic syntax', in John Weinstock (ed.), *The Nordic languages and modern linguistics*, vol. iii. Austin: University of Texas Press, 116–41.

Vainikka, Anne, and Yonata Levy (1999). 'Empty subjects in Finnish and Hebrew', *Natural Language and Linguistic Theory* 17: 613–71.

Vance, Barbara (1997). *Syntactic change in medieval French: verb-second and null subjects*. Dordrecht: Kluwer.

Vanelli, Laura, Lorenzo Renzi, and Paola Benincà (1986). 'Typologie des pronoms sujets dans les langues romanes', *Actes du XVIIème Congrès International de Linguistique et de Philologie Romanes*, vol. iii: *Linguistique descriptive: phonétique, morphologie et lexique*. Aix: Université de Provence, 161–76.

Vangsnes, Øystein (2008). 'Decomposing manner *how* in colloquial Scandinavian', *Studia Linguistica* 62: 119–41.

Vennemann, Theo (1974). 'Topics, subjects and word order: from SXV to SVX via TVX', in John M. Anderson and Charles Jones (eds.), *Historical linguistics*, vol. i: *Syntax, morphology, internal and comparative reconstruction*. Amsterdam: North-Holland, 427–45.

Vikner, Sten (1995). *Verb movement and expletive subjects in the Germanic languages*. Oxford: Oxford University Press.

Vincent, Nigel, and Ian Roberts (1999). 'Remarks on syntactic reconstruction', paper presented at the Annual Meeting of the Deutsche Gesellschaft für Sprachwissenschaft, University of Konstanz.

Visser, Frederic Theodor (1963–73). *An historical syntax of the English language*. 4 vols. Leiden: Brill.

Vogt, Hans (1988). *Linguistique caucasienne et arménienne*. Oslo: Norwegian University Press.

Wagner, Suzanne Evans, and Gillian Sankoff (2011). 'Age grading in the Montréal French inflected future', *Language Variation and Change* 23: 275–313.

Wali, Kashi, and Omkar Nath Koul (1997). *Kashmiri: a cognitive-descriptive grammar*. London: Routledge.

Walkden, George (2009). *The comparative method in syntactic reconstruction*. M.Phil. dissertation. University of Cambridge.

Walkden, George (2011). 'Abduction or inertia? The logic of syntactic change', in Chris Cummins, Chi-Hé Elder, Thomas Godard, Morgan Macleod, Elaine Schmidt, and George Walkden (eds.), *Proceedings of the Sixth Cambridge Postgraduate Conference in Language Research*. Cambridge: Cambridge Institute of Language Research, 230–9.

Walkden, George (2012). 'Against inertia', *Lingua* 122, 891–901.

Walkden, George (2013a). 'The correspondence problem in syntactic reconstruction', *Diachronica* 30: 95–122.

Walkden, George (2013b). 'Null subjects in Old English', *Language Variation and Change* 25: 155–78.

Walkden, George (2013c). 'The status of *hwæt* in Old English', *English Language and Linguistics* 17: 465–88.

Wallage, Phillip (2005). *Negation in Early English: parametric variation and grammatical competition*. Ph.D. dissertation. University of York.

Wallenberg, Joel C. (2009). *Antisymmetry and the conservation of c-command*. Ph.D. dissertation. University of Pennsylvania.

Wallenberg, Joel C., Einar Freyr Sigurðsson, and Anton Karl Ingason (2011). 'Distinguishing change and stability: a quantitative study of Icelandic oblique subjects', paper presented at the 13th Diachronic Generative Syntax conference, Philadelphia.

Warner, Anthony (1993). *English auxiliaries: structure and history*. Cambridge: Cambridge University Press.

Watkins, Calvert (1964). 'Preliminaries to the reconstruction of Indo-European sentence structure', in Horace G. Lunt (ed.), *Proceedings of the Ninth International Congress of Linguists*. The Hague: Mouton, 1035–45.

Watkins, Calvert (1976). 'Towards Proto-Indo-European syntax: problems and pseudo-problems', in Sanford Steever, Carol Walker, and Salikoko Mufwene (eds.), *Papers from the parasession on diachronic syntax*. Chicago: Chicago Linguistic Society, 306–26.

Watkins, Calvert (1995). *How to kill a dragon: aspects of Indo-European poetics*. Oxford: Oxford University Press.

Weerman, Fred (1993). 'The diachronic consequences of first and second language acquisition: the change from OV to VO', *Linguistics* 31: 903–31.

Weinreich, Uriel, William Labov, and Marvin I. Herzog (1968). 'Empirical foundations for a theory of language change', in Winfred P. Lehmann and Yakov Malkiel (eds.), *Directions for historical linguistics: a symposium*. Austin: University of Texas Press, 95–195.

Weir, Andrew (2008). *Subject pronoun drop in informal English*. MA dissertation. University of Edinburgh.

Wenisch, Franz (1979). *Spezifisch anglisches Wortgut in den nordhumbrischen Interlinearglossierungen des Lukasevangeliums*. Heidelberg: Carl Winter.

Wessén, Elias (1966). *Isländsk grammatik*. 2nd edn. Norstedts: Svenska Bokförlaget.

Westergaard, Marit (2005). 'Norwegian child language and the history of English: the interaction of syntax and information structure in the development of word order', in Kevin

McCafferty, Tove Bull, and Kristin Killie (eds.), *Contexts—historical, social, linguistic: studies in celebration of Toril Swan.* Bern: Peter Lang, 293–310.

Westergaard, Marit (2009). *The acquisition of word order: micro-cues, information structure, and economy.* Amsterdam: John Benjamins.

Westergaard, Marit, and Øystein Vangsnes (2005). 'Wh-questions, V2, and the left periphery of three Norwegian dialect types', *Journal of Comparative Germanic Linguistics* 8: 117–58.

White, Hayden (1978). *Tropics of discourse: essays in cultural criticism.* Baltimore: Johns Hopkins University Press.

White, Lydia (2003). *Second language acquisition and universal grammar.* Cambridge: Cambridge University Press.

Wichmann, Søren (2008). 'The study of semantic alignment: retrospect and the state of the art', in Mark Donohue and Søren Wichmann (eds.), *The typology of semantic alignment.* Oxford: Oxford University Press, 3–23.

Wiklund, Anna-Lena (2009a). 'In search of the force of dependent V2: a note on Swedish', *Working Papers in Scandinavian Syntax* 83: 27–36.

Wiklund, Anna-Lena (2009b). 'May the force be with you: a reply from the 5th floor', *Working Papers in Scandinavian Syntax* 84: 233–6.

Wiklund, Anna-Lena (2010). 'In search of the force of dependent verb second', *Nordic Journal of Linguistics* 33: 81–91.

Wiklund, Anna-Lena, Kristine Bentzen, Gunnar Hrafn Hrafnbjargarson, and Þorbjörg Hróarsdóttir (2009). 'On the distribution and illocution of V2 in Scandinavian *that*-clauses', *Lingua* 119: 1914–38.

Willis, David (1998). *Syntactic change in Welsh: a study of the loss of verb-second.* Oxford: Clarendon.

Willis, David (2000). 'Verb movement in Slavonic conditionals', in Susan Pintzuk, George Tsoulas, and Anthony Warner (eds.), *Diachronic syntax: models and mechanisms.* Oxford: Oxford University Press, 322–48.

Willis, David (2007a). 'Specifier-to-head reanalyses in the complementizer domain: evidence from Welsh', *Transactions of the Philological Society* 105: 432–80.

Willis, David (2007b). 'Syntactic lexicalization as a new type of degrammaticalization', *Linguistics* 45: 271–310.

Willis, David (2011). 'Reconstructing last week's weather: syntactic reconstruction and Brythonic free relatives', *Journal of Linguistics* 47: 407–46.

Wilson, John, and Alison Henry (1998). 'Parameter setting within a socially realistic linguistics', *Language in Society* 27: 1–21.

Winford, Donald (2003). *An introduction to contact linguistics.* Oxford: Blackwell.

Winford, Donald (2005). 'Contact-induced changes: classification and processes', *Diachronica* 22: 373–427.

Winter, Werner (1984). 'Reconstructing comparative linguistics and the reconstruction of the syntax of undocumented stages in the development of language and language families', in Jacek Fisiak (ed.), *Historical syntax.* Berlin: Mouton de Gruyter, 613–26.

Wright, Joseph (1910). *Grammar of the Gothic language.* Oxford: Clarendon.

Wurff, Wim van der (1997). 'Syntactic reconstruction and reconstructability: Proto-Indo-European and the typology of null objects', in Jacek Fisiak (ed.), *Linguistic reconstruction and typology*. Berlin and New York: Mouton de Gruyter, 337–56.

Wurmbrand, Susi (2004). *No TP-fronting meets Nearly Headless Nick*. MS. University of Connecticut, Storrs.

Yang, Charles (2000). 'Internal and external forces in language change', *Language Variation and Change* 12: 231–50.

Yang, Charles (2002). *Knowledge and learning in natural language*. Oxford: Oxford University Press.

Zagorin, Perez (1999). 'History, the referent, and narrative: reflections on postmodernism now', *History and Theory* 38: 1–24.

Zanuttini, Raffaella, and Paul Portner (2003). 'Exclamative clauses: at the syntax–semantics interface', *Language* 79: 39–81.

Zeijlstra, Hedde (2008). 'On the syntactic flexibility of formal features', in Theresa Biberauer (ed.), *The limits of syntactic variation*. Amsterdam: John Benjamins, 143–73.

Zupitza, Julius (ed.) (1880). *Ælfrics Grammatik und Glossar*. Berlin: Weidmann.

Zwart, C. Jan-Wouter (1991). 'Clitics in Dutch: evidence for the position of INFL', *Groninger Arbeiten zur germanistischen Linguistik* 33: 71–92.

Zwart, C. Jan-Wouter (1993). *Dutch syntax: a Minimalist approach*. Ph.D. dissertation. University of Groningen.

# Index of languages and sources

Page ranges given in bold represent the main section on that language or source.

# Index of subjects

Page ranges given in bold represent the main section on that subject.

# OXFORD STUDIES IN DIACHRONIC AND HISTORICAL LINGUISTICS

GENERAL EDITORS

Adam Ledgeway and Ian Roberts, University of Cambridge

ADVISORY EDITORS

Cynthia Allen, *Australian National University*; Ricardo Bermúdez-Otero, *University of Manchester*; Theresa Biberauer, *University of Cambridge*; Charlotte Galves, *University of Campinas*; Geoff Horrocks, *University of Cambridge*; Paul Kiparsky, *Stanford University*; Anthony Kroch, *University of Pennsylvania*; David Lightfoot, *Georgetown University*; Giuseppe Longobardi, *University of York*; David Willis, *University of Cambridge*